ANZIO

ANZIO

THE FRICTION OF WAR
ITALY AND THE BATTLE FOR ROME 1944

LLOYD CLARK

headline
review

Copyright © 2006 Lloyd Clark

The right of Lloyd Clark to be identified as the Author of
the Work has been asserted by him in accordance with the
Copyright, Designs and Patents Act 1988.

First published in 2006
by HEADLINE REVIEW

An imprint of Headline Publishing Group

1

Apart from any use permitted under UK copyright law, this publication
may only be reproduced, stored, or transmitted, in any form, or by any means,
with prior permission in writing of the publishers or, in the case
of reprographic production, in accordance with the terms of licences
issued by the Copyright Licensing Agency.

Every effort has been made to fulfil requirements with regard
to reproducing copyright material. The author and publisher will
be glad to rectify any omissions at the earliest opportunity.

A CIP catalogue record for this title is available from the British Library

10 digit ISBN 0 7553 1420 4
13 digit ISBN 978 0 7553 1420 1

Text design by Ben Cracknell Studios

Typeset in Garamond by Palimpsest Book Production Limited,
Grangemouth, Stirlingshire

Printed and bound in Great Britain by
Clays Ltd, St Ives, plc

Headline's policy is to use papers that are natural, renewable and
recyclable products and made from wood grown in sustainable forests.
The logging and manufacturing processes are expected to conform
to the environmental regulations of the country of origin.

HEADLINE PUBLISHING GROUP
A division of Hodder Headline
338 Euston Road
London NW1 3BH

www.reviewbooks.co.uk
www.hodderheadline.com

Contents

FOR CATRIONA WITH LOVE

Acknowledgements

It is my very great pleasure to thank everybody who has helped in the researching and writing of this book. Without the Anzio veterans giving so freely of their time to talk to me, my knowledge of the battle and understanding of what made those involved in it 'tick' would have been greatly diminished. I am therefore grateful to Dr John Attenborough; G. Bryant; Maurice Cheadle; Norman Clarimont; Clive Colley; Richard Dawes; Arthur Fenn; Jonathan Forbes; David Hardy; Lord Healey; Ted Jones; Bill Lewis; Joachim Liebschner; Arthur Malinson; Fred Mason; Jack Morris; E. Needham; Reginald Norfolk; Jimmy Reed; Terry Reynolds; Henry Tonks; Raleigh Trevelyan; Neil Tucker; Graham Swain; John Swain; Douglas Vickers; Ben Wallis; Fred Webster; Bert Wickes; David Williams; T.J. Anderson; David Cohen; Peter Coup; Charlie Franklin; Tony Glenister; Daniel Goldstein; Frank Kimble; Bernie Kirchoff; JPL; Norman Mohar; Eric Montrose; T.D. Morgan; David Munford; Leonard O. Peters; Peter Randall; Oliver P. Roach; David Stearns; Ivor Talbot; Paul van der Linden; Ran Williams;

Donny Wilson; Klaus Hide; Karsten Hoffmann; Gerd Jebsen; Gunther Maucke; Ralph Leitner; Gunter Pollmann; Felix Reimann; Paul Wagner; Edgar Weiss; Alonzo Badotti; Fabia Sciarillo and Antonio Zinzone. My special thanks to the Italy Star Association for introducing me to so many 'old soldiers', and to Bill Lewis and Diego Cancelli – proud citizen of Aprilia and native of Anzio – for their friendship and assistance. Diego was my guide and inspiration on the battlefield and gained me access to the areas of the beachhead that I wanted to look at, took me to memorials and museums, introduced me to knowledgeable people and was a most wonderful companion during my research in Italy.

I should also like to thank the following people for permission to quote from memoirs and diaries: Cordino Longiotti; Dr Ray McAllister; Norman Mohar; Paul Brown Jnr (for Paul Brown's memories); The Trustees of the Liddell Hart Centre for Military Archives (for the Alanbrooke diaries); Aaron Elson (for Murray Levine's memories); George Avery; F. Eugene Liggett; The Citadel Archives and Museum (for Mark Clark's diaries); The US Army Military History Institute (for John Lucas's diaries); Bob Graffagnino (for Dr Peter Graffagnino's memories); the Second World War Experience Centre (for the papers of Ron Rhodes, H. Bretherick, M.W.L. Wood, James Reeder, Roger Hill, John Herbert, Geoffrey H. Dormer, Raymond Fort and William Dugdale); Claus Wentz (for the papers of Edwin Wentz); Sarah Harris (for the diary of David Harris) and Madeline Robinson (for the diary of Kenneth Wright). Quotes from *Whicker's War* are reprinted by permission of HarperCollins Publishers Ltd © Alan Whicker, 2005; from Wynford Vaughan-Thomas's *Anzio* by Pan Books; from Lt. Gen. L.K. Truscott Jnr's, *Command Missions – A Personal Story* by Presidio; from Homer Bigart's *Forward Positions – The War Correspondence of Homer Bigart* by The University of Arkansas Press; from *Sparks – The Combat Diary of a Battalion Commander (Rifle), WWII, 157th Infantry Regiment, 45th Division, 1941–1945* by Thunderbird Press; from Robert E. Dodge's

Memories of the Anzio Beachhead and the War in Europe by Vantage Press; from Ross S. Carter's *Those Devils In Baggy Pants* by Signet, and from Ernie Pyle's *Brave Men* by Henry Holt.

I am also grateful to the archivists, librarians, curators and historians at the following institutions: Das Bundesarchiv, Freiburg; the Imperial War Museum, London; the National Archives, London; the Veterans History Project Collection, American Folklife Center, Library of Congress, Washington; 45th Infantry Division Museum, Oklahoma City; and the Liddell Hart Centre for Military Archives, London. Dr Peter Liddle and Cathy Pugh at the Second World War Experience Centre, Leeds; Jane Yates at The Citadel Archives and Museum, and Dr Richard Sommers at the US Army Military History Institute were particularly helpful. The staff at the Central Library of the Royal Military Academy Sandhurst – Andrew Orgill (who also compiled this book's index), John Pearce, Ken Franklin, Christina Claridge and Sandra Gower – deserve my special thanks. Where else would a senior librarian trawl his files and the internet in search of an obscure book having been given the scantest of information, order it, make you a cup of tea and then, if that was not enough, provide you with the address of an Anzio veteran that you are keen to interview? Thanks also to my colleagues in the Department of War Studies at Sandhurst. The heavy workload at the Academy makes it difficult to find the time to research and write, but I have always been encouraged to do so and with the help of the team found scraps of time in which to complete this book. My Alamein Company group of Commissioning Course 052 also assisted me by coming up with a number of excellent points and asked a series of penetrating questions during our Exercise Anzio Angst. I am also indebted to my agent Charlie Viney for his help and encouragement, and his partner Ivan Mulcahy and Jonathan Conway for their support. I have also been blessed with excellent editorial teams on both sides of the Atlantic: Lorraine Jerram and Emma Tait at Headline, and Brando Skyhorse and Morgan Entrekin at Grove Atlantic. Thanks also to Sally Sargeant for her copy edit and Alan Collinson at Geo-Innovations for the maps. The errors in this book, however, are mine and mine alone.

Finally, my greatest thanks are offered to my family. This book was written during an extremely busy and exciting time in my life and it took me away – physically and mentally – for protracted periods. The family suffer badly when a writer is at work and my wife Catriona, and my children Freddie, Charlotte and Henry, were all remarkably tolerant during the whole process. I hope they think that the added pressure that I forced on them has in some small way been compensated for by what I have produced. Catriona, this book is for you.

Lloyd Clark
Wigginton Bottom and Camberley, May 2006

Maps

Introduction

In 1944 Lady Nancy Astor, the first female Member of Parliament, received a letter from a disenchanted soldier of the British Eighth Army fighting in Italy. It had been signed anonymously from the 'D-Day Dodgers'. Failing to see the irony, the notoriously cantankerous politician had replied: 'Dear D-Day Dodgers'. It was a faux pas that immediately attracted the ire of the troops in Italy who believed that after the Normandy landings, the Italian Campaign had become an all but forgotten sideshow. The anonymous soldier was a representative of troops who had already been through several D-Days of their own, including landings in North Africa and Sicily, followed by those at Reggio di Calabria, Salerno and Anzio.

But the memory of these operations – together with the savage fighting in Italy – were effectively washed away in the minds of Britons and Americans alike by the wave of interest in the long-awaited cross-Channel invasion. Before long the North West European Campaign was to become the Campaign, and 6 June 1944 the D-Day. From that moment until the end of the war in Europe, fighting in other theatres receded into the background, their influence on the final outcome of the war chronically distorted by a trend to see the conflict through the prism of Overlord. Over subsequent decades it is a view that the media and Hollywood have been only too happy to reinforce. The Normandy landings remain the focal point for anniversary commemorations of the Second World War in Britain and, along with the anniversary of Pearl Harbor, in the United States as well.

To a large extent the abiding grip of Operation Overlord in the collective British and American imaginations has been at the expense of other campaigns, and might be explained by the mistaken belief that the North West European Campaign contributed to the defeat of Germany in a way that no other theatre came close to matching. On the face of it the fighting in the Mediterranean generally, and Italy in particular, contributed less to the eventual Allied victory whereas Overlord, which necessarily took the cream of both resources and commanders, was ultimately 'decisive'. Indeed, it is often said that the wider Mediterranean Campaign had at best a marginal influence on the success against the Axis Powers, and some go as far as to say that the Allies defeated Germany despite the fighting in Italy.

Veterans of the Italian Campaign have learned to live with negative assessments. Though many of them accept that theirs was a secondary theatre, they argue cogently that they were far from 'D-Day Dodgers' and that their efforts did have a substantial impact on the outcome of the European war. Having significantly weakened the Germans by trading painful body blows in fighting that was as vicious as anywhere else and in the most difficult conditions, the men of the British Eighth and US Fifth Armies declare that they played a full part in the success of the Normandy landings. Indeed, although the collective national memories of the fighting in Italy is lamentable, the bloody battles of Salerno, Monte Cassino and Anzio still have dramatic resonance. These brutal confrontations led to heavy casualties and became notorious for their intensity and the tenacity of all involved. But as part of a cul de sac campaign they lack the prominence of the battles fought in Normandy, Arnhem and the Ardennes.

The fighting in Italy demands to be understood rather than overlooked. The Italian Campaign begs to be analysed not only for issues concerned with its strategic vitality, but for the insight that it provides into multi-national fighting on land, sea and in the air against an extremely competent enemy in often-difficult terrain. It was a Herculean effort by the British and American forces at a time when their leaders felt the need to undertake offensive action against the Axis prior to the mounting of the much-anticipated cross-Channel invasion. It was the development of a Mediterranean strategy initiated by an isolated and hamstrung Britain as Germany busied itself extending its influence in the region and the Soviet Union. With no possibility of launching a cross-Channel invasion in the immediate future, Britain was inexorably drawn to the Mediterranean to protect its interests and to begin the slow process of wearing down the Germans. Just as in the First World War, the British sought to hone their fighting skills with each battle, whilst grinding down Germany's ability to sustain their war effort. However, when the United States and the Soviet Union entered hostilities in 1941, the shape and the tempo of the conflict was inevitably altered. The latent capability of both nations was obvious, but before their offensive capabilities could be unleashed, the Soviets had to repel the enemy's advances and the Americans had to find their fighting feet. The Mediterranean provided, amongst other things, the possibility to help further dilute the already stretched German resources and blood untested American forces prior to the Allied invasion of France. Thus, during 1942, having failed to overcome the Soviet Union quickly, the Axis Powers were drawn into a wider war of attrition for which they were unprepared. That autumn the Germans were struggling in the Caucasus at the southern end of an Eastern Front nearly 2,000 miles long as Stalingrad soaked up its forces, while in Egypt they suffered a real reversal at El Alamein. German potency was waning and the British and Americans were in a position to step up the pressure on their enemies by developing their operations in the Mediterranean. The Allies never agreed about the efficacy of fighting in the region, with Washington and Moscow firmly focused on the potential of the cross-Channel invasion, but London determined to squeeze every last strategic advantage out of the theatre before the demands of Operation Overlord became all consuming.

The steps from North Africa to Sicily and to Italy were not long, but they put strain on the Allies politically and militarily. The decision to invade Italy was particularly fraught with the landings in Normandy just months away (even though one of its primary aims was to pin German troops in the country) and the commitment to the campaign and its various operations remained controversial throughout. For this alone, the fighting in Italy deserves attention, but also for the light that the campaign shines on the conduct of the Second World War in Europe at all levels: from the strategic discord between Washington and London, through the application of high-risk operations commanded by captivating personalities involving multi-national forces on land, sea and air; to the tactical fighting in complicated terrain and in appalling weather against a fiercely combative and highly trained enemy in strong defensive positions.

The Italian Campaign was fought in conditions that heightened what the nineteenth-century Prussian strategist Carl von Clausewitz called 'friction', about which he wrote: 'Everything is simple in war, but the simplest thing is difficult.' This was never truer than at Anzio during the early months of 1944. This audacious scheme to land British and American forces behind enemy lines a mere twenty-five miles from Rome was as controversially conceived and conducted as any other operation in the Mediterranean Theatre. The battle quickly became a microcosm of the fighting in Italy, exuding friction in a race against time against a cluttered strategic backdrop and intense political interest in the outcome. Here British and American troops slugged it out with the Germans as though the entire war depended on it.

Anzio was a battle that gave extra bite to the song that was sung by the troops in Italy to the tune of 'Lili Marlene':

We're the D-Day dodgers here in Italy
Drinking all the vino, always on the spree,
We didn't land with Eisenhower
So they think that we're just a shower.
For we're the D-Day dodgers out here in Italy

We landed in Salerno,
A holiday with pay,
The Jerries brought the band out to greet us on the way.
Showed us the sights and gave us tea,
We all sang songs, the beer was free
To welcome D-Day dodgers,
To sunny Italy

Salerno and Cassino
We're takin' in our stride
We didn't go to fight there,
We went there for the ride
Anzio and Sangro were just names,
We only went to look for dames,
The artful D-Day dodgers
Out here in Italy

Look around the mountains
In the mud and rain
You'll find scattered crosses,
Some which bear no name.
Heart break and toil and suffering gone
The boys beneath them slumber on,
For they're the D-Day dodgers,
Who stayed in Italy.

Cast List

(Divisional commanders can be found in Appendix 1: Order of Battle)

THE BRITISH

Field Marshal Sir Alan Brooke – Chief of the Imperial General Staff

General Sir Henry Maitland Wilson – Supreme Allied Commander Mediterranean Theatre from 8 January 1944

General Sir Harold R.L.G. Alexander – Commander Allied Fifteenth Army Group

General Sir Bernard Montgomery – Commander Eighth Army to 31 December 1943

Lieutenant General Sir Oliver Leese – Commander Eighth Army from 31 December 1943

General R.L. McCreery – Commander British X Corps

Major General V. Evelegh – Deputy Commander VI Corps

Admiral of the Fleet Sir Andrew Cunningham – Naval Commander in Chief

Admiral Thomas Troubridge – Commander Royal Navy Task Force 81

THE AMERICANS

General George C. Marshall – Chief of the Army Staff

General Dwight Eisenhower – Supreme Allied Commander Mediterranean Theatre to 8 January 1944

Lieutenant General Mark W. Clark – Commander US Fifth Army

Major General Alfred M. Gruenther – Fifth Army Chief of Staff

Major General Geoffrey T. Keyes – Commander US II Corps

Major General John P. Lucas – Commander US VI Corps to 22 February 1944

Major General Lucian K. Truscott Jnr – Commander 3rd Infantry US Division to 17 February 1944 and VI Corps from 23 February 1944

Rear Admiral Frank Lowry – Commander US Navy Task Force 81 and Task Force 81

Lieutenant General Ira C. Eaker – Commander Air Forces Mediterranean

Major General John K. Cannon – Commander XII US Air Force

Major General Edwin J. House – Commander US XII Air Support Command

THE GERMANS

Field Marshal Albert Kesselring – Commander-in-Chief South West and Army Group C

Lieutenant General Kurt Mältzer – Commandant of Rome

Colonel Eugen Dollmann – General Wolff's SS Liaison Officer

Lieutenant General Ernst Schlemmer – Commander Rome Area

General Heinrich von Vietinghoff – Commander Tenth Army

Lieutenant General Fridolin von Senger und Etterlin – Commander XIV Panzer Corps

General Eberhard von Mackensen – Commander Fourteenth Army

General Alfred Schlemm – Commander I Parachute Corps

General Traugott Herr – Commander LXXVI Panzer Corps

ITALIANS

Victor Emmanuel III – King of Italy

Marshal Pietro Badoglio – Prime Minister

Prologue

The remains of a mud-encrusted Thompson sub-machine gun and Lee Enfield rifle lie together in the scrubby grass. The wood has rotted away, but despite corrosion both are unmistakable. It doesn't seem right to touch them, but I wonder how they came to be there. To have stood on this spot in the early spring of 1944 would have invited instant death, but on an icy morning sixty-one years later all is quiet. Just three miles from Anzio I stare across the ground that the British troops called 'The Fortress', trying to imagine that time, looking for clues. It was here, week after week, that the combatants fought a trench warfare their fathers would have known on the Western Front. Despite the extensive land-scaping that has taken place since the Second World War, the atmosphere of this place speaks of something awful happening.

The gorge that I am looking for opens up in front of me – an old river course where the intense fighting was hand-to-hand, and an Anzio veteran spoke of 'heaps of dead'. I detect the telltale signs of battle: eroded edges of shell holes outlined in rime; the entrances to tunnels and bunkers hollowed into the valley sides; depressions which mark the line of former trenches dug into the sandy soil; shell fragments, rusty barbed wire and spent cartridge cases – the detritus of war. Looking beyond the vineyards that now cover the old German front line, I can see the Allied objective of the Anzio landings – the snow-topped Alban Hills, tantalisingly almost within touching distance. But in early 1944 both they and Rome – a mere twenty-five miles distant – were beyond the Allies' grasp. Over four months American, British and Canadian troops failed to impose their will on the enemy, and at one point their tenuous foothold on the Anzio beachhead was severely threatened.

I make my way into Anzio past endless construction sites – it is as if the burgeoning population won't be satisfied until the whole battlefield has been concreted over. But the port remains virtually unchanged. Here is the quayside used by Allied shipping in a massive logistical effort. I squint at the grainy black and white photograph in my hand, and orientate myself to the scene in front of me, until I'm standing on exactly the same spot as the *Life* photographer back in 1944. A brightly decorated fishing boat has replaced the hulking grey landing ship, but the place once occupied by a jeep and anti-aircraft gun remains the same. That building hasn't changed at all. There is the curve of the harbour. Here are those steps. My gaze traverses along the seafront to the art deco Casino building, taken by the Rangers on the morning of the invasion. In the far distance lie Nettuno and X-Ray beaches. It is all strangely reassuring.

Along the front to Nettuno prosperous-looking Italians chat over espressos in the cafés and bars. Many from the older generation look uncomfortable when the war is mentioned and quickly change the subject. Though the determined seeker might eventually locate the few modest memorials and the dusty room in a back street purporting to be a museum, Anzio barely reflects its violent past and hardly promotes it. Juggling yet more black and white photographs, I wander through the narrow streets and stumble across the American Major General John Lucas's original headquarters. On Via Romana I find his subsequent hideaway – a humble basement below a café. There is Lucas – or 'Foxy

Grandpa' as many soldiers called him – standing by the entrance under a sign reading 'Vicolo Ciece' or 'Dead End Street'. The sign is still there.

Driving inland towards Cisterna I pull up at a particularly bloody part of the battlefield. The vineyards which have been described to me by veterans remain largely intact – though studded by new buildings – but I can take my bearings from the battle-scarred pillars that once marked the entrance to Isola Bella Farm, and it is all too easy to imagine the terrifying scene here one morning in late January 1944 when the Rangers were surrounded by a German panzer division. Walk beyond the hedge and you immediately feel exposed in a killing ground. What were those young men thinking as they hugged the cold soil that day? Only six of the 767 Rangers who started the attack ever returned.

I make my way through Cisterna towards the Alban Hills following ubiquitous 'ROMA' signs. Route 7, the road that once supplied the German Gustav Line, leads me up over 1,300 feet to the town of Albano and, just like the German defenders, I can look south and down towards Anzio 18 miles away. With my binoculars I can pick out traffic movement, even the wake of boats out at sea. I swing right, picking out various towns until confronted by the belt of smog over Rome. I head back towards Anzio, and drive under the notorious Flyover – now rebuilt after its devastation in the front line – and stop at the British Beachhead Cemetery, one of three Allied cemeteries on the battlefield. Some 7,000 Allied soldiers and at least as many Germans died as a result of the fighting at Anzio.

During the battle a farmhouse that accommodated the British Casualty Clearing Station, named the 'Yellow Bungalow', stood adjacent to this field, then in bloom with temporary wooden crosses. Portland stone now marks the graves of over 2,300 dead in a setting more reminiscent of a typical English country churchyard. In the quietness I bend down to examine the headstone of one A.H.F. Murdoch, a twenty-eight-year-old corporal in the Wiltshire Regiment. Alfred Murdoch had been from Poplar, east London. His wife, Grace, had written his epitaph: 'One day we will understand. Sleep on darling. Your loving wife and sons.'

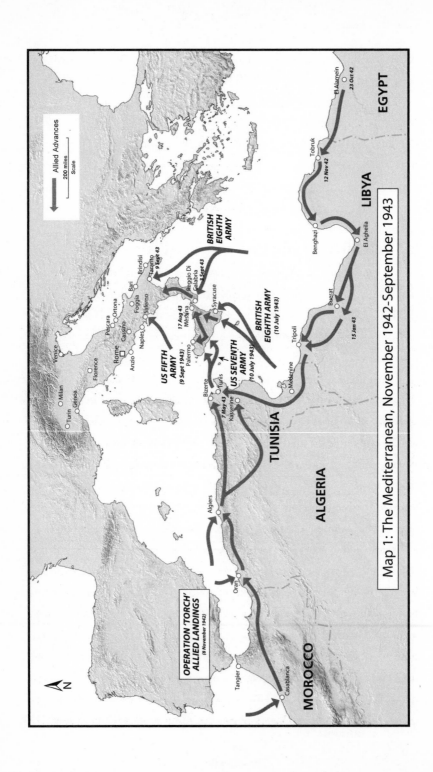

Map 1: The Mediterranean, November 1942–September 1943

CHAPTER 1

The Italian Job

(Allied Strategy and the Invasion of Italy 1942–1943)

The rockets poured over the landing craft and thundered down onto the beaches. Their lunatic shriek heralded the arrival of the Allies at Anzio–Nettuno at 0200 hours on 22 January 1944. Twenty-year-old Private Richard Dawes held his breath as explosions blistered the coastline. Just like the other thirty-five soldiers stretched out in two lines on the landing craft, Dawes felt vulnerable now that the force had announced itself so dramatically. Adrenaline surged through his body and his stomach lurched. The cacophony drowned out the growl of the engine, but from the vibrations through the soles of his boots, and the breeze on his face, he sensed movement. Then the rockets stopped firing as though giving way for a response. A wave boomed against the armoured plated hull making the men start and huddle together. Dawes tried to work out how far they were from the beach, but spray blurred his vision. He blinked hard, licked his lips and pulled his rifle tight to his chest, his heart beating furiously. There was a shout of: 'Thirty seconds!' and Richard Dawes began counting to steady his nerves. He had only reached twenty before a jolt propelled him into the man in front, and the ramp rattled down to expose them. A stentorian voice yelled 'Move!' as they scuttled down the slope and onto the beach. Another shapeless figure yelled incomprehensibly, and pushed him towards the green lamp that marked the rendezvous point. Dawes jogged heavily across the sand, inhaling a mixture of smoke and cordite, until he reached his company's position. He listened for the rip of German spandaus, but heard nothing save the arrival of panting colleagues. As the battalion assembled around him, he relaxed slightly, even allowing himself to think that everything was going to be all right.

Private Richard Dawes was a replacement who had joined his unit just after landing at Salerno, but in time for its advance towards Rome. During the autumn as part of Major General John Lucas's US VI Corps (a formation consisting of American and British divisions) he had fought his way through Italy's Apennine mountains. Every step had been a struggle. In early October Lucas – a natural worrier with a great deal to worry about – had confided to his diary: 'Rain, rain, rain. The roads are so deep in mud that moving troops and supplies forward is a terrific job. Enemy resistance is not nearly as great as that of Mother Nature.' The vile weather and mountains were difficult enough, but the Germans had made the advance tortuous. Dawes had been soaked to the skin for weeks and in almost continual combat. He had been so tired that on several occasions he had fallen asleep whilst marching to his next battle. Both hands were calloused from digging foxholes. 'This is just so awful', he wrote in his notebook, 'I think that death might be preferable. God help me. God help us all.' But he and his comrades continued their struggle, taking tiny bites out of the terrain. It was the sort of stagnation that the Germans regarded with satisfaction, but the British perceived as sinful.

Bursting with enthusiasm for the strategic possibilities that Italy offered, Winston Churchill feared that his campaign was on the verge of break down, and would perish during the winter. To revive his

Mediterranean ambitions, the Prime Minister had backed plans to land troops behind enemy lines on the beaches of Anzio–Nettuno, a mere thirty miles from Rome. The plan had considerable potential, but to the Americans it was considered 'a sideshow of a sideshow'. The situation reflected developing tensions between Britain and the United States: strong allies sharing a common tongue and purpose, but with differing priorities, perspectives and characters. At the British Embassy in Washington the philosopher Isaiah Berlin observed of the Americans: 'they have been taught to dislike [the British] in their history books. Those Englishmen who they do like are liked precisely because they do not conform to what they regard as the standard type of Englishman.' National stereotyping abounded. The experienced British pedigree gun dog felt the need to be patient with the flighty American mongrel puppy. But the Americans looked at Britain as a tired-out creature whose back legs fell occasionally from under him, and needed support. As one British diplomat observed: 'Britain and America are partners, but they are also rivals, each anxious to prove that its views on policy, indeed its way of life, is superior to that of the other. It is this element of competition which distinguishes the partnership . . .' There was rivalry, but the rivalry masked more profound differences and the Italian Campaign, with its distrust, frustration, dispute and resentment, had brought those differences to the fore. In such circumstances the strong relationship between Winston Churchill and the American President, Franklin Roosevelt, was critical.

The agreement by the Western Allies in December 1941 that their priority should be the defeat of Germany had been logical for the British. But for a United States still reeling from the Japanese attack on Pearl Harbor, it was far more challenging. Churchill had consistently argued for an attritional policy that gnawed away at Germany's ability to sustain its war effort. In this the Mediterranean loomed large and Churchill, advised and supported by the service heads who formed the Chiefs of Staff, was its patron. The Americans instinctively disliked the Mediterranean approach, not least because its Joint Chiefs of Staff believed that it was informed as much by British Imperial interests as it was by defeating Germany. But the British had begun fighting in the Mediterranean during the summer of 1940, intent on defending Egypt from Benito Mussolini's Italy. By the spring of 1942 Germany had joined the fray, and the Axis powers had advanced to within seventy miles of Alexandria. The Americans were unimpressed and despite the British extolling the virtues of patience, the Joint Chiefs were restless, wanting to seize the initiative. The American Army Chief of the Staff, the amiable-looking General George C. Marshall, had already made up his mind. The sixty-one-year-old was set on an offensive launched from Britain into mainland Europe, a cross-Channel invasion, as soon as was practicable. The British were not against this *per se,* but argued that the Axis powers had to be further weakened before it could be successful. Nevertheless, the cohorts agreed to build air and ground resources in the United Kingdom for its preparation, and a tentative launch date of April 1943 was set. With the Americans temporarily placated, General Sir Alan Brooke, the prudent British Chief of the Imperial General Staff, peddled the case for an expansion of operations in the Mediterranean. Marshall immediately took this to mean that the British were not fully supportive of a cross-Channel invasion, code named Operation Roundup, whereas Brooke maintained the need for flexibility and attrition. A decision was required and London began to work on Washington to get what it wanted. General Albert C. Wedemeyer, a senior officer on Marshall's staff, remarked of the subsequent meetings held during the spring of 1942: 'What I witnessed was the British power for finesse in its finest hour, a power that had been developed over centuries of successful international intrigue, cajolery and tacit compulsions.' But the Americans held out and nothing had been decided by the time that the Allies met in Washington in June. Here the Joint Chiefs continued to argue that operations in the Mediterranean would undermine preparations for Roundup. But the British could not be dissuaded and a frustrated Churchill began to work personally on Roosevelt's resilience. 'Here is a true Second Front of 1942', the Prime Minister insisted: 'Here is the safest and most fruitful stroke that can be delivered this autumn.' The American President was slowly convinced. He wanted to get inexperienced United States troops into battle and, in a Congressional election year, wanted to be seen as a man of action. Marshall called the subsequent decision to invade French-held North Africa – Operation Torch – as: 'a momentous change of Grand Strategy.' He was as apoplectic as Brooke was delighted. The British could now develop their Mediterranean ambitions.

Torch was the first truly Allied operation of the war, and aimed to secure the entire North African coastline. The British had cannily agreed to an American Commander in Chief of the Allied forces, Lieutenant General Dwight Eisenhower. The astute Eisenhower held the permanent rank of Lieutenant Colonel and although new to field command had nascent talents. Another soldier whose star was in the ascendant became his deputy, the ferociously ambitious Major General Mark W. Clark. Beak-nosed and with a leanness that made him seem taller than his six feet three inches, Clark was on the cusp of great fame. The two men, who had been friends since West Point, congratulated each other on 8 November as Torch made a firm lodgement on African soil, then pondered the military lessons. The learning curve had been steep, particularly for the Americans. Indeed, the dashing Brigadier General Lucian Truscott, the future divisional and corps commander at Anzio, stated that his landing in Morocco was a 'hit and miss affair that would have spelled disaster against a well-armed enemy intent on resistance.' Even so, this easy opening fixture gave the British and Americans some confidence, and as General Bernard Montgomery's British Eighth Army pushed westwards after its victory at El Alamein, the grand plan seemed to be working. However, the deteriorating weather and tenacious Germans had ensured that the campaign could not be concluded that year.

Even as the Allied dust cloud converged on Tunis in early 1943 the Afrika Korps continued to land punches. The severe blow that the Americans took at the Kasserine Pass in February was such a shock that the British raised questions about their military competence. Such inquests only served to further strain already stretched allied relations in North Africa. Brooke's dissatisfaction came spilling out in his diary: 'I am afraid that Eisenhower as a general is hopeless!' he complained on 28 December: 'He submerges himself in politics and neglects his military duties, partly I am afraid because he knows little about military matters.' General Sir Harold Alexander, the impeccably dressed Anglo-Irish aristocrat who became ground forces commander in the final stages of the campaign, was more broadly critical of the Americans: 'They simply do not know their job as soldiers and this is the case from the highest to the lowest, from the General to the private soldier.' Such attitudes were commonplace within the British officer corps and Clark in particular was singled out for special treatment as an individualist who courted publicity – a 'typical American general'. Many that worked with him were not therefore displeased to see him promoted in January 1943 and sent to command the new US Fifth Army. But Clark never forgot the barbed British remarks about him and his countrymen in Tunisia. Truscott, however, was more conciliatory:

> British commanders and staff officers impressed Americans as being supercilious, conceited, and arrogant. British officers considered the Americans to be loud, boastful and inexperienced . . . One could sympathise with the lack of understanding and mutual regard between British and American commanders, however one might deplore it. But the bitterness, personal and professional jealousy . . . and even hatred, which existed among some of the American commanders and staffs, I could never condone.

This mature outlook was one shared by Eisenhower who wrote to a friend, 'one of the constant sources of danger to us is to regard as our first enemy the partner that must work with us in defeating the real enemy.' He was quite right, for the surrender of the Axis forces in North Africa in May was not the final step towards the defeat of Germany, only the first. Nonetheless, it was a crucial success as Field Marshal Albert Kesselring – the man who was to emerge as the Allies' *bête noire* in Italy – noted: 'The Allies won a total victory. The final battles left the enemy with a sense of superiority which gave an extraordinary boost to his morale . . . at the end of this phase the Axis had lost the strategic initiative.'

The surrender *was* a watershed for the Allies, as Ernie Pyle, an American war correspondent in North Africa, recognised:

There were days when I sat in my tent alone and gloomed with the desperate belief that it was actually possible for us to lose this war. I don't feel that way any more . . . We are producing at home and we are hardening overseas . . . I can't yet see when we shall win, or over what route geographically, or by which of the many means of warfare. But no longer do I have any doubts at all that we shall win.

By the late spring of 1943 the Allies had some momentum behind them. Along with the success in North Africa came a more positive outlook on the Eastern Front and the rapidly growing military strength of the United States. In such circumstances the British were keen to extend their Mediterranean strategy before their allies' strategic desires became demands that could no longer be resisted.

The British sought to make the Mediterranean a liability for the Germans. At the Symbol Conference in Casablanca in January 1943 Alan Brooke had proposed the invasion of Sicily to finally open the Mediterranean to Allied vessels, further wear down the German war machine and – possibly – force Mussolini out of the war. If the Italians did leave the Axis, he continued, Hitler would then be forced into deciding whether to defend Italy using German forces, or withdraw. Brooke had emphasised that, if the Allies filled the vacuum, a withdrawal would provide many treasures. He listed them whilst pointing to a large map: access to partisans in Yugoslavia; valuable bomber airfields and a threat to the Austrian border – the southern reaches of the Reich. Marshall was unimpressed: his fears were becoming a reality, with the British attempting to alter the direction of an agreed strategy, and he reflected the unease of many in Washington. One British observer wrote that the Americans 'regarded the Mediterranean as a kind of dark hole, into which one entered at one's peril.' But not all agreed and, disappointingly for Marshall, Roosevelt, Admiral Ernest King, the American Naval Chief of Staff and General Henry Arnold, the Chief of the Army Air Forces, backed the invasion of Sicily. Marshall winced. The Mediterranean was to be *the* theatre of 1943 and Operation Husky in Sicily – the first opposed landing in occupied Europe – was scheduled for July. But what was to happen after Sicily? At the Washington Trident Conference in May the British suggested an invasion of Italy, at which Marshall became convinced that they were trying to scupper the cross-Channel invasion, now code named Operation Overlord, and were pursuing a hidden agenda. Kesselring, the commander of German forces in Sicily and southern Italy, concurred declaring that Churchill wanted: 'to establish a jumping-off base for an assault on Europe from the south.' This was undoubtedly the case, and to sweeten this potentially bitter strategic pill for the Americans, the British proffered a concession. Overlord was to be launched in May 1944, and seven battle-tested divisions, and most of assault shipping currently in the Mediterranean, were to be returned to England by 1 November 1943. With it also came an agreement that Eisenhower should report on further Mediterranean options. The next Allied move would depend on his findings, in concert with an appreciation of the invasion of Sicily and the delicate political situation in Rome.

As the strategists manoeuvred, Harold Alexander sought to ensure that his Army Group was ready for its next challenge. Whilst overseeing the assimilation of many lessons from North Africa, he was most concerned to improve the fighting ability of the Americans. By ensuring that their training, discipline and whole approach to battle fighting were tightened, Alexander and his team achieved his aim. And he did it without causing offence. 'We must tread very warily,' Alexander confided to Brooke in April 1943:

> if the Americans think we are sneering at them – and God forbid that – or that we are being superior, they will take it very badly, as they are a proud people. We must take the line that we are comrades and brothers in arms, and our only wish is for them to share the horrors of war (and the handicaps) and reap the fruits of victory together.

Diplomacy was one of Alexander's strengths. The fifty-one-year-old had led from the front as a junior officer in the Irish Guards during the First World War. Initially unsure whether he was cut out for military life, he had flourished and rose steadily through the ranks. In 1940 he managed the British Expeditionary Force's retreat to Dunkirk, then served in Burma before becoming Commander-in-Chief Middle East in the Western Desert in August 1942. In every respect Alexander fulfilled the American image of what a British general officer should look, sound and act like. Most comfortable when dressed in riding boots, breeches and a leather flying-jacket, he was Churchill's favourite general – handsome, bright, modest and, above all, a gentleman. Eisenhower wrote that 'Americans instinctively liked him'. However, Harold Alexander's *laissez-faire* approach to command and relative inability to initiate were weaknesses. Alexander did not 'grip' his subordinates (particularly if they were successful) nor did he discuss matters through with colleagues before coming to a decision. The Mediterranean Campaign was to probe his strengths and weaknesses to the full.

The invasion of Sicily tested Alexander, not least because of the two difficult subordinates that he had under his command: Lieutenant General Bernard Montgomery, the narcissistic commander of British Eighth Army, and Lieutenant General George S. Patton, the equally narcissistic commander of the US Seventh Army. From the outset there were problems. The more experienced British force was allotted the principal role in the invasion whilst the Americans, much to their *chagrin*, were to provide support. Bernard Montgomery aggravated the situation by throwing his weight around during planning – criticising arrangements, making demands. With his hands held behind his back, he would perambulate around the conference table at Alexander's headquarters, making speeches. Occasionally he would stop and point at a colleague or map for effect. Alan Brooke was so enraged with the situation that he had to 'haul Montgomery over the coals for the trouble he was creating with his usual lack of tact and egotistical outlook.' In the end a conservative plan had been agreed: a British-led advance to the critical port of Messina in the north-eastern corner of the island. This was unlikely to lead to the destruction of the defenders, as Germans and Italians could withdraw to Messina for evacuation to the Italian mainland, but it was the plan most likely to deliver Sicily into Allied hands. The Americans, however, remained piqued at their subsidiary role, leading to competition between the two Armies in Sicily, turning rivalries and jealousies into festering resentments.

As the Allies made their final approach to their Sicilian landing beaches in the early hours of 10 July 1943, Churchill played bezique with his daughter-in-law at Chequers. With a large Cuban Romeo y Julieta cigar between his fingers and a tumbler of Red Label whisky at his elbow, he rose abruptly on several occasions to venture into the Operations Room for the latest news. On one occasion he returned mumbling: 'So many brave young men going to their death tonight', and then scanning his cards added: 'It is a grave responsibility.' That night he slept just a couple of hours before returning to the Operations Room for the first report, clad in a silk dressing gown. The Prime Minister was informed that the weak Italian troops defending the coast had been quickly overrun by Montgomery's force. The defence of the island was now in the hands of 33,000 German forces included two half formed divisions: the lorry-born infantry of the 15th Panzer Grenadier Division to the west of the country, and the Hermann Göring Panzer Division (a future Anzio division) to the east. The Germans were a far more formidable foe than the Italians and as reinforcements doubled their number, they delayed the 450,000 Allies by skilful use of the terrain. The Eighth Army was halted on the plain of Catania and Montgomery was desperate to get moving again. He looked to bypass the blocked route by pushing westwards through Enna, but that road had been allotted to Omar Bradley's II Corps. Paying no attention to American needs, or waiting to obtain permission, Montgomery despatched his XXX Corps onto the road. As John Steinbeck, then a war correspondent for the *Herald Tribune*, declared: 'We get along very well as individuals, but just the moment we become the Americans and they become the British, trouble is not far behind.' Patton's response was inevitably pro-active. Never one to turn away from a challenge he got the suggestible Alexander to allow him to advance westwards for indecisive – but prestigious – objectives which included the capital, Palermo. His command contained two divisions that were to feature in the fighting at Anzio: 3rd US Infantry Division, a veteran of the fighting in North Africa commanded by the talented and amiable Major General Lucian Truscott; and 45th US Infantry Division, well-trained but green and newly arrived from the United States commanded by Major General Troy Middleton. Supporting Patton's other formation, 1st US Infantry Division, were two battalions of US Rangers – a third battalion was attached to Truscott. Similar to British commandos, the Rangers were an elite force which had been activated in the early summer of 1942. They had landed in North Africa and fought with distinction in the subsequent campaign commanded by their founder, the young and dynamic William O. Darby.

Patton's indulgence in the west was uneventful: Palermo was taken on 23 July, and he then received permission to turn eastwards in preparation for an assault with the British on the German defensive line in the north-east corner of the island. Patton wrote to Middleton about the coming attack: 'This is a horse race in which the prestige of the US Army is at stake. We must take Messina before the British. Please use your best efforts to facilitate the success of our race.' In fact, Montgomery had already conceded that the Americans would reach Messina first, but to Patton, there was a point to prove. The Americans won the 'race' with their 3rd Division entering Messina on 17 August – but not before Kesselring had overseen a slick evacuation of his forces.

The invasion had been a steep learning curve for the Western Allies and as Kesselring was to contend: 'the Axis Command was mighty lucky, helped above all as it was by the methodical procedure by the Allies. Furthermore, the Allied conception of operations offered many chances. The absence of any large-scale encirclement of the island or of a thrust up the coastline of the Calabria gave us long weeks to organise the defence with really very weak resources.' Alexander had compromised, stroked, consented and indulged – at the expense of effectiveness and victory. Even so, Sicily was a military success falling in a mere thirty-eight days and another boost for Allied morale. But it had also been an education, as Montgomery conceded: 'I think that everyone admitted that we learnt a great deal in Sicily. In some cases possibly all that was learnt was how *not* to do certain things. But all in all, the experience was invaluable to us all . . .' Moreover, the Americans not only rehabilitated themselves in the eyes of many British officers – including Alexander and Montgomery – but also ushered in a resurgence in their self-confidence. The fall of Sicily was a turning point in many ways, 'perhaps the decisive one on the way to defeat, a road along which other milestones had been Stalingrad and Tunis' according to

Johannes Steinhoff, the commander of a Luftwaffe Fighter Group who fought in the skies over Sicily. But another commentator observed that although Sicily was 'an Allied physical victory', it was also 'a German moral victory'. The Germans had been outnumbered, but fought a successful withdrawal leading to the evacuation to the Italian mainland of 53,545 men, 9,185 vehicles, all of their heavy weaponry and 11,855 tons of stores. Moreover, Kesselring had warned that Alexander and his men would have to be on their mettle if they were to make further progress in the Mediterranean theatre. Alan Whicker, then a teenage subaltern and director of an Army Film and Photographic Unit, believed that there was little doubt where they would end up next: 'Our last pictures of the Sicilian campaign', he recalled, 'showed Generals Eisenhower and Montgomery staring symbolically through field glasses out across the Straits of Messina towards the toe of Italy, and the enemy.' A decision had already been taken, but the nature of the Western Alliance ensured that it had not been easily reached.

While Allied High Command debated their next move, they were closely following the deteriorating political situation in Rome. Since their defeat at El Alamein in October 1942 there had been a growing feeling in Italy that they should pull out of the war. Indeed, Kesselring's Chief of Staff, General Siegfried Westphal had written: 'only a few Italians still believed that the salvation of their country lay in continuing the war at the side of their German ally . . . the distaste felt for Mussolini and the Party has become a burning hatred.' On 24 July 1943 the Fascist Grand Council met for the first time since the beginning of the war and passed a vote of no confidence in Mussolini. On the afternoon of 25 July, he went to see King Victor Emmanuel at Villa Ada, the royal residence on the outskirts of Rome to discuss the situation. The King, dressed in Marshal's uniform, the dark bags under his eyes contrasting starkly with his luxuriant white moustache, spoke frankly:

My dear Duce, it's no longer any good. Italy has gone to bits. Army morale is at rock bottom. The soldiers don't want to fight any more . . . The Grand Council's vote is terrific . . . You can certainly be under no illusion as to Italy's feelings with regard to yourself. At this moment you are the most hated man in Italy . . . I have been thinking the man for the job now is Marshal Badoglio.

Finally aware that everything had changed, Mussolini stormed out, only to be bundled into a waiting ambulance under an armed guard, which he thought at first had been provided for his personal protection, but soon realised was facilitating his arrest. Marshal Pietro Badoglio thus became President, the King took command of the armed forces and the Fascist party and its Grand Council were abolished. The Duce was escorted into hiding, eventually to be holed up in a mountain hotel at Gran Sasso in central Italy.

That night, 25 July, the news was announced on the radio to an expectant population in speeches by the King and Badoglio. Italy immediately celebrated. 'The people in the street are going mad with joy', one observer wrote about Rome, 'Pandemonium is let loose! I hurry along to have a look!' Some wept, others embraced. Young and old jostled to tear posters of Mussolini from the wall, hurl them to the ground, and crush them underfoot. Black shirts and Fascist literature were torched in street bonfires. Fifteen-year-old Alonzo Badotti lived with his widowed mother and six hungry siblings in a loft near Rome's Termini Station. That night they were given hope:

It was a wild time the news was a release, everyone was happy – but it was also a time for revenge. I saw one particularly hated Fascist lying in the gutter in a pool of blood, his face smashed, and people kicking his corpse as they went past, children as well as adults. It was a wild time.

But it did not last and a malaise descended once more. Badotti continued:

> Over the course of the next few days, there were stern faces in the
> bars and coffee shops as people tried to work out what it all meant.
> There was no more jollification. It was only at this point that we
> began to turn our minds to the possibilities of ending our involve-
> ment in the war. It was the next logical step, but we did not know
> what the government's intentions were.

At this stage even Badoglio did not know what his government's intentions would be, as he weighed up the advantages of surrendering to the
Allies against the consequences of German reprisals and occupation.
Berlin was watching Rome carefully. As it did so the President initiated
secret armistice negotiations with the Allies. The Germans had been
planning for an Italian *volte-face* since May, and had developed 'Plan
Achse' to deal with it. Kesselring, an Italophile, immediately recognised
the dilemmas facing the new regime, and sought reassurances.
Although the King informed him that Italy would continue to fight,
and indeed, their war 'would be intensified' Kesselring retained his
reservations. Hitler completely distrusted Italy without his friend
Mussolini at the helm, and German troops moved into northern Italy
under Field Marshal Erwin Rommel, the commander of a new Army
Group B. By 16 August some eight and a half German divisions had
secured important mountain passes, roads and railways vulnerable to
being blocked. If the Italians surrendered, 'Achse' would be activated,
and Kesselring's divisions withdrawn up the Boot of Italy to be taken
in under Rommel's command. This was a blow to sixty-year-old
'Smiling Albert' Kesselring, an eternal optimist who argued that
southern Italy could be successfully defended by making the enemy
struggle in the exposed, mountainous countryside. From his headquarters at Frascati near Rome, Kesselring insisted that delaying actions
would provide time to construct defensive lines which would in turn

absorb repeated blows and sap Allied resources. The Führer listened, was interested, but would not commit himself to a decision just yet. Whilst waiting on Berlin, the innovative Luftwaffe officer continued with his preparations to defend against an Allied invasion of Italy, while the newly created Tenth Army commanded by General Heinrich von Vietinghoff was ordered to anticipate an amphibious attack some-where between the Straits of Messina and Naples.

The decision taken by the Western Allies to invade Italy had been angst ridden. During the fighting in Sicily the British had pointed at an unstable Italy and proposed giving it a shove. Naturally Marshall was against the idea, but in the wake of Eisenhower's report supporting an invasion, the Joint Chiefs provided their assent. The Army Chief of Staff, incredulous to the end, then worked hard to ensure that the British were not given a blank cheque in Italy. Brooke wrote exasperat-edly in his diary at the end of July:

> Marshall absolutely fails to realise the strategic treasures that lie at our feet in the Mediterranean . . . He admits that our object must be to eliminate Italy and yet is always afraid of facing the consequences of doing so. He cannot see beyond the tip of his nose and is maddening.

When the Quebec Quadrant Conference gave the final authority for the invasion in August, the agreed goals were limited, but Brooke was not downhearted. Although initially doing little more than stretching the Germans, encouraging Italian surrender and seizing airfields, the British harboured the belief that the Americans could be talked into agreeing to more grandiose aims later. Rome – and beyond – beckoned and Churchill wanted to blaze a trail there. But recognising that the Americans needed cajoling, the British began to pave the way by agreeing to Operation Anvil, a landing in the south of France which was to act as a diversion to Overlord. Both sides left Quebec quietly satisfied, but Churchill was already thinking of 'quickly crushing Italy', thus making the risky cross-Channel offensive unnecessary.

The invasion of Italy by Alexander's 15th Army Group was to take place in early September. There were to be two main attacks. The first was to be conducted by Eighth Army on 3 September – four years to the day since Britain declared war on Germany. Operation Baytown was to land British XIII Corps on the toe of Italy, advance through the Calabria and roll the Germans north along the Adriatic coast to the airfields at Foggia. The second attack was to be conducted by US Fifth Army six days later. Operation Avalanche was to land Major General Ernest J. Dawley's US VI Corps and Lieutenant General Sir Richard McCreery's British X Corps in the Bay of Salerno thirty miles south-east of Naples and develop operations northwards via Naples. There was also to be a subsidiary attack at Taranto in the inner heel of the Boot by 1st British Airborne Division named Operation Slapstick. This assault would endeavour to secure the ports of Taranto, Brindisi and Bari thus assisting the sustenance of Eighth Army as it developed its advance. Moreover, as it was also to take place on 9 September, it was hoped that it might divert some attention away from Avalanche. This was thought to be important as there was excellent defensive terrain on the high ground surrounding the landing beaches which provided not only excellent observation, but also a barrier to exploitation operations. Moreover, Fifth Army was a new fighting organisation and its abrasive commander, forty-seven-year-old Mark Clark had never commanded troops in the field before. Brought up in Chicago, Clark had graduated from West Point 110th out of 139 candidates. He had risen from the rank of Lieutenant Colonel to Lieutenant General in just three years and was seen to be one of the most talented and ambitious officers in the US Army. His choice of Alfred M. Gruenther as Chief of Staff – at forty-three the youngest Major General in the army – reflected Clark's innate belief that this was a young man's war, although he recognised the need for experience and also surrounded himself with men that were senior in years of service – including his former War College instructor Fred Walker as commander of 36th US Infantry Division. But Clark regarded dynamism as the most important soldierly trait, and eschewed caution. Acutely aware that his handling of Avalanche would be closely scrutinised, he relished the challenge.

As his commanders got down to the detailed planning of their operations, Alexander looked towards the autumn months. Trying to anticipate future difficulties from his headquarters in a villa in La Marsa on the outskirts of Tunis was essential, but he was only just grasping the enormous difficulty of the tests that an invasion of Italy posed. Alexander – or 'The Chief' as his inner circle knew him – spread out a map of Italy on the table in his study. As he examined the mountains, valleys and rivers that dominated the landscape he instinctively knew that, if they decided to stand and fight, this terrain offered the Germans significant defensive opportunities. What were the Germans planning? Would Kesselring defend Rome? And would the Allies have the resources to break through if they did? He returned to the map and surveyed the contour lines for a second time.

In keeping with his character and previous battles, Montgomery's Baytown was a meticulously planned, methodical attack. By deciding to overwhelm the enemy with superior numbers and firepower, the diminutive general provided yet more evidence that he would do whatever he could to avoid unnecessary casualties. The landings on the beaches north of Reggio, so recently used by the Germans in their evacuation from Sicily, were successful with the defending Italians once again collapsing. 'Irresistibly the scene was like a regatta', wrote the Australian war correspondent Alan Moorehead, describing the crossing from Messina on 3 September, 'or some yachting carnival perhaps, even Cowes . . . The soldiers laughed and waved.' Alan Whicker, then making his second assault landing, agreed that it was all unexpectedly easy, 'peaceful' and 'almost gentlemanly', with the surrendered Italians assisting in the unloading of the British craft, guiding troops through minefields and cheering Montgomery when he arrived.

The news had been greeted enthusiastically by the Prime Minister, who was staying with the President at the White House. The two men got on well, but Churchill was an exhausting guest, as Roosevelt revealed to a colleague: 'I'm nearly dead. I have to talk to the P.M. all night, and he gets a bright idea in the middle of the night and comes pattering down the hall to my bedroom in his bare feet.' The invasion of Italy had given Churchill's fertile imagination a new lease of life, and when he heard that the Italians had also signed a secret armistice agreement he grinned broadly and scampered to the President's side proclaiming, like Sherlock Holmes to Dr Watson, that 'the game's afoot'. The next step was to make the armistice public and strike Italy's sixty-one field divisions from the Axis order of battle. But that was easier said than done as Badoglio continued to fear a 'spiteful' German reaction, demanding that no announcement be made until Allied troops were more firmly established on Italian soil. Already disgusted at Italian duplicity, the Allies immediately began to pressurise the President for an early declaration in the hope that the Germans would withdraw northwards before 'Avalanche' was unleashed. The discussions continued as Eighth Army eased itself into the rocky Calabria, at Italy's heel. The advance proved demanding for Montgomery's two and a half divisions who were faced by two divisions of Lieutenant General Traugott Herr's LXXVI Panzer Corps – both of which were also to end up at Anzio. By pulling away from the laborious British attack, and the skilful demolition of roads and bridges, 26th Panzer and 29th Panzer Grenadier Divisions stifled any offensive momentum. Montgomery would have to be patient, advance steadily and hope that Clark would not rely on Eighth Army assistance if Avalanche ran into trouble. Eisenhower did all that he could to limit the risk of significant problems for the attack, but grew increasingly exasperated at Badoglio's failure to disclose the armistice. Eventually the tantrum-prone Eisenhower could stand no more, and was granted permission by both Roosevelt and Churchill to broadcast news of the agreement even as the Allied armada approached the Bay of Salerno.

As Eisenhower rehearsed his short speech on the morning of 8 September, Kesselring was reading air reports about enemy shipping movements in the Tyrrhenian Sea. Although his staff officers were unsure what (if anything) the enemy were up to, it looked as if a convoy was heading from Bizerta in North Africa, to either Salerno, Naples, or the coast north of Rome. At his great walnut desk Kesselring examined the reports, pondering potential scenarios. An aide de camp squinted as he entered the room to bring the Field Marshal an update. Sunshine flooded the office through a window at Kesselring's back, and reflected off the highly polished parquet flooring, blinding staff and interlopers alike. It was an old trick but the competitive old soldier liked it. He studied the paper, checked his maps and just before noon acted decisively. Von Vietinghoff was ordered to withdraw the divisions facing Eighth Army in the Calabria more quickly, and to put all troops in the central sector of Italy on alert. Kesselring was concentrating his forces, seeking a rapid riposte to any Allied landing. He continued to shuffle formations into the afternoon until his concentration was broken by air raid sirens. As he left his office for the shelter escorted by his bodyguard, several anti-aircraft guns coughed into life. Their fire drowned out the drone of 130 approaching American B-17 bombers. The Field Marshal agonised as the hour-long raid devastated his headquarters, cut his communications and cost nearly 100 men their lives. It was an attack that dislocated Kesselring's command at the very time it needed to be in control. He had been lucky to escape with his life. He emerged from the bunker and grimaced. The raid had confirmed his suspicions that an Allied landing was imminent.

At 1830 hours, when Clark's force was just nine hours from Salerno,

Eisenhower's voice was heard on Radio Algiers informing the world of the Italian armistice. Although the announcement was not a complete shock to the Italian government, it was a surprise. Indeed, when Raffaele Guariglia, the Foreign Minister, met Badoglio at the Royal Palace after the broadcast to ask him about the severity of the situation, Badoglio candidly declared: 'We're fucked.' The Italians did not have a plan to resist the Germans. They were not organised nor were they motivated to do so. The announcement was confirmed three hours later by Badoglio: 'The Italian Government', he bleated, 'having recognised the impossibility of continuing an unequal struggle against overwhelming opposing forces, with the intention of saving the nation from further and graver misfortunes, has requested General Eisenhower, Commander-in-Chief of the Anglo-American Forces, for an armistice. The request has been granted. Consequently any act of hostility against Anglo-American Forces must cease on the part of the Italian forces everywhere. They will, however, resist any attacks that may be made upon them from any quarter.'

Italy was out of the war and the Royal Family, Badoglio, ministers and the army general staff fled Rome for Brindisi. The news of the armistice was passed on to the anxious troops in the Avalanche armada. They cheered and some sang ('Run Rabbit Run' was a favourite in the British vessels) in the belief that the Italians would at that very moment be withdrawing from the Bay of Salerno. It took the experienced, intelligent and responsible to get the men to focus on the job in hand by warning them that the Germans might be waiting for them. It was a confusing situation and Norman Lewis, then a British Intelligence officer attached to the Fifth Army Headquarters and who was later to write *Naples '44*, a seminal book on the Italian Campaign, was as perplexed as anybody: 'It was clear that no one knew what awaited us', he wrote, 'despite all the agents we had assumed to be working for us in Italy, absolutely no information had come out regarding the situation.' In spite of the warnings, some salvaged the condoms with which they had been issued. Removing them from the muzzles of their rifles, they hoped that they might now be useful in other ways.

The Italians also greeted the news with glee, but exhilaration evaporated with the swift reaction of the German troops. In their naivety, many had believed that an armistice would lead to an immediate German withdrawal, but the reality was to be very different. In order to protect themselves, the Germans unleashed the first phase of 'Plan Asche' in which they swiftly disarmed the Italians whilst occupying Rome and other towns and cities: '. . . and so began a new chapter in our living nightmare' recalled one Roman. In the Bay of Salerno, Major General Rudolf Sieckenius's resolute 16th Panzer Division replaced the jaded Italian defenders, quickly improving its defences. Kesselring's foresight had given Tenth Army an opportunity quickly to concentrate its full weight against a landing. Von Vietinghoff had five divisions within striking distance of the Avalanche coast, and the Prussian aristocrat knew just as well as Clark that the side which built up its forces fastest was likely to win any beachhead battle. Coming from the sea Fifth Army might have been considered at a disadvantage in this contest, but Tenth Army was, as Westphal recognised, 'poorly fitted to resist an attack from the sea.' The Allies had surprise mastery of the sea, and dominated the skies from where they could attack the mustering Germans as they advanced along the poor Italian roads. Nevertheless, amphibious warfare was notoriously difficult to master – particularly for a novice such as Clark – and at one point during the coming battle, it looked as if the Allies might be pushed back into the sea.

Avalanche did not start badly on 9 September, although landing in the darkness of the early hours did lead to some confusion. It was only Sieckenius's particularly strong and well-positioned defences opposite VI Corps's 36th US Infantry Division that caused difficulties. Enjoying the elevation of the mountains, clear fields of fire and pre-surveyed killing zones for their machine guns and artillery, the Germans hit Walker's division hard. American journalist Jack Belden was one of the first out of the landing craft and had a torrid time:

> This was the third landing I had made, and it was the hardest . . . Shells were flashing in the water, flames were yellowing the sky, and bullets were slapping into the boat. They snapped over our heads, rattled against the boat sides like hail and beat at the ramp door . . . the boat shuddered and the ramp creaked open . . . I stepped down . . . At last I was in the continent of Europe.

Despite obstinate German defence on the night of the landings, during the first day the situation was never desperate operationally, and the two Allied corps forged small beachheads. It was only when Clark tried to take the high ground and build a strong defensive perimeter that he ran into difficulties. The Germans had reacted quickly. Faced with Montgomery's advance in the south and the successful Slapstick landing at Taranto, Kesselring prioritised and decided to focus on Salerno. Ordering the Hermann Göring Panzer and 15th Panzer Grenadiers Divisions to mass against British X Corps on the Allied left, and 26th Panzer Division and 29th Panzer Grenadier Division against the Americans on the right, the Germans hoped to stop the Allies pushing inland, and then break them. So good was the response of Tenth Army that on 12 September von Vietinghoff was able to launch a counter-attack into the gap between Fifth Army's two corps. The carefully focused ferocity of the thrust led Clark to confide in his diary later that day: 'The situation is extremely critical.' Striking hard against Walker's beleaguered division, German armour looked set to reach the landing beaches and threatened the VI Corps headquarters, a large barn hung with drying tobacco leaves, where Dawley panicked. When asked by Clark what he was going to do the General replied: 'Nothing, I've no reserves. All I've got is a prayer.' Clark was unimpressed, but he too had a momentary wobble and had to be dissuaded from re-embarking VI Corps and sending them over to join the British. He later suggested that this was merely a contingency plan, and his memoirs went so far as to paint a picture of him taking a bold decision against received wisdom: 'I thought it over carefully as I walked along the beach', he declared: 'I was dirty and tired and worried, and finally I said, "To hell with the theory! I am not going to issue any such orders!" Furthermore, I decided, the only way they're going to get us off this beach is to push us, step by step, into the water.' Just as Clark's words reveal a good deal about his personality and obsession with image, Harold Alexander's laconic declaration says much about him: 'If the Germans had pushed on to the sea their arrival might have caused us some embarrassment.'

The Wehrmacht were eventually held by a stoical defence conducted by a mixture of troops including the 504th Parachute Infantry Regiment (which had been dropped within the VI Corps perimeter for the purpose), together with headquarters and support staff. Two batteries of artillery firing at close range also provided much needed fire power. At one point Norman Lewis was ordered to take his revolver and 'assist in the defence of Army Headquarters against Mark IV and Tiger tanks that were rolling towards us'. Lewis was not impressed. 'Outright panic now started', he continued, 'and spread among the American troops left behind. In the belief that our position had been infiltrated by German infantry they began shooting each other, and there were blood-chilling screams from men hit by the bullets . . . What we saw was ineptitude and cowardice spreading down from the command, and this resulted in chaos.' Clark bravely prowled along the frontline encouraging his men and gaining information. On one occasion he personally took charge of defences against an attack by eighteen German tanks. Seeing a Lieutenant General playing the part of a Lieutenant must have been inspirational. This was not swaggering; it was remarkable leadership that made all the difference.

For four days the battle was precariously poised, but support by 15-inch naval guns and airpower tipped the balance. Lieutenant Rocholl of the 16th Reconnaissance Battalion, 16th Panzer Division wrote in his diary: 'Nearer and nearer the shells dropped, with shrapnel flying past uncomfortably close. Involuntarily one ducked together in the armoured car, although it would not have given the slightest protection. Suddenly there was a sharp crack and a deafening explosion . . . all the earth and dirt seemed to drop into our open turrets. This was a bit too much . . .'. Rocholl's diary was later found on his dead body. Taking heavy casualties and lacking fuel, the Germans gradually began to tire. By 16 September, with some 170,000 troops and 200 tanks ashore, Clark believed that the crisis had passed and Kesselring ordered his forces to disengage – just as Montgomery was approaching from the south.

Alexander had urged the Eighth Army commander to greater efforts on 10 September in order to assist Clark at Salerno. But Montgomery was revelling in his own private war and explained that the terrain and enemy demolitions continued to hinder his advance. Clark was underwhelmed, and on 12 September as the Germans were driving towards the beach, he wrote to Alexander: 'I hope that Eighth Army will attack with all possible vigor in order to contain 26th and 29th Panzer Divisions to maximum.' Alexander hoped so too, and ordered Montgomery to get to Salerno 'whatever the risks' – but it remained a very cautious advance. It was not until 15 September that Clark received a message from Montgomery which started: 'It looks as if you may be having not too good a time, and I do hope that all will go well with you . . . We are on the way to lend a hand, and it will be a great day when we actually join hands . . . .' Clark's terse reply ended: 'Situation here well in hand'. By the time Eighth Army finally linked up with Clark's troops on the following day, it was too late to influence the battle, but just in time to take the glory. During the fighting in Sicily Clark believed that the British media had failed to give the Americans the credit that they deserved, and now BBC reports painted Montgomery's advance as 'courageously pushing aside enemy resistance' to go to Fifth Army's aid. Clark was incandescent: 'We'd get reports from the BBC that the Eighth Army was coming to our rescue,' he later complained:

> I remember sending Monty a message that we needed help. The faster he could get, and the nearer he could get, the very momentum of his Army coming up was a deterrent to the enemy and a boost to us. But there wasn't any physical joining of hands to the extent that any British came to intervene in the battle. Monty sent me some sort of personal message saying that we had joined hands, and I said, 'Well I haven't felt the grip of your hand yet.'

The difficult situation was exacerbated when Clark was told by Alexander's headquarters to: 'First, play up the Eighth Army progress henceforth. Second, the Fifth Army is pushing the enemy back on his right flank.' Clark read the missive disbelievingly and vowed not to be cheated again. After Salerno he became increasingly suspicious and critical of British officers above – and below – him, which coloured his relationship with Alexander and came to distort his operational planning. He also became obsessed with public relations and soon had fifty men working to ensure that his efforts, and those of his Army (and particularly the American part of it), were given maximum publicity. Ensuring this he ordered a 'three to one rule'. Every press release was to mention Clark three times on the first page and at least once on all other pages – and the General also demanded that photographs only be taken of him from his left side. His public relations team even came up with a Fifth Army song: 'Stand up stand up for General Clark, let's sing the praises of General Clark . . .'. He was very fond of that song. In this way Clark became as adept at using the Fifth Army to promote himself as Montgomery was with the Eighth Army. In many respects the two men were very similar, not least in their self-confidence. In fact, Clark and Montgomery got on quite well, particularly after the cagey young American had learned how to flatter the effete old Brit. Clark's diary records that he once said to Montgomery: 'The Fifth Army is just a young Army trying hard to get along, while the Eighth Army is a battle-tried veteran. We would appreciate your teaching us some of your tricks.' Montgomery was delighted with this and gave him some advice: 'From time to time you will get instructions from Alexander that you won't understand. When you do . . . tell him to go to hell.'

Salerno had been a severe test for Clark, his commanders and his troops. It was yet more invaluable experience, but Ernest Dawley was not given the opportunity to put what he learned to the test. Superiors who had visited the VI Corps headquarters during the battle were united in their doubts about Dawley. According to Clark he was prone to 'go to pieces in emergencies', Alexander dubbed him 'a broken reed', and Eisenhower considered him 'nervous and indecisive'. Dawley was sacked and on 20 September replaced by John Lucas. The crusty West Virginian was not Clark's ideal successor, older and lacking the hard edge that Clark was really looking for, but he was available and experienced. Clark was not particularly taken with McCreery either, but to have removed both corps commanders would have raised questions about Clark's ability to harness the talents of his subordinates. In any case, even a rebuke to a British corps commander in an American Army at that sensitive time would have been politically unwise. Nevertheless, some emerged from Avalanche with their reputations enhanced, prime among these being Truscott and his 3rd Division, with whom Clark had a strong affinity having served with that formation just before the war – 'the finest division in this or any other theatre' – and Darby – 'an outstanding battle leader' – and his Ranger Force. Clark was also feted. Six years younger than the average age of a divisional commander, he had revealed some inexperience, but was now a proven battle winner with a Distinguished Service Cross pinned on his chest for the extraordinary heroism that he displayed during the fighting. It was well deserved. Alexander was impressed, Churchill began calling him 'the American Eagle' and Eisenhower, although perhaps not the most objective assessor, said that he was a man of 'enormous ability, intelligence and drive.' However, the American General Jacob Devers, who was to get to know Clark well during the course of 1944, recognised both Clark's foibles and talent, observing that he was a 'cold, distinguished, conceited, selfish, clever, intellectual, resourceful officer who secures excellent results quickly. Very ambitious.' Omar Bradley was equally sceptical, remarking that Clark 'seemed false, somehow, too eager to impress, too hungry for the lime-light, promotions and personal publicity'. Both assessments are accurate – Mark Clark not only wanted to be successful, he wanted to be seen as a great war hero who Americans could relate to. In his memoir *Calculated Risk* published in 1951, he dubbed himself a 'tall and dirty Western bandit on the prowl'. The Chicago-born cowboy had made an impressive entrance, but still had much to learn.

Field Marshal Kesselring and von Vietinghoff had lost the Battle of Salerno, but their confidence was not greatly undermined. Although the beachhead had not been destroyed in spite of a propitious position, both men looked with admiration at their achievement in initially stifling Avalanche. Kesselring knew that Hitler was analysing the battle, but remained convinced that his argument for defence south of Rome had been strengthened by the landings. The Field Marshal now claimed, much to Rommel's ire, that he could stall the Allied advance for between six to nine months. Salerno became, therefore, another German morale victory and from it Tenth Army drew strength. As Fifth Army reorganised after its exertions, the Germans prepared to fight delaying actions in front of Naples. As he wanted to see more, Hitler did not rush into a decision about a withdrawal, but while he continued in his deliberations, the first important steps were being taken towards Anzio.

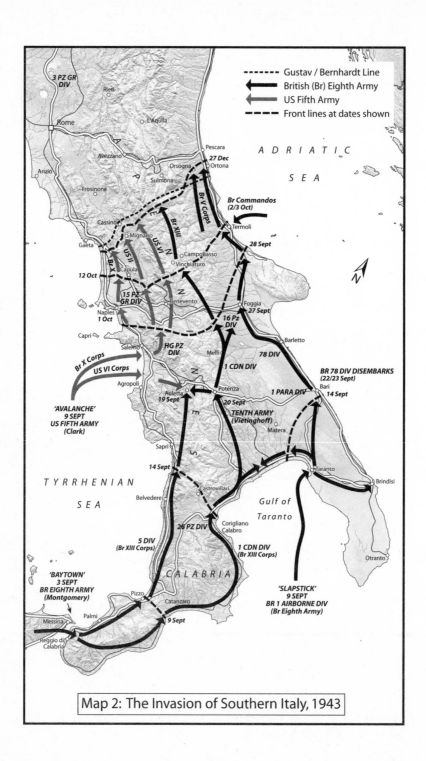

Map 2: The Invasion of Southern Italy, 1943

Gustav / Bernhardt Line
British (Br) Eighth Army
US Fifth Army
Front lines at dates shown

3 PZ GR DIV
RieB
Rome
L'Aquila
Avezzano
Orsogna
Pescara
27 Dec
Ortona
Anzio
Sulmona
Frosinone
Br Commandos
(2/3 Oct)
Cassino
Mignano
Termoli
Br XIII
28 Sept
Gaeta
US VI
Campobasso
Vinchiaturo
Capula
12 Oct
15 PZ
GR DIV
Benevento
Foggia
27 Sept
Naples
1 Oct
16 Pz
DIV
Barletto
Capri
HG PZ
DIV
Salerno
Melfi
78 DIV
Br X Corps
Agropoli
1 CDN DIV
BR 78 DIV DISEMBARKS
(22/23 Sept)
US VI Corps
Auletta
19 Sept
Potenza
20 Sept
1 PARA DIV
Bari
14 Sept
'AVALANCHE'
9 SEPT
US FIFTH ARMY
(Clark)
TENTH ARMY
(Vietinghoff)
Matera
Sapri
14 Sept
TYRRHENIAN
SEA
Castrovillari
Taranto
Brindisi
Belvedere
Gulf of
Taranto
26 PZ DIV
Corigliano
Calabro
5 DIV
(Br XIII Corps)
1 CDN DIV
(Br XIII Corps)
Otranto
CALABRIA
'BAYTOWN'
3 SEPT
BR EIGHTH ARMY
(Montgomery)
Pizzo
'SLAPSTICK'
9 SEPT
BR 1 AIRBORNE DIV
(Br Eighth Army)
Catanzaro
Messina
Palmi
9 Sept
Reggio di
Calabria

A D R I A T I C

S E A

Gulf of
Taranto

CHAPTER 2

Viktor, Barbara, Bernhardt and Gustav

(The Italian Campaign October–November 1943)

Albert Kesselring's face broke into a grin and with a wave of his hand he changed the subject. Colleagues who had just arrived from Berlin seemed more interested in the Field Marshal's narrow escape from the air raid at Frascati than examining the resource implications of his defensive scheme. Or were they just a little nervous at the prospect of scrutinising the phlegmatic Field Marshal's proposals? They chuntered on about the beautiful location of their host's new headquarters in the mysterious Monte Soratte just north of Rome, with one suggesting that such a place was wasted on the Italians. Kesselring responded by claiming that the locals believed that its many fissures were gateways to the underworld, and ushered the party into a tiny conference room with a scowl. The guests entered the dimly lit chamber laughing at Italian gullibility, but the unamused Field Marshal did not follow and made his apologies before leaving them in Westphal's hands. As coffee was served there was a consensus amongst the jilted officers that Kesselring looked tired and had lost weight, whilst at that very moment the subject of their concerns was striding so briskly down the corridor that he was outpacing his young aide. By the time that the cups of the 'obnoxious, cackling ephemera' were half empty, Kesselring was being sped away in a waiting staff car to a desolate landing strip. He glanced at his watch again – still twenty minutes late – and began to fidget with his gloves. He did not like to keep his front line troops waiting and had already cancelled this visit to Naples twice. The car eased to a halt next to a Ju-88 and the pilot saluted. Although the Field Marshal often flew himself and was well known for his forays over enemy lines for 'practice' and to 'test the temperature of the front', he had decided not to do so this time. Today he wanted to concentrate on an examination of the vital ground south of Rome. As the Ju-88 revved its engines, Kesselring spread a map out on his knees, not looking up until airborne. Peering through the perspex window, he scrutinised the landscape below: the Alban Hills; Frosinone; the Liri Valley; Cassino and the peaks towards the River Volturno. He believed that he could stop Alexander here and protect Rome until the spring at least. But would Berlin think so too?

Westphal was in full agreement with Kesselring's plans to defend central Italy. It was obvious that the Germans needed to make a stand and deny the Allies a morale-boosting seizure of Rome together with all of the military and strategic benefits offered by occupation of the region. Moreover, such a defence was eminently achievable for, as the Chief of Staff wrote: 'The whole of Italy south of the Po is mountainous and so offers good prospects of slowing down the operations of an enemy in the interior, if not stopping them altogether.' The two men were in no doubt that the Allies could be forced into an unsuitable frustrating slogging match at the very time that they were gearing up for the cross-Channel invasion. In this Vietinghoff's Tenth Army were already in the midst of playing an overture to Kesselring's requiem: Hube's XIV and Herr's LXXVI Panzer Corps were conducting a destructive fighting withdrawal against Fifth Army and

Eighth Army then pushing on to Foggia and Naples respectively. Their defensive skills drew grudging admiration from Mark Clark who later wrote: 'Our thirty-mile advance to Naples was anything but easy . . . Kesselring was a master of delaying tactics.' But whilst the Germans could hinder, they could not stop Alexander from ultimately taking his objectives. Thus, the devastated Foggia fell to Montgomery on 27 September and soon after work began to make its airfields once more operational. Within three weeks US Fifteenth Air Force was launching bomber offensives into Germany and central Europe, and US Twelfth Air Support Command was assisting the ground forces. The Allies never underestimated the important advantages of airpower, but the 300,000 tons of shipping required to resurrect Foggia severely undermined Montgomery's ability to sustain his advance. Logistical difficulties also impeded Fifth Army until Naples was captured on 1 October. As Clark's troops entered the city desperate for its port facilities, the recent four-day uprising was self-evident: destroyed vehicles, rubble, smashed glass and the remains of fires littered the streets. A ten-year-old Sophia Loren had witnessed this ferocious outburst of violence:

Ragged little boys from the slums finally rebelled against the German oppression and took matters into their own hands . . . Armed with bottles filled with gasoline they had stolen from the Germans, these boys ignited rags they had stuffed into bottles to serve as wicks, and then darted from side streets and swarmed over the huge German tanks, stuffing the bottles into the gun slits in the tanks just as the gasoline exploded . . . They attacked tanks and trucks and installations, and no German soldier on the street was immune from their swarming attacks. Their fire bombs were exploding everywhere . . . Many of these boys were shot and killed by the Germans, their bloody little bodies dotting the streets, but nothing daunted their attacks.

As the fighting in the city peaked, the Germans looted, planted time-delayed bombs and systematically destroyed anything – including food stores and the utilities – that might be of use to Fifth Army. Having already suffered at the hands of Allied bombers which had badly damaged a third of their city, it was little wonder that this so-called 'anthill of humanity' was on its knees. 'We made slow progress through shattered streets, past landslides of rubble from bombed buildings', wrote Norman Lewis: 'People stood in doorways, faces the colour of pumice, to wave mechanically to the victors, the apathetic Fascist salute of last week having been converted to the apathetic V-sign of today, but on the whole the civilian mood seemed one of stunned indifference.' Understandably bewildered Neapolitans had reservations about whether their liberators would be any more benevolent towards them than the Germans had been. Clark, nevertheless, was justifiably proud to have taken the city, not only the first to fall in Italy, but the first on continental Europe, and on 5 October wrote to his wife Maurine: 'I give you Naples for your birthday. I love you . . .' Recognising the political and military necessity of a stable Naples, he immediately oversaw a frenzy of works – and ensured that he was seen to be doing so. Clark was a difficult figure to miss on the streets, the lanky man of action, trousers tucked into paratrooper boots, with a green scarf worn jauntily around his neck. 'He loved the attention', recalls one correspondent, 'and we loved him for making our jobs so easy.' The wrecks of over 130 ships clogging the harbour were removed as the water and power supplies were improved, but food shortages remained acute. Lewis, working as a linguist in a unit dealing with security in Naples, witnessed children prising limpets off the rocks and selling them by the pint. 'If boiled long enough', he said, 'they could be expected to add some faint fishy flavour to a broth produced from any edible odds and ends . . . Nothing, absolutely nothing that can be tackled by the human digestive system is wasted in Naples . . . There is a persistent rumour of a decline in the cat population of the city.'

The situation was eased when the harbour reopened on 5 October, but was not solved. Naples, well known for its larceny, was inspired by the war and 'Allied crews', wrote Alan Whicker, 'were not geared up to deal with the mass of well-organised criminality which in a hungry lawless land had become woven into every life. It was calculated that one third of all supplies landed at this major port was instantly stolen, to reappear in the black market. So it was Christmas every day for the gangsters . . . .' Prostitution was also rife with boys acting as pimps for their mothers and sisters who sold themselves for a packet of biscuits. Venereal disease spread quickly and by the end of the year – despite warnings and the widespread availability of prophylactics – it had been the cause of more casualties than the fighting. German air raids, the random destruction caused by the time-delay bombs, and a typhus outbreak in the overcrowded back streets, added to the growing evidence that Naples was ailing. Indeed, the avant-garde American war correspondent Reynolds Packard reported a Dantesque world where 'prostitution, black-marketing, racketeering, and confidence games were rampant. Desertions became wholesale: U.S. soldiers would shack up with Italian girls and not bother to return to their regiments. Groups of these deserters banded together and became dangerous outlaws . . . Naples became a crucible in which moral values were boiled down to a residue of basic necessities and wild desires.' Naples had become a running sore, but it was vital to Fifth Army, and Clark was willing to spend time and resources nursing it.

Back in London, Churchill delighted in Alexander's progress and was in ebullient mood when he wrote to him on 2 October: 'I hope . . . by the end of the month or thereabouts . . . that we shall meet in Rome.' Alexander also felt positive and from his new headquarters in Bari replied: 'All will be well. The German will be harassed and continuous pressure applied to his rearguards all the time . . . .' The Prime Minister was so energised by the news that he bored colleagues with his plans for Italy and its strategic providence. During this time Winston

Churchill's desire to take Rome verged on obsession, proclaiming on many occasions that: 'He who holds Rome holds the title deeds of Italy.' Like a love-struck youth, Churchill couldn't get Italy out of his head. Even those that had experience of his previous passions and fancies found it tiresome. Alan Brooke went so far as to confide in his diary on 7 October: 'Churchill is in a very dangerous condition, most unbalanced, and God knows how we shall finish this war if this goes on.' But the Prime Minister was not alone in coveting Rome, for Mark Clark was also beginning to respond to the allure of the Eternal City. Both men looked forward to a steady advance and the capture of the capital in the foreseeable future, but on 4 October Hitler made his critical decision. A stand would be made south of Rome with Kesselring holding 'successive defensive positions' in the southern Apennines. The Apennines form Italy's mountainous spine, a spine that physically separated Alexander's two Armies. Over 840 miles long, 80 miles wide and with peaks averaging 4,000 feet, the area was amongst the wildest and most remote in the country. Such terrain would severely limit the Allies' ability to apply their superior firepower, armour and tactical airpower, but would enhance German defensive opportunities as winter approached. Kesselring was relieved. He could now provide his tired troops with the prospect of holding ground for the first time after their retreats through North Africa, Sicily and southern Italy. But first the necessary defences had to be constructed for them, and 'lines' were developed along the 'ribs' that thrust out from the Apennines to the coast to create barriers. Created to sustain shorter rearguard actions were the lightly fortified Viktor Line that stretched along the River Volturno in the west across the country to the River Biferno, and the Barbara Line just behind it. But behind them came the main battle position, the Winter or Bernhardt Line which emerged some seventy-five miles from Rome. Spanning ninety miles from the River Garigliano to the River Sangro, its role was to hold the Allies for as long as possible. A rearward extension to this position was eventually constructed to protect the obvious route to Rome through the Liri Valley. This Gustav Line development became an even more formidable obstacle than the Bernhardt Line. Centred on the town of Cassino with its 1,700 feet high peak topped with a sixth-century monastery, its deep underground bunkers, labyrinthine tunnels, machine gun emplacements, anti-tank ditches, minefields and barbed wire were to be the stuff of an attacker's nightmare. Yet in October 1943, these defences were mere pencil marks on Kesselring's map. Time was short, the Allies were massing and with Berlin watching him closely the work began. 'The pressure Kesselring now brought to bear upon his subordinates was colossal', his biographer has written, 'as he moved tirelessly from place to place, driving, urging and cajoling in his determination to exact every morsel of work and ingenuity from weary men and to make the best of the relatively limited resources at his disposal.'

15th Army Group struggled on after Foggia and Naples had fallen, and threw themselves into the Viktor Line during the first weeks of October. Eighth Army crossed the River Biferno on the 3rd, overwhelming the German defences soon after, whilst the Fifth Army crossed the River Volturno on the night of 12–13 October and then forced the Germans back. With Viktor cracked the two Armies pressed forward. It was a slow, painful and costly slog – just as the Germans had intended – which made Churchill's anticipated meeting with Alexander in Rome look presumptuous and preposterous. John P. Lucas's VI Corps were attacking up the valley of the middle Volturno through the Barbara Line to Verano, and found the going 'enormously difficult.' Lucian Truscott, the commander of 3rd US Infantry Division agreed, writing that 'narrow valleys were broken by the intensely cultivated plots. Rugged mountains rose to elevations of more than 5,000 feet. Our road wound its way through defile after defile, crossed over numerous bridges, and clung precariously to precipitous cliffs in many places. Off the roads, occasional cart trails led to villages nestled among the mountains.' Fighting in such terrain required special skills that neither side had anticipated or possessed. Their weapons, transport, training, tactics – everything was designed for fighting on flat ground. In spite of their experiences in Sicily, neither opponent was mentally or physically prepared for mountain warfare. Even so, the innovative Germans developed tactics based on their methods in the Calabria: carefully positioned demolitions protected by mines, booby traps and a rearguard of dug-in infantry armed with machine guns, light automatics and mortars fully supported by the artillery. Von Vietinghoff chose where and when to fight extremely carefully, ensuring that tactical geography chronically undermined Allied ability to dislodge them. It was a situation that Montgomery had warned against back in September when he observed of the enemy: 'You must never fight the battle *his* way. You must choose the ground. He must be made to fight the battle according to your plan. Never *his* plan. Never.'

For the Allies, the seemingly endless series of battles were intensely demoralising. Paratrooper Ross Carter and his comrades in 82nd US Airborne Division were extremely tough and had been well trained, but the landscape filled them with 'dread and foreboding as we sat scrutinising the gray, weathered, rotten, landsliding, precipitous, ledge-covered, waterless, barren mountain. On the peak Krautheads were hidden in caves, grottoes, camouflaged pillboxes, foxholes and behind the rocks.' They lamented that this was ground that 'God must have made when He was mad at somebody and forgot to improve after He made it.' Nonetheless, like the Germans they adapted their tactics and developed their outflanking and infiltration skills. In a classic operation, a regiment would advance along the main route until stopped by demolitions, at which point one battalion engaged the enemy and protected the deployment of the division's artillery, whilst the other battalions took to the mountains to outflank the enemy positions. During these movements the vastness of the landscape swallowed the units as they scaled the slopes, and then the broken ground fragmented their attacks.

When the enemy was eventually engaged, the fighting was often at close quarters and required considerable creativeness. 'I threw dozens of hand grenades, and even rocks,' Private Fred Ford recalled, 'and I guess I killed plenty of Germans . . . But I never had a single chance to shoot my automatic rifle.' Eventually the defenders were forced to concede a mile or two of precious Italian real estate, but it was a time-consuming, exhausting process. There was little respite for the infantry, and the occasional lulls only gave them just enough time to regroup and prepare for their next action. The battalions moved at night through a devastated landscape slipping, cursing and fumbling until the sounds of battle told them that they had arrived. Then they would dig in and snatch a few hours' sleep before attacking at dawn. The elderly-looking forty-three-year-old American war correspondent Ernie Pyle spent a considerable amount of time with the GIs here in late 1943. His stories, published in over 400 weekly and 200 daily newspapers, were as popular at the fighting front as they were back in the States. Living with the 'Fabulous Infantry' as he dubbed them, Pyle got to understand and respect these young men:

> Their life consisted wholly and solely of war for they were and always had been front-line infantrymen. They survived because the fates were kind to them, certainly – but also because they had become hard and immensely wise in animallike [sic] ways of self-preservation. None of them liked war. They all wanted to go home, but they had been at it so long they knew how to take care of themselves and how to lead others. Around a little group like them every company was built.

As Pyle revealed in his candid articles, these men shared a bond that only those that had suffered and faced death together could understand. Their needs were as basic as their hopes were fragile, and most of them accepted their fate with little more than a good-natured grumble.

Without the tenacity of the infantry, the Italian Campaign would very quickly have come to a grinding halt, but other arms were also vital. The engineers cleared obstructions, built bridges, constructed roads, cleared mines and carried out scores of other jobs that allowed the infantry to operate. Alexander said that the work of the engineers was 'without parallel' – and they publicised their successes at every opportunity. Alan Whicker was amused when drivers were 'welcomed' to a village or a river crossing by a sapper unit. 'On one mountain road where as usual the Germans had blown every bridge,' he recalled, 'the first replacement had a large sign saying proudly, "You are Crossing this Bridge Courtesy of the US Fifth Army Engineers who Built it in 3 Days 14 Hours and 26 Minutes!" At the next blown river-crossing the familiar British Bailey bridge had a small notice: "This Bridge was built by the REs in 9 hours 42 minutes". Underneath in brackets and small print: ("There is *nothing* unusual about this bridge"). They must have been the Sappers who invented Cool.' It was over these bridges and up and down the rutted roads that trucks rattled day and night carrying the necessities of war. As they approached the front, signs directing them to a plethora of units assaulted their tired drivers. One noted: 'we'd have to pull off the road and study the hodgepodge for five minutes before finding out anything.' Infantry supplies had to be unloaded at the foot of a mountain where they were picked up by mule teams. Rations, water, ammunition, telephone cable, radios, clothing – everything that was needed to sustain offensive operations was hauled forward. It was common for the last part of the journey to prove too steep even for the mules and so soldiers became the beasts of burden. It was an exhausting and labour intensive undertaking made more complicated in October when, according to Clark, 'the rain came down in torrents, vehicles were bogged above the axles, and the lowlands became seas of mud.'

The vile weather dominates the memories and diaries of those who fought through Italy during the autumn of 1943. The drenching rain and biting cold tormented the troops incessantly as they were exposed to the full ferocity of the elements and suffered wet clothes for weeks on end. The men in 3rd US Infantry Division were still wearing the uniforms that they had been issued with during the summer whilst their cold weather kit languished in Sicily due to a lack of shipping. Truscott wrote: 'Cold and wet caused extreme discomfort, and it was beginning to affect the health of the command. Respiratory diseases, fevers of undetermined origin, and jaundice were beginning to take their toll . . . Whilst our losses in battle had not been excessive, the daily toll was beginning to mount, and losses from non-battle causes such as sickness and injury were even larger and were affecting the combat effectiveness of every battalion.' Pneumonia and dysentery were commonplace, and trench foot was endemic in circumstances where men would often go for weeks without changing their soaking socks or remove their boots. But in spite of the physical and mental trauma of the fighting, psychiatric casualties were rare. Indeed Pyle wrote: 'comparatively few men *do* crack up. The mystery to me is that there is anybody at all, no matter how strong, who can keep his spirit from breaking in the midst of battle.' Even so, on top of the 40,000 battle casualties Fifth Army suffered by the end of the year, there were another 50,000 non-battle casualties and perhaps 20,000 deserters at any one time. Morale was haemorrhaging, but Clark was acutely aware of the situation and wisely instructed subordinate commanders to 'give particularly careful attention to the welfare of our troops' and 'minister continuously to their mental and physical well-being'. The Red Cross had an important role in this and many young women consequently suffered considerable hardship living in tents close to the front line. Clark wrote a glowing endorsement of their work in his diary saying that their distribution of 'newly-made doughnuts and words of good cheer to soldiers just out of combat' were much appreciated.

More substantially, however, Fifth Army began to give its men a short break from the front in a 'rest-area programme'. In Naples the lucky troops could enjoy dances, films, shows and go on sightseeing trips. The first quota of 800 men left Truscott's division for the city on 5 November. They were a sorry sight noted the general, 'Haggard, dirty, bedraggled, long-haired, unshaven, clothing in tatters, worn out boots, their appearance was appalling'. But on their return a week later, they were 'rested, clean, shaven and trimmed, and cleanly clad in new uniforms . . . The effect of this rest camp program on the morale of the battle-weary men of the command was of inestimable value, and saved many men who would otherwise have broken under the strain.'

For those still at the front, the prospects of a short leave gave them a little optimism, but just staying alive occupied them constantly. There were nasty enemy surprises at every turn. Villages in particular were viewed with suspicion, even if they were empty. When Ross Carter entered one such place the atmosphere was definitely eerie: 'The strong glacial winds blowing off a snow-capped mountain banged shutters and doors on the deserted houses in this weirdly creepy, empty, lonely village. We couldn't see a bird, a chicken or a human being. In some homes plates of half-eaten food were on the table . . . It reminded me of Pompeii.' Booby traps often took the lives of the unwary, and the mines which peppered the ground were a constant concern. On occasion the Allied troops found none of these and were lulled into a false sense of security only then to come under the concentrated fire of the patiently waiting enemy guns. More often, however, the Germans had to be prised out of buildings one by one and in this the Allied artillery played a crucial role. Ernie Pyle visited a battery of 155-mm howitzers commanded by a fifty-year-old textile plant executive who was a veteran of the First World War. His four 12-ton guns were dug in in a rough square reinforced by sandbags and covered by a camouflage net. 'They were terrifically big guns,' he wrote, 'and Lordy, did they make a noise!' With a range of eleven miles and relatively safe on the reverse slope of a hill, these weapons levelled many villages. Such acts were virtually Fifth Army policy, indeed an indignant Norman Lewis referred to Clark as 'the destroying angel of southern Italy'. On one visit to the front Lewis entered a village after an Allied bombardment and was told by an old man that 'practically nobody had been left alive, and that the bodies were still under the ruins'. It was only when he glanced down at the uneven ground that the young officer realised that he was standing on 'the charred and flattened corpse of a German soldier'. Similar damage was also done by aircraft of Twelfth Air Support Command which provided valuable support to the ground forces. Its aircraft targeted the enemy front line, supply dumps and strafed roads. 'Allied fighter-bombers were very effective,' German infantryman, Herbert Hoewa remembers: 'You couldn't walk on the road. Even if you were on a bicycle, they would come down and shoot at you. The firepower of the Allied forces was enormous.' Dive bombers were particularly feared. P-51 Mustangs were converted for the job, screaming vertically out of the skies and dropping their bombs at 4,000 feet just before their pilots blacked out. The bad weather severely limited their much-needed appearances during the autumn and winter months, but when they did fly the impact of these aircraft on the Germans was enormous.

The fighting in Italy remained a great psychological challenge to all concerned, but slowly and methodically Fifth and Eighth Armies closed in on the Bernhardt Line. Throughout this period Alexander was unwavering about pinning down the Germans to prevent their reinforcement of France but, as he wrote in his memoirs: 'I and my commanders were determined to have Rome, and were not to be deterred by the German resolve to hold it.' Both ambitions would be well served, he thought, by an amphibious attack somewhere on the long Italian coast to dislocate the Germans and reinvigorate his flagging offensive. It was an idea with which Clark had also been toying since his breakout from Salerno, and on 21 October he wrote that it was 'of critical importance to make an amphibious landing and thrust northward from some appropriate point on the shore.' Alexander first talked to Eisenhower about an assault from the sea just a few days later, and it was they and not Churchill (as has been commonly assumed), who initially explored the idea. Clark was closely involved with the subsequent development as he had already established a special amphibious operations section at his headquarters under Major General John W. O'Daniel. This unit had thoroughly examined the options – including the possibility of a landing at Anzio, a town thirty-five miles south of Rome, that offered decent beaches and a port – but they remained concerned about the availability of the necessary resources. During the autumn of 1943 only one US regiment or a British brigade and the bare minimum of shipping could be assigned to the operation due to the need to withdraw divisions and vessels to the United Kingdom in preparation for Overlord. Landing Ship Tanks (LSTs) were the most sought-after commodity. According to the British Official History LSTs became 'the perfect maid-of-all-work', transporting all manner of vehicles, equipment, supplies and troops. These 330 feet long, 50 feet wide vessels with flat bottoms could run right up on to the shore to unload 2,100 tons of cargo through the bow doors. Their shortage led Churchill to write that 'the letters "L.S.T." are burnt in upon the minds of all those who dealt with military affairs during this period'. The Prime Minister was infuriated by the situation, bellowing at staff officers from the War Office that Allied military options were forever being 'restricted and distorted by the shortage of tank landing craft'. His dreams for Italy, he said, were 'languishing for the sake of a few more assets'. Brooke was also angry, and wrote in his diary the following day:

It is becoming more evident that our operations in Italy are coming to a standstill and that owing to lack of resources we shall not only come to a standstill, but also find ourselves in a very dangerous position unless the Russians go on from one success to another.

44

Our build up in Italy is much slower than the German, and far slower than I had expected. We shall have an almighty row with the Americans who have put us in this position with their insistence to abandon Mediterranean operations for the very problematical cross Channel operations. We are now beginning to see the full beauty of the Marshall strategy!! It is quite heartbreaking when we see what we might have done this year if our strategy had not been distorted by the Americans.

On 26 October the British Prime Minister could contain his frustration no longer and in a stinging letter to Roosevelt declared: 'I feel that Eisenhower and Alexander must have what they need to win the battle in Italy, no matter what effect is produced on subsequent operations.' Churchill was directly threatening Overlord for the sake of the Mediterranean. The British wanted to retain 56 British and 12 American LSTs in the theatre until 15 December and looked to find more troops for a divisional-sized amphibious assault. London argued cogently that these concessions would not impinge on Overlord as the resources would be back in good time for the cross-Channel invasion. Marshall bristled, but the Joint Chiefs of Staff agreed to the British request. Brooke told a satisfied Alexander to plan on retaining the vessels until mid-January to allow for time to resupply as he was sure that the Americans would agree to a time extension later in the year. He also questioned whether just one division was enough to have the impact that was required. The ghosts of the 1915 expedition to Gallipoli and the calamitous Dieppe raid of the previous year still haunted a General Staff that was only too aware of the many risks inherent in amphibious operations. The employment of sufficient and experienced troops in these vulnerable 'end runs', as the Americans called them, was a necessity. The oft-fought Anglo-American wrestling match over resources was about to enter a new phase.

By the end of October Mark Clark's headquarters had pitched itself

at Caserta, twenty-one miles north-east of Naples. The palace there –
which Alan Moorehead described as 'vast and ugly' – had been the
former home of Charles III of Spain, rivalled in size and splendour
only by Versailles. Nonetheless Clark 'found no suitable accommodation within its 1200 rooms', according to Alan Whicker, 'so set up a
trailer, a converted truck, in the formal gardens behind the Palace –
which as he explained in resultant publicity, was no place for an
American cowboy.' Here he attracted visitors: generals, politicians and
other VIPs making tours of the war zone on important business, to
boost the morale of troops or just to be seen. Clark realised that time-
consuming hosting was part of the job, but later wrote: 'I sometimes
felt that we were being pushed into the tourist business.' His time
became even more precious after Alexander issued instructions on 9
November for an autumn offensive. In this the Eighth Army would
begin by launching a diversionary offensive across the River Sangro,
cracking the Bernhardt Line and pushing on to Pescara and possibly
Avezzano. Meanwhile, one corps in a series of operations would attack
from the centre of Fifth Army to breach the Bernhardt Line by taking
the high ground surrounding the Mignano Gap, advance to the Gustav
Line, cross the Rapido, storm Cassino and then advance through the
Liri Valley to Frosinone. When Clark was closing in on Frosinone he
was to launch 'an amphibious operation south of Rome directed on the
Colli Laziali, together with a possible airborne landing by one R.C.T.'
The aim of this division-sized supporting attack – code named
Operation Shingle – was not just another diversion, nor was it to
directly take Rome: it was to assist Fifth Army's offensive. By landing
at Anzio and pushing eighteen miles inland to the Colli Laziali – the
Alban Hills – Alexander hoped to dislocate the enemy and encourage
the withdrawal of Tenth Army north of the capital. The hills were an
important military objective as they overlooked two major roads
leading from Rome to the German defensive lines: Route 6 lay to the
north and led via Frosinone to Cassino; and Route 7 lay to the south

and led towards the coast and Minturno. By dominating this mass of hills, Alexander sought to cut the enemy's lines of communication, block their withdrawal route and destroy Tenth Army. Shingle was not to be launched too soon because of the anticipated weakness of the Anzio force. Alexander was clearly aware of the potential threat to Shingle, as was Clark who later testified that: 'I was convinced that it would be unwise to land behind the enemy lines unless we could feel assured of joining up the amphibious attackers with our main elements within a few days.' With the outline plan completed and Fifth Army ready and willing to take on the challenge of an amphibious assault, all that was required to turn talk into action was the confirmation from London that permission had been secured to retain the LSTs beyond mid-December.

As arrangements were being made to unhinge Tenth Army, Alexander's charges staggered forward. By mid-November the right of Fifth Army was on the Bernhardt Line whilst its left and Eighth Army were just short of it on the Garigliano and Sangro respectively. Montgomery had covered 400 miles from the Calabria and Clark 100 miles from Salerno in some of the most difficult conditions that Europe could provide. Fifteenth Army Group was tired and so there was a period of reorganisation and reinforcement before the next phase of offensive operations began. During this Fifth Army incorporated the divisions of the French Expeditionary Corps commanded by General Alphonse Juin, and Major General Geoffrey Keyes's US II Corps was inserted between British X Corps and US VI Corps to conduct Clark's main attack towards Cassino. Keyes's corps consisted of 36th and 34th US Infantry Divisions for the grinding attack and 1st US Armored Division – commanded by the insatiable Major General Ernest Harmon – for exploitation. Also attached was First Special Service Force, an outfit consisting of five battalions of American and Canadian troops equipped as light infantry and commanded by Lieutenant Colonel Robert T. Frederick. A hard, uncompromising unit that was, according to Clark, 'trained to do anything from making a ski assault to dropping by para-chute on the enemy's rear', they were not to be confused with the US Special Service Company which toured the front entertaining the troops. In reserve was an Italian unit – the 1st Italian Motorised Brigade – for on 13 October Italy had declared war on Germany and become a 'co-belligerent'. II Corps was a capable mixture of guile and brute force, but it would take a remarkable effort to attain the objectives ascribed to them. Indeed, it was remarkable that just one corps had been assigned the job of a breakthrough to Frosinone for Alexander had the forma-tions to apply a far greater concentration of force at the decisive point. It was a decision made not for a lack of information about the Winter Line, for reports from the front alone indicated the strength of the German positions. On 7 November, for example, Lucas reported to Clark: 'Enemy has continued determined defense and has clearly indi-cated that he will not give up positions without a hard fight. He has employed every means at his disposal to prevent our gaining access to the commanding terrain he is holding.' Truscott contributed to this assessment and told a correspondent:

It's by far the strongest area of defense we've run into so far in Italy . . . I could send a small patrol to pierce the defenses at any point; I could take Cassino tomorrow if I wanted to make the expenditure of men. We have learned that the Italians have been working on the German defenses for the last six weeks, and there are some strong positions. They've got the mountaintops fortified with pillboxes blasted out of the rock, and reinforced with concrete. On the lower features, they've got very deep entrenchments – wired in. In a great many places they have machine-gun mounts.

A few weeks later that correspondent, Richard Tregaskis, was to be badly wounded in the head by a shell. At six feet seven inches tall, he was one of the few men on the front who looked down on Mark Clark, but always recognised that his height was a disadvantage in the front line. There was a 'smothering explosion', he wrote of his wounding:

> it seemed to flood over me from above. In a fraction of a second of consciousness I knew that I had been hit. A curtain of fire rose, hesitated, hovered for an infinite second. In that measureless interval, an orange mist came up quickly over my horizon, like a tropical sunset, and set again, leaving me in the dark. Then the curtain descended gently. I must have been unconscious for a few seconds . . . Catastrophe had struck me down . . . there was no pain. Everything seemed finished, quiet, as if time had stopped.

The Winter Line, as its name suggests, sought to end the mobile phase of operations in Italy for several months. The Tenth Army withdrawal had been a success, with von Vietinghoff opining, 'Enemy gains contributed no great threat and every step forward into the mountainous territory merely increased his difficulties.' The construction of the defences and deployment of reinforcements within them from Army Group B were completed just in time. This influx of Rommel's men was much appreciated for it was not just the Allies that suffered from fatigue. XIV Panzer Corps alone – now commanded by Lieutenant General Fridolin von Senger und Etterlin – sustained over 3,500 casualties during the last three weeks of October which left its three divisions averaging just 2,100 front line infantry. Rommel's command remained in existence until 6 November, at which time he was transferred to France and Army Group B was disbanded and reconstituted as Fourteenth Army under the command of Colonel General Eberhard von Mackensen. This left Kesselring from 21 November as Commander-in-Chief South West and Army Group C incorporating all German forces in Italy. His delight at this new appointment was marred only by the challenge that now faced him. Partisans disrupted his lines of communication in ambushes and demolitions whilst Allied bombers went about their business largely unmolested by a Luftwaffe in Italy that now consisted of a mere 430 aircraft. Allied aircraft targeted anything German that moved. One German truck driver, Corporal Edgar Weiss, had to feel his way down to Rome from Milan carrying ammunition:

> It was the middle of November and the weather was horrible, but on that 400 mile journey I was still attacked seven times by Allied bombers and twice by partisans. There was nothing much we could do about the aircraft other than take pot-shots at them, but to defend us against the marauding partisans our convoy of twenty trucks travelled with a motorised platoon of infantry of about 25 men. We should really only have travelled at night, but we were under pressure to get to Rome as quickly as possible so we had to take a chance in daylight. By the time that we reached the capital we had lost half of our trucks and half of our escort.

Even with their ability to resupply their formations in Italy fundamentally compromised, Tenth Army still had to hold the Winter Line and Fourteenth Army still had to be ready to defend Rome against any amphibious landing that Alexander might attempt behind von Vietinghoff's men. This Allied threat from the sea was one that Kesselring took increasingly seriously, for he knew how tempting it would be for them to exploit his coastal flank to assist in an attempted breakthrough of the Winter Line. Kesselring faced a series of challenges, but was optimistic. Indeed the Führer praised his Field Marshal's mindset by declaring: 'military leadership without optimism is not possible.' The reverse is also true, and in spite of the many calls on his time, the Commander-in-Chief still spent 70 per cent of his time at the front obtaining information, listening to views and assessing situations to ensure optimum efficiency whilst searching for perfect defence. He demanded a great deal from his subordinates, later admitting: 'I was not a superior officer who was easy to get on with – but popularity is rarely the handmaiden of command.' It was a ruthlessness born of a man laden with responsibilities and with little time for the niceties of man management. There were to be no second chances, Berlin had placed its faith in him and he well knew that, as his biographer has written: 'one slip and a strong defensive position might give way and destroy the southern buttress to Hitlerian strategy.' Yet the threat to it was multi-dimensional and Kesselring also had to recognise the possibility of a popular uprising against the Germans in Rome.

The political situation in Italy was highly complicated. Kesselring was *de facto* ruler of the two thirds of Italy that Germany still occupied. Mussolini, meanwhile, had been rescued from his captivity in a hotel tucked away in the mountains of central Italy on 12 September in a remarkable glider raid. The disgraced dictator was immediately flown away in a waiting light aircraft and into the arms of Hitler who set his old friend up as puppet leader of Fascist north Italy at Salo in October. Meanwhile, Badoglio and the Royal Family were in Brindisi acting as a rallying point for anti-fascist forces and had formed a 'rump' Government under the eyes of an Allied Commission that held the real political authority in southern Italy. Both Badoglio and the King were tainted by their previous associations with Mussolini, but the Allies supported them hoping that, in Churchill's words, the two men 'would be able to do more for what had now become the common cause than any Italian Government formed from the exiles or opponents of the Fascist regime.' The aim remained, nonetheless, to reach Rome and then establish a broad-based Italian Government. Shortly after the Allied landings at Salerno, Romans had eagerly awaited the arrival of the Allies in the city, but were instead occupied by Germans under Lieutenant General Kurt Mältzer who became the Commandant of Rome. During this time scores of buildings were occupied, including fashionable hotels close to the Termini Station such as The Flora, The Excelsior and The Grand, and they established their main headquarters in Coso d'Italia. 'We were flung out into the street', remembers Antonio Zinzone who was thirteen at the time, 'because we had a large apartment near the centre of the city. We were given fifteen minutes to pack our things – that is a mother and her five children – and that was that. It was taken over by a gang of officers and the one that smelt strongly of alcohol slammed our own front door in our faces. It was terrible. Our father had been killed in North Africa and we were homeless.' The Germans did not flood the capital with troops, but immediately made their presence felt by taking control of the utilities, intensifying rationing and putting their people in positions of power which ensured that the city ran as they wished. The six parties of the underground Committee of National Liberation (CLN) worked doggedly to undermine these occupiers. Its resistance groups, and particularly that of the Communist Party's Gruppi di Azione Patriottica (GAP), left bombs wherever Germans gathered, ambushed convoys, and carried out drive-by shootings in cars and even on bicycles. When the Germans banned bicycles, they took to tricycles. Fabia Sciarillo recalls:

We were sometimes awoken by the sound of an explosion or the rattle of machine gun fire. We got used to it. I remember walking past a café one morning that had had its front blown out. There was still blood on the paving, glass scattered everywhere and a stern looking military policeman guarding the scene. That bomb killed twelve Germans and was not uncommon.

The actions of the Resistance forced Mältzer to employ far more valuable German resources on security than Kesselring would have liked, but the attacks led to more than the Romans just losing their freedom of movement: it spawned a heavy-handed German reaction. Men brutalised by the front line and serving in Rome, for example, became increasingly vicious towards the Italians and incidents of rape and the summary executions on the street were not uncommon. The Gestapo, meanwhile, conducted great sweeps of the city and arrested men on the pretext of inadequate documentation and dragged random males from their families and into forced labour. Pope Pius XII objected and was joined in his protestations by Kesselring, a devout Catholic who had no control over the Gestapo, but the raids and torture continued to the sound of Allied bombing raids against German military installations. Rome looked different, felt different and was unabashedly controlled through a climate of fear.

As the Romans gazed longingly south-east hoping that the Allies would soon provide their salvation, so Harold Alexander looked to put his Army Group within striking distance of the city through his autumn offensive. Montgomery launched his preliminary operation on 28 November and within days had forged a strong bridgehead across the Sangro and had cracked the Adriatic end of the Bernhardt Line. But his pronouncement that 'The road to Rome is open' was premature for when the offensive was brought to a halt at the end of the year, Eighth Army had advanced only fourteen miles at a cost of over 6,500 casualties. The German ability to hold Montgomery without having to resort to moving troops and other resources from Clark's front was disappointing for Alexander. His main thrust would now have to be made by a Fifth Army facing an undiluted enemy. The first phase of the offensive was to seize various hills and villages which would allow Allied troops safe passage through the Mignano Gap. It opened on 2 December with a 925-gun artillery bombardment. The subsequent attack on the Camino Mass by II Corps from the north and X Corps from the south, forced Albert Kesselring to withdraw to the edge of the Gustav Line on 6 December, but it took another eleven days before the Mignano Gap was fully opened. The fighting there was conducted in treacherous conditions, its intensity astounding visitors. Fifth Army staff often had to act as battlefield tour guides, and when Generals Vasilieff and Solodovnek arrived from the Soviet Union they were escorted to the Camino front where, according to Clark, 'troops were struggling to overcome mines, wired booby-traps, machine-gun nests, and mortar positions concealed deep in the rocky slopes'. It rained for most of the day and as they trudged uncomfortably forward on the backs of mules, their British guide was wounded by a shell splinter. On their return they looked shocked and exhausted. 'Vasilieff', Clark later wrote, 'suggested that I had misunderstood his explanation of just what the mission wished to see. "What we're most interested in," he said, "is logistics" . . . He took another gulp from his vodka-glass. "After all," he added, "we can die for Mother Russia any day in Russia. Why should we die in Italy?"' This was warfare in one of its most tortuous forms, everything took far longer than expected, the punishment absorbed by the troops tremendous. Nevertheless, Fifth Army's slog continued up to the Gustav Line during December before coming to a breathless halt. The bloody clinch of Viktor, Barbara and Bernhardt was merely a prelude to the smothering embrace of Gustav. The Australian war correspondent Alan Moorehead was horrified by what he saw the troops go through during these autumn battles, and bemoaned the fact that commanders made 'the ones that survived, do the same thing all over again at Cassino.' This slow advance put Alexander's plans in serious jeopardy for Shingle would not be launched until Frosinone was threatened, and he could not hold on to the LSTs indefinitely.

In the early winter of 1943 the Mediterranean Campaign was thus delicately poised. Since September the Allies had made considerable territorial gains in Italy, but in order to exploit its strategic potential, the British argued for more resources. Marshall riled at this 'Mediterranean Syndrome' that, as one commentator has written, meant 'always a little more needed, for a little longer and achieving a little less than previously agreed.' A decision to reinforce Italy would certainly have important, wide-reaching, strategic consequences and was, therefore, an important agenda item for a set of Allied conferences held at the end of the year. The conferences began before Alexander's offensive had been launched and were to decide the fate of the Italian Campaign and, as a corollary, Operation Shingle. Churchill began his journey to the Cairo 'Sextant' Conference from Plymouth on 12 November aboard HMS *Renown*. Amongst those accompanying him was his doctor, Lord Moran. Churchill was fatigued and off colour as a result of his inoculations and a cold, and Moran was concerned that the sixty-eight-year-old's remarkably resilient constitution was beginning to show signs of deterioration. Churchill, however, was determined not to be thrown off course by illness – or by the Americans. He felt that too many opportunities had been missed in Italy, remarking that 'I have been fighting with my hands tied behind my back', and he yearned to have them untethered. The Prime Minister was frustrated, sick and morose, making him highly volatile. Indeed, Lord Moran later wrote that 'Only a spark was needed to cause him to blow up.' The Americans had begun their voyage across the Atlantic in USS *Iowa* on 13 November. Franklin Roosevelt was also in a belligerent mood, determined to undermine Churchill by stalling discussions about Italy until after Stalin had given his anticipated support for Overlord during the second conference in Tehran. It was an eventful voyage during which the President and Joint Chiefs refined their tactics for sidelining the British, and were nearly blown out of the water by a live torpedo fired mistakenly at the *Iowa* from an escorting destroyer.

The first Sextant session provided the British with a taste of the new American manoeuvrings, dominated as it was by discussion of the Far East out of respect to the Chinese delegation. As a result, the first debate about the war against Germany did not take place until the second day of the four-day conference. During this the British argued that a start date for Overlord should be dictated only by the enemy's strength and, not dissuaded by the Americans' intransigence over discussion of the Mediterranean, that the Germans should be further weakened by operations in Italy prior to the invasion. To facilitate this Churchill suggested that shipping resources should be retained in the

Mediterranean beyond mid-January. 'Overlord remains top of the bill,' he said, 'but should not be such a tyrant as to rule out every other activity in the Mediterranean.' Alan Brooke did not always agree with his civilian boss's strategic visions, but he backed him in every conceivable way on this issue, writing in his diary:

American drag on us has seriously affected our Mediterranean strategy and the whole conduct of the war. If they had come wholeheartedly into the Mediterranean with us we should by now have Rome securely, the Balkans would be ablaze. I blame myself for having the vision to foresee these possibilities and yet to have failed to overcome the American short-sighted views, and to have allowed my better judgement to be affected by them.

Substantiating their argument, the British team emphasised the success that had been achieved in Italy, not least that German reinforcements had poured into the country (and the Balkans) after the Italians had collapsed at the expense of the Eastern Front and France. The Americans replied that they were not opposed to operations in Italy, but as the initial agreed aims there had already been taken, the priority should now be the launch of Overlord in May as had been agreed at the Washington Conference. With time short the two sides agreed to disagree, and as the Americans had planned, nothing was decided before the Tehran 'Eureka' Conference hosted at the Soviet Embassy.

There was a tense atmosphere in Iran where the 'Big Three' met together for the first time in the war. On the evening of their arrival Sarah Churchill, who was accompanying her father, wrote to her mother: 'Papa was really very tired and his voice almost completely gone. Uncle Joe was already there and he – Papa – wanted to start right there and then. However, Moran and I went into action, got our heads bitten off; but finally, luckily, no meeting and he had dinner in bed like a sulky little boy and was really very good. He was nervous and apprehensive, I think.'

On the following afternoon, the 28th, the softly spoken Soviet Premier, dressed in the uniform of a Marshal, announced that Italy was of limited strategic significance. Inevitably influenced by the possibility that the development of Allied operations in Italy could threaten the Balkans and Austria – areas of Soviet interest – he proclaimed that Overlord should have top priority. Stalin also favoured an American proposal for an amphibious invasion of southern France – Operation Anvil – to be launched before Overlord in order to draw German forces from the north and act as one arm of an eventual giant Allied pincer. It was a blow to the British, for if Anvil was to take place a month before Overlord as mooted, the Americans would require Mediterranean assets to be returned earlier than expected and thus sink their Italian proposals. To add insult to injury, there was even an American-initiated discussion about closing operations in Italy before Rome was taken. The British sensed a sea change against them as Roosevelt ruthlessly used Stalin to destabilise Churchill's position. However, on 30 November, Churchill's 69th birthday, Brooke came forward with a bold new proposal: the development of offensive operations in Italy – supported by an amphibious attack if landing craft could be retained until mid-January – facilitated by the postponement of Overlord until 1 June, and of Anvil until July. He was careful to emphasise, however, that both invasions of France were to have priority over all other operations. As a compromise this worked well for focus remained on north-west Europe, but with the possibility of taking Rome and the further weakening of German forces in the east and west. Agreement was reached on Brooke's design, but it was apparent that the Anglo-American relationship had begun a new chapter in which Roosevelt was no longer willing to be bullied by Churchill. For his part, the British Prime Minister was hurt by Roosevelt's truculent attitude, but in compensation was buoyed by the prospect of a reinvigorated Italian Campaign. Once again his persistence had paid off for as Roosevelt's biographer has said: 'Churchill's reputation as a statesman was founded on tenacity. He never surrendered. If you slammed the door shut in his face he came in through the window.' Indeed, in spite of his growing physical weakness he also grabbed at the chance to make the Mediterranean a very British theatre. With London having agreed to Eisenhower as the Supreme Commander of the Allied Expeditionary Force for Overlord, Washington agreed to make General Sir Henry 'Jumbo' Maitland Wilson Supreme Allied Commander of the Mediterranean. Just as Allied weight was beginning to shift towards France, Churchill and Brooke had one final opportunity to ensure that Italy did not become a strategic backwater.

In early December, once the conferences were over, Churchill was eagerly looking forward to the new year and the prospects of success in Italy. Brooke hoped for the same, but harboured increasing reservations about Alexander's abilities, writing: 'He is a very, very, small man and cannot see big. Unfortunately he does not recognise this fact and is oblivious to his shortcomings . . . It is hard to advise him as he really fails to grasp the significance of things.' Thus, to add zest to what Brooke perceived to be a lacklustre 15th Army Group headquarters, Alexander received a new Chief of Staff, the intelligent and dynamic Lieutenant General A.F. 'John' Harding. This appointment and the replacement of a disenchanted Montgomery – bound for Overlord – by Lieutenant General Sir Oliver Leese, went some way towards refreshing an increasingly tired front. Mark Clark was not immediately affected by the changes in command, but Roosevelt and Marshall both encouraged him to seize Rome as soon as possible in order to dent German morale before Overlord was launched. Clark did not need to be encouraged, but Washington was a long way from the Gustav Line that stood resolutely between him and his prize in early December. Operation Shingle had been specifically designed to dislocate the Germans, but with the front beginning to stagnate bloodily in front of Cassino, he increasingly doubted that it could be launched even with the LSTs extension. Clark needed more time and more resources. It was to be a sick Churchill who came to his rescue.

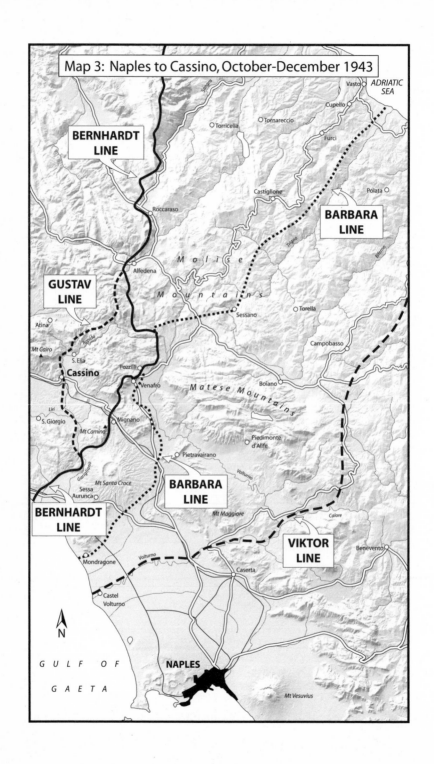

Map 3: Naples to Cassino, October–December 1943

CHAPTER 3

The Anatomy of a Wild Cat

(December 1943–January 1944)

Churchill stumbled down the steps of the Avro York as a cold wind
scudded across the deserted aerodrome near Tunis. It was a little after
daybreak on 11 December and no car had arrived to meet the British
party. During the eight and a half hour flight from Tehran the Prime
Minister's health had markedly deteriorated in the overheated cabin.
With nowhere else to go, he sat down heavily on his official boxes, took
off his hat, and surveyed the desolate scene. Perspiration ran down his
grey face and his flimsy hair flickered in the breeze. Lord Moran, his
doctor, recommended that his patient get back into the aircraft, but
Churchill scowled at the suggestion. The pilot tried to raise somebody
on his radio, but it took an hour before he could confirm that they had
landed at the wrong airfield. Eisenhower was waiting to meet them 40
miles away. With Moran's assistance the Premier struggled to his feet,
hauled himself back up the steps and into his seat. He was uncharacteristically quiet as the aircraft prepared for take off, and throughout
the ten-minute flight his eyes remained closed. Immediately on landing

the Prime Minister was bundled into a car destined for Eisenhower's villa near Carthage. During the journey the Premier turned to the American commander and said: 'I shall have to stay with you longer than I have planned. I am completely at the end of my tether, and I cannot go on to the front until I have recovered some strength.' It had been his intention to travel on to Italy to visit the front with Alan Brooke, but he was feeling so unwell that stoic as he was Churchill recognised he had reached his limit. It was an admission that further worried the British party. Brooke would continue on to Italy, whilst Churchill fought his pneumonia.

On Brooke's return to Carthage from Italy on 18 December, he did not tell the bedridden Prime Minister the worst. On one night Lord Moran had even feared for Churchill's life as his temperature had reached worrying heights and his breathing was shallow. Now he was more stable, even doing a little work, but the general did not want to unnecessarily strain him with lurid details of the thoroughly depressing situation in Italy. By mid-December, Alexander's Armies were making very limited territorial gains and Brooke did not believe that the Allies would capture Rome before the spring. On 15 December he had noted: 'My impression of the day is that we are stuck in our offensive here and shall make no progress till the ground dries, unless we make greater use of our amphibious power . . . The offensive is stagnating badly and something must be done about it as soon as I get back.' He was not impressed by Mark Clark's plans when he visited Fifth Army headquarters on 16 December complaining 'he seems to be planning nothing but penny packet attacks and nothing sufficiently substantial'. The need for something more was only underlined when he had stood atop Mount Camino. 'I was able to see quite clearly Mount Cassino and the country round,' he wrote in a note to his 17 December diary entry, 'and . . . discussed with Alex the very nasty nut we should have to crack there.' As if to emphasise these problems, Clark had signalled Alexander recommending the postponing of Operation Shingle as not only had Fifth Army not progressed far enough to make the attack viable, he also lacked sufficient resources for it. It was at this point that Churchill and Shingle became intimately acquainted. Both ailing and in need of reviving, the pair helped each other to regain their strength.

On 19 December a revitalised Prime Minister dictated a heated minute to the Chiefs of Staff, venting his anger at the situation in Italy. As the words flowed, Moran became resigned to the futility of asking Churchill to rest, and left the room. The subsequent missive read:

> The total neglect to provide amphibious action on the Adriatic side and the failure to strike any similar blow on the west have been disastrous. None of the landing-craft in the Mediterranean have been put to the slightest use for three months, neither coming home in preparation for 'Overlord' . . . nor in the Italian battle. There are few instances, even in this war, of such valuable assets being so completely wasted.

Churchill was determined that further offensive action in Italy should utilise an amphibious assault and now for the first time learned about Operation Shingle. Brooke left the Prime Minister for London the following day having been lectured on the opportunities that would arise from a strong push towards the Alban Hills, and with the distinct impression that his lecturer was feeling a little stronger. As Churchill recuperated by Eisenhower's swimming pool, he recalled his short time as a battalion commander on the Western Front during 1916 after his Dardanelles gamble had failed, and lamented that wasted opportunity. His illness had given him the time and space to think in a way that he had not been able to do since becoming Premier in May 1940. With his mind focused on Shingle, he was delighted on 22 December to receive a positive response from the Chiefs of Staffs in reply to his minute to them. The stagnation in Italy, they said 'cannot be allowed to continue' and agreed that an amphibious landing should be used 'to strike around the enemy's flank and open up the way for a rapid advance on Rome.' The Chiefs of Staff suggested that if more landing craft were made available for Shingle, then a larger strike force could be landed allowing the operation to be launched long before Fifth Army was at Frosinone. This, they claimed, 'would have a more far-reaching effect on the whole progress of the campaign, and would be much more likely to open the way forward for a rapid advance.' It was a suggestion that immediately captured Churchill's imagination, giving him an achievable objective to reach for. In an instant he was convinced that a solution to the deadlock had been found. Shingle had found a powerful patron.

The Chiefs of Staff recommended that Shingle become a two division attack which would require 88 landing craft. The difficulty was, of course, that Churchill had only just agreed that 68 would leave the theatre in mid-January for Overlord, leaving only 36 in the Mediterranean. Although another 15 were due to arrive from the Indian Ocean after the recent cancellation of an American landing on the Andaman Islands, there still were not enough landing craft for this assault. The only solution was to keep the 56 British LSTs of the 68 in the Mediterranean for a further three weeks. On Christmas Eve, Churchill had regained enough strength to hold a conference with amongst others, Maitland Wilson and Harold Alexander, to discuss these issues. They worked deep into the night and agreed that a two division plan was possible with a start date of around 20 January if the extra landing craft could be secured until about 5 February for resupply. Churchill had got what he wanted; a plan which he believed would be a 'wild cat to rip the innards out of the German army', rather than a mere diversion. At the conclusion of their discussion, the Prime Minister grinned, lit his first cigar for two weeks, poured himself a Scotch and wished the assembled senior officers a happy Christmas. He slept more soundly that night than he had done for several weeks, but awoke early full of ideas for the Anzio attack. He held another conference in his bedroom on Christmas morning to explain the plan to colleagues from all three services in the Mediterranean including Eisenhower. It was here that the frustrated General Churchill, albeit in his pyjamas, revealed his unstinting support for the Shingle scheme to a wide audience. He asked Alexander to outline the plan and the dapper general, unruffled by the odd setting, obliged by briefing on a corps-sized operation which would land two divisions initially, followed by two more over subsequent weeks. There was, he stressed, no need for an immediate link up by Fifth Army and he believed that the attack would lead not only to the destruction of the German Tenth Army, but also to the capture of Rome. The boldness of the vision and the enthusiasm of the Prime Minister's rejoinder left his audience enthralled, but blind to some of the practical difficulties concerning Shingle's ability to achieve its objectives. With hope clouding the reality of the situation, Alexander had lent his military credence to a fundamentally flawed concept. Churchill's notoriously well-articulated grand military ideas lacked pragmatism, and it had always been an important part of Brooke's job to act as a critical friend, exposing the flaws in the Prime Minister's thinking. But Brooke was in London. Harold Alexander on the other hand, was a professional soldier who should have known better. By grasping so readily at the Shingle straw, albeit under the domineering influence of Churchill and the Chiefs of Staff, he had helped to give the operation considerable momentum and rationale. In such circumstances it was difficult for somebody on the spot to ask the necessary questions. Would the thrust to the Alban Hills be sufficiently powerful to cut Routes 6 and 7 and precipitate a Tenth Army withdrawal leading to its destruction? Was it not likely that a successful German counter-attack against the stretched Allied lines of communication from the beachhead would lead to the annihilation of the landing force? Those present did not raise these issues, to a man giving Shingle their unqualified support. Churchill could not have been happier, and at Christmas lunch was in excellent form devouring turkey, plum pudding and several glasses of champagne. Harold

Macmillan, the British Minister Resident in North Africa, thoroughly enjoyed the meal, later noting in his diary: 'The old boy presided . . . clothed in a padded silk Chinese dressing-gown decorated with blue and gold dragons – a most extraordinary sight.'

But Christmas Day in the front line was grim. Grappling with the outposts to the Gustav Line, Fifth Army was not given the day by Mars and so fought on. First Special Service Force had 1,800 men in the front line that day and attacked at 0600 hours. The fighting was bloody and intense with one platoon of twenty-five men ending the day with only six survivors. Elsewhere Ross Carter was trying to come to terms with the death of a close friend whom, he later wrote, 'we mourned with aching, hating hearts'. At the front this 'special' day was much the same as any other. One 3rd US Infantry Division officer from Texas recollected:

> It was my first white Christmas, but by December 25th I was sick of the snow. We shouted season's greetings to each other ironically as the shells exploded down around us, ate our usual rations in a freezing gale and then got shot at . . . All day one of my men wore a big Santa beard, much to the amusement of the rest of his platoon. I should have told him to remove it, but as we were all covered in snow it hardly stood out, and we all needed a lift – even if it was just from a stupid beard. Goodness knows where he got it from.

For those newly arrived in Italy, such as Quartermaster Sergeant John Swain of the Royal Electrical and Mechanical Engineers who was some distance from the fighting in southern Italy, Christmas was a time to be enjoyed to the full. By this period of the war the Italian Campaign had achieved a forbidding notoriety that those due to go into action were determined to take whatever fun they could get, whilst they could still get it. Swain spent as much time as he could learning Italian, mixing with the locals and taking pleasure in their hospitality. 'Christmas Day came', he recalls, 'and to the very obvious pleasure of the troops, the Sergeants and some of the Officers turned out to serve up Christmas dinner and clean up afterwards. A good time was had by all, and our efforts were appreciated. The trouble was that this was indeed too good to be true. I found myself again asking the burning question: "Is this the lull before the storm?" It just had to be.' He was right to be concerned. That day Churchill was enthusiastically endorsing the plan that would put Swain on a ship bound for Anzio within the month.

26 December saw Churchill busy with telegrams. His first informed the Chiefs of Staff about the decisions taken the previous day about Shingle, and the second advocated the Anzio landing to Roosevelt – 'it should decide the battle of Rome and possibly achieve destruction of a substantial part of the enemy's army' – before asking him to sanction the retention of the crucial LSTs for a few extra weeks. The American President replied on the following day, agreeing to 'delay the departure of fifty-six LSTs scheduled for Overlord . . . on the basis that Overlord remained the paramount operation and would be carried out on the date agreed . . .'. Churchill had anticipated a tussle with Washington at the very least over his requirements, but there was none. A pang of guilt over the way he and Stalin had treated the sick old man at Tehran, perhaps? More likely, thought Churchill, that as the LST extension did not threaten the launch of either Overlord or Anvil, there was little to be gained from still opposing it. Operation Shingle was beginning to gain an unstoppable momentum, but there were those who opposed it. Eisenhower's British intelligence chief, Brigadier Kenneth Strong (the man who had not spotted the Germans evacuating across the Messina Straits from Sicily) was vocal in his concerns. Strong believed that Alexander's premise that Shingle would force the Germans to withdraw was unsubstantiated. The German forces were too numerous in Italy to be overly concerned by the assault, he argued, and Kesselring

would hold his line and deal with the landing piecemeal. Alexander understood what Strong was driving at, but held that the Germans would be 'so totally dislocated by the thrust that withdrawal would follow shortly after.' He also recognised the operational risks inherent in the plan, but was confident that they would be controlled during the detailed planning phase. Strong's concerns were not heeded, and the fundamental strategic flaws in Shingle were not attended to. It was a very dangerous situation that reflected badly on Alexander's myopia and Churchill's involvement. It is a matter of debate whether the Prime Minister should have got so caught up in operations, but as Alan Brooke's biographer has written:

> It is easy to criticise, with justice, many of Churchill's interventions in the running of the war, particularly his ignorance of logistic factors, his natural buoyancy which led him to goad commanders towards premature offensive moves against their will, and his general dislike for those aspects of reality which impeded his grand design for victory. These defects made him a most imperfect strategist in the practical sense, and often a sharp thorn in the sides of men no less anxious than he to beat the enemy. But it is equally easy to forget his vision . . . .

That visionary, with his penchant for difficult amphibious operations on peripheral fronts, left Tunisia for warm weather convalescence in Marrakesh on 27 December. A few days after his arrival, Churchill received Alexander's revised plan for the offensive. Operation Shingle would be preceded by an attack conducted by Fifth Army against the Gustav Line beginning on 12 January. This full-scale attack was to finally overcome the German outpost zone, grapple with their main defences and draw the enemy reserve in order to give the amphibious landing the best possible chance of success. This landing was to be conducted by John Lucas's US VI Corps. Lucas was chosen as commander as he possessed a safe pair of hands, was experienced, wise, and headed a corps that contained tried and tested formations. The parochial commander would have preferred an all-American force, but Alexander was insistent that the Allies would share the glory – and the risk. He was less concerned about co-operation with the other two services, not least because they also had Americans at the helm. Rear Admiral Frank Lowry was to be in overall command of Task Force 81 and its American contingent, whilst Rear Admiral Thomas Troubridge was to command the Royal Naval element. This Task Force would not only deliver the divisions, but also keep them supplied and provide them with fire support. In the air, the bombers and tactical aircraft of Lieutenant General Ira C. Eaker's Mediterranean Allied Air Forces would conduct a spectrum of operations from reconnaissance, through close air support, to the bombing of the German lines of communication. Alexander had conceived of a thoroughly combined and joint plan, and his instructions to Mark Clark were unambiguous:

> Fifth Army will prepare an amphibious operation of two divisions plus to carry out an assault landing on the beaches in the vicinity of Rome with the object of cutting the enemy lines of communication and threatening the rear of the German XIV Corps.

Thus, Clark's initial orders to Lucas issued were:

1. Seize and secure a beachhead in the vicinity of Anzio.
2. Advance and secure Colli Laziali.
3. Be prepared to advance on Rome.

Preparations were now moving apace, and there was considerable excitement in the various headquarters, but some commanders began to reveal their concern about the suitability of the VI Corps commander for such a challenging operation. The British historian

Raleigh Trevelyan has written, 'Several higher ranking British officers were worried about Lucas, whose so-called caution appeared to them to be merely a pathological slowness.' The Chiefs of Staff were also concerned, but Alexander reassured them that Lucas was 'the best American corps commander' – although he might well have meant that he was 'the best American corps commander *available*'. He was also the senior corps commander and came with 'Eisenhower's hearty recommendation.' The amiable fifty-four-year-old Southerner was immensely proud to have been given Operation Shingle, but his outward satisfaction cloaked his weariness. 'Foxy Grandpa', as Lucas was known to his troops, was balding, wore a short grey moustache and smoked a corncob pipe. Slow in movement and speech, Shingle's pilot was as far removed from a dynamic, charismatic leader as could be imagined. Considering Clark's credo that this was a young man's war, Lucas's appointment was noteworthy. Sensitive and self-effacing to a fault, Lucas admitted to his diary whilst fighting his way through the mountains:

> I am far too tenderhearted ever to be a success in my chosen profession . . . . I don't see how our men stand what they do . . . they are the finest soldiers in the world and none but an humble man should command them. My constant prayer to Almighty God is that I may have the wisdom of success and the minimum loss of life.

Lucas aspired to be a bold general, for he knew that it was a characteristic linking all great commanders, but he also accepted his own limitations. Clark also accepted them, for rather than seeing his subordinate's caution and thoroughness as hopeless weaknesses, he was attracted to them. The Fifth Army commander was also drawn to Lucas's relative docility for he was dedicated to imposing his will on the battle, and Lucas's temperament would allow him to do that. He was not too worried about what Alexander wanted, the man was 'a peanut and a feather duster', but was more concerned that VI Corps survived long enough to help take Rome. Both Clark and Lucas, neither of whom had been involved in the development of the scheme since Christmas, believed that Shingle was trying to do too much with too little.

The detailed planning for the Anzio landings began on 1 January and had to be completed in just three weeks. The VI Corps staff blanched at the resources assigned to the operation, but had no option to try and 'make a hearty and sustaining broth with just a few tired vegetables and no meat.' Attempts were again made for more sustenance. On 3 January Alexander asked Churchill on Clark's behalf, whether he might retain 504th Parachute Infantry Regiment that was due to leave the theatre for England, and Marshall grudgingly approved this. On the following day Clark asked for an additional ten LSTs to be retained beyond 5 February to strengthen the assault divisions with artillery, tanks and other supporting arms, and a further 14 LSTs for the period after the Anzio force had linked up with the Fifth Army for logistics. Both he and Alexander understood that these requests would impact on Overlord, but as the Army Group commander said in a telegram to Churchill: 'surely the prize is worth it.' Churchill secured what was asked for, not because the Americans had a sudden change of heart and became as positive about Italy as the British, but because there had been a revaluation of global resources and the outcome was to the benefit of Shingle. The Italian front could be reinforced without adversely affecting Overlord. The argument that there would not be enough resources for the cross-Channel invasion and strong Allied offensive operations in Italy during the first half of 1944 had been severely overstated.

On 7 January, Lucas's operations officer and his chief logistician gave a detailed briefing on the VI Corps plan to Alexander and Harding in Algiers. There were to be landings on a twelve-mile front: Major General W.R.C. Penney's 1st British Infantry Division and attached 2nd Special Service Brigade were to come ashore six miles north of Anzio, Major General Lucian Truscott's 3rd US Infantry Division and 504th Parachute Infantry Regiment were to land five miles east of Nettuno, and Colonel William O. Darby's Ranger Force and the independent 509th Parachute Infantry were to be inserted in between them on the beaches at Anzio itself. Anzio, formerly 'Antium', had been the birthplace of Nero and Caligula and the town in which Coriolanus had died. The locals fished, and the Romans went to Anzio to relax in the summer, a tourist trade that had subsequently spawned a casino, some fine restaurants and some hotels, but it was cold and quiet in January. The neighbouring Nettuno was larger with a medieval castle on the seafront, but a similar sleepy feel to it as its sister town during the winter. Neither they nor the Germans expected them to be the focus of such sustained military action as was being planned by Allies in the New Year. Landing at Anzio–Nettuno was a considerable challenge, for they were exposed to winter gales and obstructed by German and Italian mines which would have to be swept before the assault, but there was a harbour that, if it could be taken intact, would massively improve Lucas's ability to reinforce and resupply his corps. There were a smattering of field defences manned by little more than two or three companies of German troops and some minefields, but nothing that would overtly cause major difficulties for Lucas if the troops were landed on the correct beaches, at the correct time and with the requisite equipment. Penney was concerned, however, about a sandbar which had been discovered a couple of hundred yards off his sector of shoreline, and sand dunes which would make 1st Division's exit from the beach difficult, but neither were insurmountable problems. Truscott had no such difficulties and was pleased with his clear run up to the shore and a flat exit, whilst Darby examined the challenge of landing on a beach overlooked by buildings and which led straight on to a promenade. On leaving the beaches, the three forces would move inland: Penney into the Padiglione Woods, Darby into Anzio and Nettuno, and Truscott into the open countryside. The ground beyond the beaches was flat and dismal. Formerly all marshland, Mussolini had drained it during the 1930s, and the fertile earth was now studded with farms and several towns. Aprilia lay adjacent to the Via Anziate leading to the Alban Hills some eighteen miles to the north of Anzio, and the Via Appia (Route 7) ran through Cisterna with its Lepini Mountains backdrop. Lucas's first task after the landing was to secure a perimeter against any enemy counter-attack, and this was to be established on the Moletta River (although actually not much more than a stream) on the left, beside a lateral road which passed over the Via Anziate in the centre, and along a branch of the heavily embanked Mussolini Canal of the right. Any breakout to the Alban Hills would have to come after the construction of this perimeter and a phase of consolidation. Alexander declared the plan 'eminently sensible' and said that it 'laid solid foundations for an exploitation phase.'

From Algiers Lucas's staff officers took the plan on to a conference in Marrakesh hosted by Churchill. It was an all British affair attended by the Mediterranean service chiefs, and marked by a lack of dissenting, or even challenging, voices. The Prime Minister dominated the meeting, radiating such confidence that it became difficult to raise fundamental concerns about the efficacy of the plan. Neither Clark nor Lucas had been invited. Kenneth Strong was present, however, and remained uneasy. Although ULTRA – the top secret British signals intelligence acquired from the breaking of Axis military codes – had suggested that the landing would be virtually unopposed, Strong was concerned about a rapid German reaction to the landing. The Germans had twenty-three divisions in Italy, fifteen of which were part of Tenth Army which was opposing the eighteen Allied divisions of 15th Army Group. While this in itself was a cause for concern as the Allies only had a very slight advantage in any attack on the Gustav Line, it was what lay behind von Vietinghoff's men that caused Strong to worry. General der Flieger Alfred Schlemm's I Parachute Corps reserve, consisted of the newly formed 4th Parachute Division largely positioned between Florence and Rome, together with 29th and 90th Panzer Grenadier Divisions refitting just north of the capital. Surely, Strong thought, if the Allies had seen the potential for an amphibious strike, the Germans would have done the same and prepared their reserve to deal with it. The Brigadier was correct, Kesselring did have a plan. Each possible landing place was given a code name and a staff table drawn up showing what units would move to the area, and by what routes, as soon as the alarm was given. The alarm units would most often be the division's reconnaissance unit. The code word for an amphibious attack in the Rome area was 'Richard'. Hitler planned to reinforce Kesselring with troops from France, the Balkans and Germany, although the time required to do this meant that the initial threat would have to be dealt with by Kesselring's existing I Parachute Corps resources. Strong feared that these divisions would be able to race to Anzio and deliver a fatal blow to the beachhead whilst VI Corps was still building its strength. He was not convinced that the attack on the Gustav Line would be successful enough to demand that a large proportion of the German reserve would be needed to reinforce the defences there. There was the good possibility, therefore, that the Germans would recover quickly from the surprise landings, and react ruthlessly against a vulnerable VI Corps as they pulled in formations from the Adriatic front and North Italy and further afield. A successful counter-attack against the Allied landings would provide the Germans with a golden opportunity to avenge Sicily and Salerno, and damage Anglo-American confidence prior to a cross-Channel attack. After several attempts to be heard, Strong plucked up the courage to make his point which he outlined in his memoirs:

Although the landing force might make an initial deep advance, it could not achieve a decisive success in the face of the opposition which could be expected. I also believed that the strength of the Gustav Line was being seriously underestimated . . . I estimated that the Germans could hold it without taking any units or formations away from the Anzio area. I was strongly supported by members of General Clark's staff, but we could make little impression on the others there.

Alexander was unmoved, arguing that the Allies had more guns than the enemy and virtually controlled the skies. Moreover, he was confident that his attack on the Gustav Line would be a success, and that the German ability to react swiftly to anything would be undermined by their participation in a winter relief programme. Harding, however, was unconvinced, privately concurring with Strong's position, but felt it sensible to keep his counsel as he was new to his post and, in any case, recognised that there was not the time, nor the desire to undertake the fundamental reassessment of Shingle that was required. It was a silence that he lived to regret. Churchill listened to Strong's words intently and whilst agreeing that Shingle was a risk, ended his speech by saying: '. . . without risk there is no honour, no glory, no adventure'. Strong was overridden.

After this conference there was no doubt that Operation Shingle would now take place and the Prime Minister proudly wired Washington: 'A unanimous agreement for action as proposed was reached by the responsible officers of both countries and of all services.' On 8 January Clark noted in his diary, 'Operation Shingle is on!' Two days later, at a final commanders' conference chaired by Alexander, Clark and Lucas were told that Shingle would be launched on 22 January. By this time, in spite of his reservations, the Fifth Army commander knew that it would be futile to raise concerns about the operation's objectives and looked to Lucas to control the risks as best he could. Lucas had his own concerns, such as 'the diminutive size of the proposed expedition as well as the distance to which it was projected', but said nothing as 'General Clark, evidently under pressure, said emphatically that the operation would take place, and after that I could only obey orders.' Lucas was disconsolate and thoroughly disillusioned with Operation Shingle, confiding in his diary that, 'the whole affair has a strong odour of Gallipoli and apparently the same amateur was still on the coach's bench.' He felt that he had been left out of the decision-making cycle and given a task that was 'foolhardy and ill conceived'. Lucas left the conference having been told by Alexander that he was the best man for the job, although in truth he had little confidence in the corps commander whom he perceived as a grumbling Eeyore figure, who immediately saw the risks in an enterprise rather than the opportunities. After the meeting Lucas further noted in his diary:

> Apparently Shingle has become the most important operation in the present scheme of things . . . Alexander quoted Mr. Churchill as saying, 'It will astonish the world,' and added, 'it will certainly frighten Kesselring.' . . . I have the bare minimum of ships and craft. The ones that are sunk during the operation cannot be replaced. The force that can be gotten ashore in a hurry is weak and I haven't sufficient artillery to hold me over but, on the other hand, I will have more air support than any similar operation ever had before. A week of fine weather at the proper time and I will make it.

Lucas was determined to do what he could to make the plan work, but nothing could convince him that it was wise to order his corps to strike out for the Alban Hills until it was at full strength and the sting had been taken out of the enemy's potential to counter-attack. Along with most of the VI Corps and Fifth Army staff, he believed that Shingle was properly a two corps or even a full Army task. He could not get the two corps Salerno attack out of his mind and although there were no mountains encircling the invasion beaches, he had quickly spotted that the Alban Hills overlooked his projected beachhead. He was therefore greatly relieved when Clark's orders arrived on 12 January and they stated that VI Corps was to:

1. Seize and secure a beachhead in the vicinity of Anzio.
2. Advance on Colli Laziali.

Clark had consented to Alexander's instruction, but with this order was evading it – a tactic that he was to hone over the coming weeks and months. The first objective was easy to understand, but the second had been made deliberately vague. By telling Lucas to 'Advance *on* Colli Laziali', rather than move on '*to*' them, Clark had given VI Corps the opportunity to retain its flexibility. Lucas could now decide on the speed of his advance to the hills depending on the situation. Indeed, he was told by Brigadier General Donald W. Brann, the Fifth Army Operations Officer who personally delivered the orders, that 'much thought had been put on the wording of this order so as not to force me to push on at the risk of sacrificing my Corps. Should conditions warrant, I was free to move and seize the Colli Laziali.' Brann said that the VI Corps aim was first and foremost, to seize and hold the beach-head – no more was expected. It was a weight lifted from Lucas's shoulders – although his confidence immediately suffered a setback when he was told that Clark wanted to establish a small Fifth Army command post in the beachhead just as soon as it had been secured. Fearing that his ability to control the battle would be compromised by Clark sitting on his shoulder, he confided in his diary: 'I wish to hell he wouldn't.'

As the days passed Lucas continued his preparations, holding meetings with subordinate officers, and representatives from the naval task force and the air forces. The process went well, but his concerns about the relative weakness of his corps played on his mind. 'They will end up by putting me ashore with inadequate forces and get me in a serious jam', adding presciently, 'Then, who will take the blame?' He continually badgered Clark for more tanks – only one battalion of armour was to land with each division – and more infantry. Gruenther stalled him by saying that none could be spared due to the attack on the Gustav Line, but a week before Shingle was launched Clark complemented VI Corps with two armoured regiments from Combat Command A of 1st US Armored Division, 179th Infantry Regiment of the 45th US Infantry Division and more artillery. Lucas would now have the equivalent strength of four divisions and if more strength was needed, Clark reassured him, Fifth Army would send the remainder of the two divisions to the beachhead. With this resource issue settled, VI Corps then concentrated on ensuring that its troops were in the best possible position to conduct the offensive even though it had but one rehearsal. Lucas had made his only complaint at Alexander's commanders' conference about the prescribed start date of 22 January. He contended that it did not give him enough time for rehearsals and felt strongly that adequate time to consider problems arising from sufficient practice was 'vital to the success of anything as terribly complicated as this'. His protest came to nothing in spite of the fact that 1st Division's last landing had been virtually unopposed more than six months previously and had not seen action since, and 3rd Division had landed in Sicily in July against fierce opposition and had hardly been out of action since. 'Another week might save dozens of lives', Lucas reflected, 'but the order comes from a civilian minister of another nation who is impatient of such details and brushes them aside . . . .' When the time came for the rehearsal, 1st Division's landing was satisfactory on 17 January, but 3rd Division's attempt ran into numerous problems two days later. Truscott, an expert on amphibious warfare, largely blamed the navy for the mistakes that included the worst possible start when not one battalion landed on time or in the correct location. In another incident the landing craft were released so far out to sea that it took them three to four hours to reach the shore and then forty valuable DUKWs amphibious vehicles and nineteen 105-mm guns sank. Clark was so furious that he was unapproachable for an hour after he had heard the news whilst Lucas, knowing that there was not another opportunity to refine their techniques did all that he could to ensure that the relevant lessons were learned from the experience.

As VI Corps massed around harbours in the Bay of Naples the atmosphere was like a festival. A mass of military paraphernalia arrived: baggage, guns, every conceivable type of vehicle and piece of equipment, boxes of supplies, ammunition, rations – all that an army in miniature required to fight on its own and to be sustained in action. 'There was a great deal of rushing around getting everything prepared', recalled Sergeant Bert Wickes of the Royal Artillery:

> The roads were clogged with troops and vehicles bearing their individual flashes, and guns of every calibre. It was an amazing spectacle, fascinating, exciting – it got your adrenaline running. It was only after it went dark and you were left alone with your thoughts as you tried to get to sleep that your mind turned to what it was all for. We were going into battle. We didn't know where and we didn't even know when, but we were going and with every passing hour the tension rose.

Private T.J. Anderson, an American combat engineer from 3rd Division, agreed:

> Boy we were nervous, but we were just bustin' to go. We replacements had to prove ourselves to those experienced boys. Everything had been building up to this moment, and we just wanted to get into action. These were mighty intense days that zipped by in a flash. One day I was on a troop ship from the States, the next it seemed like I was in North Africa, the next in Naples and then a landing ship bound for Anzio. Crazy days.

Briefings were regularly held all over the assembly area to give orders and pass on the latest intelligence, and many units made their men study models of the ground containing vital objectives and key terrain features. Security was tight. Military Police stood resolutely outside the buildings being used for the corps and divisional briefings, whilst guards were always posted outside the warehouses, barns, and tents utilised for unit briefings. Movement was restricted, identities were checked, and information given on a need to know basis only. It was, therefore, something of a shock when senior officers were told that children were selling postcards of Anzio down at the harbours where Task Force 81 was collecting. That armada comprised 374 vessels, including 2 command ships, 5 cruisers, 24 destroyers, 4 Liberty ships, 84 LSTs and 96 LCI (Landing Craft for Infantry). Embarkation was presided over by Admiral Frank Lowry. Lowry's attention to detail was minute having been squarely blamed for the 3rd Division rehearsal fiasco and he, of course, passed on the compliment to his subordinates demanding that they 'sharpen up their act.' This was a critical phase of the operation – the correct vessels had to be loaded with the correct cargos, in the correct order or else there would be such chaos on the beaches that both the operation and the lives of those in the landing forces would be placed in jeopardy. It was an immensely complex job, with time and space at a premium. Everything that had to be loaded had to be prioritised, checked off on manifests and loading tables. The VI Corps troops were the last to embark and they waited patiently in their assembly areas, checking their kit, cleaning their weapons, chatting, playing cards and writing letters home. 'I wrote three letters to my Mum and Dad in those last hours', remembers Corporal Clive Colley of the Royal Engineers:

I had landed in North Africa, Sicily and Salerno and seen men die all around me, but I had come away without so much as a scratch. I'd been extremely lucky. I truly believed that I was destined to die on the beach on the next op. I dreamt it, I thought it and I even talked about it to my mates. I wasn't frightened, in fact the belief that I was going to die made it easier for me. I was doomed and I accepted it. But the problem was, how to write what I thought was going to be my last letter home without worrying my parents. I wrote two, and re-read them, but they were either too frightening for my folks, or too senti-mental. The one that I decided to send read: Dear Mum and Dad, Everything here is alright. Don't worry about me, I'm surrounded by good men. Take Care. Your loving son, Clive. I know what I wrote because I still have the letter – I forgot to post it.

Meanwhile, Mark Clark's attack on the Gustav Line had begun well on 12 January. The French Expeditionary Corps on the right gained several miles and made a dent in the German positions before being halted, US II Corps moved up into a position to make the main attack across the Rapido in the centre, and British X Corps on the left managed to forge bridgeheads over the Garigliano and looked threat-ening. This was the ideal position for Clark as he had hoped to draw von Vietinghoff's reserves and succeeded on 18 January when Kesselring made the decision to release 29th and 90th Panzer Grenadier Divisions to counter-attack the British. It was an important decision that the Field Marshal did not take lightly because the two divisions formed a vital part of his defence against an amphibious assault, but he committed the divisions believing that it was safe to do so. This belief was rooted in the claim of Admiral Canaris, Chief of the Office of Foreign Intelligence in Berlin, who told him: 'At the present time there is not the slightest sign that a new landing will be undertaken in the immediate future.' Another report confirmed that the Allies did not look like launching a major naval offensive stating that: 'The number of ships in the Naples harbour may be regarded as quite normal.' With previously reliable intelligence sources telling him that an amphibious landing was highly unlikely, Kesselring decided to use the two panzer grenadier divisions to counter the move on the Garigliano that threatened to roll up the German positions from the south and outflank Cassino. The Germans, therefore, had failed to discover the Shingle preparations in spite of their size. It was a major intelligence blunder, but can at least in part be explained by the destruction of the Luftwaffe's long-range reconnaissance squadron base. Between 1 and 21 January, in preparation for Shingle, General Eaker's aircraft dropped 12,500 tons of bombs in 23,000 sorties on the roads, railway lines and Luftwaffe airfields north of Rome. The Germans had been effectively blinded in the air. To exacerbate this, the Allies also engaged in complex deception operations, which not only fed the enemy false information on the radio, but also got them interested in naval developments in North Africa and Sicily which pointed towards an invasion of southern France in the coming months. By shielding the Germans from the true picture and offering a convincing false one, Kesselring had been comprehensively deceived.

Having sent two of his reserve divisions along and I Parachute Corps headquarters south, Kesselring's reserve was limited to 4th Parachute Division stationed north of Rome. The defence of the capital was left in the unwilling hands of Brigadier General Ernest Schlemmer, but this uninspiring staff officer was deemed to be so out of his depth that Kesselring imposed a detailed plan on him. 4th Parachute Division was put on a high state of alert and told to prepare a rapid reaction battlegroup which was to race to the site of an Allied landing, block the roads, obtain intelligence, and stall the enemy advance for as long as possible whilst other formations were moved into the area. On 18 January the parachute division formed *Kampfgruppe* Gericke, named after its outstanding commander Major Walther Gericke. It was made up of battalions commanded by Captain Friedrich Hauber and Major Erich Kleye, and contained a high proportion of experienced soldiers. On receiving the news that they were to provide the vanguard of the German defence in the Rome area, the division was delighted. One new soldier with excellent signals skills in Kleye's battalion recalls:

We were biding our time by training, going on exercise, trying to make some of our vehicles and equipment serviceable. We had a good *esprit de corps*, high morale. We were highly trained aggressive troops. We had become parachutists to see action – and were not worried about engaging the enemy. Most of us welcomed it.

To ensure that they were well positioned for their task, *Kampfgruppe* Gericke was moved from Perugia – an ancient town between Florence and Rome – to an assembly point at Isola Farnese, near Lake Bracciano several miles north of the capital. Kesselring issued further warning orders through Fourteenth and Tenth Army that divisions were to make provision to send mobile units at short notice to assist in the event of an enemy landing. In this way he remained convinced that in spite of having despatched a large proportion of his reserve, he could still mass tens of thousands of troops around an Allied beachhead within a few days of their attack. What Kesselring most feared was an amphibious landing followed by a swift move inland which could do damage before he had an opportunity to react.

The arrival of the Fourteenth Army reserve on 19–20 January successfully stopped British X Corps from making greater progress, but was deployed before II Corps had even started to make the main Fifth Army attack on the evening of 20 January. The prospects for an Allied breakthrough looked extremely good as Keye's troops prepared for their assault river crossing. However, 36th US Infantry Division was so decisively stopped in its attempt to cross that Rapido that a Congressional Enquiry was established after the war into the handling of the operation. Its failure meant that by 21 January, on the eve of Operation Shingle, all momentum had been taken out of Mark Clark's attack and once again the front was on the verge of stagnation. Fifth Army had suffered 26,000 casualties since mid-October, and these losses, together with the weather, the sodden terrain and the strength of the enemy positions, made further advances unlikely in the foreseeable future. In such circumstances Shingle became an operation to initiate a Tenth Army withdrawal. But if von Vietinghoff managed to hold on to the Gustav Line, and von Mackensen managed to contain or destroy the Anzio landing, Alexander and Clark faced the nightmare scenario. The Fifth Army commander was in an invidious position on the eve of Shingle. He needed VI Corps to pose a threat to German communications whilst believing that it would be suicidal to advance too far too fast. Lucas, therefore, would need to be menacing, but patient. It would be a delicate balancing act and Clark was confident that the decision that he made to watch his subordinate closely had been further vindicated by events.

The Task Force in the Bay of Naples was ready to sail for Anzio–Nettuno before dawn on 21 January. Lucas had conducted a final briefing with his senior commanders the previous afternoon and watched the last of his corps board the various craft to the sound of the divisional and regimental bands. It was an emotional scene as a seemingly never-ending stream of green, their rifles and sub-machine guns slung over their shoulders, left the quayside and were swallowed up by the grey steel. Lucas eventually joined Truscott on board Lowry's USS *Biscayne,* having satisfied himself that he had done everything in his power to prepare his divisions for the operation. He probably had. He was a perfectionist, with an eye for detail and had overseen the preparations with a critical eye. There was little that he could do now, for until disembarkation VI Corps was in the hands of a restless Frank Lowry. Lucas tried to occupy his mind, but failed at this, writing:

I have many misgivings, but am also optimistic. I struggle to be calm and collected and, fortunately, am associating intimately with naval officers whom I don't know very well which takes my mind off things . . . I think we have a good chance to make a killing but I wish the higher levels were not so over-optimistic. The Fifth Army is attacking violently towards the Cassino line and has sucked away many German troops to the south and the high command seems to think they will stay there. I don't see why. They can still slow us up there and move against me at the same time.

Mark Clark, who was also extremely nervous and touchy before the invasion, might well have exacerbated Lucas's understandable concerns. Maitland Wilson thought that the Fifth Army commander had what he called the 'Salerno Complex' caused by a bloody nose in September, and leading to the symptom of 'over caution'. This may well have been true, but if it was then Clark's lack of confidence in Operation Shingle heightened it. Back at his Caserta headquarters, he waited in his caravan with Gruenther. There was nothing that he could do now until his planned visit to the beachhead with Alexander on the morning of the landings. There was nothing much that the troops could do aboard their vessels either. They had all received double rations at breakfast that morning, and plenty of tea and coffee. Lance-Bombardier Terry Reynolds of 1st Division artillery recalls:

> The army tried to coat the bitter pill of an invasion with egg, bacon and tea. It was pathetic really, but we enjoyed it. I was a bit nervous and couldn't eat much, but an old lag told me to either stuff it down or fill my pockets because you could never tell when you were going to be fed again. This really didn't help my situation. That sounded pretty serious stuff, and I took myself off for a quiet vomit behind the latrines.

On board the men made themselves as comfortable as their surroundings would allow. The senior NCOs wandered round to make sure that all was well, the officers and men chatting in groups whilst veterans knew that they should try and sleep. Many could not settle as plans, jobs, and everything that could possibly go wrong dominated their thoughts. Some tried to occupy themselves by checking and rechecking their equipment. TNT for blowing doors; phosphorus grenades for clearing confined spaces; fuses; magazines; pistols; coloured lights for the beach rendezvous. George Avery of 84th Chemical Mortar Battalion remembers:

Aboard ship we were invited to make ourselves at home. Part of the LST was occupied by some soldiers of the 3rd Division but, for the most part, we and they kept to ourselves. Having no sleeping quarters, we were fed hot Navy food on deck in mess gear with unlimited coffee served in galvanized garbage cans heated over gas burners and left on deck all night. I have never forgotten that thoughtfulness. I chose to sleep under a truck carrying who knows what on the open deck. We were issued with bandoliers of rifle ammunition, hand grenades and three chocolate bars. Now we really knew. These chocolate bars were given to us almost always when there was to be a prolonged battle and food might be short. The chocolate is as hard as rock, has to be cut to be eaten, never melts, can be carried in your pocket for days and substituted for food.

The night of 20–21 January was cold and clear with the majority of the corps managing at least some fitful sleep. By dawn, the armada quietly slipped out of its harbours and headed at 20 knots into the Tyrrhenian Sea preceded by a cruiser. Visibility was good and the water calm. The warships were ready for action and smaller vessels clung to the flanks of the convoys ready to ward off enemy attacks. But none came. As it got light, the sight of the assembled fleet was awe inspiring. 'It was only when we were at sea that I really had a idea of what I was involved in,' recalls Private First Class Leonard O. Peters of 15th Infantry Regiment, 3rd Division, 'there were ships of all shapes and sizes for as far as the eye could see. I looked around and aircraft patrolled the skies and gunners manned their weapons. It was exciting – but frightening at the same time.' Commander Roger Hill on the *Winchester Castle* said: 'I walked through the decks where there were all these American soldiers who were the Rangers, and to see them just prior to going into action was eerie. They were all cleaning their weapons and all looked very solemn, hardly any jokes.' The convoys sailed parallel to the coast and passed the Gustav Line. The day passed slowly. 'We just wanted to get on with it by that point', remembered Terry Reynolds, 'but it was as though we were moving in slow motion. We never thought that we'd arrive. The day was a blur, but a long blur. We didn't want time to think about our fate, we just wanted to get to our destination and do our jobs.' Alexander cabled Churchill on the evening of 21 January: 'Just back with Admiral Cunningham from visits to convoys at sea about seventy miles from Naples. All well by 4 p.m. No sign of enemy air . . . I am leaving Naples at first light tomorrow in a fast motor boat to visit the landings and see General Lucas . . .'. In Downing Street Churchill was like an anxious father awaiting news of a birth. He later wrote in his history of the war: 'It was with tense, but I trust suppressed, excitement that I awaited the outcome of this considerable strike.' The convoys turned towards Anzio–Nettuno after nightfall. There was no interference from the enemy and Lowry and Lucas were pleased to learn that the forecast for the following day was good.

By around midnight the great invasion fleet had edged its way silently towards the shore and dropped anchor three miles off Anzio. A stillness fell on the ships which rocked gently in the swell as their occupants anxiously awaited H-Hour. The senses heightened a natural reaction to dangerous situations and the men went through their personal routines, chatted a little and listened for any information that they could glean from any source. On one landing ship there was a rumour that the attack had been called off, but that was quickly squashed. The immensity of what was about to happen struck most of the men dumb and conversation dried. Alan Moorehead recalled that: 'The strain and fear which exists in every front-line before attack is probably brought to its highest pitch in a night sea landing.' Imaginations ran riot with one Irish Guards officer later writing: 'Nobody had a clear idea of what the landing was going to be like, beyond a hazy picture of wading up to their necks through water churned to foam by bullets and stained scarlet by blood, to cling to a few yards of sand in the teeth of two German divisions.' BBC war correspondent Wynford Vaughan-Thomas waited nervously with British 2nd Brigade's headquarters. 'My only weapon of war,' he wrote, 'was the new, cumbersome portable recorder which I was to be the first to take into action . . . On it I hoped to capture the strange, tense atmosphere of a landing at night from the sea.' He found the silence that immediately preceded the attack 'uncanny'. Why were the German guns silent? The invasion fleet were perfect targets.

Did the Germans know that they were there? Surely it was too quiet? Was it a trap or had they managed to slip through without the Germans knowing? Was that a wave crashing into the hull, or something else? Lucas went through the landing routine with Lowry for one final time on the *Biscayne*. The minutes passed slowly, and then suddenly there was movement.

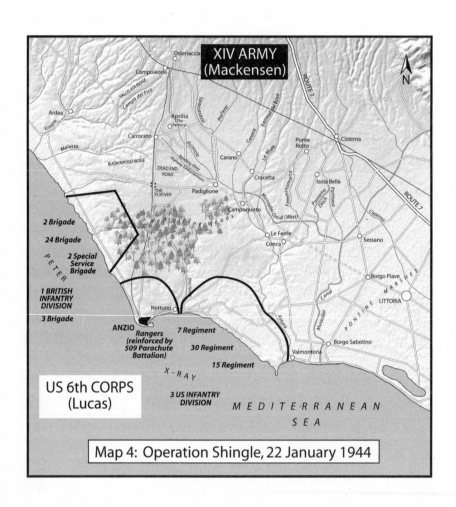

Map 4: Operation Shingle, 22 January 1944

CHAPTER 4

Style Over Substance

(22 January 1944)

On the evening of Friday 21 January 1944, Berthold Richter, a nineteen-year-old engineer in 29th Panzer Grenadier Division, wrote a letter to his parents. 'I am looking forward to some leave soon and hope to see you both. I miss you terribly . . . I have not been able to write as often as I would have liked and fear that I am not much of a son nor a brother. Please send my love to Anna and tell her that I miss her too. I would imagine that she has grown since I last saw her.' He signed off 'Your loving son, Bertie' and attached a recently taken photograph of himself in uniform posing by the Coliseum. Grenadier Richter was a good-looking young man, with a shock of black hair and bright blue eyes. He had left his family in Hamburg for basic training twelve months before and had not been home since. Had he returned, those that had known him would have noticed that he had changed – he had lost a little weight, but he also stood differently, and there was something unfathomable about his expression. Richter had seen his officer blown up during the fighting in Sicily, cradled his dying best friend in his arms at Salerno and been wounded twice during the fighting in the mountains. His division had eventually been pulled out of the line for a refit and a time in reserve near Rome. Here Richter had briefly – but fully – sampled the pleasures of the capital city where he drank and smoked heavily, and lost his virginity to a prostitute. He had no time to waste. Now he was at Anzio, one of a 380-man unit that had only the previous day been enjoying the sea air, conducted a little training, and making preparations for the demolition of the harbour. Richter slipped the sealed letter in his breast pocket, as a comrade staggered through the door of their seafront billet with two cases of 'liberated' wine. With the town evacuated and offering so little to entice the men, they settled in for some drinking, singing and gambling. Berthold Richter enjoyed himself, at one point falling off a table as he danced with a wooden chair, before falling fast asleep fully clothed on a mattress on the floor. It is likely that he was awoken by the sound of the approaching Allied landing craft and had gone to investigate. The shots that killed him had propelled his comrades out of bed and into the waiting arms of the Rangers. Before being escorted into captivity, Richter's friends saw his body curled in the foetal position surrounded by a large puddle of blood on the esplanade.

Nearly 800 5-inch Allied rockets had crashed into the buildings and along the waterfront of all the invasion beaches. The wall of explosions killed and wounded some of the sentries, dropped masonry down onto the sleeping, cut telephone lines and detonated some of the mines. But its psychological effect on the enemy was even more impressive, sending those still capable of a fight reeling into the first waves of VI Corps. Their confidence boosted by the pyrotechnics, Lucas's assault waves stormed the beaches to the sound of their own descending might, but silence from an overawed enemy. Assisted by lights (set up on the sand by two-man teams launched from submarines) the assault craft had landed accurately and on time. Wynford Vaughan-Thomas recalls:

I braced myself for the shock of the searchlights stabbing out from the shore, followed by the tracers pouring over the waters. But again a silence more intense than ever held the whole area as the assault craft crept in . . . The incredible had happened. We had got the one thing we had never bargained for, utter, complete surprise.

The Allied landings were an unexpected success. An Irish Guards officer wrote: 'It was all very gentlemanly, calm and dignified', whilst a less restrained 3rd Division officer declared: 'We hit the beach and shook Hitler's breeches . . . It sure was a relief after Salerno and that God awful practice.' The real thing was far more successful than the rehearsals because Lowry and Troubridge had worked tirelessly to ensure that the same mistakes were not repeated, and assisted by the benign conditions, they were not. Lucas noted in his diary: 'We achieved what is certainly one of the most complete surprises in history. The Germans were caught off base and there was practically no opposition to the landing . . . The *Biscayne* was anchored 3½ miles off shore, and I could not believe my eyes when I stood on the bridge and saw no machine gun or other fire on the beach.'

The landing was an important first step which had been made accurately and securely in order to provide a stable base for further phases. The next step was to push Lucas's troops and vehicles swiftly across the beaches to instil the attack with some forward momentum. In this intense task the Military Landing Officers (MLO) played an important role. Captain Denis Healey, a future Chancellor of the Exchequer, was an MLO on the British Peter beach. A veteran of landings in North Africa and the Calabria, Healey did not take part in the Salerno landing (where his replacement was killed), but he was an expert in his field. He landed as the engineers were clearing lanes in the minefields when his job was then 'to make sure that the troops followed the white tape through the lanes, and the vehicles were on the laid metal tracks to stop them bogging . . . My three days at Anzio were busy, but not dangerous.' The beaches were extremely busy, with bulldozers creating breaches in the sand dunes, loudspeakers directing the troops, whilst vehicles and guns spilt out onto the sand. Healey and his team ensured that 1st Division's paralysis was kept to a minimum, although there was little that they could do when the sand bar that had concerned Penney during planning caused delays. Lucas was not happy and visited an irritated Penney to demand greater efforts as troops waded ashore or were lifted by DUKWs. Had the German defences been stronger they may have been able to exploit such difficulties, an accurate artillery barrage for example might have caused Penney serious problems, but instead the Panzer Grenadiers were rounded up within minutes of the landing. Vaughan-Thomas wrote, 'The only Germans we saw were a forlorn group standing under guard at a farmhouse door. They had been fast asleep when we landed and clad in pyjamas had jumped into their car and driven it through the door of the barn and had been rounded up before they had gone a hundred yards.'

The three Ranger battalions and the supporting parachutists were extremely grateful for the lack of opposition on Yellow beach in Anzio. Lucas had expected a tough fight to take the harbour and the Rangers had been specially selected for this mission after their excellent performances in Tunisia and Sicily. Their commander, Colonel William O. Darby of Arkansas, 'a broad-shouldered, thick-chested man', who 'moved quickly and spoke with decision', recognised the nature of the challenge that faced his force as the beach was narrow and overlooked by buildings. He told the planners at Caserta: 'When I run out of the landing-craft I don't want to have to look right or left', and that is exactly what happened. When Darby disembarked from his landing craft he ran straight up the beach, across the road and into the Paradiso sul Mare, the large white twin-domed Art Deco casino built in the 1920s. As he set up his command post, his men, followed by 509th Parachute Battalion, fanned out and within minutes were bringing back prisoners. It was during this time that Berthold Richter had been killed. Richter's friend Ralph Leitner recalls: 'I was lucky not to be shot like him. These soldiers had adrenaline pumping through their veins and itchy trigger fingers. They looked fearsome. I recognised them as Rangers from their dress and the black, red and white insignia on their sleeve and knew instantly to respect them.' The newly arrived Town Commandant also lay dead nearby. He had been driven down the coastal road from Anzio to a headquarters in Nettuno in the company of a Lieutenant to ascertain the source of a droning noise that could be heard out to sea. Minutes into their journey they were caught up in the rocket attack which forced them to take evasive action, but at its conclusion they sped on. As their vehicle entered Nettuno the Rangers ambushed them, drilling them with fire. The driver tried to barge through, but crashed into a ditch. The commandant was killed, the driver was badly wounded, but the Lieutenant cowering in the back emerged unscathed and was taken prisoner. Within minutes he was standing in Anzio harbour, watching the continued landings. He told his interrogators back in England that he had been impressed with what he saw: 'he never heard a word of command', they reported, 'and yet it seemed that everything went clock-work-like'. He could appreciate the careful planning: 'it was like a big business without confusion, disorder, or muddle.' The speed and surprise of the attack had given the Germans no time in which to react. *The Times* later reported on one illustrative action: 'At a German command post, from which the occupants fled when the Rangers landed, rooms were left in disorder, even to the remnants of a meal which had included sardines, Czech beans, and Danish bacon. Near by lay two German soldiers, shot as they ran from their machine-guns.' Some Germans did not even have time to get dressed. One American private remembers bumping into a half-naked man in the darkness of Anzio:

As our squad entered a gloomy narrow street I could see a pair of fleshy white buttocks wobbling in the opposite direction and I shouted 'Halt!' as loud as I could. The man stopped, raised his hands, turned and walked towards us. We could tell that he was shocked – and perhaps a little embarrassed – because he was only dressed in a vest. At first I thought that he might be an Italian, but he found his confidence when he knew that we were not going to shoot him and started swearing at us in German. His thin legs were shivering below a great pot belly. It was my first encounter with the Master Race.

The Germans were quickly overrun, and Anzio was secured by 0800 hours, with Nettuno secured two hours later.

Soon after 3rd US Infantry Division and 504th Parachute Infantry Regiment had landed on X-Ray beach, they began to push forward. 'Once we knew that the division was going to get ashore in one piece and without any hindrance from the enemy,' recalls Oliver P. Roach who was a Staff Sergeant with 15th Infantry Regiment headquarters, 'our minds were on our next objective. Making a beachhead was very important, because we just didn't know when or where the enemy would counter-attack us.' This was a concern which was shared by the entire corps on the morning of 22 January, and in anticipation John Lucas had planned to create an initial beachhead area some two and a half to three miles deep which could be defended. To facilitate this, reconnaissance platoons were thrown forward and patrols were sent out by units in an attempt to 'join hands' across the front as quickly as possible. The probes forward were cautious, but firm. The Americans felt vulnerable as they moved through the open, flat, scrubby marsh-land on the right of the front towards the Mussolini Canal and an unmade road known as the 'disused railway bed' which ran across their front. The British, meanwhile, were circumspect about the prospect of traversing the dark Padiglione Woods. Leading the way on Penney's left flank was 2nd Battalion, North Staffordshire Regiment which advanced with two companies forward using a track through the

Umbrella Pines that became known as Regent Street. 'It was a little nervy being at the forefront of a corps attack striking out for Rome', recalls an officer from battalion headquarters. 'It was literally a shot in the dark. We didn't know what was in front of us and had to constantly co-ordinate ourselves with the rest of the brigade. We were told to speed up then slow down, then speed up again. All we could really do was push on at a steady pace. The Colonel knew what he was doing.' They ghosted through the darkness, their senses aching, their hearts pounding and their breath freezing at their mouths, expecting to be ambushed at any moment. But the division found no resistance in the wood and their attack developed unhindered in a breaking dawn towards the Moletta River, the Via Anziate and the flyover at Campo di Carne. The first organised German troops were encountered by the vanguard of both divisions after dawn. This weak defensive screen was established by the first German forces to be sent to the area and a number of their 88-mm guns opened fire on the beachhead and the landing vessels. It was the least that Lucas had expected and by mid-morning, as a weak sun gently warmed the embryonic beachhead, he had good reason to feel thoroughly satisfied. The landing had been a great success, and his divisions were forging a beachhead against negligible opposition.

Churchill wanted to be in London when Operation Shingle was launched and had arrived back at Downing Street on 18 January. He was still weak from illness, but his high expectations for Shingle helped sustain his morale. However, on the eve of the attack the Prime Minister was in a contrary mood, snapping at staff and colleagues alike, and clearly anxious about the operation. He found it difficult to concentrate on his work that evening, but within minutes of the first wave landing he received a message: 'Personal and Most Secret for Prime Minister. From General Alexander. Zip repeat Zip' – Operation Shingle had been launched. The lack of any further word on the situation at Anzio for several hours did not help the Premier's mood.

Having only slept fitfully for a couple of hours that night, he pounced on Alexander's next communication at 0900 hours. 'We have made a good start', it read. 'We have obtained practically the whole of our bridgehead and most of the supporting weapons will be ashore tonight I hope.' With that the Prime Minister relaxed – but he demanded frequent updates fearing German counter-attacks. Alan Brooke, meanwhile, went shooting. The newly promoted Field Marshal did not feel paternalistic towards Shingle which he viewed very much as Churchill's baby; he allowed the Prime Minister to enjoy the ordeal of its delivery alone. 'Very good shoot, only 4 guns: Cobbold, uncle Philip, Barney and I', he recorded in his diary for 22 January. 'Howling wind, almost gale force. Shot 172 pheasants. At lunch was called up by War Office and told that landing south of Rome had been a complete surprise. This was a wonderful relief!'

It is not certain who raised the alarm, but by 0300 hours the news had reached Kesselring's headquarters in Monte Sorrate. The Field Marshal had been awoken with the words: 'Case Richard.' As he dressed hurriedly a staff officer appraised him of the situation – there had been a landing in the Anzio–Nettuno area, but details were scant – but it could be up to four divisions. Kesselring's mind lurched into action, running through the implications of the news and various scenarios that it could lead to. But he made no assumptions until he had the facts. There had obviously been a massive intelligence failure. Spies had failed to spot Allied preparations, and its armada had not been spotted approaching Anzio. He had been wrong-footed, and it was now his job to restore stability, and to strike back. Within minutes he was in a large briefing room with Siegfried Westphal, where a clutch of befuddled officers were talking animatedly over a map of Italy. The briefing by the intelligence officer was short and at its conclusion Kesselring launched immediately into questions. Making his apologies, an NCO bearing papers interrupted proceedings with new information.

Civitavecchia, a promising invasion area sixty miles to the north of Anzio, was being bombarded. Kesselring smiled and nodded; the Allies were toying with him. Already unsure whether the landings were a raid, a feint or a full-scale attack, this complicated matters. Albert Kesselring strode over to the map table and leaned heavily over it. 'We have a problem,' he announced, 'but not an insurmountable one', and proceeded to launch into a speech which those present later recalled as a bravura lecture on Allied intentions. The Field Marshal declared that the landing at Anzio was the opening gambit of an attempt to seize the Alban Hills, which would cut Tenth Army's lines of communication fighting in the Gustav Line thus blocking their route of withdrawal. He remained calm throughout, even joking occasionally at the expense of his colleagues. 'We have been caught a little off-guard,' he explained, 'as we are over-stretched trying to contain the fighting in the south. But we can recover. The British and American aim is to threaten Rome, have no illusions about that, but can they seize the city swiftly? Not, gentleman, if I have a say in the matter – and I intend to be very vocal.' Pausing, he turned to Westphal and demanded to know what assets he had between Anzio and Rome. 'Virtually nothing in the landing area,' came the reply, 'and perhaps another 800 men in the vicinity in total.' Kesselring nodded again and then smiled. Throughout he exuded a confidence that infected all those who listened to him that morning. Kesselring acted as though this was merely a long expected – and eagerly anticipated – exercise. His *sang-froid* was securely rooted in his anticipation of Allied landings, albeit not necessarily at Anzio and at that time, and the preparations he had made for it. The terse instructions that he issued that morning were not a knee-jerk reaction to events, but had been carefully prepared for such an eventuality. The aim was to have 20,000 troops in the area by evening.

By 0430 hours the words 'Case Richard' had been signalled all over Italy, alerting commands that an Allied amphibious assault was under way at Anzio–Nettuno and ordering certain units and formations to move to contain it. The military commandant of Rome, Lieutenant General Kurt Mältzer, was to block routes in to the city with all available forces, and the Commander-in-Chief of the Air Defence District of Rome (who was also the commanding general of all Luftwaffe forces in the Mediterranean theatre), General Max Ritter von Pohl, was to move all his flak formations stationed south of Rome into defensive positions. Major General Heinrich Trettner's 4th Parachute Division, the majority of which was still north of Rome, was to move without delay to the beachhead whilst its spearhead, *Kampfgruppe* Gericke, was to be sent immediately to block the Via Anziate and the secondary roads in the area. A *kampfgruppe* from 29th Panzer Grenadier Division stationed near Velletri, as yet uncommitted against British X Corps on the Garigliano, was sent towards Cisterna to block the only other main Allied exploitation route. Thus by the time that Adolf Hitler had been informed of the landings at around 0600 hours, a small, but highly mobile force had already been deftly despatched to contain the Allies. That morning the Führer was at his *Wolfschanze* (Wolf's Lair) headquarters in an East Prussian forest east of Rastenburg. Although still under development it covered an area the size of twenty-one football pitches. Only a small percentage of the *Wolfschanze* contained underground bunkers, but these were impressively built with a shell of reinforced concrete six feet thick. Narrow corridors connected the rooms which all had electric heating, running water, fitted furnishings, and ventilation machinery which drew fresh air through the ceiling. Hitler's personal bunker – the *Führerbunker* – also boasted air conditioning. It was cramped, claustrophobic, but safe. On receiving the news of the attack Hitler had been calm but intense, for Kesselring had shrewdly forewarned him about the likelihood of just such a landing. He had watched Mark Clark's recent offensive develop with interest, but was confident that Kesselring's defence would hold firm. He now relied on the Field Marshal to deal a blow to the Anzio–Nettuno landings, and provide a victory that would shake Allied faith in their ability to conduct successful amphibious warfare.

Hitler's composure allowed him to maintain his usual routine without interruption on 22 January. There was the usual pre-breakfast situation report in the Map Room at which he was given the latest news about the landings, followed by a communal breakfast with his staff. Here Hitler always sat facing a large wall map of the Soviet Union and spoke passionately about the Eastern front and the evils of Bolshevism, but the main situation conference that morning was dominated by the situation south of Rome. By this time it was clear that the attack was no feint, but a major strike, and the meeting decided to send formations from other theatres to deal with it: 715th Infantry Division was to be moved from the south of France, the 114th Jaeger Division from the Balkans, three independent regiments – including the highly regarded Infantry Lehr Demonstration Regiment – from Germany, and two heavy tank battalions from France. The meeting also gave Kesselring the authority to use any division from Fourteenth Army in northern Italy, which were under the control of the Chief of High Command of the German Armed Forces (OKW), Field Marshal Wilhelm Keitel. As a result the larger parts of 65th Infantry Division and 362nd Infantry Division, together with elements of the newly formed 16th SS Panzer Division, were ordered south of Rome. Kesselring also ordered Tenth Army to stop counter-attacking British X Corps and go onto the defensive all along the Gustav Line in order to facilitate the release of as many units for Anzio as possible. Von Vietinghoff was displeased, arguing strongly that Mark Clark's offensive was still a threat, but was forced to concede. Tenth Army subsequently released 26th Panzer Division and elements of 1st Parachute Division from its left, and units from the Hermann Göring Panzer Division, 71st Infantry and 3rd Panzer Grenadier Divisions from his right. The newly arrived I Parachute Corps headquarters was also returned to Fourteenth Army with Schlemm ordered to take command at the beachhead Anzio–Nettuno until General Eberhard von Mackensen's Fourteenth Army headquarters could be moved from

Verona. Hitler was impressed with Kesselring's continuing *sang-froid* and the fact that his headquarters had not mentioned the word 'withdrawal'. In the late afternoon, the Führer took tea with his secretaries and then sat down to dinner with Keitel and his aides where their strategy was discussed. There had been no panic at either the *Wolfschanze* or Monte Soratte.

The race between the belligerents to build up their forces at Anzio–Nettuno had begun. Several units had formed the defensive screen which the Allies had run into that morning. These included the 29th Panzer Grenadier Division *Kampfgruppe* which used its five armoured cars south of Cisterna to block the road from Nettuno. At 0715 hours it engaged an American reconnaissance force and took the first Allied prisoners of the battle. Shortly after the first troops from the Hermann Göring Panzer Division arrived at Cisterna, and the spearhead of 4th Parachute Division's *Kampfgruppe* Gericke on the Via Anziate. Battalion Hauber blocked the road at Campoleone Station and sent a patrol out to Ardea where it stopped the British 1st Reconnaissance Troop as it drove up the coastal road. In a matter of hours the Germans had not only recognised Alexander's intentions for Operation Shingle and set in motion a plan to heavily reinforce the area, they had also focused their activity on roads that Lucas would rely on to exploit the success of his initial landings. Moreover, by occupying Ardea, Campoleone Station and Cisterna, the Germans retained strong foundations for a counter-attack. As if to underline Kesselring's intent, several German Messerschmitt 109 fighters and Focke-Wulf 190 fighter bombers broke through to strafe the beaches, and drop light bombs on VI Corps at its most vulnerable point. Ross Carter of 2nd Battalion 504th Parachute Infantry Regiment wrote:

The deck of our LCI was crowded with troops standing around waiting to unload into the icy water and make the three hundred yards to the beach. Just as Berkely was reaching for one of Pierson's cigarettes, a dive bomber came in and hell opened its doors. The bomb missed the bow by five feet or so, but the explosion lifted the boat clear out of the sea and blew a column of oily water into the sky which fell back on the boat and left us oil-coated for several days.

Stranded off the beach, one of the men swam ashore with a rope and tied one end to the strut of an amphibious Piper Cub, a light aircraft, sitting on the sand. Loaded up with equipment, weapons and ammunition, the men held the rope, jumped into the water and pulled themselves along. 'The water', the young paratrooper recalled, 'was eight to ten feet deep and icy as a spinster's heart.' It was a fitting introduction to Anzio, for the men emerged from it 'wet, cold, miserable, mad, disgusted and laughing,' a list of adjectives that accurately reflect what troops were to feel during the coming battle. Indeed, as Carter says, he and his comrades had 'embarked upon an adventure that staggers the mind.' Private Robert E. Dodge, meanwhile, managed to get off his LCI safely, only to come under immediate aerial attack:

> We doubled-time off the L.C.I. and kept going. We had run for quite a distance when Jerry planes came in strafing and bombing. Our anti-aircraft guns sent up such a cloud of aerial bursts, you wouldn't think anything could fly through it. We instinctively hit the ditches. All around you could here the zap of shrapnel from our guns' shells hitting the ground. The noise of the planes and guns was really frightening. This time no one was hurt, but now we realised it was for real. Before we could get out of the ditches, we were being urged on with shouts of 'Move it'.

The Luftwaffe disturbed some of the Allied new arrivals on the first day of Shingle, but caused no significant damage due to their small numbers and the success of Allied Spitfire and Kittyhawk fighter patrols which accounted for seven enemy aircraft for the loss of three Allied. Thus, although the Germans had begun to move troops into blocking positions, and the Luftwaffe had been active, by noon the assaulting forces had reached Lucas's initial beachhead line. British 2nd and 24th Guards Brigade were firmly lodged in the Padiglione Woods and patrols had reached the Campo di Carne flyover. It was a damp and exposed spot with a few farmhouses, but little else. 'It gave me goose bumps', says the 5ft 2in Corporal 'Lofty' Lovett of the North Staffordshires, 'and it did not help when I was told that "Campo di Carne" translated to "Field of Flesh". Here we were in the middle of God knows where, with precious little cover, waiting for something to happen. It was as still as could be, just the occasional boom of a German gun, or the noise of an aircraft, but otherwise quite quiet.' Meanwhile, to Lovett's right, 2nd Special Service Brigade had taken a position astride the Via Anziate two and a half miles north of a defensive line around Anzio–Nettuno created by the Rangers and 509th Parachute Battalion. The Americans had also occupied its soggy initial beachhead area with 7th Infantry Regiment on the left, 30th in the centre and 15th on the right, with patrols pushed forward to the Mussolini Canal where they prepared bridges for demolition to secure the flank.

Included in the invasion force into Anzio were 150 Carabinieri whose job it was to maintain public order in the towns after the landings. They were understandably extremely apprehensive at being part of a dangerous amphibious assault, but were relieved to walk ashore knowing that the Americans were already in control. Setting up a headquarters in a restaurant on the seafront, this armed police force, resplendent in their black uniforms, found that they had very little to do as the populations of Anzio and Nettuno had been evacuated. However, these native Italian speakers became extremely useful when refugees from elsewhere on the battlefield started to congregate in towns during the day. The first had started to arrive mid-morning, some carrying suitcases, children, and even family heirlooms. But there were others who had only too obviously run from their homes in a hurry, some without coats, and one or two still in nightclothes. A proportion of these were injured, their bruised and bloody bodies covered in a thick layer of dust. Many spoke of the dead that they had left behind. These people had lived with the war for years, but the violence had come with appalling suddenness on 22 January. Antonia Paolo who lived with her husband and four children on the edge of the Padiglione Woods recalls the experience:

> Our farmhouse was sturdy, but not strong enough to stop the rockets. Only one hit our roof, but brought it down. Luckily nobody was hurt. The children were screaming and my husband grabbed them into his arms and carried them down into the cellar. We sat in the dark listening to the bombardment. It was the worst moment of my life and we prayed together. But it ended as quickly as it had started and within what seemed like minutes, a British officer who spoke fluent Italian was standing in our parlour apologising for the damage, and promising that somebody would be along soon to help us. My husband thought that they would help rebuild the roof and our demolished wall, but what he meant was that we would be escorted down to the port.

Once down at Anzio, the Paolo family were quickly put on an LCI with around twenty other families, and by evening were being administered to by the Allies in Naples. Some families left the danger area at the first opportunity, others as the battle spread, but many had to be prised from their homes or waited until the fighting was on their doorstep before electing to leave. Wynford Vaughan-Thomas witnessed one family which only fled once their house was under direct German fire: 'The battle was a mere few hundred yards down the road', he wrote, 'and the bewildered civilians, clutching their bedding and a few battered suitcases, would stumble through the darkness, the noise and the shell-bursts to the dubious safety of the rear.' Over the coming weeks a constant trickle of civilians asked to be taken to safety and at times it was a major task feeding and sheltering several hundred often frightened refugees. A church on the outskirts of Anzio was eventually used as an embarkation centre, although it was frequently overflowing with people, a significant number of whom were very young, very old or sick. Occasionally there was panic when a shell landed close by, and sometimes the evacuees had to wait several days before a ship could be found to take them to safety, but eventually 20,000 were taken to Naples.

As the first refugees were being evacuated from Anzio, Generals Alexander and Clark, together with a host of other high-ranking officers, were arriving. The two men had received a positive report from Lucas at 0300 hours that the landing had been successful and good progress was being made. Thus, as soon as it was light, the party from Caserta made their way to Naples harbour and were taken by fast PT boats to visit VI Corps. The news en route continued to be heartening with Gruenther staying in close contact with Clark who was encouraged that no German armour had yet been encountered. The flotilla arrived at the *Biscayne* at 0900 hours, and after a detailed situation report from Lucas, the group ventured onto the beachhead. Alexander visited 1st Division and spent considerable time with 24th Guards Brigade. Lieutenant William Dugdale, commander of a Grenadier Guards Anti Tank platoon, was one of the first to encounter Alexander whilst on the beach having dealt with some local difficulties:

> The naval Lieutenant who commanded our Landing Ship hit a sandbank about 200 yards off the beach and we came to a shuddering stop. The Carrier Platoon roared off and disappeared beneath the waves but by their snorkel tubes they survived by dint of much revving of the engines the carriers all got ashore. The Anti-tank Platoon was less lucky and two of the six tugs sank and stopped in

the water with their guns behind. After two hours of hauling and heaving we finally got a tow line on them and pulled them through the surf. I emerged from the water soaking and cross to be confronted by an immaculate General Alexander in field boots who said, 'You look extremely scruffy' to which the only answer was 'Sir' and a salute.

Dressed in his trademark fur-lined jacket, riding breeches and peaked officer's cap, the dapper, imperturbable Harold Alexander was instantly recognisable. A group of guardsmen were impressed that the general did not break his stride when a salvo of exploding 88-mm shells showered him with soil. 'He brushed off the soil like he would the drops of water having been caught in a shower of rain', one said, 'and continued on his way chatting to his aide who looked as though he'd seen a ghost.' Like Clark, Alexander did not lack physical courage and had been wounded and twice decorated for leadership and gallantry during the First World War. He thought that it was important to show the troops not only that he was willing to share their danger, but that it was important to be calm under pressure. His companion, Admiral Troubridge, was not afraid to show his concerns however, and as he pulled himself up from a nearby ditch was heard to complain: 'I don't feel safe except at sea. This is most unfair, as really I am a non-combatant on land.' Whether the General's tour was a boost to the troops' morale or merely distracted them from their duties is a moot point, but it was certainly remembered. The Scots Guards official historian writes: 'General Alexander made a tour of the beach-head that morning, wearing his red hat and riding in a jeep followed by his usual retinue. We were again reminded of the likeness of the operation to an exercise – the Chief Umpire visiting forward positions and finding things to his satisfaction.' He seems to have found 'satisfaction' in most of what he saw that morning and Clark felt the same. Meeting Truscott at the 3rd Division command post, the two men discussed events over a breakfast of eggs, bacon, and toast prepared over an open fire by Private Hong. No sooner had they finished than Lucas and his Chief of Staff arrived and Hong had to start cooking again. Throughout the morning a succession of visitors enjoyed breakfast, but left Hong fuming 'Goddam, General's fresh eggs all gone to hell.' Clark visited Lucas again before he left for Naples that afternoon and praised what had been achieved so far, but also offered the advice: 'Don't stick your neck out, Johnny. I did at Salerno and got into trouble.'

VI Corps had made a solid start, but even in the earliest hours it was conservative. Whilst there was ample opportunity for Lucas to push out further and faster, his innate protective mentality allowed the Germans to establish strong defensive foundations. Although the enemy were about as weak as anybody could have anticipated for much of 22 January, and in spite of the fact that VI Corps headquarters understood that the enemy would only get stronger, Lucas remained focused on fulfilling Clark's primary aim of a secure beachhead in a methodical and workmanlike manner. Even if it was imprudent to strike out for the Alban Hills at this stage, Lucas seemed blind to the possibility of taking as much important ground as possible in order to create a launch pad for offensive action and to provide defensive anchors. There seemed to be a lack of urgency about the advance when with a little more derring-do, VI Corps could have threatened Aprilia and Cisterna. Penney in particular felt that a wonderful chance was being wasted and his respect for Lucas rapidly diminished from that moment on. In the Padiglione Woods the Guards Brigade waited for orders, but none came. They built fires, ate their stale rations, drank tea and smoked as new German arrivals seeped into defensive positions on more advantageous ground. As Vaughan-Thomas wrote of that day, 'We held the whole world in our hands on that clear morning of January 1944.' But John Lucas was not the only General to reveal a lack of boldness at Anzio. Another was on his way from Verona.

*   *   *

Eberhard von Mackensen grumbled throughout his flight from Verona that 'a withdrawal of Tenth Army was the only way to save the German army in Italy.' Arriving with the Fourteenth Army headquarters advance party to take possession of a nondescript building at the heart of German-occupied Rome, the General lost his temper at the mess that had been left by its previous occupants. Von Mackensen was a deep-thinking officer, highly professional and capable, but he had a superficial side to his nature. As German forces in Italy frantically sought to respond to the gauntlet thrown down at Anzio, this austere Prussian aristocrat, whose father had been Field Marshal during the First World War, announced that he would not move into the building until it had been tidied. While cleaners swept he and the vanguard of his staff took over a local café that had just one telephone but – this being Italy – three coffee makers. Kesselring, who disliked von Mackensen's attitude and pessimism, had given his subordinate clear orders: 'set up a temporary headquarters in Rome, and as soon as you are ready move to the Alban Hills and establish a permanent base . . . Prepare a plan to pin the Allies in their bridgehead with a view to a counter-attack as soon as was possible.' As his staff climbed the stairs to the newly dusted second floor 'Map Room' that afternoon, they were greeted by the sound of a dozen ringing telephones. Satisfied that his office was the largest and with the best view, von Mackensen got to work. As Mackensen played the *prima donna*, an ever-growing number of German troops were being conveyed towards the beachhead. Many did not know where they were going, why and what they would find at their destination. One officer being thrown about in the back of an aged Renault truck that afternoon was Rittmeister Edwin Wentz, the commander of a replacement company in the Hermann Göring Panzer Division. At the time of the Allied attack the fifty-year-old had been sitting in the company kitchen drinking ersatz coffee. The bitter weather had aggravated an old shoulder wound that Wentz had picked up in 1916 on the Somme, and the intense pain had woken him early that morning. As he sat rubbing the scar where the shell fragment had entered his body all those years ago, he reminded himself that battles were a young man's game. Wentz was happy enough to provide a finishing school for young infanteers before they went into the line, but he didn't want to fight any more. Just as he was pouring himself another coffee, a clerk burst in and breathlessly reported that a Major was on the telephone. Curtly informed about the Allied landings, Wentz received his orders: 'You must take your company and move them towards the Anzio beachhead. You will receive further instruction later.' He could not believe what he was hearing – his men were keen but had only the most basic military skills. But Wentz's men were not representative of the wider Hermann Göring Panzer Division which, commanded by Generalleutnant Paul Conrath, had been hardened by its experiences in Sicily and the Gustav Line.

Everything had been loaded in under forty-five minutes and one hour later, just after noon, they left having been told to get to the battlefield before dusk, giving enough light to reconnoitre the positions they were to take up. However, Edwin Wentz worried about movement in broad daylight due to enemy aircraft. Clattering around in the back of the trucks that afternoon, these men were dazed by the speed of events. The wooden seats provided little comfort, and the soft-skinned vehicles scant shelter from the icy weather, but some managed to sleep, their heads lolling over their colleagues who tended to ignore them. Most just sat back, quietly smoking or bent forward over their packs staring out at the frozen countryside, lost in their own thoughts. There was little talk, although the inexperienced were prone to give a running commentary about the position and progress of the convoy. The veterans tended to keep their own counsel until provoked. One sergeant, who had seen action at Stalingrad, recalls: 'The youngsters were like little children going on an adventure, excited and apprehensive in equal measure and prone to asking every fifteen minutes, "Are we there yet?" God, they were annoying, but like parents we had to remain patient and try and take their minds off the present by talking about other things. I tried not to get too close to them. Experience told me that once in battle their chances of surviving for more than a couple of days in action were extremely limited.' At one point they were subject to a fleeting air attack and the drivers sped up and pulled off the road. 'Dismounting, the men took cover and fired on the aircraft with machine guns and rifles. It made one run strafing the road and then departed. After that, it became quieter and we reached the objective without further incident.' Alighting at Cisterna, the company found some units of the division had already arrived and were digging in, whilst others were being deployed further forwards. A Panzerjäger Battalion from 1st Regiment armed with towed 7.5-cm Paks, for example, was moving closer to the front line. By the time that Wentz and his men had received their orders, this battalion was fighting an American patrol which advanced to Isola Bella, just two miles south of Cisterna. Lieutenant Ernest Hermann recalls:

> The 1st Platoon opened fire and stopped that movement. The enemy pulled back to Borgo Montello and the 1st Platoon pushed on close behind him as ordered. It advanced to just before Borgo Montello. The enemy had dug into the town and opened fire with machine guns, small arms, antitank guns and tanks, making a further advance unthinkable . . . The platoon found the best positions available and went over to the defence.

As soon as the Allied guns were able, they targeted the enemy as it endeavoured to organise its defences in the open, but the Germans returned fire just as soon as they were able. And so began the first of the deadly artillery duels which were to characterise the Battle of Anzio.

As Cisterna was occupied, *Kampfgruppe* Gericke was being strengthened on the other side of the beachhead by the arrival of Battalion Kleye. With the ability to hold more ground with two battalions, Kleye was sent to defend Ardea, whilst Hauber was to concentrate on the Via Anziate. Joachim Liebschner, an eighteen-year-old Lance-Corporal from Silesia, says that the road attracted fire from the outset:

> I was a runner which meant that I had to try and keep communication between my own company and battalion headquarters. We were issued with a bicycle and it was really a great big joke because when we moved forward, the harder the artillery fire became and we were then attacked by aeroplanes. When everybody jumped into ditches to the left and right I was left with the bicycle. Eventually I went to the Sergeant Major and said look when am I going to use my bicycle here, and he said 'You signed for it, you're responsible for it!' typical German kind of answer to a question . . . I left it against a tree and thought I could find the tree again when we get to the front line. Not only had the bicycle gone but the tree had gone as well. The artillery fire in this sector, people were saying, was of comparable strength to that in the 14–18 war.

The shells crept ever nearer, tearing up the ground with a blast of such intensity that its sound waves were soaked up by the chests of the paratroopers. But it was not the men new to battle that struggled most with the bombardment; it was the veterans and, as Liebschner says, one sergeant in particular who had been wounded and traumatised on the Eastern Front:

> He lost his nerve altogether. Most of us didn't know what we were letting ourselves in for, but this fellow had been in the front line several times and the closer we got, the more he started shivering and complaining of a headache and sickness and his legs were

giving out. He couldn't move. We left him underneath a small bridge shivering and crying and he was hysterical. I never heard of him again.

That evening a strong patrol from Battalion Hauber was sent down to Aprilia. As it was such a vital town that had not defended all day, Gericke expected to hear that it was occupied. To his amazement he learned at 2030 hours that it was not and passed the information on to the recently arrived Lieutenant General Fritz-Hubert Gräser. Gräser was the commander of a 3rd Panzer Grenadier Division *kampfgruppe* which had been ordered to take over the defence of the Via Anziate from 4th Parachute Division thus allowing Gericke to concentrate his forces on the west side of the road. The critical road in the beachhead was to be defended by a more experienced division. Although Gräser's force also contained some replacements, 3rd Panzer Grenadier Division was of more varied stock for, at its heart, were veterans of the Eastern Front, with a proportion having served at Stalingrad where the original division had been all but wiped out. The division had fought well at Salerno and was reaching the peak of effectiveness. Gräser immediately occupied Aprilia.

By the time that the panzer grenadiers were preparing the buildings of Aprilia for defence, Schlemm had established his I Parachute Corps headquarters in the Alban Hills and was in full command of the German forces at Anzio. Kesselring was furious with his predecessor's efforts that day. Although the untalented Schlemmer was obviously out of his depth in such an operation, his inability to carry out simple orders was inexcusable. Monte Soratte had instructed Schlemmer 'to push all units as they arrived as far south as possible so as to help the flak slow down or halt the enemy advance', but instead he formed a strong ambushing force in the Alban Hills in case of a push on Rome. The 20,000 men that had made it through to the beachhead were either surplus to his requirements, had slipped through his net, or had ignored his orders. Through the incompetence of one man in a position of power, the Germans' carefully laid plans could have failed. Had the Allies chosen to advance swiftly soon after their landing, they would at the very least have been able to seize valuable ground for an expansive beachhead. As Kesselring later wrote:

> Every yard was important to me. My order, as I found out on the spot in the afternoon, had been incomprehensibly and arbitrarily altered, which upset my plan for immediate counter-attacks. Yet as I traversed the front I had the confident feeling that the Allies had missed a uniquely favourable chance of capturing Rome and of opening the door on the Garigliano front. I was certain that time was our ally.

As was the Field Marshal's style, on the day of the invasion he had been decisive in his actions and visited the front personally. Far from doing what the Allies had wanted him to do and withdraw in a panic from the Gustav Line, Kesselring had remained unfazed by Operation Shingle. Anything else would have been distinctly out of character. In spite of von Vietinghoff's whinging that with so many troops having been taken from him he could not hold his front, and advocating an immediate withdrawal, Kesselring literally and metaphorically held his ground. There was no need to withdraw and in any case, as he told von Senger und Etterlin 'the present line is shorter and therefore more economical, than a line running directly in front of the gates of Rome straight across Italy.' Kesselring was not minded to act as the Allies wanted him to and was determined to regain the initiative. First he would build up a critical mass of troops, and then he would push the Allies back into the sea. The American historian Carlo D'Este has written: 'Kesselring symbolised the German defense of Italy, and he became the bedrock upon which it was built. Where others would have drawn the wrong conclusions and overreacted, Kesselring remained composed and was quite literally the glue that held the German Army in Italy together . . . Kesselring excelled in the art of improvisation, and Anzio may well have been his finest hour.'

John Lucas was feeling comfortable that evening. Reading the reports that were coming through to the *Biscayne* it was apparent that the divisions were secure and were not under any immediate threat. By the end of the day, as British Guards officers played bridge and slept in their pyjamas, Lucas read with quiet satisfaction that 36,000 men and 3,000 vehicles had been landed. Casualties had been very light – 13 killed, 97 wounded and 44 captured or missing, and the defending panzer grenadiers had been dealt with clinically, producing 227 prisoners. He was also pleased to hear during the afternoon that the port had been opened after the navy had pulled away the hulks of sunken vessels and swept the harbour. As a result of this unexpected speed, supplies were flowing ashore far quicker than anticipated, allowing British vessels to land in Anzio rather than having to struggle with the sand bar. The beachhead was quiet. Exhausted after a trying day, Geoffrey Dormer, a First Lieutenant on the minesweeper HMS *Hornpipe,* noted in his diary:

> D-Day Evening. Things have been very quiet, and it has been a lovely, calm, sunny day, with almost cloudless blue skies. The multitude of ships off the beaches look more like a Review than an Invasion Fleet . . . There are a few columns of smoke rising from the shore, and now and then a dull thud. Sometimes a Cruiser does a bit of bombarding, or a few enemy planes approach.

To the troops on the ground, the beachhead had an ethereal quality to it. Lieutenant Ivor Talbot was in a foxhole close to the Mussolini Canal when he wrote in his diary that evening:

> It has been a remarkable day. We landed at 0430 in the darkness and made our way inland. There were the inevitable pauses in our advance, but we were eventually told to dig in for the night. It is now

2200 and I am dog tired but must get round to the men before I sleep. All is quiet as it has been for most of the day. I was not expecting this and I think that I had expected to die. I think that we must be careful that we keep our concentration. The Germans will not allow us to remain here without a fight, but we seem to have won the first day.

Talbot was incorrect in his assessment of 22 January. The Allies had not 'won the first day'. It had been a draw. What the young Lieutenant had not taken into account was the skilful German reaction to Operation Shingle for whilst the Allies were in an excellent position to develop and consolidate a strong beachhead in preparation for a breakout, Kesselring had successfully begun to build a counter-attacking force intent on destroying it. Kesselring drew strength from the knowledge that his build up rate would increase significantly henceforward, whilst the Allies were not only dependent on supply from the sea, but were also under time pressure to link up the two disparate parts of Fifth Army. Lucas, meanwhile, felt confident that he could quickly establish an immovable force at Anzio–Nettuno and could rely on the support of powerful naval guns and airpower. By the end of the first day there were opportunities for both sides, and as such much depended on the actions over the coming days of two risk-averse commanders – John P. Lucas and Eberhard von Mackensen.

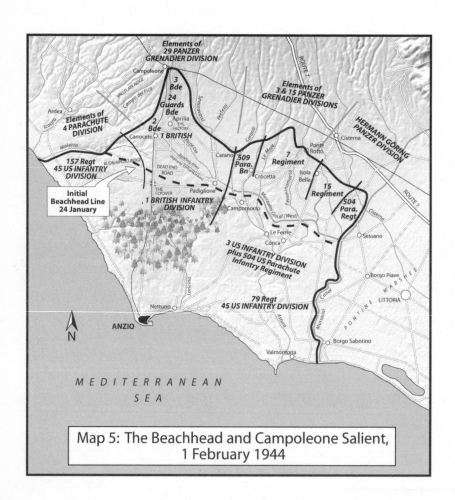

Map 5: The Beachhead and Campoleone Salient,
1 February 1944

CHAPTER 5

The Nudge

(23 January–2 February)

Rome was throbbing with activity on the morning of Sunday 23 January. The peal of bells calling parishioners to mass was lost in the din of shouting German voices and hundreds of vehicle engines. Staff cars, armoured cars, half-tracks, tanks, and trucks all vied for space on the *Corso D'Italia* heading east, and there was a heady atmosphere in the capital as the Italians witnessed the Germans gripped by surprise. One witness spoke of German-occupied hotel foyers looking like 'poorly directed mob scenes in provincial operas.' The news of the landings at Anzio–Nettuno swiftly passed on from various German headquarters to their subordinate commands had also spread quickly amongst Romans after anti-fascist groups had been sent a message by the Allies: 'Your aunt is ill and about to die.' It was the code for the Allies having landed close to the capital. Kesselring was so worried that the attack might precipitate a popular uprising that Waffen SS Colonel Eugen Dollmann had been summoned from his boarding house by the Spanish Steps to an emergency meeting at Monte Soratte.

Within the hour Dollmann (a liaison officer for General Karl Wolff, the head of the SS in Italy) was standing at Kesselring's side. Did the Colonel think that the attack would lead to an uprising in the capital? 'No,' replied the astute officer, 'the Romans are not brave enough and will not fight until Alexander's army is on the city boundary.' During the day there had been rumours that the Germans were preparing to withdraw from Rome; that the Allies were just a couple of miles away; that the Communists were about to seize power. But there had been no uprising. By the end of the day it was clear that the Allied arrival was not imminent and that the Germans were not leaving. Indeed, a spate of summary roadside executions, and an increase of heavily armed patrols was an obvious challenge to any dissension. The night passed without even the hint of an insurrection, and the following morning Dollmann drove down quiet secondary roads towards Anzio with his dog to see how the battle was progressing. Just outside Campoleone he pulled over by a bedraggled-looking collection of soldiers and spoke to their officer. The Major told him that yesterday morning he had been on convalescent leave in Rome enjoying the sights, and by the evening had been placed in command of 150 soldiers from a VD hospital. Only half possessed rifles, he complained, and several looked like dead men walking. Wherever this unhealthy horde was deployed would be an extremely lean part of the thin field-grey line that was building up around the Allied beachhead. Even so, the Germans used whatever was on offer to create a defensive line for they expected an imminent Allied breakout. As Siegfried Westphal later wrote: 'an audacious and enterprising formation of enemy troops . . . could have penetrated into the city of Rome itself without having to overcome any serious opposition.'

Far too concerned with defence, neither Rome nor the Alban Hills were troubling Lucas during the first two days of the operation. In some places the Germans had already launched local counter-attacks. The Hermann Göring Panzer Division, for example, lashed out violently against 3rd Division's 30th Infantry Regiment necessitating the rapid development of defensive positions. The inexperienced replacement Private Norman Mohar was the member of an Ammunition and Pioneer Platoon and had soon found himself in the thick of the action:

> The first night I was sent out with booby-traps and mines to lay in 'No Man's Land'. 'NO MAN'S LAND'!! I couldn't believe that I was only a few hundred feet away from German machine guns. Now and then the Germans would fire flares, which hung for what seemed like hours floating down on a small parachute . . . Sometimes the Jerries would open up with their machine guns at the same time as launching the flares. The German machine gun tracers were only a few feet above the ground.

In well co-ordinated attacks combining German tanks and infantry, General Paul Conrath's division successfully pushed south of the Mussolini Canal in the darkness, taking most of its bridges. Conrath continued to apply pressure on Truscott's men throughout 23 January with strong patrols, but the Americans hit back sharply that evening, recovering most of the lost ground. These were tit for tat actions that successfully managed to reacquaint the two formations after their previous encounters in Sicily and at Salerno and were 'an ominous harbinger of the trial of strength that was shortly to take place.' On that day there was only a small increase in the size of the beachhead as units consolidated the ground won the previous day. When patrols were pushed out to reconnoitre the ground ahead, however, they invariably reported increased enemy activity. Patrolling was one of the many aspects of soldiering that the 504th US Parachute Infantry Regiment excelled at. Commanded by the blond haired, barrel-chested Colonel Reuben H. Tucker, the 504th were hard men and good soldiers, as Ross Carter declared:

The thing that distinguished us from most other soldiers was our willingness to take chances and risks . . . Each man had supreme faith in his ability to take care of himself whatever the odds. For this reason paratroopers were at times quarrelsome because they could never believe that anybody could beat the hell out of them.

Lieutenant Toland of 2nd Battalion carried out a seven-man patrol on the night of 23 January 'to look for trouble'. At 2000 hours, dressed in dark clothes with their faces blackened, the men crossed the Mussolini Canal and slipped into No Man's Land. Deep inside enemy-held territory, a place that they called 'Jerryland', they dropped down into a ditch to check a map just as a tank across the road opened fire on the beachhead. Carter wrote of the incident:

The powerful *whoosh* of the projectile passing overhead set our heads ringing. A hundred yards to the left a truck drove up and unloaded a lot of men who went into the field and began to dig holes about fifty yards from us . . . a digging German left his group and had the bad luck to pass near the end of our patrol. Casey, tensely coiled like a giant snake, enveloped him, slit his throat with his eleven-inch dagger and silently crouched on the ground.

The patrol made their way back to friendly lines, passing German machine gun teams as they went, their 'breasts bursting with excitement and thrilling with exultation.' The experience had left their 'nerves limp' and they were so tired that they could 'do no better than splutter in aimless conversation', but their information was gratefully received and fitted cleanly into an intelligence picture that spoke of a rapid German response to the landings.

There was no attempt to take Aprilia, Campoleone Station and Cisterna on the second or even the third day despite the evidence that resistance was building. Kesselring later wrote that during this period the defence had been a 'higgledy-piggledy jumble – units of numerous divisions fighting confusedly side by side', and so this was the time to seize vital ground. Just a few thousand German troops had arrived on the 23rd, but their number had swollen on 24 January to 40,400. The incoherent force was developing into something capable of giving Lucas a bloody nose. Schlemm had managed to fashion a continuous, though slim, defensive line around the sixteen-mile long, seven-mile deep beachhead. His main line of resistance was centred on Campoleone and Cisterna, but outposts had been pushed five miles further forward for protection. Schlemm's commanders had developed strong defensive positions utilising all of the advantages that the ground had to offer for tactical advantage. Barns, outbuildings and farmhouses had been fortified and connected by trenches. The armour had been camouflaged and everything was covered by carefully sited artillery. Denis Healey on his third and last day, out of curiosity, decided to drive to the front in his amphibious jeep: 'But when I got there', he says, 'I saw our soldiers in trenches being bombarded and so turned round sharpish and headed back to the beach.' Healey was convinced by what he had seen that the best opportunity for exploitation had already passed, although back in England *The Times* headlines proclaimed: 'LANDING SOUTH OF ROME ESTABLISHED. ALLIED TROOPS SEVERAL MILES INLAND. SERIOUS THREAT TO GERMAN LINES OF COMMUNICATION'. On the following day the newspaper's claim that the beachhead was 'being rapidly increased in depth' was still untrue. *The Times* seems to have been producing copy based on what it thought should be happening rather than what was actually happening. In reality VI Corps had been caught in an unseemly limbo between attack and defence. Defending the Mussolini Canal on the right (twenty feet wide with thirty feet high banks), was 504th Parachute Infantry Regiment, to its left was 3rd Division holding a nine mile front along the west branch of the Mussolini Canal, with Ranger

Force taking the American sector along the Lateral Road up to the Via Anziate. 1st Division straddled this important highway and continued the line down the western section of the Lateral Road and then along the mouth of the Moletta River to the sea. In reserve Lucas held the 3rd Brigade of 1st Division, two battalions of 7th US Infantry Regiment and 509th Parachute Battalion. The corps was still awaiting the arrival of a regiment of 45th US Infantry Division and Combat Command A of 1st US Armored Division before the end of the month, and Lucas was not tempted to try anything aggressive until they arrived. Frustration was growing, a feeling that Vaughan-Thomas picked up on as he toured the British front: 'As D-Day turned into D plus 1, then into D plus 2, a slight unease began to possess the Allied rank and file. The exhilaration of the Great Surprise had worn off. The men could not share the thoughts of the Corps Commander and knew nothing of the factors which had influenced him to consolidate on the Beach-head. They only sensed that for the moment there seemed to be no strong enemy before them.' Why give the enemy the initiative and waste the initial surprise? Lieutenant William Dugdale of the Grenadier Guards could not under-stand it:

> The only excitement was Lieutenant Michael Hargreaves and his Carrier Platoon who, sent on a recce, drove completely unopposed up the local minor roads to the south west suburbs of Rome. He finally turned round as he thought he could be cut off at a street corner.

Yet Lucas, secreted in his Nettuno headquarters close to the seafront, thought that he was doing rather well bearing in mind Mark Clark's orders. He noted in his diary on 25 January, the same day that von Mackensen's Fourteenth Army took over command of the beachhead from Schlemm: 'I am doing my best, but it seems terribly slow. I must keep my feet on the ground and do nothing foolish.' Something 'foolish' might have been a major offensive thrust to the Alban Hills, but on the 25th the agitated VI Corps commander did allow himself an attempt by 1st British Division to take nearby Aprilia, and 3rd Division to advance several miles towards Cisterna.

Aprilia was desirable to Lucas both as a stepping-stone towards the Alban Hills and a defensive anchor. The evacuated town was a potential fortress that sat on a slight rise beside the Via Anziate, dominating the boggy ground surrounding it. The troops called it the 'Factory' for although it was a small model Fascist town of two and three storey buildings, the geometric design and tower that rose out of the Fascist headquarters made it look like an industrial site. The attack on the Factory was to be 'the first warning to the front line soldier that the Anzio adventure had lost its early bloom'. At dawn British armour began moving up the Via Anziate flanked by a marching Guards Brigade, spearheaded by the Grenadiers, stretching back as far as the eye could see. A smattering of local farmers standing on the frosty verge clapped nervously as the troops passed them, whilst Penney and his brigade commanders watched the spectacle from the Flyover. It was to be the last time in the battle of Anzio that it would be a safe place to do such a thing. The Grenadiers continued up the road for a further two miles, then deployed on their start line – the Embankment of the 'Disused Railway Bed.' Here they came under increasingly heavy German fire and Lieutenant Michael Hargreaves, the hero of 'The Rome Patrol', was killed by one of the first shots fired that day. Their first task was to take Carroceto and to use it as a base from which to assault the Factory. An attempt to enter the village, however, led to the officer of the lead platoon, Lieutenant The Honourable V.S. de R. Canning, being wounded in the head and all of his section commanders, bar one, becoming casualties. It was not until a couple of Shermans provided covering fire that a second platoon managed to infiltrate the village and clear the buildings in vicious hand-to-hand fighting. The preliminary action had already cost the battalion dearly. As the historian of the Grenadier Guards has written: 'Carroceto was in our hands. With how much less cost could it have been captured two days before!' The main attack on the Factory began at 1415 hours. Two companies advanced across the open ground assisted by a barrage of smoke, high explosives and a low sun that was glaring in the faces of the defenders. Nevertheless, one of the company commanders was killed leading his men forward, and the other wounded. Sapper Stanley Fennell watched the attack: 'I cringed at the sight, because I was sitting in an enormous armoured car, and they were completely soft-skinned, as it were. The shells burst amongst them, and they marched steadily forward in the attack . . . to see them go forward was awe-inspiring.' The Grenadiers reached the town and immediately began clearing the buildings. It was an unpleasant task, 'a deadly game of hide-and-seek, of sudden encounters at close quarters and of unexpected stumblings upon well-armed enemies. Shutters and doors had to be smashed in and grenades flung quickly into rooms where the Germans might be hiding, the Guardsmen ducking hurriedly to avoid the flying fragments. In some houses terrified civilians crouched in shallow cellars praying that the fight would sweep past them.' Slowly the Germans were overwhelmed and the battalion took 111 prisoners that day. One Nazi officer, whilst being led through Carroceto under armed guard, pointed to a Sherman and said in English 'if I had that, I would be in Rome by now'.

It rained heavily that night, weather which was to undermine the ability of the Allied forces to support VI Corps during the last week of January, and under its cover the Germans prepared to retake the Factory. At dawn on 26 January the panzer grenadiers opened fire on the Grenadiers with machine guns and five self-propelled guns from some large huts a couple of hundred yards to the north-east of the town. There was no infantry attack and the armour was stopped by anti-tank guns and the supporting artillery, but the huts continued to provide cover for the enemy. A platoon from Captain T.S. Hohler's company was sent to relieve the Germans of the huts, and it succeeded, but two German tanks almost immediately forced its eight survivors out. The battle continued, however, as the Grenadiers' historian has written:

There was no choice but to attack again, and there were no other troops available than Hohler's company, who by this time were extremely weak, their headquarters having received a direct hit from a shell while the wounded from the first skirmish were being treated inside. Capt. Hohler returned with his new orders, to find that a Guardsman who had been blinded some time previously in the huts, had had his leg blown off while lying on a stretcher; another had lost both legs; and several others, including the Company Sergeant-Major, were also wounded.

Hohler led another attack across the bare, flat ground during which five of his men were killed. But he managed to occupy the huts. Whilst organising his defences a tank opened fire with its machine gun and a stream of bullets smashed through the wooden walls. There were several casualties, including Hohler whose forearm was shattered. Alone and feeling faint he scrambled over to another hut where he joined another wounded man and a Guardsman whose Bren gun had jammed. Through the fug he heard shouting which indicated that the tank was now moving forward and rising gingerly to his feet saw the beast descending through a hole in a wooden panel. By the time he turned round, the German infantry were rounding up his men. The Bren gunner had been caught with his weapon in pieces and was being led away with a Schmeisser jammed into his ribs. Hohler knew that he would be next unless he acted quickly. 'Captain Hohler rather carefully laid down', the Battalion War Diary explains, 'put his steel helmet over his face, turned up his toes, and lay as one dead. The wounded Guardsman was led off as well, but the ruse worked, and Captain Hohler was not disturbed by any German.' He eventually reached safety, but the enemy retook the huts. The casualties had been heavy, 130 rank and file alone, but the battalion's determination to hang on to the Factory was undiminished. The Grenadiers' attention to detail remained as acute as ever, for even as their Commanding Officer lay wounded barking orders, Lieutenant William Dugdale, the junior officer who had been lambasted for his appearance by Alexander on D-Day, received another ticking off: 'I found Col. Gordon Lennox lying on a mattress in the Factory compound directing the repulse of the counter-attack', he recalls. 'As "Left Out of Battle" I was not in battle order or wearing a steel helmet. Col. Gordon Lennox beckoned me over and enquired why I was not properly dressed.' Within minutes Dugdale was properly dressed and found himself in the front line under a German bombardment. Throughout the remainder of the day the Germans put the Brigade under such heavy artillery fire that it was largely responsible for the 119 casualties Irish Guards lodged at Carroceto. There were some enemy infantry attacks that caused the Grenadiers difficulties on their open right flank, but an advance by Ranger Force and 509th Parachute Infantry Battalion clinically eliminated the problem. The battle had been bloody, but Penney had secured a valuable objective.

The first battles of Carroceto and the Factory became a benchmark for the grisly tussles that were to take place in the Anzio beachhead. Father Brookes, the Irish Guards' padre, who had served on the Western Front during the First World War, said that 26 January compared unfavourably to any of his wartime experiences. Brookes spent the day at the British Casualty Clearing Station (CCS) that had been established at a Yellow Bungalow close to the Via Anziate between the Flyover and Anzio. It was overwhelmed with wounded and as shells were falling all around, some had to be administered in the relative safety of a drainage ditch. The author of the Irish Guards history, D.J.L. Fitzgerald, a captain at Anzio, later wrote:

The patience and gratitude shown by the wounded men is one of the few things which it is worth being in battle to see. Not only on this occasion, but at all times, the silent courage of maimed, battered, bleeding Irish Guardsmen lying in the open or, if they were lucky, in some muddy ditch, was a living monument to the strength of the human will in the depths of human misery. A man drained of blood gets very cold, there is not much a man with a shattered thigh can do for himself; a man whose chest has been torn to ribbons by shell splinters would like to be moved out of the barrage. But they did not say anything, they didn't ask for anything; they smiled painfully when the orderlies put a blanket over them or gave them a drink of water and a cigarette, and just shut their eyes for a moment when a shell exploded particularly close.

It was on that day that the field adjacent to the Casualty Clearing Station began to spawn wooden crosses.

Just as the Guards Brigade was blooded at the Factory, 3rd Division was carrying out its attack towards Cisterna. Standing on Route 7 and boasting a road that led to Valmontone on Route 6, the town guarded the supply routes to Tenth Army and so had been incorporated into the German main defences. The battle to move 3rd Division to within striking distance of Cisterna lasted for nearly four days and advanced front line by up to three miles, but ultimately left Truscott's division another three miles short of the town. During the fighting, one of the most remarkable feats of heroism to be witnessed in the beachhead occurred. The unlikely hero was T/5 Eric G. Gibson, a cook from the US 30th Regiment who often volunteered for combat duties. On 28 January Gibson was part of a squad attack in which he had asked to be lead scout. Leading the men through an irrigation ditch, he almost immediately contacted the enemy:

The squad had proceeded only a few steps when a blast of machine-pistol fire opened up from a clump of brush along the ditch bank. Gibson did not even take cover, but ran twenty yards up the ditch, firing his tommy gun from the hip as he went. He poked the gun muzzle into the brush and finished the Germans hidden there. Under a heavy artillery concentration the squad again moved out. Knocked flat under the concussion of one close shell, Gibson had no sooner risen than he was fired upon by a machine pistol and rifle. Again he charged down the ditch, to fire his submachine gun into another pile of brush.

With that threat dealt with Gibson then tackled two machine guns that had opened fire on the squad. He crawled toward the strong point as shells exploded all around him and got to within thirty-five yards before hurling two grenades into the position. Before the second grenade had exploded Gibson leapt up and charged, killing two Germans and capturing another. Quite unperturbed he returned to the ditch and continued in the lead. Within moments he rounded a corner and squad following heard a machine pistol fire followed by Gibson's tommy gun. Rushing to the scene they found Gibson's dead body lying beside the two Germans that he had killed. Eric Gibson was awarded a posthumous Congressional Medal of Honor. The 3rd Division, meanwhile, would have to try again to seize Cisterna. Truscott, who on 24 January had himself been wounded by a shell splinter in his foot, recommended a more concentrated attack on the town as 'more power was needed'.

Alexander and Clark were also keen to see a more concentrated effort. When they had visited the beachhead on 25 January, they had been satisfied that Lucas was at least beginning to move forward. Both men wanted to see the main German defences broken. Alexander had become increasingly uneasy at Lucas's lack of movement, and even Mark Clark had been surprised that the VI Corps commander had not put together an early offensive to take Campoleone and Cisterna. Lucas had not stuck his head out too far. He had not stuck it out at all. To calm Lucas's fears that a major offensive would leave him without a reserve, Clark informed him that the remainder of 45th Division and

1st Armored Division would be sent to the beachhead, along with 168th Brigade of 56th British Infantry Division and First Special Service Force. Lucas was confused and seemed either unwilling or unable to ask Clark the obvious question. Why was the Fifth Army commander pressurising VI Corps into a major offensive? The pressure was not appreciated and that night Lucas confided to his diary: 'This is the most important thing I have ever tried to do and I will not be stampeded.' He wanted to continue with his cautious, methodical advance just as originally instructed, rather than launch an impulsively premature strike before the German counter-attack. But if Lucas was under pressure from Alexander and Clark, it should be noted that Alexander was in turn under severe pressure from Churchill. On 26 January the Prime Minister cabled Fifteenth Army Headquarters: 'I am thinking of your great battle night and day', and so he was. He had already demanded to be informed why there had been no breakout at Anzio and was told that it was 'not due to lack of urging from above'. As usual, Brooke was feeling the full force of the Prime Minister's displeasure, noting in his diary on 28 January: 'Churchill was full of doubts as to whether Lucas was handling this landing efficiently. I had some job quietening him down again.' The Prime Minister's mood was at least partly fuelled by a cable received that same day from Alexander saying that he was also unhappy at Lucas's efforts. Clark, meanwhile, had been despatched to the beachhead in an attempt 'to urge General Lucas to initiate aggressive action at once'.

Mark Clark was in a foul mood during the journey to Anzio, and was only to get worse. Initially he had been irritated by reports that the attacks by 1st and 3rd Divisions had proved so 'challenging', but by the time that he was nearly killed by an American minesweeper opening fire on his motor-launch, he was furious. One of the shells had hit Clark's stool and although he was not wounded, there had been casualties amongst the crew. The subsequent meeting with Lucas was frosty, but he thawed a little when presented with the plan for a major attack that was to take place that night, 28–29 January. He was told that 1st Division were to take Campoleone Station, whilst 3rd Division was to seize Cisterna. The meeting broke up amicably, but Lucas still felt compelled to write that night:

> Apparently some of the higher levels think I have not advanced with maximum speed. I think more has been accomplished than anyone had a right to expect. This venture was always a desperate one and I could never see much chance for it to succeed, if success means driving the Germans north of Rome. The one factor that has allowed us to get established ashore has been the port of Anzio. Without it our situation by this time would have been desperate with little chance of a build-up to adequate strength. As it is, we are doing well and, in addition to our troops, unloaded over 4,000 tons of supplies yesterday. Had I been able to rush to the high ground around Albano . . . immediately upon landing, nothing would have been accomplished except to weaken my force by that amount because the troops sent, being completely beyond supporting distance, would have been completely destroyed. The only thing to do was what I did. Get a proper beachhead and prepare to hold it. Keep the enemy off balance by a constant advance against him by small units, not committing anything as large as a division until the Corps was ashore and everything was set. Then make a co-ordinated attack to defeat the enemy and seize the objective. Follow this by exploitation. This is what I have been doing, but I had to have troops in to do it with.

Lucas's preoccupation with resources can clearly be seen in this diary entry, and he certainly could not be criticised for lack of attention to the resupply of the beachhead. It was a sophisticated operation in which a convoy of six LSTs departed from Naples every day on the 100-mile trip to Anzio. Each vessel contained 50 trucks loaded to capacity usually with 60 per cent ammunition, 20 per cent fuel, and 20 per cent rations. These vessels were supplemented each week by 15 LCTs and every ten days by four Liberty ships, loaded with over 9,000 tons of cargo. There had been some poor weather in which 'Liberty ships lay tossing and the LCTs rolled and pitched continuously', but it was the Luftwaffe attacks that caused more concern. As the harbour was critical to the Allies, it was an obvious German target. Between 23 January and 3 February whilst Kesselring gathered his ground forces, he massed a substantial bomber force: 140 long range bombers had been moved to Italy from north-west Germany, France and Greece, and the anti-shipping force in the south of France was reinforced by an additional 60 aircraft. Torpedoes, bombs and radio-controlled glider bombs (a general purpose bomb which was rocket-powered and radio-controlled) were all dropped in and around the harbour. The first major raid came on 23 January when the medium bombers launched glider bombs against a Landing Ship Tank. On this occasion their weapons failed to respond to the radio controls, but the anti-aircraft guns, barrage balloons and smoke screens failed to deter future attempts. Allied fighter patrols ruled the skies during the day, and so most German bomber raids were launched after darkness. Lucas wrote on 26 January: '8.45 p.m. The biggest yet. The Hun's determined to ruin me and knows that if I lose Anzio harbor I am in a hell of a fix. I went to look at the mess. Trucks are burning and the town is in a shambles, but ships are being unloaded. Casualties have been heavy I am afraid.' Ross Carter watched the show with grim fascination from the Mussolini Canal: 'All night the enemy dropped long-burning parachute flares over the harbour', he wrote. 'Night after night we watched the awesomely spectacular fireworks and shivered at the sight of burning planes falling to the earth or into the sea.' The navies soon got the measure of the bombers, however. Commander Roger Hill on HMS *Grenville* recalls:

With the glider bombs I found that if I started to turn, the bomb would start to follow me, but the bomb had a bigger turning circle than I did and they all missed us. I could see them sort of turning somersaults and landing in the sea and I had people on the Bridge who were spotting the next one that was roaming and when that was finished they left a plane over the top who was obviously taking photographs, so we made a very rude signal to them.

Before long the Task Force 81 destroyers had the means to detect and jam the Luftwaffe's radio beams. The German pilot prowled the harbour looking for a likely target and then, staying high and clear of the heavy flak that poured from the anti-aircraft guns, released his bomb. From that point on this was a battle of wits between the pilot with his joy-stick trying to guide the bomb onto its target, and the jamming team. Often the navy managed to bring the missiles down into the sea – but not always. Before the end of the month the Germans had sunk the cruiser *Spartan* – 'Spartan lies on her side, the bilge just showing . . . For miles the sea is full of blackened, bloated corpses', the destroyers *Janus* – sunk in 20 minutes with the loss of its commander and 150 men – *Jervis* and *Plunkett*, the minesweeper *Prevail*, the hospital ship *St David*, and the troop transporter *Samuel Huntington* containing 7,181 tons of equipment and materials. But although these losses were disquieting, VI Corps had successfully taken delivery of 68,886 men, 508 artillery pieces and 237 tanks by 29 January, and Lucas was justifiably pleased with this effort.

Amongst the new arrivals had been the 45th US Infantry Division commanded by Major General William W. Eagles, and 1st US Armored Division commanded by Major General Ernest N. Harmon. Eagles according to Lucas, was a 'quiet, determined soldier, with broad experience' whilst Harmon, although also determined and experienced, was far from quiet. Born into poverty in New England and orphaned at the age of ten, this ambitious character was the embodiment of the American Dream. Now in his fiftieth year, Ernest Harmon was a bull of a man who sported two pearl handled revolvers. He lacked tact, but demanded respect, and had been carved from the same granite as Patton. It was without any sense of irony, however, that Lucas welcomed Harmon to the beachhead with the words, 'Glad to see you. You're needed here.' His Combat Command A was just in time for the attack on the night of 28 January and was to support 1st Division's attack towards Campoleone. On 27 January the Scots Guards had pushed on from the Factory and taken what the officers called 'Dung Farm' and the men called something else on account of the smell of rotting animals and manure. From this foul place the Scots were to secure a road between the farm and Campoleone, with the Grenadier Guards attacking on their left. Once this road had been taken 3rd Brigade were to launch an assault to Campoleone Station. Combat Command A was to support the attack by swinging across the Vallelata Ridge west of the Via Anziate and south west of the station. In a secondary but simultaneous attack, two battalions of Ranger Force were to infiltrate Cisterna during the night whilst its third cleared the Conca–Cisterna road in preparation for the main onslaught on the town by 15th Infantry Regiment the following morning. Subsidiary attacks by 7th Infantry Regiment and a company of 30th Infantry Regiment on the left to cut Route 7 north of Cisterna, and 504th Parachute Infantry Regiment on the right were to further occupy the enemy defences. If Lucas's offensive was successful then Tenth Army would, at last, feel the impact of Operation Shingle. By the end of January with 34th Division having managed to create a small bridgehead over the Rapido, and the French 3rd Algerian Division threatening in the hills to the north, Alexander was sensing a breakthrough. By reinforcing Clark with the New Zealand Corps and co-ordinating an attack on the Gustav Line to coincide with the attacks at Anzio, the Fifteenth Army Group commander still hoped to force Kesselring into a withdrawal.

With Clark rubbing in the need for immediate offensive action to Lucas at their meeting on 28 January, it was extremely unfortunate that, even as he spoke, an incident took place in the beachhead which was to lead to the postponing of the attack. That afternoon a party of eight Grenadier officers and three other ranks were driving up the Via Anziate to Dung Farm for an Order Group prior to their attack. Missing the turning to the farm their jeeps had continued up the main road and run into automatic fire and hand grenades from a German outpost. Three officers and a Guardsman were killed, one officer and two Guardsmen wounded and taken prisoner. The four officers that escaped did so courtesy of an incompetent German machine gunner and the pall of smoke that blew across the road from a burning jeep. As a result of the episode both 1st and 3rd Division attacks were postponed for twenty-four hours and the Irish Guards had taken the place of the devastated Grenadiers on the left of the attack. The postponement had been no mere inconvenience. On 29 January another 17,000 German troops arrived taking their total to 71,500 men. Amongst them were 7,000 soldiers from the 26th Panzer Division that reinforced Cisterna.

As von Mackensen's defences absorbed the newly arrived troops on 29 January, 1st and 3rd Divisions were making the final adjustments for their postponed attack. The weather was atrocious causing Combat Command A to slip and slide their way through difficult country to their jumping off point. Their problems were exacerbated when a German artillery observer spotted their laboured movements, calling down a bombardment. Harmon's preparations were ruined, the deployment took far longer than he anticipated and continued long after darkness had fallen. There was no reconnaissance, orders were rushed and the whole experience had been thoroughly miserable. To make matters worse a British officer from 2nd Brigade was captured with a set of 1st Division plans after he had got lost and wandered into the German lines. It was a very tense time. Across VI Corps there was at last a feeling that something positive was being done to push forward, but there were also concerns that it had been left too late and the enemy would be waiting for them in numbers. One platoon commander in the Guards Brigade remembers his company commander being uncharacteristically anxious:

Joseph Stalin, Franklin D. Roosevelt and Winston Churchill at the Tehran Conference, 28 November 1943. The ever watchful General Sir Alan Brooke stands just behind the British Premier and the US President. IWM A20713

Field Marshal Albert Kesselring, who masterminded the German defences in Italy and ensured a rapid reaction to the Allied landing at Anzio–Nettuno. IWM RY66846

The urbane General Sir Harold R.L.G. Alexander, who struggled to stamp his authority on the Italian Campaign and contain his increasingly single-minded American subordinate, Lieutenant General Mark Clark. IWM NA7957

Churchill posing in his dressing gown after hosting a Christmas lunch at Carthage, 25 December 1943. He is flanked by General Dwight Eisenhower *(left)* and by General Sir Henry Maitland Wilson *(right)*. Those standing behind include: Air Chief Marshal Sir Arthur Tedder *(second from left)*, Admiral Sir John Cunningham *(fourth from left)* and General Sir Harold Alexander *(sixth from left)*. IWM NA10075

Never one to miss a photo opportunity, Lieutenant General Mark Clark hands a Christmas parcel to an American soldier in Italy, December 1943. IWM NYP13269

British troops
embarking for Anzio
at Naples on the
afternoon of
20 January 1944.
IWM NA10899

General Alexander
(seated on extreme left)
and Admiral Thomas
Troubridge *(pointing)*
en route for the British
landing beach at Anzio
on 22 January.
IWM NA11052

Mark Clark on his way to Anzio in his PT boat on
22 January. IWM EA16866

Troubridge, Major General John P. Lucas and Major General W.R.C. Penney confer
on 22 January. IWM NA11049

John Lucas in his Nettuno headquarters looking considerably older than his fifty-four years. US NATIONAL ARCHIVES

General Eberhard von Mackensen, who was tasked with the containment and then the destruction of the VI Corps beachhead. BUNDESARCHIV

3rd US Infantry Division land on X-Ray beach on the morning of 22 January. An LST is on the left and an LCI on the right. US NATIONAL ARCHIVES

An LST is unloaded in Anzio harbour. It was to become the fourth largest port in the world during the battle. DENIS HEALEY

Civilians awaiting evacuation from Anzio during the battle. IWM NA12560

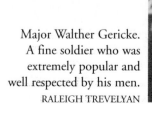

Major Walther Gericke. A fine soldier who was extremely popular and well respected by his men. RALEIGH TREVELYAN

Irish Guardsmen march to battle along the Via Anziate on 25 January. They were to suffer heavy casualties taking Carroceto later that day. IWM NA11442

A British 25-pounder gun is loaded. The Padiglione Woods can be seen in the background. IWM NA13316

A British M4 Sherman medium tank makes its way to the front line at the end of January. These workhorses of the Allied armoured divisions had 75-mm guns that could fire high-explosive and armour-piercing ammunition, but were vulnerable to bursting into flames if their thinly armoured petrol tanks were hit. IWM NA11308

A British sniper armed with a Lee Enfield rifle in the ruins of Aprilia (the Factory). IWM NA14849

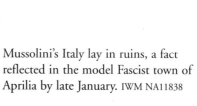

A Bren gunner and riflemen cover a British house-clearing team from a shell hole in the Factory. IWM NA15417

Mussolini's Italy lay in ruins, a fact reflected in the model Fascist town of Aprilia by late January. IWM NA11838

He had already been through a great deal during the war, and the constant bombarding that we were suffering played on his nerves. He seemed to tremble, and had definitely developed a stammer, but he got on with his job and ignored it, and so did we. We were all on the edge and knew that it could happen to any one of us at any moment . . . As I left he put his hand on my shoulder and asked how my feet were – I had some blisters caused by some new boots – and he gave me a knowing smile saying that I could wear them in by giving Jerry 'a jolly good kick up the arse'. That evening I made sure that I stayed with the men for as long as possible. They were all nervous and needed reassuring. Some needed a reassuring word, others just a wink, or a smile. I was new to this leadership lark, but I seemed to feel what they needed, and was well aware that I could very well provide the last kindness of their lives. It struck me then that leadership is not about shouting and screaming, it is about empathising, understanding, and motivating – just as my company commander had cleverly done when asking about my rotten boots.

On the evening of 29 February Ranger Force were bivouacked in a pine forest four miles behind the front line. Here Darby briefed the Ranger Staff and his battalion commanders about their mission. Moving his finger slowly over a map spread out on the bonnet of his jeep, he explained that 1st and 3rd Battalions were to infiltrate Cisterna using the Pantano Ditch which cut through the German lines, whilst 4th Battalion, followed by his own headquarters, were to advance directly up the Conca–Cisterna Road. Darby emphasised that the force in the ditch were not to be intercepted for not only were they vulnerable there, they also needed to maintain surprise in order to successfully cross the one and a half miles of open ground between the end of the ditch and the town. It was an operation fraught with danger and Darby's stomach had turned over when Truscott had tasked him with it earlier that day, but he believed that his men were the best in the beachhead for the job.

Marshall and Truscott had founded the Rangers in 1942 as a fighting elite (based on the British Commandos) and although William Darby was only in his early thirties, he was given the task of selecting and training the men. He had subsequently led them in Tunisia, Sicily and Salerno where they had developed a formidable reputation, and became known as 'Darby's Rangers'. Now he had to look his battalion commanders in the eye and convince them that they had an achievable aim. He told them that he recognised that the lack of detailed maps of the area and the short reconnaissance time were problematical, but he thought that the risks were acceptable. The operation was exactly the sort of 'Snoop and poop night work, followed by street fighting and hitting the enemy' for which they had been trained and in which they excelled. The men, meanwhile, had been relaxing after the previous night's ten-mile march out of the front line by the Via Anziate to the woods. At 2030 hours they had a hot meal, and half an hour later made their final individual preparations for battle. Each man stripped to the bare essentials of equipment, packed his belongings and placed them in a tent. The company clerks collected the letters, and after a brief pause for a smoke, they began their three-hour march to the jumping-off position.

As Darby's men moved through the cold, moonless night Captain David Williams, a British staff officer in the 1st Division headquarters in the Padiglione Woods, began to feel tense. It had been 'an exciting, but draining experience':

My job was to summarise the intelligence that was coming into the headquarters and put it in a report. Although I was not responsible for the quality of the information that I was working with, I still felt a massive weight of responsibility on my shoulders as I had to interpret it . . . Everybody got quite short with each other during 29 January. They were tired, over-worked and under a great deal of strain. We were also working in quite cramped conditions in tents that leaked and were cold. I can remember feeling quite faint during that day and could not understand why. Then it dawned on me. I had not had a meal for nearly 24 hours. I grabbed a ration pack and carried on . . . The worst moment came that night, once the attack had been launched, waiting for the first word on progress – or the lack of it. We had been taught no plan survives the first contact with the enemy. I could not get that out of my head.

At 2300 hours, the Irish and Scots Guards advanced behind a ferocious creeping barrage. The aim was to keep the enemy's heads down long enough for the infantry to pounce on them unchallenged. A mixture of the dark, smoke and battlefield debris, however, combined to slow the two battalions and they fell quickly behind the protective wall. The attack covered half a mile before the Germans illuminated the battle-field with flares and Very lights. Small groups of Guardsmen could be seen scuttling along in the slowly falling light, to be cut down by German machine gunners. An NCO shouted an order whilst silhou-etted by burning scrub and he too was poleaxed. The battalions had walked into a killing bowl. Mesmeric tracers hissed, supply vehicles exploded turning their drivers into charred mummies, shells burst spraying deadly fragments into soft bodies and the wounded screamed. The platoons made an attempt to reach the enemy that were firing from all around them, but the attack quickly became fragmented. The officers tried to bring order to the chaos, but often became casualties themselves whilst leading their men in the face of the German guns. The two commanding officers, Lieutenant Colonel C.A. Montagu-Douglas-Scott of the Irish Guards and Lieutenant Colonel David Wedderburn of the Scots Guards, were both at Dung Farm trying to control the battle through radio links with the companies, but they had difficulty trying to work out what was happening as shells began to tear their headquarters to pieces. The two battalions staggered forward in small unit actions, firing and manoeuvring. It was a messy battle, as one Guardsman recalls:

Such a lack of information, and no cover in those vines. Shells screaming and whirring like mad, vicious witches. Sprays of fire all over the place. Shrapnel like hail. Bullets whizzing from nowhere. And on top of that the bloody rain. We were so cold. Half the soldiers disappeared – mown down, captured, or just fucked off, everything you can imagine.

Gradually the Guards managed to get close enough to their enemy to use their bayonets and grenades in vicious hand-to-hand fighting, but by midnight they only had a tenuous hold on the lateral road either side of the Via Anziate. Digging in as best they could, they managed to hold on to their positions for the rest of the night, but with dawn threatening, armoured support was required if they were not to be overwhelmed. Brigadier Alistair Murray promised tanks to the Scots Guards advising them by radio, 'I'm going to send up our heavy friends to see what they can do. Stand by!', but just five Shermans arrived from a weakened 46th Royal Tank Regiment, and there were none for the Irish Guards. One Irish Guardsman wrote that he had been trying to dig a shell scrape for hours to give himself a precious few inches of protection, but mortars and shells constantly inter-rupted his work. 'The most frightening moment came just before dawn', he recalls, 'when a ruddy great Tiger tank appeared about 150 yards in front of me. We had no weapons to attack it with and so I prayed that the thing would go away and it did. It clanked across the field and disappeared. Some other poor sod had to deal with it.' Two Tiger tanks engaged the Irish Guards and the situation was becoming critical for them, but just when they needed guidance from battalion headquarters most, radio communication was lost. Radio operator Lance Corporal G. Holwell dismantled his 18 set to try and solve the problem, laying out a plethora of fragile pieces on a ground sheet. Using the thin beam of a shaded torch which attracted fire, he reassembled them and got the radio working again just in time to receive the order to withdraw at 0615 hours. The remnants of the battalion pulled back down the railway line but Holwell was not amongst them, a shell fragment having killed him.

Penney had to strike back at Campoleone quickly, for by dawn on 30 January the Scots Guards were firm but vulnerable around the lateral road. At 0900 the artillery threw down another bombardment and the Irish Guards, supported by a company of King's Shropshire Light Infantry, again attacked. They pushed through a scene of devastation – smouldering vehicles, destroyed buildings, the wounded crying for help and the dead. The air was acrid with smoke and the smell of cordite. The renewed effort linked up with the Scots Guards and the five Shermans supporting them and together they clattered into the German defences. It was enough to dislodge the tired defenders who retreated back to the embankment below Campoleone Station. The British needed to maintain their momentum and so at 1500 hours 3rd Brigade leapfrogged the exhausted Guards and struck towards the embankment – 1st Duke of Wellington's Regiment (Dukes) on the left and the 1st King's Shropshire Light Infantry Regiment (KSLI) on the right. The men screamed and shouted at the enemy as they attacked to give themselves courage, but many fell trying to cross the open ground. Sergeant Ben Wallis recalls the moment when he attacked:

I had never been so frightened. We were all frightened, don't believe anybody that says he wasn't. We'd heard the fighting earlier in the day, seen the dead and dying – now it was our turn. I turned to my mate before the off and we shook hands. The order was given to advance, and we walked into bullets, mortar bombs and shells. They were waiting for us, we didn't stand a chance. My mate, Billy, was killed by a sniper. I was shot through the shoulder and evacuated out. I was lucky as I later heard that out of our platoon – which was about 35 men – only 10 survived.

After two hours the KSLI and Dukes were still short of the embankment. Exposed and vulnerable at the end of a long salient, the battalions did what they could in the growing darkness to dig in. That night 3rd Brigade continued to suffer casualties as Private David Hardy of the Dukes explains:

> We were shelled and mortared throughout the hours of darkness, unable to move. I was in a shell hole with another bloke which we managed to deepen a little. Others were in far worse positions and had no real protection. The lads on our left and our right copped it that night.

When one Dukes officer who was contacted on the radio by brigade headquarters and asked about their situation replied, 'We feel like the lead in the end of a blunt pencil', he was told not to fret because the armour would force its way through with the next drive forward. The officer was not impressed and said, 'The bastards said that they would be here today, but I've seen nothing of them.'

The attacks that day would have been assisted by strong armoured support, but Harmon made no impact on the battle. Having struggled to get his tanks to the start line immediately prior to the attack on the 29th, he did not begin his advance until seven hours after the infantry. When the tanks, tank destroyers and half-tracks eventually began to move, they were again held up by the terrain and picked off by German anti-tank guns on the Vallelata Ridge directly in front of them. It was a natural tank trap. A number got stranded in irrigation ditches. Harmon tried to help, but only succeeded in diluting his resources:

> I ordered an armored wrecker to pull them out. The wrecker was ambushed by the Germans. I sent four more tanks to rescue the wrecker. Then I sent out more tanks after them. Apparently I could learn my first Anzio lesson only the hard way – and the lesson,

subsequently very important, was not to send good money after bad. Because I was stubborn, I lost twenty-four tanks while trying to succour four.

One by one the stranded vehicles were destroyed and evacuating crews cruelly picked off by snipers. Harmon's attack had failed even before it had got going:

> Half of me was seething and the other half was shattered. When I moved up to the front line at 8 o'clock that morning, nothing was moving and I was greeted not by rapidly moving armoured fighting vehicles, but by their smouldering wrecks and scores of dead and wounded.

On hearing that Harmon had called off his attack Penney immediately radioed him and said: 'Would you mind putting some of your tanks on to the Campoleone road so that they might help out my 3rd Brigade in the morning?' The 1st Armored Commander replied: 'Show me the way!', and that night moved 25 light tanks onto the Via Anziate to assist with the attack on Campoleone Station the following morning.

The renewed thrust began at dawn on 31 January, when the 3rd Brigade's reserve battalion, 2nd Sherwood Foresters Regiment (Foresters), supported by Penney's tanks, pushed through the Dukes and KSLI and endeavoured to get to the railway embankment. Wynford Vaughan-Thomas watched the attack from the north of Dung Farm:

> All we could see were the quick fountains of black smoke thrown up along the railway line, a tank belching fumes from behind the walls of a broken farm and a cloud of white dust hanging over the spot where we imagined the station to be. The Alban Hills seemed startlingly near. The noise ebbed and flowed over the leafless vines,

now rising to a general thunder as the guns cracked out on both sides, now dropping to a treacherous lull. Small figures now appeared, popping up from holes in the ground and half crouching they ran. There seemed so few of them . . . We saw them drop out of sight and heard the swift outburst of the machine-gun fire that welcomed them. Were they over the railway line? Was Campoleone ours?

Campoleone was not theirs. The Germans had been reinforced overnight with two extra battalions of infantry, six Mark IV tanks and three 88-mm guns and defended stubbornly. When the attack was put in it was immediately devastated. In just ten minutes 265 Foresters became casualties along with fourteen tanks. Some managed to get to the embankment, but no further. One of the battalion signallers, Sergeant Thomas Middleton, got separated from his colleagues during the attack:

I was alone in my lonely world . . . The noise of the place was incredible, the smell was foul and I could hardly think straight. I moved forward half crouching, half stumbling, I was totally disorientated. I came across one of our boys locked in an embrace with a German, hit by shells whilst grappling with each other. Their entrails smothered the ground. The knowledge that the Germans were in the area put me in a spin. Was I moving towards them or they towards me? Where was the headquarters? I tried to raise someone on the radio but could not hear anything as shells landed around me. I may have been wandering for 5 minutes or 2 hours, I do not know, but I finally found myself back with the battalion. I was told to take up a defensive position and only then did I realise that I had been wandering around without having touched my Sten gun which was still slung over my shoulder.

The remnants of the battalion pulled back, reorganised, and another attempt was made to burst through, but with the same predictable results. The American tank crews were amazed at the stoicism of the British troops. Kenneth Hurley, a loader, later wrote:

> From that day on I vowed never to knock the Limeys again, bless their black hearts. The British went on and on, with just their courage, soup bowl helmets and rifles for protection. Crazy, but brave like I'd never seen. 'Give it up won't you?', I thought, 'for God's sake don't try again!' But they did. A British officer was walking between the tanks, crying out something to his men huddled around. I wanted to shout, 'You silly bastards, get down!' It was a different concept, a different attitude. The British lieutenant strolled across the front of my tank, bobbed down out of sight, then waved his swagger stick. They charged, about 20 of them. None returned.

The Sherwood Foresters did not give up and attempt after attempt was made to cross the embankment, but the men just melted away. A desolate Harmon visited the battlefield that morning and later wrote:

> There were dead bodies everywhere. I had never seen so many dead men in one place. They lay so close together that I had to step with care. I shouted for the commanding officer. From a foxhole there arose a mud-covered corporal with a handle-bar moustache. He was the highest-ranking officer still alive. He stood stiffly to attention. 'How's it going?' I asked. 'Well, sir,' the corporal said, 'there were a hundred and sixteen of us in our company when we first came up, and there are sixteen of us left. We're ordered to hold out until sundown, and I think, with a little good fortune, we can manage to do so.'

But the battle did not last until sundown; Penney brought it to a close on Lucas's orders in the early afternoon. The Sherwood Foresters had started out as 35 officers and 786 other ranks and ended the day with 8 officers and 250 other ranks. The battle had come to a halt on the body-littered embankment before Campoleone. The British attempt to threaten the Alban Hills from the Via Anziate had failed.

The Rangers, meanwhile, had been running into severe difficulties themselves. At 0100 hours 1st Battalion, their faces blacked and lightly equipped, with grenades crammed in pockets and combat knives stuffed into their boots, entered the Pantano Ditch in single file. They were followed fifteen minutes later by 3rd Battalion. The night was freezing, inky black and overcast with occasional enemy artillery fire. Dobson's battalion groped their way along the narrow channel filled with six inches of icy water and reached the point of no return as they passed behind enemy lines. The journey had been slow and difficult and the two battalions lost contact with each other. Darby had emphasised the need for stealth, and so was livid when radio operators called him to say that they were lost. If they were ambushed now they would be caught like rats in a trap, and the main attack would be in jeopardy. Passing within feet of German mortar and artillery positions the Rangers had to stifle their instinct to engage the enemy. 'We could have taken them in the blink of an eye', recalls Corporal Ben Mosier, 'we heard them talking in German and it was just so tempting, but we couldn't show our hand.' 1st and 3rd Battalions continued to advance ever deeper into the German lines in a snake formation one and a half miles long from head to tail. At one point 1st Battalion could hear some fighting to their rear, and Dobson received a message from a runner shortly after that 3rd Battalion had been involved in a fight with a German Mark IV tank which had spotted its movement. Although a bazooka quickly destroyed the tank, its machine gunner had killed Major Miller and three others. It was fortunate that this encounter did not raise a general alarm.

Just a mile to the north-east of Dobson's advancing battalion, in the outbuilding of a ruined farm which served as a command post, Edwin Wentz was worrying about his men stuck under their camouflaged netting in their trenches and their tactical positioning. 'I was told where I was to set my defences and then to get on with it,' he remembers. 'I even had to wander to my left and right to find out who was on my flanks. On the day before the attack my right flank was wide open and I had to cover it by spreading my forces, but 12 hours before the attack began it was taken over by some parachutists. This allowed me to concentrate my company on a narrow front of 400 yards. I had seven MG-42s, three 7.5cm mortars and over 90 rifles. I crafted a killing zone.' That morning the Rangers were going to blunder straight into it.

Meanwhile at 0200 hours 4th Battalion started their move up the Conca–Cisterna road. Darby was not expecting any significant opposition in this area for at least a mile, but within minutes his men had run straight into a German strong point and a tempestuous fire fight ensued. The leading companies tried to attack and break through, but the Germans were well dug in with interlocking fields of fire making any advance suicidal. The position could not be forced and after three and a half hours of increasingly futile platoon attacks, with nothing to show for them except scores of casualties, the battalion commander ordered his men to dig in. Darby endeavoured to alleviate 4th Battalion's problems by trying to arrange artillery support in order to suppress the German machine guns and mortars, but the gunners were not happy to open fire due to the close proximity of the Rangers to the Germans. 1st and 3rd Battalions continued their advance: there were still two miles to cover – one and a half of them over open ground – before Cisterna was reached. Sentries and patrols had slowed them down. Leading the way was a large squad of twenty scouts, men honed in trail finding and the art of silent killing. Led by Lieutenant Jim Fowler – who revelled in the strange, dangerous work – they dealt with the Germans, leaving the slumped bodies of several German sentries in grey-green overcoats with their throats cut. Many Germans had inadvertently joined the Americans thinking that this was a friendly patrol and no prisoners could be taken. Dobson stepped up the pace and the head of his battalion reached the end of the Pantano Ditch at just before 0400 hours. What Dobson found was not what he was expecting – it was busy, German vehicles moving up the road, artillery firing – it was at this point he realised that the Germans were far stronger than he had been led to believe. He tried to raise Darby on the radio, breaking radio silence. He wanted to clear this position of guns. But he could not raise the Force headquarters. He carried on with his mission as ordered and left the guns. It was now just about to get light and they still had 800 yards of open ground to get across and into Cisterna – the most difficult part of the mission. They began to move.

It was at this moment that Edwin Wentz received a telephone call from the Obersturmbannführer in the regiment on his left. A patrol had just reported that three men at their listening post had been found with their throats cut and he advised the company to be on full alert. Just as Wentz stepped outside his farm building to ensure that the dawn stand had begun, the silence was broken by a scream. Jim Fowler had killed a German sentry, but he had died noisily – screeching as his throat was cut – and in his death throes he provided the alarm. The Germans came alive. An MG-42 opened fire just yards away and out of the gloom the Rangers charged with fixed bayonets screaming like banshees. Tracers burned the air; mortars crumped in volleys, automatic fire swept the wet fields and tanks opened up from their hidden positions behind haystacks. There was enormous confusion. There had been no gap in front of Cisterna – it was filled with Germans. If this was not an ambush then it was as good as. Dobson attempted to regain some control, but his men were still struggling to deploy in an attempt to take up firing positions, much of 1st Battalion and 3rd Battalion were still in the ditch, pinned down by deadly accurate machine gun fire. It severely constrained their movement – it had provided protection but was now a death trap. Many broke out into the open to avoid this and the battle fragmented into small actions. Some managed to get into farmhouses, but the majority fought from the ditch. He tried to inform Darby of the situation but still had difficulty raising the headquarters; however, at 0835 hours there was a brief conversation which was logged in the 'Ranger Battle Journal': 'Call received from 1st and 3rd Battalions, in south edge of Cisterna. Can't adjust fire; enemy in buildings; town strongly held.' Darby radioed back that 4th Battalion was also pinned down and could not be relied on for support and advised that Dobson should try and break into the town. The advance party of 1st Battalion consequently charged on to force their way forward, but were hit hard by enemy fire from every direction and sought shelter in a shallow drainage ditch by the side of the road.

By around 0900 the Rangers had been effectively immobilised and the Germans had begun to outflank the battalions using their tanks and infantry. Dobson wrote:

> The Germans' first counterattack came from the rear – from the direction of our own lines – in the form of seventeen tanks and armored, self-propelled guns. They overran our position, but we knocked out fifteen of them with bazookas, grenades and about everything else we could lay our hands on. I saw one of our sergeants trying to plaster a sticky bomb on a German tank turret when a bazooka shot hit the opposite side. It knocked him into the air and he did a complete somersault but landed running. All these tanks, and guns were burning, and exploding in the middle of our position at one time – a beautiful sight.

Dobson himself shot dead the tank commander of a Mark IV tank with his pistol and then climbed up and threw a phosphorus grenade in. He was hit in the hip jumping down when the grenade exploded. He was captured and taken to a German casualty clearing station, where he was operated on without anaesthetic. The Americans had travelled light, possessing scant protection against armour, but they used their bazookas, grenades and the anti-tank 'sticky bombs' to great effect. The courage required to tackle an enormous Panzer with any of these weapons was immense. Private 'Lacey' Smith spotted a tank with the commander's hatch ajar and rushed it with a grenade. Just as he was clambering aboard, the opposite side was hit by a bazooka. 'It felt like I had been hit in the face with a sledge hammer', recalls Smith, 'and I landed on my back winded. As I looked up, the beast was moving towards me and the commander's head was sticking out of the top. Frank Steele shot him, straight between the eyes, and I attached a sticky bomb to its track and ran for cover. That baby worked a treat, it threw the track and then a bazooka finished it off.' 3rd Battalion units tried to get up to 1st Battalion and remove the blockage in front of Cisterna – but failed as their ammunition got dangerously low and it was clear that both battalions were surrounded.

Those of 3rd Battalion still in the Pantano Ditch were faced by a number of German Mark IVs and a Tiger tank with an 88-mm gun which the Germans ran up to its edges and just blasted away. The results were appalling. 'I never thought that I'd survive,' recalls Ranger Fred Davis: 'I saw the big gun pointing straight at me and tried to dig with my bare fingers into the bottom of this wet ditch. I felt a hot blast above my head, fell face down into the water, and when I got up the five men that had been behind me were not there, not a trace.' As the tanks chased and destroyed, the German artillery also opened up with devastatingly accurate bombardments. Mosier remembers: 'They were firing into us. After the first volley you felt naked. You knew that they could see you and you could do nothing about it.' Slowly but surely the Rangers were being strangled. At one point German paratroopers advanced towards the ditch, overwhelmed its occupants and then forced their prisoners to move with hands raised towards the rest of the battalion. Those still fighting quickly organised an ambush which killed several of the escorting Germans (as well as some of their own men) and knocked out the two accompanying tanks and an armoured car with the last of the bazooka ammunition. Nevertheless, the event prompted many of the remaining Rangers to capitulate. The fighting was becoming increasingly desperate, but J.P. O'Reilly of 3rd Battalion was inspired by one of his company officers, a Lieutenant Newman who led an attack on a machine gun position:

He sure had a lot of guts. He was a little fellow with big thick glasses. But boy he loved to fight . . . He broke his glasses when he jumped the machine gun nest with only his pistol. With his glasses broken he couldn't see worth a damn. That's how he was captured. He never would send his men where he wouldn't go. And there was never a place, however hot, that he would hesitate going.

The battle was coming to an end as the Germans attacked from all sides round and more tanks arrived. With no ammunition and the situation hopeless, increasing numbers surrendered. 4th Battalion could not help and were pinned down south of Isola Bella. Taking over the radio in the shell hole that was serving as 1st Battalion headquarters, Sergeant Major Robert Ehalt, one of the original NCOs in the Rangers who knew Darby well, called up Darby at 1215 hours and said, 'They're closing in on us, Colonel. We're out of ammo – but they won't get us cheap!' Darby replied, 'Issue some orders but don't let the boys give up! . . . Who's walking in with their hands up? Don't let them do it! Get some officers to shoot! . . . Don't let them do it! . . . Do that before you give up! . . . Get the old men together and lam for it . . . We're coming through. Hang onto this radio until the last minute . . . Stick together . . . Use your head and do what's best . . . You're there and I'm here, unfortunately, and I can't help you but whatever happens, God bless you.' By mid-afternoon Darby radioed Truscott and said, 'Sir, it's over. 1 and 3 Battalions no longer exist.' That afternoon, after he had extracted the remnants of 4th

Battalion and his Ranger Force headquarters from the field of battle, Darby went to see Truscott and, according to the 3rd Division commander, 'he just sat and sobbed.' He blamed himself for not being with them, leading from the front. Of the 767 men of 1st and 3rd Battalion sent out, just six men returned. Just 12 men were killed and 36 wounded, but 743 were captured. But Dobson was told by his interrogators that 400 dead Germans had been found in front of Cisterna. Edwin Wentz survived to fight another day. At roll call that evening he discovered that his company had suffered just six casualties, and made a melancholy entry in his diary: 'My men are helping to bury the dead . . . It is sickening.' On 31 January Darby went to the Rangers bivouac area in the Pine Wood 'his eyes rimmed with red and a two days' growth of beard on his face. He stood silently looking at the pile of bedroll and barracks bags, studying the stencilled names and serial numbers of the men. Then he went away.' He was never the same man again and was killed, aged thirty-four, by a stray artillery shell in the rear area on 30 April 1945 two days before all Axis troops in Italy surrendered. Days later President Truman promoted William O. Darby to Brigadier General.

Lucas also had to cope with his failure. Campoleone and Cisterna were still in German hands. Both Alexander and Clark were unhappy. There would not now be a push to the Alban Hills and the Gustav Line continued to be supplied. The Fifth Army commander arrived in the beachhead on 30 January and went immediately to his newly established forward headquarters in the grounds of Prince Borghese's Renaissance palace between Anzio and Nettuno. Lucas was dispirited: 'Clark is up here and I am afraid intends to stay for several days. His gloomy attitude is certainly bad for me . . . I have done what I was ordered to do, desperate though it was. I can win if I am let alone but I don't know whether I can stand the strain of having so many people looking over my shoulder.' During an edgy meeting the following day, Clark heavily criticised Penney, Truscott and Darby for their plans.

Once Clark's rant was over, Lucas stepped forward and announced that, as corps commander, he had sanctioned the divisional plans and should take any blame for their failure. Ignoring Lucas's noble gesture, Clark launched into another stinging attack on Darby and Truscott for the way in which they had used the Rangers. It was Truscott's turn to put up a defence and he replied that as he had been responsible for organising the original Ranger battalion, and that Darby had commanded them through so many battles, nobody understood their capabilities better. Mark Clark turned mutely on his heel and departed, leaving a bitter atmosphere hanging in the air. That evening Lucas wrote:

I don't blame him for being terribly disappointed. He and those above him thought this landing would shake the Cassino line loose at once but they had no right to think that, because the German is strong in Italy and will give up no ground if he can help it . . . The disasters of the Rangers he apparently blames on Lucian Truscott. He says they were used foolishly . . . Neither I nor Truscott knew of the organized defensive position they would run into. I told Clark the fault was mine as I had seen the plan of attack and had OK'd it.

Clark, meanwhile, noted:

I have been disappointed for several days by the lack of aggressiveness on the part of the VI Corps. Although it would have been wrong, in my opinion, to attack to capture our final objective on this front, reconnaissance in force with tanks should have been more aggressive to capture Cisterna and Campoleone. Repeatedly I have told Lucas to push vigorously to get those local objectives. He had not insisted on this with the Division Commanders . . . I have been harsh with Lucas today, much to my regret, but in an effort to energize him to greater effort.

The failure of Lucas's offensive sent shock waves back to London. On 1 February Alan Brooke wrote despondently: 'News from Italy bad and the landing south of Rome is making little progress, mainly due to the lack of initiative in the early stages. I am at present rather doubtful as to how we are to disentangle the situation. Hitler has reacted very strongly and is sending reinforcements fast.' On the same day Churchill wrote to Alexander: 'It seems to have been a bad show. Penney and Truscott seem to have done admirably considering what they were facing. Does Lucas have any idea what a mistake he has made?' There was a very strong feeling now that Lucas had waited far too long to make this push and numerous opportunities had been missed. The VI Corps commander knew that his bosses were frustrated and when Alexander visited him in the beachhead on 1 February, Lucas feared for his command. Lucas recalled that Alexander had been:

> . . . kind enough but I am afraid he is not pleased. My head will probably fall in the basket but I have done my best. There were just too many Germans here for me to lick and they could build up faster than I could. As I told Clark yesterday, I was sent on a desperate mission, one where the odds were greatly against success, and I went without saying anything because I was given an order and my opinion was not asked. The condition in which I find myself is much better than I ever anticipated or had any right to expect.

The 'condition' in which VI Corps now found itself was having to defend. In a move agreed by Alexander and Clark, Lucas ordered that the new enlarged beachhead should be defended and a 'final' defensive position should be developed on the line of the original 24 January beachhead.

By the first days of February, Operation Shingle was foundering. Rather than having the strategic impact that Churchill and Alexander had desired, the two men were left to ponder two vulnerable salients, a narrow British one towards Campoleone and a wider American one towards Cisterna. VI Corps was worse off than before Lucas's attacks had started. The correspondents sought enlightenment at Lucas's villa in Nettuno. 'He sat in his chair', wrote Wynford Vaughan-Thomas, 'before the fire, and the light shone on his polished cavalry boots. He had the round face and the greying moustache of a kindly country solicitor. His voice was low and hardly reached the outer circle of the waiting Pressmen. They fired their questions at him, above all Question No 1, "What *was* our plan on landing and what had happened to it now?" The General looked thoughtful. "Well gentlemen, there was some suggestion that we should aim at getting to those hills" – he turned to his G-2 – "What's the name of them, Joe? But the enemy was now strong, far stronger than we had thought." There was a long pause, and the firelight played on the waiting audience and flickered up to the dark ceiling. Then the General added quietly, "I'll tell you what, gentlemen. That German is a mighty tough fighter. Yes, a mighty tough fighter."'

So ended the first phase of the Battle of Anzio. The next phase was to be even more violent, and to introduce it the Germans would launch a series of counter-attacks. The pallid and quietly spoken Gruenther said of the Germans, 'You push the accordion a certain distance and it'll spring back and smack you in the puss. The Germans are building up a lot of spring.' The enemy now had the initiative. Private James Anderson, a replacement for 30th Infantry Regiment, arrived at Anzio harbour on 1 February as it was under air and artillery fire. 'I remember plainly', he recalls, 'a British officer screaming at us, "What's the matter with you blokes, do you want to live forever?"'

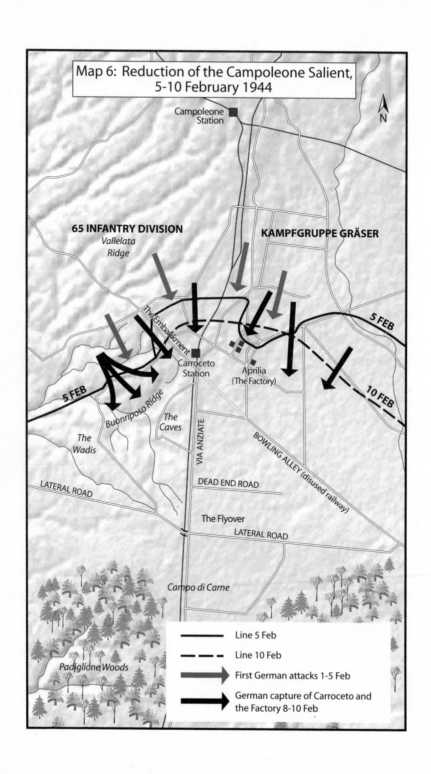

Map 6: Reduction of the Campoleone Salient,
5-10 February 1944

N

Campoleone
Station

65 INFANTRY DIVISION
*Vallelata
Ridge*

KAMPFGRUPPE GRÄSER

The Embankment

5 FEB

Carroceto
Station

Aprilia
(The Factory)

5 FEB

10 FEB

Buonriposo Ridge

*The
Caves*

*The
Wadis*

VIA ANZIATE

BOWLING ALLEY (disused railway)

LATERAL ROAD

DEAD END ROAD

The Flyover

LATERAL ROAD

Campo di Carne

Padiglione Woods

———	Line 5 Feb
- - -	Line 10 Feb
⟶	First German attacks 1-5 Feb
⟶	German capture of Carroceto and the Factory 8-10 Feb

CHAPTER 6

The Spring Released

(3–19 February)

By 3 February Oberfeldwebel Felix Reimann was nursing a broken index finger that had been trapped under a shell, but despite all the action he had seen, was otherwise unharmed. Reimann had just rearmed and refuelled his StuG III self-propelled gun nicknamed 'Lucy', and was chatting to his commanding officer. As part of *Kampfgruppe* Gräser, the young NCO had been in the front line since its arrival at Anzio on 23 January, excelling himself in the defence of Carroceto and Campoleone by knocking out five Shermans with his 75-mm gun. Both he and his driver, Walter Scherling, had fought together on the Eastern Front during 1942 where they had been wounded in a Soviet air raid (that had killed twenty-six others), been neighbours in hospital during their recovery and had rejoined their unit on the same day. Their almost telepathic understanding had held them in good stead at Carroceto where Scherling turned a couple of words from Reimann into life-saving manoeuvres. They had also been lucky. At Campoleone a British shell smacked against their forward armoured plating, but had not exploded. Now that the fighting had died down and pulled from the front line, the crew had an opportunity to examine what the projectile had done. Calling colleagues over to inspect the damage, they looked proudly at 'Lucy's' scar, even posing for photographs beside it. The snapshot recalled for posterity a small group of grimy, unshaven soldiers aged between nineteen and twenty-five, but all looking at least twenty years older. The men were fighting their tiredness, but an officer told them to get some rest and they shuffled off. Reimann lay down but could not sleep. Images of the battlefield filled his mind, together with the fading memories of his wife and children. He opened his eyes to see Scherling crouching beside him, smiling and holding a bottle of brandy. Both men drank deeply and reminisced for a while. Later Reimann scribbled in his diary: 'The intensity of the fighting has been remarkable and I have never seen such determination in battle . . . We are now all very tired. Battles sap a man's strength without him knowing. When it is over, your body wants to sleep, but your mind sometimes will not let you. I am sure that the next battle – or eternal sleep – is not far away.'

Lucas's thrusts at the end of January had caused Eberhard von Mackensen to postpone his counter-attack against the beachhead by forty-eight hours to 3 February. Having amassed nearly 100,000 combat troops against the Allies' 76,400, this relatively slim offensive superiority would first have to 'iron out' the front line. The British salient – three miles long by one and a half miles wide – was 'positively demanding' to be counter-attacked according to the Fourteenth Army Chief of Staff, Major General Wolfgang Hauser. But von Mackensen demanded caution. The son of a First World War Field Marshal, von Mackensen looked every inch the Prussian general – stern, high cheek boned, with slicked back greying hair and monocle. Only the duelling scar was missing. A foil to Kesselring's chronic optimism, here was a man who did not like to take chances. He had organised his forces carefully, Schlemm's I Parachute Corps controlled the western sector of the line, while Lieutenant General Traugott Herr's LXXVI Panzer Corps commanded the middle and eastern sectors. Their attacking troops had moved into position during 2 February and morning of the 3rd. 'It was good to feel that we would be striking back', says one German grenadier. 'We had taken considerable punishment and wanted to get the job done as soon as possible. There was nobody that did not think that within a few weeks the Anzio beachhead would be vanquished.' To the west of Via Anziate *Kampfgruppe* Gericke and 65th Infantry Division's *Kampfgruppe* Pfeiffer concealed themselves in the barren 'wadi country', whilst *Kampfgruppe* Gräser took up positions across the main road and on the eastern side of the salient. The weather was vile – heavy rain, sleet and a freezing wind. Captain Gerd Jebsen, a grenadier company commander, remembers:

> It was a struggle to keep anything dry. Weapons rusted unless constantly attended to, there was filthy mud everywhere – it got into your hair, your eyes, your food – our feet were constantly wet and our clothes clung to our bodies. We turned into human icicles at night. There were times when I thought that death on the battlefield would be a welcome release.

The fields became waterlogged, the ravines filled with water and the roads turned to ice. Von Mackensen asked Kesselring for another postponement, but the Field Marshal turned him down stating that the bad weather would negate Allied air superiority and that an early attack would ensure that British defences were weak. There was no front line as such, no maze of trenches like in the Great War's Western Front, just a scattering of positions. In some places these positions were evenly spaced, in others clustered together, and sometimes there were wide gaps between them. Their location and strengths depended on the terrain and resources, but they always sought to form a web that if touched, would lead immediately to a reaction. Ideally each position contained a company with every man dug into a slit trench within sight and sound of his comrades. The company commander would be 100 yards to the rear with a signaller on a portable set in touch with battalion headquarters. The ground between these positions, and between companies, would be covered by fire and often laced with barbed wire and mines. Further back in support were the machine guns, mortars and field guns and tanks in case the enemy overran the positions or there was need of a counter-attack. Several miles to the rear lurked the heavier divisional guns, ready to fire at a few minutes' notice. 1st Division had spun a fine web, but as they did so they could hear the enemy organising a few hundred yards away. They knew that a German attack was imminent, and cursed Lucas for leaving them in a salient.

An artillery bombardment hit the nose of the salient during the late afternoon of 3 February and when it lifted a panzer grenadier company from *Kampfgruppe* Gräser advanced. It was merely a probe down the road towards the Dukes, KSLI and Foresters, but when the British artillery returned fire they gave their positions away or confirmed them. By dusk all was quiet again, but the Germans had learned much about the British defences. All was quiet until 2300 hours when a five-minute hurricane bombardment announced the opening of the next phase of the attack. Lieutenant Edward Grace's 6th Gordon Highlanders platoon were at Dung Farm which to them became known as 'Horror Farm'. 'Shells were falling all around with such frequency that they merged together like the rolling of a drum', he later wrote. 'One could do nothing but crouch down as far as possible into the slit trench and listen to the spiteful hiss and crash of each shell. Then came the attacking infantry screaming war cries: 'Sieg Heil!' and 'Gott mit Uns!' as they attacked through the sleet behind a supporting artillery barrage. 'We could never have imagined the intensity of machine gun fire which suddenly shattered the waiting darkness', Grace continued. 'From both our flanks bullets swept over our heads with the fierceness of a great hailstorm.' Gräser pushed forward, but the defenders were assisted in their task by blazing haystacks that had been ignited by white phosphorus mortar rounds and illuminated the battlefield. The Germans crumpled – as though squashed by an immense weight – as bullets and mortar fragments bit into them. The noise was stupendous when the shrieking rockets of the six-barrelled Nebelwerfers were launched. Voice control of the battle became impossible. There was some infiltration of the British positions, but both the Gordons and 1st Reconnaissance Regiment on their right held firm. Meanwhile, Gericke and Pfeiffer were pushing against the salient from the west against the Guards Brigade. Paratrooper Corporal Joachim Liebschner recalls the scene:

> It had been raining that night and we were soaking wet, food hadn't come forward to the front line; we were pretty exhausted because we were on guard day and night. We got very little sleep, the artillery fire was incessant, it was pretty exhausting even before we started attacking. But things moved on very quickly . . . It was the first time in my life that I had seen people blown up and killed. The first four I saw killed was whilst I was carting a message from one place to another through a wadi. They had three mortars there when I passed, but on my way back there were only two left. One of them had exploded when a bomb had been put in the barrel and four youngsters were all dead. A fearful sight, all blown to pieces. They fell thick and fast after that.

The Guards came under heavy pressure, and the fighting continued after dawn on 4 February, but they repelled the attack. Having failed to break through with their initial push around the salient, the Germans retired and gave the British an opportunity to retake some of their lost ground in a series of short, sharp counter-attacks. The 1st Reconnaissance Regiment, for example, attempted to clear the enemy from some farm buildings. Their Commanding Officer, Lieutenant Colonel E.A.S. Brett, later wrote:

The leading assault troop cleared out the first house without much trouble, although the Germans tossed hand grenades at us from the upper windows. The next farmhouse was 20 yards away; and a machine-gun firing on a fixed line about two feet off the ground, pinned the assault party to the ground between the houses. The fire from this machine gun was nasty, and it annoyed Lieutenant J.A. McNeil. So he collected a Bren gun and walked calmly forward, firing it at everything and then running the last 50 yards. There was not very much moon about, but he spotted the slot the machine-gun was firing through and rolled three hand grenades into it. Another trooper with a 2in. mortar gave them the bombs as well. That stopped the trouble from the machine-gun . . . then everything came down on the assault parties. We put down a smokescreen and got them back.

The jostling for position continued throughout the day and the security of the salient remained in great peril from a concentrated German attack which could slide into and through the defenders. But this did not happen. Von Mackensen planned for the salient to be slowly – but surely – ground away, rather than attempting its rapid destruction with one focused, but potentially misplaced, incision. This was a mistake, for 168th Brigade of 56th British Infantry Division landed that morning and Lucas had time to use it to bolster Penney's defences. It also allowed 1st Division the time to withdraw 3rd Brigade from the nose of the salient where it was vulnerable to being pinched out, and into reserve. The radio message 'Every man for himself!' was picked up from the Dukes' forward company that evening by the Germans. The battalion was very pleased to be out of their exposed position. One of their number remarked to a war correspondent on 5 February:

That salient – I'll tell you what it was like. We were in the slit-trenches – a whole day of it without being able to lift our heads . . . I had to do everything, filth and all, where I was. I've never seen such machine-gun fire. It was taking the heads off the daisies . . . In the night we couldn't see a darn thing in the rain. All I did was to pop my head up from time to time to see if a Jerry wasn't going to stick a bayonet into me. Then came yesterday morning. Nothing but shells, and the smoke drifted across to us . . . Then, after we'd been firing at everything that moved, I was going to open up on a new mob coming out of the smoke, when someone shouted, 'Christ, those are our boys!' They were prisoners, shouting in English, not German, 'It's hopeless. You'd better join us.' Some of our lads got frightened and started to climb out of their slit trenches to throw down their guns, but the CO shouted, 'Get back into your trenches', and he would have shot the first one that moved. We shouted to the prisoners, 'Run and we'll fire on your guards.' Some did, others lay down, so we fired. We killed a good many Germans, maybe some of our boys too. I tell you, that shook me more than anything. Then, at last, we got the order, 'Get out quick!' . . . We came running down that main road and all the shells in hell came down on us. Lots of bodies there, too! I fell over one that groaned, but what could I do, I couldn't stay? And then we passed a whole row of burning tanks, all oily waste smoke . . . and what smelt like the stink of burning bodies . . . and now we're perfectly happy, as you might say. You don't know of a job going as Sanitary Man at Corps, do you?

The salient had now assumed a stubbier shape, but was more easily defended and the Factory and Carroceto remained in British hands. Moreover, Lucas had received more reinforcements which allowed for a slightly more comfortable situation. His reserve consisted of Combat Command A of 1st US Armored Division near the Via Anziate in the Padiglione Woods behind the British, and two regiments of 45th Division behind 3rd Division. These formations readied themselves to strike when required, but also helped to create the Final Beachhead Line that was centred on the steeply embanked Lateral Road. The heart of the position was the Flyover for it straddled the Via Anziate, the preferred German axis of advance. This was the line behind which there was to be no VI Corps withdrawal. At night wire and mines were laid and mutually supporting strong points developed on the stone farmhouses. The upper floors were to be used by snipers and artillery observers and the lower floors were reinforced with sandbags promising shelter for machine guns and anti-tank weapons.

The reality of a small beachhead battening down the hatches against a German offensive was very different from Winston Churchill's fanciful musings in Marrakesh just a few weeks earlier. The Premier was not at all pleased with progress and on 4 February his Junior Private Secretary, Jock Colville, recorded in his diary: 'The P.M. is suffering from indigestion and also very perturbed by Shingle's lack of success . . . He cannot understand the failure to push inland from the beach-head. While the battle still rages he is refraining from asking Alexander the questions to which the P.M. can find no answer, but his faith in A., though not dissipated, is a little shaken.' That same day the newspapers began to take a more pessimistic tone with *The Times* reporting:

> The operations in Italy are moving slowly. The Anzio beach-head has again been enlarged, but, it may be gathered, only in a limited measure and in face of strong opposition which had included a number of local counter-attacks . . . There are no signs of a swift excursion from the beach-head; and it seems equally likely that the allied forces in it may shortly have to face a hostile counter-offensive.

For the reason behind the failure, Churchill and Alexander looked no further than Lucas. The whole 'mess' as the Prime Minister increasingly insisted on calling Anzio in private, called into question whether Lucas was up to the job. Churchill inquired of Wilson why the American had been chosen in the first place. Alexander wrote to Brooke: 'What we require is a thruster like George Patton . . . It is one thing to command a Corps when everything is going in the right direction and quite another to regain the initiative when lost.' Clark also admitted in his diary that Lucas 'had lacked some aggressiveness after the landing, although allegations that he could have gone to his objective or to Rome were ridiculous, for had he done so with any force he would have been cut off from his bridgehead.' There was a growing feeling that Lucas would have to be removed at the earliest opportunity, but in the meantime he had to deal with the growing threat to the beachhead's very existence.

In the next phase of the German counter-attack beginning after dark on 7 February, von Mackensen decided that the remaining part of the salient would be engulfed with a main effort to take Carroceto and the Factory. *Kampfgruppe* Pfeiffer was to attack across the Buonriposo Ridge just to the west of the Via Anziate between Carroceto and the Flyover and then push on to take the Factory, whilst *Kampfgruppe* Gräser was to attack the Factory from the east side. The ridge ran along a sector of British front defended by 2nd North Staffordshire Regiment in the south and the Grenadier Guards in the north, whilst 1st London Irish Rifles occupied the Factory. During the 5, 6 and 7 February, both sides used their artillery and bombers to try and unbalance their enemy's preparations, and despatched patrols to collect information about his positions and activities. As Kesselring wrote of VI Corps: 'Penned in as they were on the low-lying, notoriously unhealthy coast, it must have been damned unpleasant; our heavy artillery and the Luftwaffe with its numerous flak batteries and bombers alone saw to it that even when "resting" their soldiers had no rest.'

At 2100 hours on 7 February an intense artillery and mortar barrage began to fall on the British line. The waiting was over for the shivering troops and the attacks now came at the salient from all directions in yet more driving rain. Pfeiffer pushed against the Buonriposo Ridge and infiltrated the positions held by the North Staffordshires and the Grenadier Guards with infantry, tanks and self-propelled guns. The action led to fighting at close quarters and in such circumstances, the poor weather was a distinct advantage to Grenadier Guards Lieutenant William Dugdale:

> The frost and the wet meant that wherever the enemy went there appeared a cloud of steam above them which enabled us to see what was going to happen next . . . After much puffing and swearing a German emerged a few yards from me on my side of a stream. I had my Tommy gun on single shots and taking aim for his midriff I pulled the trigger. I heard the bullet hit him and he dropped and all went still . . . I had some hand grenades in a sandbag so I chucked two or three to more screams. Another German eventually arrived on our side. Again there was a crack and he dropped. This happened many more times until there was quite a pile of corpses. The Germans seemed to lose their enthusiasm and again there was silence. After an interval they made several more attempts and each time anyone arrived on our side he was shot.

But gradually the Germans expanded their penetrations and carved into the British defences through the ravines to push them off the Buonriposo Ridge. The two battalions suffered heavy casualties but although forced to withdraw, did not crumble. On a map, their line fell back towards the Via Anziate, but to the individuals the confusion that they experienced was akin to the battlefield being put into a bottle and shaken. These troops were embroiled in a terrifying experience that overwhelmed their senses but demanded fight rather than flight. In such circumstances leadership and acts of heroism can make all the difference. When the Grenadier Guards withdrew to a quarry known as 'The Gully', Major W.P. Sidney was at times all that stood between the Germans and the epicentre of the salient. Here he defended the mouth of the Gully against an attack by a company led by Leutnant Heinrich Wunn. He beat off its initial assaults with his Tommy Gun and hand grenades assisted by a handful of men from his Support Company, but when an enemy party managed to get to within twenty yards of his position via a ditch, he was forced to rush out and gun them down on his own at point blank range. Later, whilst some of his men were replenishing their rapidly diminishing ammunition supply, he and just two others held the position. In the next attack Sidney was hit in the face by a German grenade that exploded, wounding him and one of the guardsmen and killing the other. Bleeding badly from his thigh, Sidney fought on for another hour and helped to drive the enemy off before receiving medical attention. For his 'superb courage and utter disregard of danger' Sidney was awarded the Victoria Cross. One of his men later said of the award: 'Well, if he was as tough on the Germans as he was on us, he deserves the VC.'

During this phase of the battle the British lost a large number of prisoners, including Lieutenant Paul Freyberg of the Grenadier Guards, son of the Lieutenant General Sir Bernard Freyberg then commanding the New Zealand Corps near Cassino. Others included Private James Reeder of the North Staffordshires who was taken after a brief struggle. He recalls that it was all over very quickly:

> We all knew our end was nigh as our ammo was almost exhausted and we only had five men active. At that moment we expected to be dead within the next hour or so . . . The only thing left to do was await being overrun by the advancing enemy. When the Germans arrived, we were gathered together and told that we were now all POWs. We were then held on a large farm on the outskirts of Anzio. For us the war was over.

Men often became prisoners when they were at their most vulnerable having been taken by surprise, or after a long fight. Joachim Liebschner, who was himself captured by the Americans later in the battle, says that new captives were characteristically dazed, frightened, exhausted and upset:

> Before you are taken prisoner you are often involved in close fighting, often hand to hand fighting . . . and then to be taken prisoner it's like your whole world collapsing on you. You are in such a different, unknown and frustrating situation, that you simply don't know if you are coming or going. People were usually almost deranged, as if they could not believe or make sense of what had just happened to them . . . There was no spirit of defiance left at that point although it might return later, after 24 hours . . . People are very glad to be out of it and to be alive. I never experienced any trying to escape.

Meanwhile, with Pfeiffer pushing to the west side of the salient, Gräser attacked towards the Factory from the east. Here his men ran into the defences of the London Irish Regiment protecting the town, and the Berkshire Regiment on its right flank. Camouflaged by a semi-demolished house alongside the Via Anziate, Felix Reimann's StuG III provided fire support for the attacking grenadiers. 'Every time our gun fired', he says, 'a few more bricks would fall onto us with a clang.' Within an hour the Germans had penetrated between the British positions in small groups, cut their communications and organised small pockets of resistance deep within the enemy's line. The Berkshires War Diary states:

> The steady, deliberate, thump-thump-thump of Bren-guns, always so easily distinguished from the ripping sound of the German spandaus, bore testimony that stout hearts were keeping up the struggle in the forward positions. For three hours they fought and held off all attacks. Ammunition was rushed up by cooks, drivers, and anyone else who was available. Sergeant Griffin, the cook-sergeant,

stayed with his old company until 2.30 am killing Germans and providing great inspiration to the company . . . Artillery defensive fire, tanks, rifle, and bren-gun fire, the explosion of grenades, all combined to create a terrific and noisy scene. Gradually as dawn broke the fighting died down with both sides exhausted.

It was at this point, at dawn on 8 February, that the defenders received much needed fire support from the cruisers *Brooklyn, Mauritius, Orion* and *Phoebe* and several destroyers. Throughout the morning these vessels bombarded the ground north of the Factory and fragmented the German attacks. In the later morning, as the weather cleared, German concentrations were also targeted by Allied bombers. Reimann recalls 'three and a half hours of sheer hell. There is nothing worse than waiting to be killed, but that is what we had to do. By a miracle we survived as all around us heavy shells and bombs landed destroying whatever they touched.' This firepower helped to thwart German attempts to take the Factory that day, but the fighting was often at such close quarters on the western flank that it was difficult to provide even field gun support. That afternoon, however, the sector having been reinforced by 3rd Battalion 504th Parachute Infantry, a counter-attack was launched by the Foresters against the Buonriposo Ridge. It managed to regain a foothold on the southern slopes, but once again the battalion suffered heavily losing over 30 per cent casualties. 1st Division was holding on, but only just. Ensconced in his headquarters Lucas confided in his diary: 'I wish I had an American Division in there. It is probably not my fault that I don't understand the British better. I think they suffer excessive losses. They are certainly brave men but ours are better trained, in my opinion, and I am sure that our officers are better educated in a military way.' It seems that VI Corps commander did not see fit to leave Nettuno and visit Penney's headquarters.

The British awaited the next German move with some trepidation.

The division's front was pitted and dented and the enemy's unrelenting pressure had sapped their strength. William Dugdale was exhausted, but there was no respite from the fighting or the weather and he recalls that 8 February was the 'longest, coldest and wettest day of my war'. It was a dangerous situation, as he explains:

Any movement provoked a tornado of German spandaus machine gun fire. We were ordered not to expose ourselves and not to shoot unless Germans attempted to cross the watercourse. Guardsman Slater had an entrenching tool and we passed it from hand to hand to dig ourselves each a small hole in the sandy soil. This was just as well as at regular intervals we were shelled and mortared and it was comforting to be able to duck below the surface. As we had not had any food or drink for two days, we were glad to be able to jump about a bit after it got dark to restore our circulation. It continued bitterly cold and as the shooting had ceased at dark, silence fell until at about 9 o'clock preparations were made for another attack. When it arrived there were noticeably fewer Germans than the night before . . . We all shot away and hurled hand grenades and the attack petered out and we were left alone in the rain.

On the following day, the Germans tried once again to penetrate the east side of the salient. In the first minutes of 9 February 725th Regiment of 715th Infantry Division and *Kampfgruppe* Gräser advanced to contact and a protracted battle developed. By dawn the Royal Berkshires were fighting with just their battalion headquarters and forty other men. The Germans could have finished them off but not realising how close they were to success, orders were given to disengage. In the town, meanwhile, the London Irish were under a sustained attack which gradually pushed them back. It was during a rearguard action that Reimann's luck eventually ran out. 'We pulled out of our cover to support the attacking infantry', he remembers, 'and advanced towards the northern outskirts of the town. We fired on the move and I kept a careful eye on the ruins as we approached. We were vulnerable and the traverse of the gun on the StuG was not too good . . . Then from the right I saw a flash followed by a massive white explosion right in front of my eyes. An anti-tank round had caught us. I was blinded, but could hear the screams of Scherling, Paulsen and Weber as they burned to death . . . I somehow managed to get out and fell to the ground unconscious. The next thing I remember was waking up in a field hospital two days later. The screams of my friends have haunted me all my life.' As Reimann's beloved 'Lucy' blazed, the London Irish were overrun and a mere two companies of survivors pulled out to a position just south of the town. The 'Factory' had fallen, and with the Grenadier Guards withdrawn down the Embankment, it was left to the Scots Guards at Carroceto to hold on to the last remnants of the division's hard won gains. Lucas recorded in his diary that evening: 'The British are badly disorganized and knocked to pieces. It seems to me they are in worse shape than they should be, considering what they have done.'

On 10 February, Mackensen attacked again to take Carroceto station and the village. A *kampfgruppe* from 29th Panzer Grenadier Division advanced west from the Factory, Pfeiffer pushed along the Embankment from the north-west, and Gericke slotted in between from the Vallelata Ridge. At the station the 75-mm gun and machine gun of a Mark IV opened up in the bright moonlight forcing its defenders down into the cellar. The Scots Guards adjutant reported to brigade: 'There is a fucking great German tank sitting outside my door demolishing my house brick by brick.' The Commanding Officer, Wedderburn, and a captain decided to go for help. Risking their lives they slipped back to the Embankment where several US M-10 tank destroyers and Shermans were sheltering. The German tank was just 200 yards from them – but none would go to his aid. He pleaded for four hours, but eventually returned empty handed and was forced to pull back over the Embankment. It was the end at Carroceto, and the end of the salient. The Germans had achieved their aims – but it had taken them three days of hard fighting. Both sides had sustained heavy casualties. When the Dukes relieved the Grenadier Guards on 11 February they replaced just 60 men. One of them was William Dugdale. He immediately took a jeep and went to visit his good friend, 'Chucks' Lyttleton, who had been wounded and taken to the Casualty Clearing Station. It was a sombre experience:

> I asked to see him and a sister said he was not there but waved towards a line of about 30 blankets. I walked down the line looking at the labels until I saw one that said 'Lt. J.A. Lyttleton 5G.G.'. I knew the worst – I was the only survivor of Support Company. I walked back to my jeep and got in to drive back to the Battalion but there was a touch on my arm and it was the sister with a cup of tea 'have this before you go' she said, and I did.

Penney never forgave Lucas for what he deemed to be disinterest in 1st Division during this crucial period. He could not understand why Lucas had not visited his headquarters during the battle in order to acquaint himself with the division's specific difficulties and requirements. It was as though the British spoke a different language, for as soon as the salient had been lost Lucas went up to meet both with General William Eagles, the commander of 45th Division, and Penney to arrange for a counter-attack. The meeting took place at the Guards Brigade headquarters and prompted Captain Nick Mansell to write in his diary: 'A real flurry. Would you believe it? Old Corncob Charlie has actually *been* near here to see Penney and the Guards HQ.' After Penney had given a situation report, Lucas turned to Eagles and said, 'O.K., you give them the works' and left. The 1st Division commander could not believe it and later wrote: 'No operational appreciation, no orders, no intention, no objective, no nothing.' Lucas returned to Nettuno without seeing the battlefield and without understanding. This was delegation on a grand scale, so grand that it was almost a dereliction of duty. Penney later savagely recalled the meeting as 'a travesty, pathetic and tragic'. In the event, the counter-attack was a disaster when it finally took place at dawn on 11 February. Having reinforced the Factory after intercepting an American radio transmission giving details about the assault, Gräser then conducted a stubborn defence against Eagles's 179th Regiment. The infantry attacked without the tanks that they had been promised from 1st Armored Division as they had been spotted by the German artillery moving up the Via Anziate and were immediately targeted. Another attempt to seize the town took place in the early hours of the following day, but was also unsuccessful.

Having failed to take his opportunities he watched helplessly as von Mackensen wrenched the initiative from his frail grasp; Lucas's position looked weaker than ever. His situation was not helped by events on the Gustav Line. Had Fifth Army managed to break through to the Liri Valley then VI Corps would not have been in such a precarious position, but it was Clark's attack, started on 1 February, that had failed to take Cassino and force a German withdrawal. The First Battle of Cassino ended ten days later with II Corps a spent force and Kesselring's defences looking stronger than ever. Churchill received the news of the setbacks in Italy with resignation. He was particularly upset about Operation Shingle which he had fervently believed could 'unlock' the front. The Premier had also to endure a frail corps commander with a talent for missing opportunities and a talented Army Group commander who lacked the strength to grip his subordinate. On 10 February the Prime Minister despatched some advice to Alexander:

I have a feeling that you may have hesitated to assert your authority because you were dealing so largely with Americans, and therefore urged repeat urged an advance instead of ordering it. You are, however, quite entitled to give orders and I have it from the highest American authorities that it is their wish that their troops should receive direct orders . . . Do not hesitate to give orders just as you would to your own men. The Americans are very good to work with and quite prepared to take the rough with the smooth.

On 14 February Alexander returned to the beachhead to tell Lucas that he wished for there to be a breakout as soon as the tactical situation allowed. Lucas took refuge in his diary after their meeting: 'Alexander never sees the logistics of a problem. The picture he sees is such a big one that none of the difficulties appear in it.' The tables, it would appear, had been turned on the VI Corps commander who now believed that a British officer did not fully appreciate his difficulties and requirements. Alexander, meanwhile, wrote to Brooke: 'I am disappointed with VI Corps Headquarters. They are negative and lacking the necessary drive and enthusiasm to get things done. They appeared to have become depressed by events . . .' This innate pessimism was further reflected in Lucas's diary entry from 15 February when he grumbled: 'I am afraid the top side is not completely satisfied with my work . . . They are naturally disappointed that I failed to chase the Hun out of Italy but there was no military reason why I should have been able to do so. In fact there is no military reason for "Shingle".'

By mid-February Alexander was clearly discouraged by VI Corps. The operation was not progressing as he had wished or, it seems, as the media had expected. Newspaper and radio correspondents gathered every morning at Lucas's headquarters to be briefed by Colonel Joe Langevin. He had always been candid with the journalists, although could never be accused of sounding negative, but the War Office was increasingly concerned at the gloomy tone of the stories emanating from the beachhead. On 8 February *The Times* commented: 'Even . . . without putting in a full counter-offensive, the German command has succeeded in compelling the landing force to stand for the time being strictly on the defensive . . . It is clear that the landing was undertaken in the hope of quicker favourable development of a powerful offensive than has actually occurred.' And on 11 February, its headline was 'FIERCE EFFORTS AGAINST BEACH-HEAD . . . HEAVY FIGHTING IN PROGRESS . . . DANGER TO ALLIES IN BEACH-HEAD'. On the night 11–12 February the CBS correspondent Charles Daly reported: 'The situation in the bridgehead is grim: we have been forced to give ground . . . the Germans have massed strong forces against us.' References to Dunkirk abounded leading to Churchill having to make a reassuring speech to Parliament. Alexander met with the correspondents during his visit on 14 February, including Wynford Vaughan-Thomas:

> For once he was not his urbane self. He spoke to the assembled group with the firm tone of a headmaster disappointed at some misdemeanour in the Upper School. He admitted that the Beachhead landing hadn't gone as planned . . . The correspondents listened politely . . . but when he went on to say that the reports sent from the Beachhead were causing alarm, there were emphatic protests. General Alexander looked sternly at the protesters. 'Were any of you at Dunkirk?' he asked. 'I was and I know that there is never likely to be a Dunkirk here.'

The result of this farrago was the banning of the direct transmission of news from the beachhead. Which meant that for much of the battle news from Anzio–Nettuno was replaced by anodyne stories based on Fifth Army reports written in Naples and Algiers. Alexander had grasped the wriggling correspondents harder than he ever did his military colleagues.

Whilst the Allies bickered, the Germans organised themselves for their major offensive which was to begin on 16 February. Operation *Fischfang*

('Catch Fish') sought to destroy the Allied bridgehead by attacking towards Anzio down the Via Anziate. There were to be two waves supported by armour: Infantry Lehr Regiment, *Kampfgruppe* Gräser and 715th Division were to make the breakthrough, and 29th Panzer Grenadier and 26th Panzer Divisions were to exploit the penetration and drive to the coast. There would also be subsidiary efforts to conceal the German main effort and to pin and fix the enemy conducted by 4th Parachute and 65th Infantry Divisions west of the Via Anziate and the Hermann Göring Panzer Division at Cisterna. Hitler believed that the beachhead was an 'abscess which had to be lanced', and the tenor of his order of the day for the attack was, as General Walter Warlimont, Deputy Chief of the Operations Staff at OKW, said 'like the call of a revolutionary fanatic.' On 28 January the Führer had demanded:

The enemy landings at Nettuno are the start of the planned invasion of Europe for 1944. All German forces must be possessed with a fanatical desire to emerge victorious from this battle and not to rest until the last enemy is eliminated or thrown back into the sea . . . It must be fought with bitter hatred against an enemy who wages a ruthless war of annihilation against the German people and who, without any higher ethical aims, strives for the destruction of Germany and European culture . . . It must be driven home to the enemy that the fighting power of Germany is unbroken and that the invasion of the year 1944 is an undertaking that will be crushed in the blood of British soldiers.

Aware that von Mackensen was now in a position from which to strike his blow against VI Corps, Lucas hastily reorganised his defences: 56th Division were in the line from the mouth of the Moletta to the Via Anziate, 45th Division was astride the road and to its east, a short sector of front was defended by 509th Parachute Battalion, 3rd

Division remained below Cisterna, 504th Parachute Infantry defended the bend in the Allied line, and 1,800 Americans and Canadians of First Special Service Force, which had arrived on 2 February, held the Mussolini Canal down to the coast. The remnants of 1st Division was held in reserve with 1st Armoured Division. The VI Corps commander now also put the finishing touches to his Final Beachhead Line with a commendable attention to detail. It was the moment for which he had been assiduously preparing, but just as the critical period arrived, his future was ambushed. At a conference on 16 February hosted by Alexander and attended by Wilson, his deputy General Jacob Devers and Clark, it was decided to appoint two deputy corps commanders: Major General Lucian Truscott, who was to eventually take over command of the corps, and the British Major General Vivian Evelegh. When Lucas was told about the deputies on the following morning he at last had the proof that his time was running out. 'I think this means my relief', he wrote, though then adding, 'I hope that I am not to be relieved'. Von Mackensen, meanwhile, would have liked nothing better than to have been relieved. He had no confidence in a *Fischfang* plan that had largely been an invention of OKW. He particularly disliked its concentration down the Via Anziate and complained incessantly to Kesselring about the paucity of his resources. Although he had 125,000 troops against the Allies' 100,000, he believed that quantitatively and qualitatively the margin was too narrow. His pessimism was becoming wearing to Kesselring, who toyed with sacking him – particularly after a request to postpone the attack – but was disinclined due to his inability to get a suitable replacement into position at such an important point in the battle. On the eve of the attack Mackensen offered his resignation, but it was turned down.

At 0430 hours on 16 February the Allies intercepted a radio message which, when combined with their belief that a major German counter-attack was in the offing, led to the entire VI Corps artillery opening up – the largest bombardment yet in the beachhead. Peter

Graffagnino, a doctor with 2nd Battalion, 157th Regiment of 45th Division, recalled: 'Every artillery piece on the beachhead opened up at one time, our naval guns joined in, and for the next 45 minutes the steady thunder of guns and exploding shells rolled on. The front lines disappeared under dense clouds of drifting smoke and dust.' Shortly after, 452 German guns began their own work to shatter the cohesion of the VI Corps defences. In scenes reminiscent of Verdun in 1916, and with the same important symbolism to the belligerents, the battle began. The focus of the fighting on 16th was south of the Factory with 715th Division attacking from its ruins against 45th Division's 179th Regiment, and Gräser pushing out of Carroceto against the 2nd Battalion of the 157th Regiment which was blocking the Via Anziate. Company E of 2nd Battalion, consisting of 230 men including a machine gun platoon, one anti-tank gun and tank destroyers was in the vanguard. When the bombardment lifted to the Allied rear assault groups moved forward supported by tanks that advanced on the road and across the fields. Captain Felix L. Sparks commanding Company E remembers:

As the barrage lifted, I peered out of my foxhole and was greeted by the sight of three German tanks which had already penetrated through my left platoon. I yelled at my tank destroyers to engage them. This they did with devastating effect. At a range of about 150 yards, they literally blasted the German tanks to pieces. Following the tank attack there was a lull of three or four minutes. Then the German infantry came pouring in, several hundred of them. As one group approached my command post, a sergeant in one of the tank destroyers strapped himself to a .50 caliber machine gun on the side of his tank destroyer. At a range of about forty feet, he scattered Germans around the landscape. Then I saw dust coming in spurts from the back of his field jacket as a burst from a machine pistol hit him squarely in the chest. His heroic action, however, saved the command post from being overrun. A few minutes later, one of my two tank destroyers went up in flames as the result of a direct hit from a German tank. There was no forward artillery observer with my company, but I did have an artillery radio. Acting as my own forward observer, I requested the 158th Field Artillery to place heavy fire on my company position. This came in with devastating effect on the advancing Germans. They broke off their attacks on my company but started coming around on both flanks.

By about 1100 hours about half of Company E had become casualties along with one of their tank destroyers, but they were not overrun in spite of the Germans having to push much of their armour on the road. This concentration of vehicles on the Via Anziate was far from ideal as the road was narrow and heavily shelled, but it was necessary since the sun had thawed the ground which had initially provided a firm base for the attack against 179th Regiment, turning it into a quagmire. The afternoon saw the Germans trying to refocus their attack and cope with the Via Anziate choke point. It was the breathing space that this provided that allowed E Company to survive. 'By nightfall, we still held our position', Sparks recalled, 'but less than 100 men were left in the company.' The Germans had made a dent in the 45th Division line at the conjunction of the two regiments, but they had not achieved a breakthrough. 180th Regiment, meanwhile, remained comfortable in its defence against the weaker German attacks further to the east. The greatest penetration of the day was unexpected and, as a result, went unexploited. The attack by 4th Parachute Division and 65th Division against the British ploughed forward almost two miles, nearly reaching the Lateral Road before running out of steam. Major General Gerald Templer's 56th Division had to rely on the 1st Division in reserve to counter-attack. By this time there was considerable synergy between the two divisions as Templer held temporary command of 1st Division after Penney had been wounded in the head by a shell splinter earlier that morning. By the end of the day the line had been restored, but the thrust had been as much a shock to Lucas as it had been a wasted opportunity to the Germans. Meanwhile, the 3rd Division adroitly handled the attack from Cisterna by the Hermann Göring Panzer Division. Truscott had waited with tanks and tank destroyers in the front line and as the Germans advanced artillery fire annihilated their leading companies. It had been some revenge for the division's losses at the end of January. The battle continued throughout the day with heavy casualties on both sides, but the Panzer Division made no territorial gain.

The impact of the Allied artillery and naval guns on the German advance that day would be difficult to over-emphasise. Some 65,000 rounds were fired into the enemy to fragment their attacks and slow their momentum. One American divisional gunner, Charlie Franklin, says:

We fired all day, from dawn until dusk, without a break. We had stacks of ammunition, but we still had to send out for some more. We would be given one set of co-ordinates, fire on it, destroy whatever it was, and then fire on something else. It was all very precise. I never did see what we were firing at, but I'm sure that those guns did a lot of damage.

XII Air Support Command was also active sending fighters and bombers into action on interdiction and close air support missions. One 157th Regiment soldier who experienced a raid on the Via Anziate recalls: 'It was a massive morale boost to see a huge formation of aircraft fly over and drop their bombs on the road. We could see the enemy scattering as they exploded. The noise was immense, like rolling thunder. When the dust cleared great holes had appeared in the enemy lines. Some of the bombs dropped just yards in front of us and we threw ourselves to the ground. When we got up we were all completely deafened.' Conversely the bombardments were mentally and physically draining to the Germans. Captain Gerd Jebsen recalls:

The shelling was awful and sent two of my men 'over the edge'. They cowered in ditches shaking and crying. As I tried to reassure one of them, a good man who had served since France in 1940, the other took his own life with a pistol . . . Then came the bombers which caused blasts that killed anybody within 30 yards. I saw one man atomised in front of my eyes. It was terrible for the wounded who were taken away only to then be blown up in their trucks on the Via Anziate.

Kesselring was not happy with the day's achievements. At the very least he had hoped to see cracks appearing in the Allied line by the evening of 16 February but, instead VI Corps had remained solid. He thought that the Infantry Lehr Regiment – which had been attached to Gräser – had performed 'disgracefully'. This Demonstration Company, used to illustrate to troops in training how to execute an assault, was untried in battle but had come very highly recommended by Hitler himself. During the attack it had collapsed under shellfire and fled back to its jumping-off point. Kesselring was also angry that von Mackensen had not listened to his advice to send in the second wave during the afternoon to regain momentum. The Fourteenth Army commander was adamant that that wave was for exploitation only and would not use them until a breakthrough had been secured. His plan for the second day was to send the first wave forward again in the belief that if anything could create a breach in the VI Corps line, then more of the same and in the same place was the best option. Some infiltrations were made that night under the cover of darkness by 715th Division on the Via Anziate around the flanks of Sparks's Company E, and also in the 'wadi country' – 'a special, intricate kind of obstacle, hell to attack, hell to defend' – by the parachutists against 56th Division's 168th Brigade, but these were contained. The main attack began at 0740 hours on the morning of 17 February when the German artillery, infantry and armour endeavoured to drive themselves between 157th and 179th

Regiments. Supported by thirty-five fighter-bombers, the impact on the Americans was considerable, and as some of their cohesion was lost units were attacked and destroyed piecemeal. This initial success was followed up at 1100 hours by another Luftwaffe attack consisting of forty-five aircraft that bombed and strafed the disorientated troops and afforded the attackers several hundred more yards of ground. Eagles's headquarters tried to discover what was happening, but the situation was so confused with enemy tanks and infantry running amuck that the only conclusion that they could come to was that his front was collapsing. As Lucas wrote that evening, 'many events occurred which will never be part of recorded history.' 179th Regiment was withdrawn in broad daylight and was cut to pieces as Private First Class Rick O'Toole, a rifleman in 2nd Battalion, remembers:

It was a turkey shoot. What began as something quite organised quickly became a free for all. When my squad started to withdraw we were eight men, half a mile and one hour later and there were two of us. By the time I had dug in, I was the only survivor. I didn't know who was on my flanks, but I recollect the voice of someone – I think he was an officer or a senior NCO because he seemed confident – telling me what to do, keeping my confidence up. I never saw him, but if he had not been there – well, I don't know what I would have done.

The infantry defended stoically and the artillery pounded away, but by noon the Germans had created a wedge two miles deep and a mile wide across the Via Anziate. Even the impact of heavy bombers in close support of ground operations could not stop the enemy's advance. *The Times*:

The full power of the allied air forces was to-day thrown against the German positions facing the Anzio beach-head in the greatest air-ground co-operation assault since the Salerno landings . . . Fortress and Liberators to-day dropped 1,000 fragmentation bombs on enemy troops, their gun emplacements and transport, the chief objectives being along the main road . . . Nearly twice the number of Fortresses and Liberators were in the sky as were over Salerno on September 14, and the assault was a record for the number of sorties flown by the heavy bombers.

The remnants of 2nd Battalion 157th Regiment had congregated around the Caves at Buonriposo and, as the Germans swept by, were surrounded, leaving 3rd Battalion to defend the road. During the afternoon the Infantry Lehr Regiment regained some respectability with an attack that took them up the Via Anziate close to the junction with Dead End Road, and then began attacking with armour towards the Lateral Road. One tank was knocked out on the approach to the Flyover, and another underneath it. The Germans were on the verge of a breakthrough, but the Americans – assisted by some of Harmon's armour – stoutly refused to disintegrate. Spurred on by the inspirational Eagles who was to be found for much of the day in the front line, the 45th Division line was held. The 180th Regiment again remained relatively unscathed, maintaining a strong line on the right of the German penetration. One of its number, Private First Class William J. Johnson, was awarded a Congressional Medal of Honor for his actions that day after remarkable selflessness in covering his platoons' withdrawal despite being wounded. One of the great advantages of 180th Regiment's immovability was their threat to the German right flank as the enemy created a salient towards the Flyover. That night thousands of anti-personnel mines were sown in front of the Lateral Road, engineers prepared to crater the Via Anziate and lorries filled with concrete were moved into position to block the underpass. Men were sent from all over the beachhead to reinforce the Final Beachhead Line as the battle still raged a mere 600 yards in front of it. Cooks, drivers and clerks fought side by side with the infantry. 18 February was going to be the critical day.

As Lucas, Templer, Harmon and Eagles grappled with defensive conundrums, von Mackensen debated whether to discontinue his attack, or send in his second wave. The fact that he was even thinking about calling a halt to *Fischfang* at this point reveals that he was concerned about VI Corps's stubbornness, particularly as he had yet to fully draw its armoured reserve. He was also worried about his supply situation (as his lines of communication had been devastated by Allied bombing raids) and reports that he had received telling him that his first wave battalions were now at just company strength. Bringing the offensive to a halt at this point would maintain the integrity of the exploitation force for a later offensive. But then what if the Allies were on the verge of collapse? Kesselring settled the matter by ordering von Mackensen forward with his attack. Even though the Field Marshal believed that the best opportunity for a breakthrough had already passed, Berlin demanded that he fight on. *Kampfgruppe* Gräser and 715th Division, therefore, made further infiltrations into 45th Division during the night, whilst the second wave – 29th Panzer Grenadier Division and 26th Panzer Division – moved up to the front line. Private Cor Longiotti, a machine gunner in 179th Regiment's Company D, says of one probe:

> There we were only two squads of machine guns and no one else in sight, we had a terrible feeling of abandonment . . . This was the worst battle of the war that I have seen; it was like being in hell itself . . . About 200 yards to our right . . . there was a German tank firing 88 mm shells at us at point blank, knocking out my machine gun before daybreak in the morning, which left us with no fire power except a carbine, a rifle and my .45 automatic pistol.

Instead of exploiting a breakthrough, the two fresh divisions were to make the breach themselves and then exploit their own penetration. There was a diversionary attack in the area of the Caves and ravines west of the Via Anziate where 2nd Battalion of the 157th Division had been squeezed into a tighter perimeter, but still carried on fighting. Company E had just one machine gun left in action, and having been 230 strong on 16 February, had now been reduced to just twenty-eight riflemen and two officers. Sparks noted: 'There we stayed for the next several days, while the battle raged on about two miles to our rear. We were without food or water and almost out of ammunition, and the Germans could have overrun us at any time. However, they were concentrating on the final push to the sea. This left me free to direct artillery fire on German troop concentrations.' Just before dawn, the second wave, with the remnants of the first, made its attack from the Dead End Road in the fog. Defending in this area were the Loyals from 1st Division's 2nd Brigade which was almost on the Lateral Road near the Via Anziate, with I Company of the 157th Regiment adjacent on their left. On their right and a little in front were battalions from 179th and 180th Regiments. The first attack was by the Lehr Regiment through the minefields and barbed wire in front of the Loyals. 'Emerging out of the morning mist', recalled Staff Sergeant Norman Clarimont, 'were shapes throwing stick grenades. A wall of men. When they were about 30 yards away mortars fell on us. It was difficult not to seek cover in our water logged slit trenches, but when I next looked up the Germans were on top of us. I raised my hands and was led away. I hadn't fired a shot – it was all over in an instant.' One of the British platoons was wiped out, but the battalion held its position during close quarter fighting as dawn broke out. A counter-attack by some 46th Royal Tank Regiment armour was a relief to the struggling Loyals, but the Germans did not give up and later in the morning re-formed again, this time en masse. The historian of the 1st Division testified that:

Waves of German infantry poured across the open ground below the Dead End Road, only to meet a veritable hail of artillery, mortar and machine gun fire. The enemy suffered appalling casualties, yet there appeared to be no limit to his resources in manpower and whenever a German soldier fell, there always seemed to be another ready to take his place.

The Loyals fought for fourteen hours, but did not give a yard of ground. The ferocity of these incessant assaults was replicated all along the Lateral Road and the positions held by 180th Regiment. Why von Mackensen decided to dilute his force and attack the still relatively fresh 180th Regiment is a matter of conjecture, but it seems that having failed to break the Allies close to the bridge, he was hoping that the line would give elsewhere. Whatever it was, the plan did not work and although 180th Regiment were pushed back south-east and 179th Regiment south to the Lateral Road in line with the Loyals, the only result was to broaden the salient. The Germans were finding the last reserves of their strength to dismember VI Corps and open the Allies up in the centre of the battlefield. Private Cor Longiotti recalled being overwhelmed by the enemy that morning:

Shortly after daybreak in the morning of the 18 February 1944, things were happening so fast and everything was in such a big turmoil that it was all we could do to keep our heads down low to prevent being hit from shrapnel and at the same time try to defend ourselves while looking for an escape route . . . We never knew that the Germans had broken through and were already behind us until it was too late. When all of a sudden out of nowhere five German soldiers took us by surprise, coming from the rear with bayonets on their rifles and inches from our backs shouting . . . As soon as I stood up a German soldier, like lightning, jumped in the foxhole and grabbed my .45 automatic, he wasn't taking any chances . . . There were enemy troops behind us and in front of us. Then what we saw a few minutes later was just like out of the history books of World War I. About 200 yards in front of us heavily armed German soldiers under cover of artillery and mortar barrage were coming in droves, I mean droves. Twelve to fifteen waves of German soldiers were charging forward across the open fields shouting and yelling and with bayonets drawn on their rifles ready for close combat . . . there were thousands . . . They kept coming until they were hit, either wounded and knocked down or killed, never making an attempt to try and avoid the mortar or artillery fire. I honestly believe that if it wasn't for those five German soldiers that crept up on us from the rear and got to us first, we would never have made it out alive.

The performance of the exhausted 179th Regiment commander was causing Eagles some concern and so William Darby replaced him. The commander of 3rd Battalion, which had been wiped out that morning, visited regimental headquarters for instruction and did not expect compassion when he spoke with Darby:

'Sir, I guess you will relieve me for losing my battalion?' With a friendly pat on the back, the intrepid ranger replied, 'Cheer up son, I just lost three of them, but the war must go on.' The remark was not at all flippant, but admirably achieved the desired effect of relieving the tension and injecting new hope in the listeners. Colonel Darby then stepped outside and then invited us to do the same. 'Just look back of us,' he said, pointing back at the artillery . . . 'No one can continue to attack through that.' He then invited us to get back to the business of fighting. His confidence, energy and enthusiasm were just the tonic for an exhausted, discouraged command.

The afternoon saw some of the heaviest fighting yet in the battle, as the Germans desperately tried to push beyond the Lateral Road and VI Corps put everything that they could spare in the way to stop them. The Final Beachhead Line held. Darby was quite right when he indicated that the artillery would be the discriminator. The fact that the Germans did not manage to break through was testament, once again, to the co-operation between the infantry and the artillery. There was no bomber support because the weather was poor, but artillery support was excellent, firing 10 to 20 times more shells than the Germans. There was plenty of ammunition, good communications and pinpoint accuracy. This precision had much to do with the Forward Observation Officers such as Lieutenant F. Eugene Liggett supporting 157th Regiment. His job, he says, was to: 'calculate and direct artillery fire on targets ahead of the companies.' Living and working in the front line, he was not surprised to learn that the life expectancy of a Forward Observation Officer was about six weeks. Also assisting was Captain William H. McKay who was an observer in a small L-4 Cub aircraft which buzzed over the lines. During the day he spotted 2,500 Germans and a column of tanks moving from Campoleone and radioed his findings to the artillery headquarters. Within twelve minutes 200 British and American guns opened up on the target and destroyed it. McKay did this several times and stopped many German battalions from either getting to the battlefield or successfully launching an attack.

Whilst the Final Beachhead Line was under siege on the 18th, Lucas held a meeting with his divisional commander at his headquarters in Nettuno. The corps commander was glum, his divisions were on the verge of a major reversal and Clark was there to oversee his agony. Urging Lucas for positive action to rectify the perilous situation, a decision was made to counter-attack. On the following morning – 19 February – 30th Infantry Regiment from 3rd Division together with 6th Armored Infantry Regiment and a battalion of tanks from 1st Armored Division, would attack along the Bowling Alley. This was to be co-ordinated with an assault by the fresh 169th Brigade of 56th Division that had landed only that morning, which would advance up the Via Anziate. The aim was to put pressure on both ends of the Dead

End Road and to end the threat to the Final Beachhead Line. Once Lucas had overcome his fear of using his reserves, he saw the sense in the plan and later noted: 'My only recourse was to attack. The only recourse of the weaker of two opponents is to attack unless he stands still and be cut to pieces.' Meanwhile, von Mackensen looked at his situation and felt more pessimistic than ever. He had created a vulnerable salient, his troops were on the verge of exhaustion, his supplies had all but dried up and the enemy's reserve was still largely intact. He spoke to Kesselring declaring that he would continue to attack during the night, but adding that he did not rate his chances of success very highly. For once Albert Kesselring could do little more than concur with the aristocrat's assessment, but asked him to do his best nonetheless.

That night the German attacks continued to harass, probe and infiltrate giving the defenders no time to recuperate from their previous exertions – but the same was also true for the attackers. Both sides were at the limits of endurance. Gunter Pollmann, a veteran of the 715th Division says: 'Our eyes stung with tiredness. Our bodies were unwilling to do anything and had to be dragged around by the force of our minds. We ached, our heads pounded. Many of us were carrying injuries and wounds. This is the lot of an infantryman in battle.' At 0400 hours two battalions of 1st Panzer Grenadier Regiment supported by tanks targeted the Loyals again. They were initially repelled at the cost of 100 German lives and their reinforcements were later spotted and stopped by the artillery. A local counter-attack was launched by the Loyals and North Staffordshires and although at first was held, eventually yielded 213 German prisoners. An attack was also initiated against Lieutenant Colonel Lawrence C. Brown's 2nd Battalion 157th Infantry which was tying up valuable resources some way from the front line at the Caves. Throughout the night German patrols had searched for weak points in the battalion's defences, and then attacked them just before first light. The Americans cut them down. Once again the Germans were guilty of failing to concentrate their forces and a series of poorly co-ordinated actions resulted in their failure to break into the position. The fighting was intense with heavy mortar bombardments falling like a blanket over the position causing great anxiety to not only the American troops, but also the local men, women and children that still sheltered there. The conflict produced a new batch of casualties for Captain Graffagnino to treat. During his two and a half days in the Caves he had treated over 200 men, some of whom were in the 'corridors' of the stone medical aid station. 'We were out of plasma, morphine and bandages and almost out of food', he wrote later. 'We had to recruit some of the peasant women to help nurse the wounded, and set others to work cooking soup out of the few chickens and dried beans they had brought with them into the caves.' Brown was unsure for how much longer his unit could hold out. He hoped that a VI Corps attack that would sweep the line back past them, failing that that a reinforcing or relieving force would turn up, what he did not want to do was surrender or to have to make his way back to friendly lines through German held territory.

As *Fischfang* went through its death throes, an Allied counter-attack was developing. Having taken so much punishment over the previous three days there is no doubt that the Clark inspired jab at the enemy would be a welcome reviver for Lucas's beleaguered troops, but it had started badly. 169th Brigade was unable to attack that morning as it had been landed without its heavy weaponry and the subsequent attack up the Via Anziate using tanks alone got nowhere. Harmon's armour, meanwhile, attacked up the Bowling Alley supported by eight British artillery regiments and another eight battalions of corps artillery. The spectacle of the tanks moving forward was a splendid sight for the men of 180th Regiment. Captain Nathaniel Duncan witnessed 1st Armored Division's advance:

There was a loud cheer as the Shermans passed through our positions, their machine guns blaring and their guns blasting. The Germans scattered and we helped knock a couple down as they ran.

They were a little exposed on that narrow track, but it seems that our bombers must have been distracting their artillery because few shells hit their targets.

It was the day when many Germans recognised that their attempt to push the Allies back to the sea had not succeeded. For all Hitler's uplifting words, von Mackensen's force had failed to get within seven miles of Anzio. Gunter Pollmann recalls:

By the afternoon of 19 February we had had enough. We were being shelled, bombed and attacked by the enemy's armour. I had not slept for over 72 hours, not had a meal for 48 hours and was having to scrounge rifle rounds from anybody that I bumped into. 19 February was the day that we broke, and it was the day that I thought for the first time that we might lose the Battle of Anzio.

The tanks pushed slowly on and by mid-afternoon had reached a point on the Bowling Alley in line with Dead End Road. Harmon took over 200 prisoners that day and had reinstilled in VI Corps a belief that they could turn things round. Lucas noted:

German dead were piled in heaps all along our front. This was the Hun's last all-out effort. A message from Clark to me read in part: 'Congratulate Harmon on his success today. Again I want to tell you that your accomplishments today have been outstanding. Keep it up.'

To Lucas the fact that the major German counter-attack had been defeated was a source of great personal satisfaction but to Clark, with his wider responsibilities, there was little to celebrate. It had been a difficult week for the Fifth Army commander, with the long-expected German thrust at Anzio reaching its climax just as his second attempt to breach the Gustav Line had failed. The monastery at Cassino was now in ruins after Allied bombing and artillery bombardments, and the town was still in German hands. The two fronts remained inextricably linked and in mid-February the future did not look particularly bright for either side. Alexander and Clark were irredeemably restless for, whilst Lucas may have directed a battle of critical importance to a satisfactory conclusion, they remained focused on breaking a deadlock in Italy which seemed no closer now than it had done two months earlier. In such circumstances Major General John P. Lucas's position became more vulnerable than ever.

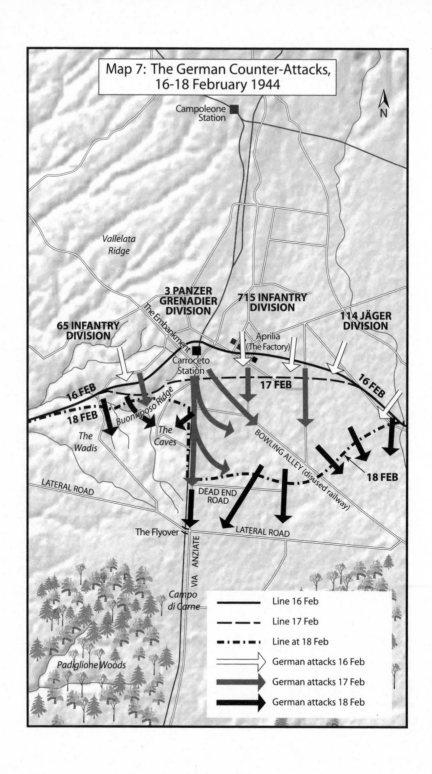

Map 7: The German Counter-Attacks,
16-18 February 1944

N

Campoleone
Station

Vallelata
Ridge

3 PANZER
GRENADIER
DIVISION

715 INFANTRY
DIVISION

114 JÄGER
DIVISION

65 INFANTRY
DIVISION

The Embankment

Aprilia
(The Factory)

Carroceto
Station

16 FEB

17 FEB

16 FEB

18 FEB

Buonriposo Ridge

The
Wadis

The
Caves

BOWLING ALLEY (disused railway)

18 FEB

LATERAL ROAD

DEAD END
ROAD

The Flyover

LATERAL ROAD

VIA ANZIATE

Campo
di Carne

Padiglione Woods

	Line 16 Feb
	Line 17 Feb
	Line at 18 Feb
	German attacks 16 Feb
	German attacks 17 Feb
	German attacks 18 Feb

CHAPTER 7

Changes

(20 February–mid-March)

Adolf Hitler was beside himself that *Fischfang* had failed. In the Map Room at the *Wolfschanze* he slammed his fists down on the briefing room table, his face a frighteningly deep red. The bearer of the bad news, Field Marshal Wilhelm Keitel, tried to remain calm as the Führer launched into a twenty-minute tirade against his generals, how their incompetence was 'conspiring to undermine the effectiveness of his brave troops.' Straining for self-control, Hitler then announced that he refused to believe that the attack was over – another should be launched immediately. He stalked off shouting for charts, reports and General Jodl, declaring that if von Mackensen could not deliver then he would have to direct the battle himself. These were tendencies that Corporal Hitler had shown many times before, outrage at battlefield setbacks followed by an overriding impulse to personally direct operations. The fact that he was in a bunker in East Prussia, had not had schooling in the art of military command and lacked a true understanding of the battlefield's terrain and the fighting conditions, did not concern him. Churchill was similarly inclined, but in most cases stayed his dabbling hand when it came to detailed operational matters, or had it stayed for him when he was showing a dangerously close interest. Both leaders found it difficult to believe that any given situation would not be greatly improved by their own involvement. But one was a dictator and the other had fought for democracy as hard as he had fought the Germans. For a short period during the First World War the two men had served opposite each other on the Western Front near Ypres, Hitler as a private and Churchill as a Lieutenant Colonel, with neither relishing the control of superiors and both men truly believing that they could do better. Now with their armies facing each other in Italy, Churchill's initiative demanded that Hitler react. In different ways both men were angered by what had recently happened in the Anzio beachhead, but only Hitler tried to actively take military matters into his own hands; Churchill got military colleagues to do it for him.

Albert Kesselring was far from immune from Hitler's tirades and interference, but he was pragmatic and saw them as part of his job. Whilst there was plenty of urgent activity at his headquarters, there was also an atmosphere that engendered self-control. The Field Marshal remained positive and tried to ensure that his staff were too. There was no question that *Fischfang* had failed to undermine the Allies' confidence in amphibious warfare by pushing VI Corps into the sea, but the offensive had gone some way towards the attainment of his own aims. Kesselring saw the task of his command as holding on to central Italy for as long as possible. With Alexander thwarted by the Gustav Line and on his heels at Anzio, Rome would be safe for some considerable time. Indeed, when a staff officer from 4th Parachute Division visited Monte Soratte at the end of February he recalled that the Field Marshal was 'ebullient and full of praise for what the troops had achieved.' Kesselring could not afford the time to rake through the embers of *Fischfang* looking for evidence of its weaknesses; he had to re-energise a disconsolate Fourteenth Army and ascertain its capabilities after a protracted period of exertion. Both he and von Mackensen were realistic enough to recognise that in the wake of its prohibitive losses and chronic supply problems, the Army could not be relied upon to do much. They hoped that, despite a record for expecting a great deal with few resources, Hitler would also comprehend this.

There was no immediate threat from Clark and Lucas, not least because the VI Corps had suffered heavy casualties during *Fischfang*. The offensive had cost the Germans 5,400 men and prodigious amounts of armour and equipment, but VI Corps's loss of 3,500 men (on top of their losses during the battle for the salient) had been a body blow. With both sides having lost nearly 20,000 men at Anzio–Nettuno since Operation Shingle began a month earlier, and the weather still dreadful, the battlefield commanders of both sides believed that a period of consolidation was inevitable. Lucas, however, would not be there to oversee it. He had been sacked on 22 February and replaced, as planned, by Lucian Truscott. Lucas may have been beginning to believe that the noose had loosened a little from around his neck after the repelling of the German counterattack, but in fact the hangman was merely waiting for an opportunity to kick away the chair. The drop had been a shock to Lucas; indeed when Clark informed VI Corps headquarters on 21 February that he was going to pay a visit the following day Lucas was moved to write: 'Message from Clark. He arrives with eight generals. What the hell.' It had not been Clark's intention to remove Lucas initially, partly because he felt that his subordinate was being misjudged, but largely because he felt protective towards a man who had been given an invidious mission. He had eventually agreed to it at the meeting on the 16th after he felt the massive and irresistible weight of opinion against the VI Corps commander. Clark believed that much of that weight was down to Churchill, and had initially railed against British pressure to remove the man he had recommended. But both Churchill and Alexander had Lucas in their sights as Operation Shingle's spoiler and demanded satisfaction. One commentator, General W.G.F. Jackson, has written of the Prime Minister's influence:

It is difficult to escape the feeling that Mark Clark's sacking of Dawley at Salerno and Lucas at Anzio may have had a common factor – the need for a scapegoat. Someone had to be sacrificed to quieten Churchill's restless criticism of the tactical handling of his strategic brain-children.

In fact the replacement served Clark's purpose. The Fifth Army Commander no longer wanted to be tainted by association with John Lucas and, after the threat to VI Corps had passed, was willing to be the hangman. Clark could see the possibilities of Truscott's dynamism. Even so, he endeavoured to make his old friend's relief as comfortable as possible, making him deputy commander of the Fifth Army while a position was found for him back home in the United States. There had been no direct reference made to Lucas's sacking in Clark's diary – in one paragraph the commander of VI Corps had been John Lucas, in the next it is Lucian Truscott. Even so, the duplicitous Clark later wrote in his memoirs: 'I had for some time been considering a change. My own feeling was that Johnny was ill – tired physically and mentally – from the long responsibilities of command in battle.'

Although he never admitted it, Lucas must have felt let down by Clark. He thought that he had been doing what Clark had wanted him to do. 'I thought I was winning something of a victory', he recorded in his diary. Lucas considered that he had carried out Clark's orders to the best of his ability, but had been sacked for failing to carry out Alexander's. To this end he wrote:

My orders were, to me, very clear and did not include any rash, piecemeal effort. These orders were never changed although the Army and the Army Group Commanders were constantly on the ground and could have changed them had they seen fit to do so.

This is a strong argument, although it misses the point that there are degrees of caution just as there are degrees of rashness. Lucas was by nature ultra-cautious, and thus failed to secure a beachhead anchored on critical towns from which he could attack or defend. He had delivered far less than most had reasonably expected. Lucas's idea of success, considering his resources, was mere survival after a German counter-attack. Despite resources, success to others was the capture of the Alban Hills and withdrawal of Tenth Army. John Lucas exuded caution. His timid face, soft voice and furrowed brow failed to inspire confidence. Truscott later wrote: 'I was not blind to the fact that General Lucas lacked some of the qualities of positive leadership that engendered confidence . . . His was a lovable personality.' Templer was more brutal, declaring: 'Lucas was absolutely full of inertia, and couldn't make up his mind . . . He had no qualities of any sort of commander, absolutely no presence; he was the antithesis of everything that a fighting soldier and general ought to be.' The 'too tenderhearted' Lucas departed the beachhead on 23 February a broken man: 'I left the finest soldiers in the world when I lost the VI Corps', he wrote, 'and the honour of having commanded them in their hour of greatest travail cannot be taken from me.' He served for three weeks as Clark's deputy before leaving Italy for home. He died on Christmas Eve 1949 aged fifty-nine.

The sea change from Lucas to Truscott was dramatic. Lucian K. Truscott Jnr was a bright, confident figure, with a bright, confident outlook – albeit (and he himself was the first to admit it) built on the firm foundations that Lucas had provided. Lucas's lack of boldness may have put the beachhead in peril, but having survived, its future looked far rosier. The three immediate tasks that Truscott set himself were to: keep the beachhead secure, reassure the British that all was well, and make VI Corps headquarters more dynamic. Truscott was liked and respected by the senior American commanders in the beachhead, but he knew that the VI Corps headquarters had to win over the British. His deputy commander, Major General Vivian Evelegh, an

Englishman, helped him to achieve this and together they made frequent visits to the British sector. Truscott was a great advocate of 'getting out and about' as he put it, to see and be seen. Within a day of taking command he had visited every formation in the beachhead. The British soon came to respect Truscott for he listened, and was sympathetic to their problems, making sure that he understood their working methods. British officers would often spend an evening with Truscott at his headquarters chatting to him, and he frequently visited them in the field. Gradually a mutual trust was built and never again was the judgement of VI Corps headquarters to be clouded by a failure to understand the British. Revitalised by Truscott's appointment, the headquarters became an empathetic, positive body reflecting their commander's character. Even Truscott's physical appearance gave hope. The handsome forty-nine-year-old dressed in cavalry boots, breeches and a leather jacket and tied a white scarf around his neck – actually a silk map of Italy purloined from an airman's escape kit. With a .45 pistol hanging in a leather holster at his side, he cut a dashing figure. Wynford Vaughan-Thomas wrote of the first meeting between reporters and Truscott at Nettuno:

> We've got a new head at Anzio, tough . . . husky-voiced and with slightly greying hair. But he looks – as we hope every general should look – like a two-fisted fighter and not like a tired-out old businessman. He was honest, outspoken, and completely realist. 'No,' he said, 'I don't reckon that everything is for the best, we're going to have a tough time here for months to come. But, gentlemen, we're going to hold this Beachhead come what may.' And he stuck out his jaw in a way that convinced you that any attack would bounce off it.

As soon as he was able Truscott cast a critical eye over the beachhead and his first priority was its security. He had little doubt that as soon as the Germans were able they would launch another attack. Undoubtedly

Kesselring and von Mackensen still had an opportunity to cause problems. VI Corps had to be in a strong position to deal with the Germans and prepare for its own breakout at some date in the future. In order to do this he needed to tidy up the front. The most obvious piece of house work was already underway – the rescue of 2nd Battalion 157th Regiment still surrounded in the Caves at the base of the Buonriposo Ridge. With *Fischfang* having come to an end, it was only a matter of time before the Germans overran the perimeter and finished Lawrence Brown's unit off. By 21 February, conditions inside the perimeter had deteriorated considerably. With so little food, water and ammunition having managed to get through to the Caves since five days earlier, the battalion's ability to fight was undermined with every meal and enemy probe. Water was being taken from a stream that ran red with the blood of dead Germans, but was boiled and drunk nonetheless. Some of the men had not eaten for forty-eight hours, having long since consumed their emergency ration of iron hard chocolate. There were a handful of mortar bombs, a box or two of hand grenades and two belts of ammunition for the lone machine gun, offset by a spirit of defiance. Lieutenant Colonel Brown had been shown to be out of his depth during the siege and so Executive Officer Captain George Kessler had organised the defences. On 21 February there had been two attempts to break through to the Caves. In the first, Templer sent armour up the Via Anziate but lost three tanks and an anti-tank gun without success. In the second, 2/7 Battalion Queen's Royal Regiment (Queen's Regiment) of 169th Brigade set out after dark to try and penetrate the line. They had not gone far, however, when they were caught up in an air raid in which the Germans' hideously effective anti-personnel 'Butterfly' bombs caused them seventy-six casualties. The battalion had forged on regardless, fending off enemy patrols that stumbled across their path, and smashing their way through startled Germans to reach the Caves. On their arrival they found an on-going battle with their adversaries who had infiltrated their perimeter. The Germans launched ferocious attack after attack and D Company of the Queen's Regiment in ground nearest the Via Anziate disappeared. At the Caves the fighting was incredibly frenzied, as Peter Graffagnino remembers:

> Our predicament . . . was still critical. There were German forces all around us, and they were still fighting to dislodge us by storming the cave opening. Men were fighting hand to hand with knives, bayonets and rifle butts. To keep the Germans out we had to call on our own artillery to blast the cave entrances. The din within was terrific, and the concussion waves left most of us with shattered eardrums.

That night the artillery saved the newly enlarged force from being overrun. The following morning scores of dismembered and horribly damaged corpses littered the battlefield. A withdrawal could not come too soon for the shattered Americans. 22 February was a tortuous day for the Allies in their ever-shrinking perimeter. Snipers were a particular danger, with the crack of a rifle almost always ending in the death of another soldier. The attacks came in waves: a flurry of fevered activity, and then a lull, followed by more violent commotion, and then quiet again. One wounded soldier, Private Paul van der Linden, listened to the battle raging away as he lay on the floor of one of the Caves:

> It was a curious experience. There I was lying on a hard cold floor quite safe really, whilst outside it was hell . . . My arm and chest were painful. The doctor had taken some of the shell splinters out, but others were too deep. I floated in and out of consciousness. I preferred it when I was out, because then the pain went away and I couldn't hear what was going on . . . The sounds were confusing. I'd hear a yell, then rat-a-tat-a-tat followed by the boom of a grenade. It was a real scrap . . . Sometimes I woke up to find our own guns targeting the Caves trying to keep the Germans at bay. A massive

explosion would rock the floor and suck the air out of the place. The noise was so great that you'd be deaf for minutes or hours afterwards. And so on it went.

That evening, and under the cover of darkness, the Americans began to withdraw. A number were killed along the way, with some captured. Others left the following morning, 23 February, leaving the thirty wounded who had been unable to attempt the journey with Graffagnino and five medical orderlies. The column moved slowly towards the Allied lines but, just as they felt that they were going to make it, an ambush was sprung from some houses ahead. Machine gun fire ripped into the group which split as everyone sprinted for cover. Individuals and small parties subsequently found their way to safety during the rest of the day. Again, many failed to make it, although Brown and Sparks, the commander of Company E, were among those that did. Sparks had been the only survivor from his unit until he was joined a couple of days later by an NCO. 2nd Battalion had gone into the line on 16 February 1,000 men strong, one week later they numbered just 225, of whom 90 were walking wounded. Meanwhile, back at the Caves the Queen's Regiment found that their positions had been badly infiltrated and C Company overwhelmed in a flamethrower attack. The remaining men of the battalion were forced back to the Caves and here the Germans threw everything that they had at the Englishmen. At various times the entrances came under attack from three Mark IV tanks, egg grenades, mortar bombs and machine gun bullets. In a great crescendo of violence the defenders stood, crouched and lay firing their weapons hoping that Allied artillery would do enough to thwart the attacks. The Caves themselves were choked with dust covering fighting troops, wounded, medical staff and civilians alike. It was only when darkness came that there was some respite and only then the battalion took their chances and attempted a withdrawal. The Germans soon saw what was happening, as the Queen's regimental history describes:

All hell broke loose . . . suddenly there were Germans everywhere and it was impossible to avoid completely their positions and patrols: the party led by Lieutenant Colonel Baynes at one time lay flat on a wadi bank while Germans with automatic weapons walked up and down immediately behind them while another party was fortunate in being mistaken for Italian refugees and walked right through an enemy position without being fired at.

Baynes made it back to friendly lines, later to be awarded the Distinguished Service Order for valour, along with twenty-one others. The Queen's had lost 362 officers and men in a mere two days, a staggering 85 per cent of their strength. In one week the Caves had ensured the virtual destruction of two battalions – but its story does not end there. On the afternoon of 24 February, the 157th Regiment's charismatic dentist, Captain Hugo Fielschmidt (American, but German named), was so concerned about the welfare of the wounded still at the Caves that he attempted to rescue them. Striding out into No Man's Land with just a Red Cross flag for protection, Fielschmidt continued through into the German lines. At one point during a bombardment he flung himself into a foxhole already occupied by two Germans. When the shells had desisted, he grinned, said good-bye and continued on towards the Caves waving his flag. When he arrived Germans were swarming over the area, but he was not troubled and according to Graffagnino 'stumbled flushed and wild-eyed into the caves'. Having made the wounded as comfortable as possible, the journey began with Fielschmidt leading the way. Graffagnino later wrote:

After ten days of underground darkness, the late afternoon daylight was almost blinding. Most of the litter-bearers, all utterly exhausted from the sleepless days and nights of battle, were unable to carry their loads more than a few yards at a time without stopping for a rest. After the constant cold of the caves, the warm, oppressively humid air sapped our remaining energies. The column proceeded slowly. The whole area through which we struggled was an incredible panorama of desolation and destruction. Wrecked vehicles and armor, uprooted trees and blasted vegetation, discarded ammunition and equipment, not one foot of ground unmarked by shell craters and, lying everywhere, the dead.

The Germans seemed curious about the forlorn group dragging itself across the torn ground, but Fielschmidt remained unchallenged until a German Major and Staff Sergeant abruptly stepped out from a house concealing a tank. The officer stated that they could not proceed, Fielschmidt protested and a protracted argument ensued. By the time the men had entered into a heated discussion about military law and ethics, both sides saw the ridiculousness of the situation and burst out laughing – but the Americans were all taken prisoner.

As Germans filled the pocket at the Caves, fighting around the beachhead continued as the belligerents conducted local attacks to obtain the greatest tactical advantage. The line was straightened and enemy positions mopped up as the two sides readjusted themselves after three weeks of bitter combat. The casualties continued to mount in an arena that was gaining a reputation for unrelenting awfulness. Private Murray Levine was a Browning Automatic Rifleman who had only just arrived at the front:

> I only lasted two or three days. On February 26 I looked out of my foxhole and could see them coming. Attacking. I opened up on them naturally. Everybody, the heavy equipment, everybody who was alive was firing at them . . . They surrounded my foxhole, and one of them tossed in a concussion grenade that landed near me and exploded. It just knocked us cold, and also caught me in the left shoulder . . . Then all of a sudden I heard a machine gun spraying, and my sidekick was killed and I caught a couple of bullets in the

back. They must have gone through him into me . . . My shoulder bothered me more because it was ripped, you know, the bullet was clean . . . and I was spitting blood from the concussion. I was a bloody mess.

Levine heard the Germans discussing his fate and then – chillingly – one cock his machine pistol: 'That's when I thought "Goodbye Charlie", when another shell exploded right amongst us and just blew them away. Killed them all . . . and part of my hand was blown off.' Whilst there was no grand attritional design, the determination to hold ground and undermine the enemy's ability to defend led to a chronic bloodletting. Battalions already severely depleted by the battles of the first three weeks of February continued to suffer because they were either still in the line or, particularly in the case of VI Corps, still so close to the front line that they were prey to air raids and artillery bombardments. On the eve of his sacking Lucas had been badgering Clark for the relief of the Guards Brigade. All three of its battalions had suffered similar casualty rates, with the Scots Guards, for example, having lost 15 officers and 122 other ranks killed, 9 officers and 303 other ranks wounded, 4 officers – including the padre and doctor – and another 213 other ranks missing. Clark was sympathetic to calls for the brigade to be replaced, but said that he could not find a forma-tion to replace it with and so the Guards had to remain in the beach-head until 9 March. The Germans had even greater difficulties finding replacement units and formations and, moreover, their troop move-ments were being constantly monitored and bombed. 65th Division straddled the Via Anziate in late February and had been placed in that position of great responsibility because it had not been part of the main *Fischfang* force. General Helmuth Pfeiffer's division had been heavily involved in the reduction of the British salient earlier in the month and engaged in diversion operations ever since, but as General Schlemm replied when he tried to object to such an obviously hazardous position: 'somebody has to do it and that somebody is you.' Pfeiffer set up his forward headquarters in the Caves recently vacated by the two Allied battalions. He was instructed to carefully watch the broad British salient which jutted out into 'wadi country' and was surrounded both by 4th Parachute Division and his own division. Corporal Joachim Liebschner made many trips to the Caves ferrying messages between the two divisions so as to ensure their close co-operation. This close country with no fixed front line was a challenge to Liebschner who, despite his job as a runner, had a very bad sense of direction. He worked long hours in dangerous conditions and on one occasion was chased and machine-gunned by a fighter whilst cycling along a track. 'That', he says, 'proved Allied superiority. To spend time and resources on one man on a bicycle – amazing.' Here there were no tanks, there was no possibility of the great sweeping manoeuvres conducted by rapidly moving troops so familiar to the German forces. 'Wadi country' was a different type of battlefield, a tortuous place where one was never quite sure where the enemy were, where there was constant movement but little mobility, and patrols were sent out and never returned. It was an intense type of fighting which demanded great concentration and unique skills. As one officer who fought in the wadis has written: 'People lived like savages, faces smeared with mud, clothes never changed, creeping and pouncing in the darkness, lunging with bayonets, firing blindly into bushes at the least rustle.' It was into this perilous world that the already under-manned 1st Irish Guards was slipped for their final spell in the front line. For three days and four nights the battalion was subjected to numerous attacks in a position called 'The Boot'. Captain D.J.L. Fitzgerald later wrote:

It was a savage, brutish troglodyte existence, in which there could be no sleep for anyone and no rest for any commander. The weather was almost the worst enemy, and the same torrential rain, which sent an icy flood swirling around our knees as we lurked in the gullies, would at times sweep away the earth that covered the poor torn bodies of casualties hastily buried in the Boot. Wallowing in a network of gullies, isolated by day and erratically supplied by night, soaked to the skin, stupefied by exhaustion and bombardment, surrounded by new and old corpses and yet persistently cheerful, the Guardsmen dug trenches and manned them until they were blown in and then dug new ones, beat off attacks, changed their positions, launched local attacks, stalked snipers, broke up patrols, evacuated the wounded, buried the dead and carried supplies. The bringing up of supplies was a recurrent nightmare. Carrying parties got lost, jeeps got bogged and, as the swearing troops heaved at them, down came shells.

The Irish Guards were further whittled away in the ravines, and taking casualties to the very last minute of their time in the Boot. Even as they were handing over to the Dukes, thirty-seven-year-old Sergeant Jimmy Wylie from Belfast was killed in a German bombardment. When they left Anzio harbour two weeks later the battalion had suffered 94 per cent casualties. The 'wadi experience' was something that every British unit was eventually exposed to as battalions were rotated through the line. The already shattered Foresters entered a particularly nasty area at the end of February with a strength of 250 officers and men. The unit was immediately subjected to all manner of bombardments and infantry attacks and at one point the Germans were rolling hand grenades from the edge of a gully down into their slit trenches. When they were relieved five days later the Foresters, too tired to climb out themselves, had to be pulled out of their slit trenches. Their sunken eyes spoke of the most immense trauma. There had been just thirty survivors.

The Foresters had been caught up in an unsuccessful attempt by Schlemm to destroy the British salient in late February and early March. It was part of a wider German offensive heavily endorsed and orchestrated by Hitler. Although Kesselring and von Mackensen had tried to explain that a period of rest and reorganisation was required before Fourteenth Army could attack again, OKW had insisted that it attack again on 28 February. The Führer was demanding that this time the main effort should be made against the Americans' salient in the east with a subsidiary attack down the Via Anziate. It was his opinion that VI Corps was on the verge of collapse and would find it impossible to relocate their paltry reserves over to the eastern side of the beachhead to contain a rapid thrust over good tank country. Having dislocated their enemy, another major attack would be launched down the Via Anziate to split the enemy, and reach the sea. There was to be no argument and no negotiation; these were Hitler's wishes, to be carried out energetically and successfully. This was a brand of optimism that even Kesselring found difficult to comprehend. Like von Mackensen he could see no sense in the plan whatsoever. Were extra resources being offered for this offensive? What about the morale of the troops? What evidence was there that the Allied ability to react would be as poor as had been assumed? These obvious questions were asked, but with no helpful answers emanating from OKW, Fourteenth Army got on preparing for an offensive that it was spectacularly poorly equipped to fight.

As the Germans prepared to attack, the Allies were receiving excellent intelligence about their activities, strengths and locations from an American Office of Strategic Services (OSS) operative in Rome. Twenty-three-year-old Harvard graduate Peter Tompkins – code name Pietro – had landed 100 miles north of Rome from a torpedo boat on 21 January and by the time that Operation Shingle had been launched had made his way in to the capital dressed as a Fascist auxiliary policeman. Since that time Tompkins had helped to co-ordinate the activities of the Italian Resistance and had established an excellent intelligence network. Assisted by over 100 Socialist workers watching the twelve major roads in and out of Rome, and a plant in Kesselring's headquarters, Tompkins had been able to radio the OSS section at Fifth Army headquarters with accurate and timely information. His work gave VI Corps a crucial insight into German movements throughout the beachhead's most vulnerable days, and during *Fischfang* it played a major part in the Allies' ability to plan their response. On 17 February, for example, Tompkins reported: 'Traffic through Rome going south on 15th. 230 freight cars loaded with material, 50 loaded with personnel, 100 horse carts, 11 Mark VI tanks, 6 medium tanks . . .' As a result of his work the vast majority of the German attempts to deceive the Allies with dummy tanks, false troop movements and fake radio transmissions in late February were a largely wasted effort. The clandestine work was dangerous and challenging, and despite having to operate in a city where the Germans were feeling increasingly sensitive and were therefore becoming ever more repressive, Tompkins and his colleagues continued to risk their lives daily. The repression took many forms: General Mältzer established a curfew which meant that civilians had to be in their homes by 1700 hours with transgressors to be shot on sight, food was scarce, prices soared, the gas and water were often cut off and the dragnet search for a work force continued. Towards the end of January, for example, the Germans sealed off the Via Nazionale area, and arrested every adult male between the ages of eighteen and seventy. Two thousand were arbitrarily removed to forced labour camps, half for construction work on the Anzio and Cassino fronts, half for Germany. It was, as Trevelyan has argued, 'a major psychological mistake. Rome looked as if it had caught the plague, and from then onwards people would flee if they saw a group in German uniforms. One could feel the hate and fear. All young men were virtually in hiding.'

These German excesses did little to pacify the Romans. Initially Operation Shingle had given them hope, and though as Colonel Dollmann had predicted, there had not been an armed rising, there were more acts of opposition. The trend was recorded by the

American nun Mother Mary St Luke who noted in her diary: 'Sabotage goes steadily forward.' The British Minister at the Holy See, D'Arcy Osborne was often awoken during the night by shooting: 'I heard some shots', he wrote, 'so went and looked out of the salon window over a dead, moonwashed Rome; it was disconcerting but romantic to hear the silver silence shattered by a mysterious machine-gun, very close indeed, spitting death anonymously at nothing but silence and moonshine. Grim and beastly and sinister and evil and symptomatic.' Throughout February German vehicles were ambushed, telephone lines cut, hit and run attacks launched using every conceivable mode of transport, lone Germans were stabbed or shot if they wandered off the main thoroughfares, and bombs continued to be left wherever Germans gathered. On 1 March, a seventeen-year-old woman, Carla Capponi, one of the most active partisans, was incredibly daring when near The Excelsior Hotel on the Via Veneto she shot a German in the back and seized his briefcase. Not satisfied with this she subsequently organised with her boyfriend to blow up a column of 150 German police on their daily march through the centre of Rome. It was to take place on 23 March, the twenty-fifth anniversary of the founding of Fascism. Allied bombers also did their best to destroy German military sites in Rome. The historic centre of the city was not deliberately targeted, but some bombs inevitably went astray and devastated antiquities whilst others missed barracks and killed civilians. Fabia Sciarillo recalls:

> The Allies' bombers were hated – and feared. They were bombing our city and our people were being killed. A hospital was hit, houses – many innocent people died. We felt as though we didn't have a friend in the world, that we were being used by the Germans, Americans and British . . . The bombs exploded in the cafes, the bombs were dropped from the air. It was all the same to many of us.

The Allies refused to recognise Rome as an Open City due to the information that they were receiving about buildings being used for military activities. There had been considerable lobbying by the Catholic Church to get the bombing stopped, but Roosevelt's official response was uncompromising: 'Everyone knows the Nazi record on religion. Both at home and abroad Hitler and his followers have waged a ruthless war against the churches of all faiths. Now the German army has used the Holy City of Rome as a military centre.'

The Allied bombing raids, the attacks by the Resistance and the heavy-handed German reaction, all had raised the temperature in Rome during the winter of 1943–44. Tompkins continued his work, hoping that the Allies would make a breakthrough soon, for he believed that it would not be long before his network was broken. He was also concerned about the fighting spirit of the increasingly beset Romans. Although the sound of exploding bombs and the rattle of machine gun fire may well have given the impression that Rome was a city on the verge of an uprising, this was very far from the case. Resentment was beginning to grow against the Allies for their inability to liberate Rome, their bombing and the destruction of the beloved medieval monastery Monte Cassino. As one wall daubed in white paint clearly explained: 'We do not want Germans or Americans. Let us weep in peace.'

By 27 February, the day before the German attacks were to be launched at Anzio, von Mackensen was frustrated. In spite of his best efforts the weather had upset his preparations as he could not move his armour off the road to its line of departure. Kesselring agreed to a twenty-four-hour postponement having received reports that water was pooling all over the battlefield and that the ground was so soft in some areas that tanks were immediately becoming immobilised. The Field Marshal's face was stern as he sat at his desk in Monte Soratte. He drummed his fingers on the shining wooden surface as he read von Mackensen's latest despatch about ammunition supplies. Westphal walked in looking harassed and clutching a sheaf of papers handed them to Kesselring saying, 'The Hermann Göring are reporting the loss of 12 tanks to artillery fire, 26th Panzer have not yet . . .'. 'Yes, I know,' Kesselring interjected, 'I have just spoken to Mackensen and he has explained the situation.' 'There is no way of stopping this?' said Westphal referring to the attack. Kesselring did not answer and returned to his reading. A feeling of despair was washing over the Field Marshal, and he knew that von Mackensen was similarly despondent. Neither man believed that Hitler's aims for the offensive were achievable – the attack was under-resourced, the troops exhausted and thoroughly deflated. The pair consoled themselves with the hope that a concerted effort could compress the beachhead and, in particular, destroy the large American salient that had formed in the east – but von Mackensen had his doubts about achieving even this. On the morning of the attack Kesselring received more desperate reports, and decided that he should make a visit to the front. When he got there the rain was still falling heavily. It was so bad that he was minded to postpone the attack again, but the commanders to which he had spoken emphasised the demoralising effect to Allied aircraft of low cloud. The offensive would begin that night.

During the afternoon the Germans released a smoke screen to conceal their final movements up to their line of departure. It mingled with the low cloud to produce a dense wall. 1st Sergeant Eric Montrose with 509th Parachute Infantry called it 'a mysterious and unsettling experience'. The Allied troops waited for the attack which they knew must surely follow. Hour after hour, they strained their ears for the sounds of an advancing enemy, expecting to be shelled at any moment. 'Doing nothing in those circumstances was almost as bad as fighting', explains Montrose, 'it was draining. Every little sound put you on your guard. I tried to tell myself that I would know soon enough when the enemy were coming, but I sat there in a hole filled with water waiting for the sound that would signal the beginning of my last few minutes of life on this earth.' The men had to wait until midnight before their anxious wait was ended when a concentrated German artillery bombardment fell on 3rd Division. Neither Truscott nor the new commander of 3rd Division, Brigadier General John W. O'Daniel, was surprised considering the intelligence that they had received. O'Daniel was a commander similar to Truscott in style, but very different in looks. He bore a large scar across his left cheek from a First World War bullet, and was stocky, and barrel chested. Although known by his nickname of 'Iron Mike', he looked and sounded just like a bull-dog. Just before dawn the Allied guns replied targeting German concentration areas and routes of advance just as the attack began. The Germans later stated that 66,500 rounds had been fired at them on 29 February. Rittmeister Edwin Wentz of the Hermann Göring Panzer Division went into battle that cold, wet late February morning, and says that the experience was unforgettable:

> I suppose that we had been given a fairly easy ride at Anzio up till now and were still relatively strong . . . But this battle carved us into little pieces. The response of the enemy artillery was fantastic. It made us all think that either the enemy knew that we were coming or had such a weight of guns that they could target anything that moved at short notice. Either way, it was not good for us. Rather than rushing on, as you might say, we limped into the attack.

Vital early momentum was taken out of General Traugott Herr's LXXVI Panzer Corps's attack as it began to move and it never recovered. Throughout the day the Germans tried to push on, but had little success. In the centre 7th and 15th Regiments immediately repelled the Germans and gave no ground. On the right, however, 504th Parachute Infantry Regiment had an intense tussle with 715th Division and two battalions of the 16th SS Panzer Grenadier Division. Ross Carter watched the attack develop from across the Mussolini Canal:

Four or five hundred yards away, marching steadily forward in four broad skirmish lines . . . came approximately nine hundred Nazis . . . My reaction was one of absolute amazement – and wounded pride. To think that the Nazis could have the brazen effrontery and suicidal stupidity to attack *us, us, us,* who feared nothing on earth or in hell . . . We began to pour devastating mortar, rifle and machine gun fire into their ranks, which they reformed without pause over the bodies of their dead and wounded . . . Hypnotized to murdering action, we all fired with deadly precision at the iron-nerved, obedient men walking across the field to the certain death of sheep following the leader to the slaughter pen . . . every soldier participating in that brave, foolhardy attack lay on that brown meadow shattered or ripped or decapitated or torn in half.

Resolute defence and accurate artillery fire again proved devastatingly successful. The Forward Observation officer with 2nd Battalion 504th Parachute Infantry Regiment was a man called Jordan. He had taken up a position in the second storey of a house – a vulnerable position but vital for observation. At one point, fearing that the Germans were about to make a minor tactical breakthrough in front of him, he called up the guns as Carter explains:

He grabbed the telephone and said 'In thirty seconds fire "Concentration 52" and throw the book at it.' Jordan dropped the phone, jumped out the back window and anteloped it to hell away, 'Concentration 52' being the house he was in. He barely got out before the artillery fire levelled it.

The attack here made no inroads into the 504th's line. On the American left flank, however, 362nd Infantry Division bolstered by tanks from 26th Panzer and the Hermann Göring Panzer Divisions did manage to overrun an outpost company of 509th Parachute

Battalion and Eric Montrose was taken prisoner. He recalls:

> Dawn was breaking and we could see the shapes of tanks with
> infantry running along side them. We tried to pick off the men and
> hoped that somebody else would deal with the tanks . . . I can
> remember one tank being taken out by a bazooka, and another by
> shell fire, but there were just too many for us to cope with. One of
> these brutes rolled right up to us and we lifted our hands. I was quite
> roughly handled by a huge German with fists like clubs . . . He had
> fight in his eyes and I was lucky that his officer was close behind
> him or else I think that I might have been shot.

This was a setback for the 509th, but it was not an incurable problem
for the hole was soon plugged as the German tanks began to struggle
with the very wet low lying ground and crumbling ditches. A counter-
attack was launched that night and by dawn on 1 March, all of the lost
ground had been successfully recaptured.

29 February was not a successful day for Traugott Herr. His formations had run themselves into the ground for very little territorial gain.
He had no answer to the power of the Allied artillery and, when the
weather cleared during the afternoon, Allied close air support. Even so,
Herr continued his attacks through the night and during the following
day, but he was only reinforcing defeat. By thrashing away at strong
defensive positions in open country the Germans were made to pay for
their folly. 1 March had been the bloodiest day of the Anzio battle so
far for the Germans who lost 202 killed, 707 wounded and 465 missing.
One of the missing was Edwin Wentz who explains:

> By the second day of the attack we had made very little ground, but
> were ordered forward again. I protested saying that out of my
> company there were only 20 men left. I was told that I could either
> let my men face the enemy commanderless, or I could lead from the

front as I should. There was no way that I would leave my men, even though I truly believed that it was suicide to continue, and so we set off again . . . At around 10 o'clock a barrage landed on our objective and we attacked. I had gone about two yards before I was knocked off my feet. A round hit me in the shoulder and left me on my back. I tried to get up but couldn't . . . All around me was chaos. I must have passed out for the next thing I remember was lying on the cold hard ground in the dark. I got slowly to my feet. I did not know which way to point – and was immediately taken prisoner by an American squad. I felt that it was a rather pathetic way to end my war – but I was grateful to still be alive and the Americans treated me extremely well.

In just two days the Germans had suffered casualties of nearly 2,500 men and at least 30 tanks without any worthwhile gains. It had been a mighty effort by the Americans and Truscott congratulated O'Daniel for the defensive stand that his division and the airborne units had taken. The VI Corps commander had found it a wrench to leave 3rd Division, but by dusk on 1 March the feeling that he had left the formation in safe hands had been confirmed. Von Mackensen knew that the attack had been comprehensively defeated but although his attacks began to wind down that evening, they continued fruitlessly for another two days, to appease Hitler. As if to underline the futility of further offensive action, the Allies launched a massive air strike on 2 March which targeted troop concentrations, roads and gun positions across the beachhead and into the rear areas. Lieutenant John Herbert RNVR witnessed the air armada from his destroyer:

There was flight after flight of four-engined Liberators and Fortresses with Spitfires diving and weaving above them. These fliers must have got a tremendous feeling of power as they roared north in their tight formations; but for the German in his slit trench it must have been a terrifying sensation as first he heard and then saw these planes coming in an invincible wave.

As Hitler again blamed the 'reprehensible actions' of a few commanders who had not 'driven home their advantage' for the failure of the latest offensive, Kesselring assessed the damage to Fourteenth Army. If *Fischfang* had destroyed the last vestiges of offensive fighting potential in one half of Fourteenth Army, then the other half had had it bludgeoned out of them in the latest attack. Herr's Corps had been cut down by VI Corps defences and crushed by the Allied bombers, and Schlemm's foray against the British salient in the west had suffered a similar fate. In spite of Hitler's protestations, Kesselring could no longer see any offensive potential in von Mackensen's command save patrolling and raiding. Indeed, with spring beckoning the Field Marshal feared an Allied breakthrough at Cassino and a breakout from the beachhead. He could do little more, therefore, than strengthen his defences to the best of his ability, and hold on to his ground. He had never expected to hold on to the Gustav Line much beyond the winter, and even if he had failed to destroy the Anzio beachhead he had managed to successfully contain it. Kesselring was clear in his own mind that Fourteenth Army needed to move onto a defensive footing, but he despatched Siegfried Westphal to the Berghof in Bavaria with the important task of convincing Hitler. He believed it necessary that somebody from the front explained in detail what the situation was, the relative strengths and weaknesses of the two sides, the impact of the weather and the terrain and the extreme limitations on Kesselring's options. The Führer had to be thoroughly – but carefully – disabused of the notion that Fourteenth Army could continue attacking indefinitely. Westphal had a number of meetings with Hitler, the last spanning three hours on 6 March. The envoy was expecting a tough time for he had heard the stories about the Führer's temper and now, as the Soviets were bombing the *Wolfschanze* and with an Allied invasion of France looming, he was expected to convince Hitler that his forces in Italy were only just clinging on to their ground. To his great surprise, and relief, Westphal found Hitler calm and measured in his response to what he was being told. 'At the end', wrote Westphal, 'the Führer said, with obvious emotion, that he knew well how great was the war-weariness which afflicted the people and also the Wehrmacht.' Keitel was amazed and remarked to Westphal as he left, 'You were lucky. If we old fools had said even half as much the Führer would have had us hanged.'

To test what Westphal had said, OKW demanded that twenty officers of all ranks be sent from the beachhead to account personally for recent failures. The group was led by General Walther Fries, commander of 29th Panzer Grenadier Division, and Hitler grilled them for two days. The party confirmed what Westphal had said and put the failure down to Allied air supremacy; the Allied artillery and their inability to commit heavy armoured forces at the critical time and place because of the soft ground. He objected to the idea that his troops' morale had been low, although he said that reinforcements had been insufficiently trained and that even the best troops would not be able to achieve success against massed artillery and air attacks. Only 10 per cent of German losses were due to infantry weapons, 15 per cent had been due to enemy bombing and 75 per cent to artillery – virtually identical figures generated during the First World War on the Western Front. Westphal's visit worked; there would be no more offensive operations at Anzio–Nettuno and Hitler instructed Kesselring to look to 1918 for lessons on what to do: 'remorseless pressure must be put on the enemy by the long-forgotten techniques of storm-regiments and artillery bombardments.' This was fine in theory, but as was often the case with Hitler's ideas, not in practice – Kesselring had neither the artillery ammunition nor the men to undertake such action. Instead he turned firmly towards tried and tested defensive methods – patrols, harassing probes and an ability to delay the enemy in a fighting withdrawal. He had already ordered a new defensive line to be constructed across the Italian peninsula in anticipation of a Fifth Army attack in the spring. Known as the Caesar Line, it stretched from the west coast near the mouth of the Tiber, through Cisterna to guard Route 7, around Valmontone to protect Route 6, behind Avezzano to protect the road leading to Rome from the north east, ending at Pescara on the east coast. It was to be completed no later than 20 April. When Tenth and Fourteenth Armies were forced to withdraw, then they would fight side by side in the Caesar Line and delay the fall of Rome. When the time came, Rome would fall and his two Armies would then withdraw north in an organised manner to another defensive line. Kesselring was on his guard against anything that would lead to the destruction of Tenth and Fourteenth Armies south of Rome. He immediately began to reorganise his forces: 26th Panzer and 29th Panzer Grenadier Divisions were moved into general reserve between the Gustav and Anzio fronts and the Hermann Göring Panzer Division was pulled back to rest near Leghorn to cover the continued threat to the area of another possible Allied landing. The divisions at Anzio were thinned out to 4th Parachute Division, 65th Infantry Division, 3rd Panzer Grenadier Division, 362nd Infantry Division and 715th Infantry Division. Von Mackensen continued to place a defensive emphasis on the Via Anziate at the expense of other areas, particularly the road to Cisterna.

Meanwhile, Alexander was conducting his own assessment of prospects for the front in early March. He firmly believed that the Germans were no longer capable of major offensive action at Anzio, but also recognised that until VI Corps had regrouped, reinforced and reorganised, they were similarly impotent. Even so, Fifteenth Army Group was already developing plans for a spring offensive in the expectation that the corps, and the wider Fifth Army, would be in a position to launch a strong attack. During late February Lieutenant General John Harding, Alexander's Chief of Staff, had prepared an appreciation upon which future plans would be based. In it he advocated a renewed offensive in Italy to pin the Germans in the Mediterranean during Operation Overlord, and to put Kesselring's Armies under such pressure that they would be required to draw formations from France and the Eastern Front to stop a rout. These were exactly the sort of proposals that Churchill wanted. The Prime Minister retained his passion for the Italian front, albeit recognising that his hopes of making Overlord redundant had been dashed, and announced to the House of Commons on 22 February that 'a large second front in Italy is not unwelcome to the Allies. We must fight the Germans somewhere.' He referred obliquely to Overlord saying, 'This wearing battle in Italy occupies troops who could not be employed in other great operations, and it is an effective prelude to them.' To Churchill, this was the saving grace of Operation Shingle – the fighting at Anzio had forced a German reaction which had weakened their forces on other fronts. In a telegram to Field Marshal Jan Smuts, the President of South Africa, on 27 February he wrote:

> Naturally I am very disappointed at what has appeared to be the frittering away of a brilliant opening in which both fortune and design had played their part. I do not in any way however repent of what has been done. As a result the Germans have now transferred into the south of Italy at least eight more divisions, so that in all there are eighteen south of Rome. It is vital to the success of 'Overlord' that we keep away from that theatre and hold elsewhere as many German divisions as possible, and hard fighting in Italy throughout the spring will provide for the main operation a perfect prelude and accompaniment.

Preparations for an Allied spring offensive began just as soon as the German attacks had petered out in early March. VI Corps was in position though it required some nurturing, but the rest of Fifth Army at the Gustav Line still needed to attain a base from which it could make an attack towards Rome. Cassino was proving extremely stubborn, but Alexander and Clark had agreed that the town was the key to the German defences and must be seized at all costs. On 15 March after a raid by 500 bombers and a three and a half hour artillery bombardment, General Freyberg's New Zealand Corps launched a new ground attack. The Indian Division managed to make some progress up to the ancient monastery, but in the rubble of the town below the New Zealanders were firmly repelled. By 23 March, the Third Battle of Cassino was over, and the road to Rome remained stubbornly closed. In the Anzio beachhead and on the Gustav Line there was exhaustion. The spring would bring new opportunities – but first there was stalemate. Winston Churchill was bitterly disappointed at how Operation Shingle had been handled and on 3 March, whilst at Chequers he summed up his feelings in one sentence to Air Marshal Coningham: 'I thought we should fling a wild-cat ashore and all we got was an old stranded whale on the beach.'

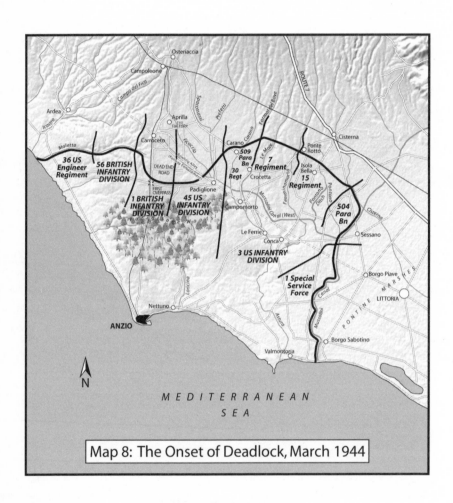

Map 8: The Onset of Deadlock, March 1944

CHAPTER 8

Entrenchment

(Mid-March–10 May)

Because the light was good for typing the American war correspondent Ernie Pyle had taken the room at the top of a four-storey villa at the water's edge in Anzio. Pyle shared the building with thirty other journalists and the Fifth Army Public Relations Staff, and everybody had become superstitious about mentioning that the building had never been hit by a bomb or shell. At seven o'clock on a sunny morning in mid-March, Pyle was woken by the sound of brisk anti-aircraft fire and the nasal whine of German Dorniers. Dressed in his underwear, a pair of slippers and a steel helmet, he casually walked over to the window to investigate. It exploded in his face, the force picking him up and throwing him violently into the middle of the room. Debris flew after him: glass, wood, brick and mortar. Pyle quickly shuffled to the corner where, as he later wrote, he 'squatted down and just cowered' as the bombs exploded. Realising that he had lost his helmet in the blast, he covered his bald head with his hands. Peering over his forearms he saw that an entire wall had collapsed on to his bed. Ernie Pyle's world had buckled around him:

The wooden doors were ripped off their hinges and crashed into the room. Another wall started to tumble, but caught partway down. The French doors leading to the balcony blew out and one of my chairs was upended through the open door . . . I had several unfinished dispatches lying on my table and the continuing blasts scattered them helter-skelter over the room, and holes were punched in the paper.

The whole episode had lasted mere seconds, but long enough for Pyle to believe that he had met his doom. Then, just as suddenly, it ended. As dust billowed around him, he remained motionless, allowing a trickle of blood to drip off his chin. The villa had been destroyed, but he had only suffered a tiny cut on his cheek and nobody else in the building had been badly injured. As he recovered what he could from the shattered room, Pyle reflected on his good fortune to still be alive. He did not think that the incident had affected him too badly until that afternoon when he went to take his comb out of his shirt pocket, but instead took his handkerchief out of his hip pocket and tried to comb his hair with it.

By the early spring of 1944, both Anzio and Nettuno had been badly damaged by German artillery and air raids. Most mornings revealed another long, narrow street clogged with the rubble of buildings that, in many cases, had been hit several times before. John Herbert (son of the First World War poet A.P. Herbert) then the Captain of HMS *Grenville*, later recalled of Anzio:

The buildings near the harbour resemble a wasp's nest that had been ravaged. Every window had been shattered, the walls chipped and pock-marked by shell-splinters and the roofs transformed into skeletons of splintered boarding. All that was left of where there had been a direct hit was the jagged outline of four walls with a confusion of bricks in its midst. Seen through our glass from seaward, the whole waterfront had a very moth eaten look about it.

The home to numerous headquarters and organisations, Anzio and Nettuno were anchors that fixed VI Corps to the coast and were a gateway to the beachhead. They were also obvious targets and as such their inhabitants became adept at the 'Anzio Shuffle', which meant diving for cover and covering your head. The towns were so frequently shelled that troops believed them to be only about as safe as the front line. Ross Carter of the 504th Parachute Infantry Regiment explained:

> On our infrequent trips to the rear to take a shower we were always in a sweat to get back to the front line. We felt safer up there, where we had to endure only machine guns, machine pistols, rifle, mortar, small antitank gun, 75, 105, 88 and occasional 150 and 170 mm fire. Infantry on the front line offered targets that were too scattered to be worth throwing many extremely heavy shells.

Everybody in the beachhead was within the range of the German heavy artillery that maintained excellent observation from the Alban Hills. Any obvious movement was likely to bring down artillery fire. As a consequence, the troops did not relish visits from the likes of Alan Whicker's Army Photographic Unit, of Mark Clark's massive entourage or, as one GI described Harold Alexander, 'the guy in the Red Hat'. Shipping was sometimes so accurately targeted that, as John Herbert wrote, the shells followed the ships 'in a most suspicious manner' making him wonder 'whether there was someone hidden in the town observing the fall of shot for the enemy, and informing them of the necessary corrections.' Nowhere was safe. VI Corps were, as one soldier observed succinctly, 'Like bacteria in a bottle.' The Germans possessed a formidable array of long-range artillery, the most famous being two railway guns dubbed 'Anzio Annie' and the 'Anzio Express' that could fire a 280-mm shell up to 36 miles. The two monstrous Krupp manufactured weapons had arrived at the front during the first week in February, to be secreted in the Alban Hills' tunnels. Wynford

Vaughan-Thomas described the sound of one of their shells:

> First you heard a distant, almost discreet cough, away behind the
> enemy lines, then a slight pause, during which you knew the shell
> was on its way. Fear wound up your guts as if they were on a fisher-
> man's reel. Then came the sickening crump of the explosion and the
> sound echoed away like a tube train pulling out of the station down
> a long, black tunnel.

Those who lived and worked in the towns got used to the constant
bombardment, much to the *chagrin* of occasional visitors such as
Corporal Ron Rhodes. Rhodes went into Anzio to see the Dental
Officer complaining of toothache:

> He gave me an injection and started to drill when suddenly we heard
> the shells whistling overhead near us. They were getting nearer and
> nearer, he kept drilling with his right hand, he reached for his own
> steel helmet, then reached under the chair and put my helmet on,
> with his left. 'Oh, well! Let's finish off'. He put some filling in and
> then said, 'Now let's bugger off!'

To protect themselves from the worst that the enemy and the weather
could throw at them, the inhabitants of the beachhead tried to make
themselves safe and comfortable. There was a skill to making a good
'dug-out', as the British called them. They had to be deep enough, at
least seven feet deep – to protect against a 150-mm shell, and with a
sturdy metal or wooden roof covered with a deep layer of soil. These
'lids', as they were called, also protected the inhabitants from the
shrapnel of air bursts. Quartermaster Sergeant John Swain's dugout
was topped off with a quarry wagon. As soon as he arrived at Anzio
he started to dig his new home with a friend: 'We went down six feet',
he remembers, 'and shuttered up the sides with odd pieces of wood in

the area, making ourselves very comfortable. We had two bunks, and an area at one end where we could brew up. It was great.' Some dugouts were better than others. One American private from 3rd Division constructed a shelter that was shallow and leaked:

> The bottom was squashy. It wasn't a very big hole, about chest deep. The hole got about six inches of water, and you couldn't do anything but try to bale it out with your helmet. We wrapped shelter halves and blankets around us but they didn't do much good. They got soaked with rain and then you sat on a piece of wood or something and shivered and cussed . . . You couldn't get out of the hole once the sun came up, or even show the top of your head . . . Jerry threw in a lot of artillery and mortars. The best thing to do was to pull in your head and pray.

One Irish Guards officer with imagination used an umbrella to keep him dry. 'Major Young's "brolly"', the Irish Guards' historian reports, 'was the envy of all and kept him snug and dry. He dug a small deep hole and lowered himself carefully into it, pulling his umbrella down on top of it, like a big, black mushroom.' The officer's device would not have provided any protection from shrapnel and shell fragments, but he was unlikely to be buried alive. Corporal Ron Rhodes dug in with a companion, Nick, and surveyed his work: 'It looked like a bloody grave, in fact it nearly was a bit later . . . we put doors on the top of the pit and put some sandbags on top to try and stop the rain peeing in, but it didn't.' One night Rhodes heard the retort of 'Anzio Annie':

> Subconsciously I started to count but I got to about twelve seconds when there was a hell of a bang and a bright flash. The next thing I remember was that the dug-out fell in on us. It happened so fast we were both buried in the sand, the weight of the wet sand on my

body was tremendous. I could see a small hole above my head, sand was coming through like an egg-timer, it was building up at the bottom of my chin. I couldn't move a muscle, the sand came up to my bottom lip. Somehow, I didn't panic, I thought, 'This is it. I'm not lucky this time.' I told myself I could hold my breath for two minutes then that would be it. I was thinking about my darling wife Joyce, how would she be told, would they find my last letter to her? Suddenly, the small hole widened and I saw a hand scraping away the sand like mad then a voice shouted, 'Ron is alive! Come on, dig like bloody hell!' The lads got me out and laid me on a stretcher. They then went back for Nick. Unfortunately he was dead. He had a big piece of shrapnel sticking through his neck. Poor Nick. I don't think he suffered. It was a quick death.

Artillery shells were not the only long-range threat to the beachhead. As Ernie Pyle's brush with death revealed, the depleted Luftwaffe had retained some potency. By the spring of 1944 the Germans had less than one tenth of the 4,500 operational aircraft available to the Allies in Italy – but the Luftwaffe air raids continued. In addition to the fighter patrols and barrage balloons, an impressive collection of anti-aircraft guns provided considerable firepower, where smoke generators produced artificial fogs. The raids continued to be most likely after dark, but the Germans came at all times of the day as well as dropping high explosives and anti-personnel bombs. On occasion raids were synchronised with attacks by the German navy which remained troublesome. Lieutenant Geoffrey Dormer was sweeping for floating mines aboard HMS *Hornpipe*, and noted in his diary on 12 February: 'We have just sunk a mine, this time in 15 minutes with 150 rounds of armoured piercing, from 6 rifles.' John Herbert in HMS *Grenville*, meanwhile, patrolled the waters 'on the look out for any E-boats or U-boats that might try and attack the anchorage'. E-boats launched a few successful torpedo raids, but most were foiled. Their 'human torpedoes' were a complete failure. These attacks in which a pilot rode on one torpedo with another slung underneath which he would launch were notoriously unreliable and claimed no victims. Throughout the battle the Germans failed to break VI Corps's lifeline to Fifteenth Army Group, and though there were intermittent losses of shipping, there were never any supply shortages. 500,000 tons of supplies were landed during the battle, and by March 1944 Anzio had emerged as the fourth largest port in the world.

Through Anzio harbour came not only resupplies, but also the means with which to reinforce and relieve VI Corps. Amongst the new formations arriving was Major General Charles W. Ryder's 34th US Division which replaced the 504th Parachute Infantry Regiment, 509th Parachute battalion and the Rangers; 18th Brigade of 1st British Armoured Division which relieved the Guards Brigade, and Major General P.G.S. Gregson – Ellis's 5th British Division which took over from 56th Division. Lieutenant M.W.L. Wood, a gunner in 5th Division, had a troubled voyage from the Bay of Naples:

> Much advance publicity of the horrors of Anzio had reached us on the Garigliano, and much sympathy was felt for our neighbours, 56th Division, when they were moved there. We little thought that it would be us, who less than a month later, would be sent to relieve the battered remains of that division.

Lucian Truscott welcomed the arrival of new formations even though there was no time to ease them into the fighting. However, the individual troop replacements (which during March alone had totalled 14,000 men) used to fill the depleted ranks of units already in the beachhead did cause some difficulties. Trying to get the correct mixture of old heads and new bodies in units led to men being shuffled along at an unedifying pace. The issue prompted General Penney to write to Alexander in mid-March:

our first problem is the literal rebirth of units with raw, inexperienced officers and men often already bewildered by their continual reposting to a succession of units . . . I dare say Gerald Templer will have told you of the driver who has been in 16 units.

Forewarned with horror stories about the fighting in the beachhead by naval personnel, a replacement would often arrive at Anzio under shell-fire. They would be swiftly disembarked to be greeted by Military Policemen hurrying them along to assembly points. The men passed quickly through the town, gawping at the broken buildings, beginning to think that everything that they had been told about the place was true. When they arrived at the 'Reception Centre', unsentimentally situated just outside the town between the cemetery and the field hospital, the men would be assigned to a unit. It was not uncommon for a soldier to be placed in an unfamiliar outfit to perform an unfamiliar task. Private David Cohen had been trained as an airborne signaller, but as soon as he got to the beachhead he was told by a sergeant major: 'Son, you ain't flyin' nowhere, you ain't jumpin' on nothin' and you ain't radioing nobody. You are now a rifleman in the best division in the United States Army.' He joined 3rd Division and stayed there for the rest of the war. From the Reception Centre the men marched or were transported to their new unit. The American war correspondent Homer Bigart wrote of one such journey in a piece published in the *Herald Tribune*:

The truckload of replacements turned off the black-surfaced road and went bounding along a muddy track to the battalion bivouac . . . They had seen dead cows and sheep beside the road and they were crouching down to the floor of the truck when the first shells came in, rattling like a runaway coal truck . . . We knew the truck would draw fire, for we had been on road before . . . It was one of those grim March days that hold no hope of spring . . . On such a day you

The Via Anziate on 25 January from the Flyover looking north towards the Alban Hills. The Factory can be seen beyond the house on the right. IWM NA11525

A disabled German Marder III self-propelled anti-tank gun (Sd Kfz 138) on the Anzio battlefield. It is armed with a 75-mm gun and a 7.62-mm machine gun. IWM NA15570

Major General Lucian Truscott confers with
Alexander in the back streets of Anzio during April.
IWM NA14593

Lucian Truscott, a loyal soldier and
a gritty general. IWM NYP47849

A soldier of 3rd US Infantry Division
shares his rations with an Italian boy.
US NATIONAL ARCHIVES

Colonel William O. Darby during a
break in the Rangers' training at
Achnacarry, Scotland in July 1942.
US NATIONAL ARCHIVES

Anglo-American
fraternisation at Anzio.
IWM NA11967

A typical American foxhole
which provided some
protection from the German
artillery and the elements.
IWM NA12625

Men of 46th Battalion
Royal Tank Regiment at the
funeral of Lance Sergeant
Leonard Ottewell. Thirty-
two-year-old Ottewell died
of wounds on 27 January.
IWM NA11693

War correspondents working in the spring sunshine on the balcony of an Anzio villa. IWM NA13321

The notorious 'wadi country'. Loathed by the Allies and the Germans alike. IWM NA14753

A little relaxation in the beachhead. Note that many of those pictured continue to wear their helmets as such activities were not exempt from German artillery bombardments. IWM NA14344

An aerial view of Cisterna after its capture. Along with Cassino, it was one of
the most heavily bombed and shelled towns in Italy. IWM C4397

An American M5A1 'Stuart'
light tank passes a British
Bren gun carrier on the road
to Rome at the end of May.
IWM NA16004

German prisoners of war
during the breakout phase of
the battle being verbally abused
by a local. IWM NA15822

'It's a great day for Fifth Army.' Mark Clark poses near the village of Borgo Grappa in one of the photographs telegraphed around the world on 25 May 1944. IWM NA15395

British troops from the beachhead 'link up' with American troops at Borgo Grappa. IWM NA15399

Defending Route 6.
A German parachutist with the
excellent MG-42 and an egg
grenade. BUNDESARCHIV

Clark and Major General Geoffrey
T. Keyes pose under the 'Roma'
city limits sign, complete with
recent bullet hole, on 4 June.
IWM TA26381

Germans fighting
in the suburbs of
Rome on 4 June.
BUNDESARCHIV

A 3rd US Infantry Division soldier is greeted by rather war-weary Romans on 5 June. IWM NA15931

Sergeant R.H. Holden drives Mark Clark through Rome on 5 June with the Fifth Army Chief of Staff, Major General Alfred M. Gruenther, sitting smiling behind. IWM NA15941

Alan Whicker's photograph of Mark Clark, General Geoffrey Keyes and Lucian Truscott mounting the steps of the Capitol in Rome. IWM NA15901

expect death more than on bright days . . . The shells came down in pairs, landing just to the right of the truck . . . At the bivouac the men climbed down and stood on shaky pins. A platoon sergeant looked over them. There is a fiction that front-line sergeants are ruthless butchers who send recruits out on hopeless missions before they have been properly introduced. But it is the sergeant who gets it in this war . . . The sergeant saw that they were nervous, and told them to go ahead and dig themselves in for the night.

Replacements, many as young as eighteen, hung on the veterans' every word in the hope of surviving long enough to pass on the benefit of their experience. In a typically lucid assessment Alan Moorehead saw the reactions of these new men who had to try and fit into a closely bonded fighting family:

They were afraid of the unknown, the mystery represented by the front line. This you could read clearly enough in the dread in their faces. It is a dread of going up to the abyss and looking over into the unknown, and of risking the chance of falling over into the unknown . . . Then later when you see the man return safely he appears to have gained in stature. He has been to the edge and looked over and come away. There is a tide of happiness as he takes back his life and all the things he hopes to do with it.

Veterans often abhorred the responsibility of having to educate the newcomers. One Sergeant told Ernie Pyle, 'I know it ain't my fault that they get killed . . . and I do the best I can for them. But I've got so I feel like it's me killin' 'em instead of the Germans. I've got so I feel like a murderer. I hate to look at them when the new ones come in.' Sometimes the new men mistook the natural reticence of veterans to become too friendly with replacements as contempt for them. Ross Carter wrote of them:

We pitied the scared, bewildered, shy, eager youngsters who acted awestruck around us old boys. We felt sad when it became our duty to lead them into battle, because a large percentage got killed before they learned how to woo the narrow percentage of safety accorded by lady luck to discerning and sagacious warriors. They would die in the damnedest of ways: One would trip over a mine and get a leg blown off; another would shoot himself or get accidentally shot; a third would let his foxhole cave in and smother him. And in the first battle they usually died in heaps.

Many were to die without those around them even knowing their names.

Within weeks Anzio had gained a reputation for being one of the most dangerous places on earth. Troops arrived not expecting ever to leave. Alan Whicker later wrote: 'The Anzio Experience has remained with me, mainly because I never expected to live through it.' Like Ypres on the Western Front during the First World War the beachhead quickly became notorious and there were those who craved a battlefield tour. To the Americans these people were known as 'Gadabouts', to the British as 'Swanners', and they included Senators, Members of Parliament, journalists and military observers. There was even a 25-pound gun just outside Anzio for visitors to fire. They were shown shell holes, collapsed buildings, a headquarters, and the cemeteries. If a shell exploded somewhere near them it allowed them to depart fulfilled with the 'Anzio Experience' and plenty of good stories for their newspapers or dinner parties. One British officer, despatched by the War Office on a deeply obscure mission, wrote of his brief visit to the beachhead on his return to London:

Just returned from Anzio. What a place! All bombs and brick dust. We were immediately issued with tin hats and were given a tour of some of the rear area. We witnessed some German dive bombers going about their work a few miles off at the front and could see smoke billowing up soon after. A couple of shells landed on the town whilst we were elsewhere . . . It rained during the afternoon, and the water collected in great pools within minutes . . . . . . There is a busy atmosphere. The harbour is hectic and trucks dash about on their errands. Troops march quickly to their destinations. The Military Police do not allow any loitering . . . Five hours was four and a half hours too long for me. We did not stay the night – thank the Lord – and saw enough to make us wonder what on earth we are doing there. We are sitting in a marsh under constant artillery attack.

There was to be a good deal of 'sitting' during this period for, whilst there were some set piece battles, they were to be the exception. The period of stalemate that lasted from early March to the middle of May, was a time of rebuilding to provide the Allies with the wherewithal to attack and the Germans to defend. The men quickly developed a routine. In conditions that more resembled the trench warfare of the First World War, they endured persistent artillery bombardments, boredom, and the elements. Daytime was the time of work for troops in the rear area, but in the front line it was a time to sleep, maintain weapons, and write letters home. At the front there was little water with most needed for drinking. Personal hygiene was a low priority, with the men wearing the same clothing for weeks and washing only when they could. Raymond Fort, an infantryman in 5th Division explains:

We got to change our underwear very rarely. In fact, we were full of lice at times. We just couldn't keep clean . . . The only time we got some respite was when we went back to our rear area because that was where we had our headquarters and there was a camp and it was near the sea. So we used to get in the sea and that was about the only time we could wash really. We only got a hot shower once, and that was only by mobile shower . . . It wasn't very pleasant, but it didn't bother me because I was more bothered about surviving than anything else . . . We did get a change of clothing every now and again and that was very nice, and they used to give us delousing powder and we had to take our underwear off because it was usually wool . . . Although we wore long Johns and vests and we used to turn the vests inside out and spread them on your knee and you used to go along the seams with this powder to get rid of the lice.

The men learned to improvise, making paraffin lamps out of empty tins, lighters out of cartridge cases and using their helmets for a multitude of purposes. Ray McAllister of 45th Division recalls:

We used our helmets for everything. I ate out of mine when we got the occasional hot chow. When we had time to shave I shaved from mine. We heated water in it for a bath and, yes, when we were pinned down in a foxhole, we went to the john in it and dumped it over the side of the foxhole during a lull in the fighting.

When conditions allowed hot food was brought up to the front, but the troops came to rely on prepacked rations which, if required, could be heated on little stoves. The British survived on bully beef, Maconachie's stew and 'hard tack' – nutritious biscuits which caused problems for those with false teeth. The Americans had K rations or 'lights' – biscuits, dehydrated coffee, hard candy – and C-rations or 'heavies' consisting of cans of meat with potato, beans or vegetable stew. The men quickly tired of the same food, particularly as it was not unknown for them to have the same meal three times a day for weeks, and looked around them for some variety. Some wrote home asking for curry powder or other spices to enliven their dishes, whilst others used whatever they could find on the battlefield. On one occasion Ross Carter and his squad dined on a cow that had been killed by shell fire only to cut their gums on the shell fragments. Harmon himself slithered on his belly across open terrain with a shotgun to raid a pheasant farm close to the German lines. On one frosty evening in March there was a row between adjacent British and American troops over which of them shot a sheep that had wandered across No Man's Land. 'It was remarkable', recalls British Private Jimmy Reed, 'we shot the beast on the previous evening and one of our blokes went out to retrieve it after dark. He crawled out fine, but after a few minutes we could hear raised whispers. It turns out that an American party were trying to steal our mutton and claiming that the sheep was their bag!' Perceptions of one's ally tended to be worst amongst those that had no contact. One British soldier declared:

> We stayed away from the Americans. We were on the same beachhead, but worlds apart, never the twain shall meet. Different rations, different weapons, different ammunition, different tactics – just different. We never mixed. There were more Americans than British, and they suffered more casualties. One British soldier could achieve the same as ten Americans. They were useless.

Americans voiced similar opinions about the British:

> We had nothing to do with the British and wanted nothing to do with them. They were stuck up, too inflexible. They would make a mistake and then make it ten more times before changing how they did things. We Americans learned much more quickly and were better soldiers for it.

However, relations quickly improved between the two units squabbling over the sheep as they had to work closely together. Jimmy Reed recalls, 'They were a good bunch. Fine soldiers, and good men. At first we didn't want them on our flank, but we soon came to rely on them.' Bill

Lewis, a signaller in a Royal Air Force team which directed close air support operations, noted perceptively: 'The Americans were brash, but jovial and we were a little stand-offish, but amenable. We were different, but doing the same job and it was not difficult to work with mutual toleration. From this respect grew, and then friendship.' Ron Rhodes became friendly with an American soldier who liked to swap food and drink:

> The Yank came in one day and asked if we had any beer, I said sure, he could have my two bottles of Black Horse beer which we managed to scrounge, I didn't drink . . . He was very grateful and said that they only got sent whisky from American Red Cross parcels . . . The next day he brought me a brand new pipe, the Sherlock Holmes type, and six pearl-handled cut-throat razors. They were marvellous.

A bottle of beer or a good shave could make all the difference to troops seeking a little comfort. Trapped in a highly dangerous environment with little to look forward to, a great deal could be attained from very little. It was therefore, not uncommon for 'live and let live' agreements to develop locally, as the German Corporal Joachim Liebschner describes:

> In the evenings we could hear Tommy and we used to shout to each other . . . He would say 'Keep quiet Jerry, we're trying to sleep!' We knew people by names, some of our positions were only 30, 40, 50 yards from the enemy . . . Whatever food was brought forward at dusk and the clanking of the mess tins meant Tommy thought something was going on and we started shooting at each other. But as soon as you started that racket, you fired away with rifles, machine guns, grenade throwers, you didn't get anything to eat because the people that carried the food wouldn't come forward.

Then when Tommy got his rations, we fired on him, and so eventually it became quite obvious that it was idiotic and if we carried on like this we were never going to get anything to eat so eventually there was an unwritten law that if you heard clanking of mess tins, you stopped shooting. And for the three or four weeks we lived there, the war finished at dusk because feeding took place.

Because these were 'unwritten rules', it was sometimes the case that they were accidentally flouted. Lieutenant F. Eugene Liggett, a Forward Observation Officer with 157th Regiment, admits:

On Easter Sunday I was up with the infantry in their trenches next to no-man's land. The Germans on their side of it, about 300 feet away. A rather unusual thing happened. The Germans were not shooting at us, and they were acting a little strange in that they were crawling back and forth to men in other trenches or holes. Before we knew what they were doing, we shot several of them with rifles. After capturing one or two, they told us what was happening and we quit shooting them. Because it was Easter Sunday, they were given a liquor ration and orders not to shoot at us.

Some deliberately broke the 'rules', however, and nearly paid the price: Robert Dodge of 15th Regiment, 3rd Division says:

I remember a BAR (Browning Automatic Rifle) man telling me of when he watched a place where Jerries would go to relieve themselves, thinking they were in defilade (protected). This BAR man said it wasn't worthwhile to fire on one man, as he would have to change his position. He happened to see three guys there talking, smoking, and taking care of other needs; he fired, and believes he got two of them. He then grabbed his BAR and rolled into the ditch. That night he dug a new hole; his old one had been obliterated.

Sometimes the local arrangements went as far as meetings between the combatants to swap cigarettes, photographs and stories, but it was not necessarily the case that a new battalion in the line would maintain a convention. The Irish Guards made one German very unhappy when he approached them soon after the battalion had entered the line and was immediately taken prisoner. The Irish Guards historian wrote:

> The German was most indignant; he had come, he explained, on the usual errand, to exchange brandy for tinned meat. Sergeant-Major Pestell explained that the trade agreement was cancelled 'as from now'. The German spent an unhappy day digging Major G. Fitzgerald's trench and asking at intervals why Irishmen were in Italy at all. The failure of their agent's mission clearly annoyed his colleagues, for soon afterward they started lobbing mortar bombs into the gully.

But it often didn't take long for violence to return to a sector. It seemed to be the Anzio beachhead's natural state. In such circumstances the men did what they could to bring a little extra comfort to their lives by evading tiresome orders and scrounging. 'When we were sent to the stores for something', recalls Corporal Bernie Kirchoff 3rd Division, 'we'd make the most of it – have a smoke, visit some friends – and then return saying the Quartermaster didn't have whatever it was we'd been sent to find. When we did go to the stores, we'd always try to get a little something from somebody there to ease our suffering. Another pair of socks, a book of pin-ups, a bottle of whiskey. All could be found if you knew where to go.' The initiative that some soldiers showed was remarkable. Harmon could not understand why the lights in his headquarters were getting dimmer and asked a technician to investigate. He reported back the following day that 250 men had tapped lines into his electricity supply to light their shelters. As Truscott said, 'Life was tense as it always is when men are close to death. But we learnt how to survive.' But many men involved in the business of killing in the front line became changed men, dehumanised by their environment and cruel circumstances. At first a man might fight it, such as Raleigh Trevelyan did when he first entered the line. He wrote to his brother:

My first shock was the sight of no less than eight dead Jerries in various stages of decomposition. They were too far gone to be removed. Anyway perhaps they were a useful deterrent to any more hostile patrols. But the smell of them – and the smell of human shit and empty tins – was atrocious. Eventually I got used to these bundles with wax faces. People had been looting their wallets, and photographs were scattered around. I picked up a photograph but was ashamed to pinch it, and couldn't even take a postcard of Romulus and Remus.

Trevelyan had been ashamed to take anything from a corpse but others, such as Norman Mohar, who had felt the same way just weeks before soon changed. Coming across four dead Germans he says, 'I looked in their pockets. I took a few badges and a belt buckle, some pictures and postcards.' Others found themselves at ease in surroundings that prior to Anzio had been unimaginable. Ray McAllister recalls:

Dog tired and overworked, ministering to both American and German wounded, I needed a drink and a bit of food, I had a can of C-ration cheese but no water. I walked to a nearby creek and dipped up a canteen cup of water. There was a dead German bleeding into the water about 20 feet away and another who had been dead long enough to be completely covered with maggots, also a few feet away. I ate the cheese with a hand covered with dried blood, sitting on the body of yet a third dead German, totally insensible to the carnage around me.

For some the fighting brutalised them in such fundamental ways that they carried out heinous crimes. One American sergeant candidly testified that:

> Looking back to Anzio, I can hardly believe that it was me. The battle made people do things that they would never think of doing under normal conditions. But I have had to live with terrible memories of certain things that I did. Killing a German in battle, that was nothing, I must have killed dozens, but once I took some prisoners, disarmed them, put them in a shell hole and shot them. Nobody reprimanded me, no one ever mentioned it again, although many people saw me do it. But it was wrong. Wrong not only because I took the lives of unarmed men, but wrong as it sent out the wrong message to my men. Once you have crossed that boundary, you are capable of anything . . . Two weeks later we were having 'difficulties' with our platoon commander. He led a patrol one night and we did not encounter the enemy – but he never returned.

After dark the beachhead came alive. It was during this time that work was carried out on defences, units reinforced and relieved, supplies brought forward. This was therefore the time for enemy air raids, mortar attacks, artillery bombardments and patrols. For patrols to seize a prisoner, obtain information about enemy positions, or to simply act as a deterrent gave the truth to John Herbert's belief that the Anzio experience during this period was: 'nothing very spectacular . . . mixed with periods of intense excitement, when all hands had to be awake and on their toes.' The troops did not like having to carry out patrols, but commanders believed that they were helpful in maintaining an 'offensive spirit' and honed skills. They certainly kept the enemy off balance. Indeed, before the 504th Parachute Infantry Regiment left Anzio, a diary was found on a dead German officer facing the unit which stated: 'American parachutists – devils in baggy pants – are less than 100 meters from my outpost line. I can't sleep at night; they pop up from nowhere and we never know when or how they strike next. Seems like the black-hearted devils are everywhere . . .' The Germans also feared the First Special Service Force, specialists in patrols and raiding. With their motto 'Killing is our Business', at times it seemed that Brigadier General Robert T. Frederick's men were fighting their own private war. Known to the enemy as 'The Devil's Brigade', these 'unemotional cutthroats' infiltrated their lines and conducted their business with stealthy efficiency. One German wrote in his diary, 'They are all around us every time we come into the line, and we never hear them come.' They also had a knack for returning laden with alcohol, food and souvenirs. It has been claimed that some even found time for local girls behind the enemy lines. Frederick was an excellent commander of a difficult group of men, many of whom had criminal records, or were rejects and misfits from other units. These men completed the usual three-month parachute training in six days. Frederick completed his first jump in his bedroom slippers after ten minutes' instruction.

Patrols would start their preparations at dusk, a time when many in the front line were beginning to wonder who among them would survive the night. Joachim Liebschner who fought in the 'wadi country' says:

At the beginning we used to go out at midnight or early morning, ten of us, we'd spy out where Tommy was lying and we'd choose the one that was most forward and isolated because we thought that we could grab him.

Liebschner's patrols targeted Raleigh Trevelyan's battalion, which led the British officer to write:

Dusk, and these awful nights. A Jerry patrol slipped behind one of my forward sections and nabbed a corporal. We were very uneasy. I'm determined we shall be offensive from now on, and I'm laying ambushes, snipers everywhere, booby-trapping the wire. My knees are sore from crawling.

Patrols were tense affairs, which had to be carefully prepared in order to avoid friendly fire incidents as well as the enemy. Those that survived soon picked up the skills, which then made them invaluable to further nighttime forays. Private Fred Mason describes one patrol which took place in March near the Flyover:

It was a carefully planned fighting patrol, and our orders were to move silently and swiftly through the night, attack a position and return by first light. The patrol consisted of one officer, one sergeant, one corporal and nine other ranks . . . I checked my equipment. 50 rounds of ammo, rifle ready and loaded with ten rounds, one of which was in the spout, two hand grenades, one in each pouch . . . I was beginning to tremble now, not only with cold, and I am not afraid to admit it, with fear . . . We crept through a hole in our wire and into No Man's Land. From now on we had to crawl on our stomachs. The ground was hard and cold . . . There was a slight breeze now and the bushes round about were beginning to sway. We cursed this for everything that moved now became an enemy in our minds.

It took an hour before Mason and the patrol were within 200 yards of the enemy front line. At this point the officer went to investigate some enemy outpost, that they did not know about:

The noise of our leader crawling away faded out and we lay, waiting for the unmistakable snarl of a German machine gun, or perhaps a grenade. But there was only the breeze, our breathing, and yes, my heart was thumping, and seemed to be hitting the hard ground and bouncing back . . . When the officer returned he said that the positions were empty but for a couple of dead Germans. He cursed the waste of time, but we couldn't help but admire the courage of this man. I for one, felt here was a man whom it was safe to be with.

Crawling up to a German position Mason's trepidation had been replaced by aggression:

> The officer spotted a figure. 'This is it', I thought, and strange to say, the fear had gone and I was ready to kill or be killed . . . A phosphorus grenade was thrown at the shape and it bust and quickly started to flare. The figure was, in fact, a bush. I think at that moment I almost stopped breathing, for I felt that the Germans must surely see us in the light of the grenade. I lay there not daring to move an eyelid. At any moment I expected to hear the crack of bullets above my head – but there was only silence. At last the light went out, but my stomach began to turn over and I felt sick.

By this time it was so late that the patrol had to return to their lines:

> We moved swiftly now. After all we were going in the right direction. Close to our line we were able to lift our weary bodies from the ground, and walk in a crouched position towards our wire. The whole of my body ached now, and I was bitterly cold. We dropped down into our trench. It was almost light now, and I was glad to stretch out in my hole in the ground. I was given a mug of tea and lit a cigarette. My thoughts returned to the events of the last four hours. I wondered whether it had been a wasted effort, or should I first be glad that we were still alive.

Such were the stresses and strains of patrols, that the experienced often feigned their having taken place. Liebschner recalls:

We'd wait until midnight, crawl out into No Man's Land – make sure that we had good cover somewhere, and make a din of a noise. Tommy would wake up and shoot at us, but we were safely behind some sort of protection, and when he had fired on us for about half an hour, we used to crawl back and supply a report that it wasn't possible to get a prisoner.

Raleigh Trevelyan certainly put up a vigorous defence against these patrols. One night he heard Germans creeping through the undergrowth, making bird noises:

Ten yards away from me there was a distinct movement. We positively hared into our trenches, and I belted off with a tommy, and Corporal Humphrey with a bren. Then Corporal H. chucked a grenade and one was thrown back at us. This went on for a bit. Next morning Davis said he had seen a dead Jerry where I'd fired. My first kill!

After this, killing became second nature to Trevelyan, even enjoyable, a situation which when he realised it shocked him into remedial action. He reimposed a level of control over what was becoming in his own words 'a child's game on a large scale'.

Trying to remain in control whilst one's ability to withstand the strains of life in the beachhead were being systematically eroded was far from easy. Some of the stresses were specific events, such as a shell exploding close by, the death of a friend, or just a dangerous situation; others were chronic such as fear, tiredness, the weather, the sight of dead and dying. The 'horrors of war' were inescapable at Anzio. Norman Mohar saw many horrible sights whilst he retrieved bodies from the battlefield:

I had to pick up these dead bodies, which were now at the blue-bellied stage. The buttons were ripping from the pressures of the gas inside. I rolled one body out of his position partly submerged in sand. His hand had been in the sand for whatever length of time he had laid there. When I pulled on that arm to free it, the flesh fell off the bones of his hand.

Corporal Ron Rhodes was attached to a field ambulance, and witnessed some horrific scenes:

Jerry hit an ammunition dump, it was hell on earth, lads running, screaming, on fire, some lay there with limbs shattered . . . We carried some of them back on a 3-ton lorry where the Medics were doing quick amputations. I never thought I could do it, but I was holding arms and legs partly blown off while the Medics sawed them off and cut the last bits of skin off with some scissors, the poor sods.

Collecting wounded off the battlefield under a Red Cross flag and without fear of being fired on was fully accepted in the beachhead. Liebschner wrote:

It was sometimes necessary to leave the wounded behind in No Man's Land because you could not bring them in at night. They were screaming, and shouting, or crying for mother. So that you had to plug your ears because you couldn't stand it any longer. But as soon as dawn came and the light was good enough for the other side to see you, all you had to do was wave a little Red Cross flag, go out into No Man's Land, pick up your wounded and cart them back. That Red Cross flag would be respected in either side and you would be walking past Tommy's fox holes, or he would pass your fox holes 10 or 15 yards from you.

The belligerents had similar systems for dealing with battle casualties: first aid in the front line followed, if necessary, by surgery by a specialist unit, and then on to a hospital for further care prior to evacuation. The wounds were very largely from fragmentation missiles – mortar bombs, hand grenades, artillery shells and bombs dropped from aircraft, or from mines and booby traps. A very much smaller percentage were from bullets and anti-tank shells. Bayonet wounds were almost unknown. One surgeon later wrote of a typical scene in a British casualty clearing station:

> The wounded lay in two rows, mostly British but some American as well in their sodden filthy clothes . . . soaked, caked, buried in mud and blood; with ghastly pale faces, shuddering, shivering with the cold of the February nights and their great wounds . . . some (too many; far too many) were carried in dying, with gross combinations of shattered, limbs, protrusions of intestines and brain from great holes in their poor frames torn by 88-millimetre shells, mortars and anti-personnel bombs. Some lay quiet and still, with legs drawn up – penetrating wounds of the abdomen. Some were carried in sitting up on the stretchers, gasping and coughing, shot through the lungs.

Cases were prioritised by triage. Casualties with abdominal wounds were said to have a 50:50 chance of survival and treated as quickly as possible. The average time that it took from wound being received to the operating table was seven hours. The surgical teams worked tirelessly to save lives for, as one British surgeon stated, 'There is no such thing as a corpse until the funeral.' A surgeon would often operate for eight hours, take a couple of hours' sleep, and then start another eight hours. It was not uncommon for a surgeon to conduct a dozen operations in each shift. The medical teams often worked in the most appalling conditions, not only in tents that leaked and with mud on the floor, but also under artillery bombardment. The field hospitals were on the outskirts of Anzio and Nettuno and, as a consequence, bombed on several occasions. On 7 February Alan Whicker returned some nurses to 95th Field Hospital after a party in the correspondents' villa. 'We passed an excellent evening', he wrote later, 'discussed everything except the war, drank everything available, and much appreciated the company of the pretty young women in their fatigues and make-up who had made an effort to become glowing replicas of peacetime party goers . . . We planned future escapes for them, said our farewells affectionately, and I drove them back . . . where in stunned horror we confronted havoc and disaster.' It was the night when the hospital was bombed by a German aircraft whose pilot, in an attempt to gain height, had released his bombs which landed on the hospital. They killed 28 staff and patients, wounded a further 64 and did a great deal of damage to important equipment. Nearly 100 Allied medical personnel were killed in the Anzio–Nettuno beachhead, including six nurses, 67 were wounded and a further 79 were captured or missing.

The Allied dead were registered by graves-registration units and buried in official cemeteries. The Americans used one site in Nettuno, and the British used two, one on the outskirts of Anzio and the other adjacent to the Casualty Clearing Station in the Padiglione Woods. The Germans buried their dead at a cemetery at Pomezia, between Anzio and Rome. Burials were conducted almost every day. Guardsman Bretherick of the Grenadier Guards recalls one of his duties as a newly arrived replacement:

The worst task we had to do was with two three ton trucks go to the Casualty Clearing Station to pick up 12 bodies of dead Grenadiers wrapped in a single army blanket fastened with large safety pins and having their identity tags in bags also pinned to the blanket. It was quite gruesome their hobnailed boots sticking out of the other end. In due course we met the battalion's Padre at the burial site, we then dug twelve fairly shallow graves and commenced the interment. I'm afraid the blankets were wet with blood and this was our first baptism of dead men killed gruesomely in this war but it certainly wasn't to be our last.

Sometimes it was not possible to recover the dead from the field of battle, particularly from the 'wadi country' and by the time the bodies were retrieved they were often decomposed, identifiable only by their dog tags. Many were never recovered, and some were lost having been buried in temporary graves which were never recorded and subsequently lost their markers and were forgotten. Death was an ever-present stress that troops had to live with. Inevitably different people coped in different ways. Some grieved for a while, a few were angry and sought revenge, others tried to forget and moved on. On one occasion, Ross Carter recalls that a soldier in his platoon 'foresaw his own death in an attack and gave all of his money to a friend and said "get stewed in Naples . . . spend it on yourself, and each drink you take have another one for your old pal, and I'll be watching you do it."' He was killed in the next attack and the money was spent as he wished. Death was an absolute fact in the Anzio beachhead. Everybody recognised that within seconds they could be a corpse and hoped that luck was with them. Norman Mohar went to see the medics to get something for his 'dystenty' and whilst he was away, his platoon's barn was hit by a salvo of shells. 'We lost 8 dead and 11 wounded. It was a wipeout of my platoon . . . The devastation from the shells was terrific!' John Swain was also extremely fortunate one night, although he did not realise it until the following morning:

I got up at first light as usual, and climbed out of the dugout to get some water to wash and shave. On the Anzio town side of the dugout lay a German 88-mm shell. I looked on the other side of the dugout and saw a hole or indentation in the ground. The shell had come to rest about twenty feet from the dugout entrance . . . I believed our shell had landed on one side of the dugout and bounced over it without exploding, and I should indeed thank the Lord.

Sometimes such incidents led to 'battle shock', an individual's nervous collapse. In such cases a soldier became immediately useless, unwilling and sometimes even unable to move. 'I saw a number of those cases', says Arthur Malinson of the Royal Army Medical Corps, 'men of previously good character literally collapsing from the stress of it all. Grown men weeping like children. Sometimes it was one incident that changed them, sometimes it had been building up for weeks. Whatever the cause, they couldn't stay in the front line and had to be cared for like any other casualty. They were usually shipped out to a hospital in Naples.' But whilst battle shock cases were evacuated, those suffering from the physical and mental symptoms of stress just had to try and soldier on. On 14 February Lieutenant Geoffrey Dormer confided to his diary whilst at sea:

Tonight I feel the strain of this existence, having once more been alarmed by the roar of an unseen plane. I feel a delicacy about the ears, hard to explain, almost a tenderness, and an inclination to jump at shadows . . . All four of us Officers have been frequently hearing, feeling, imaginary explosions in the last few days . . . My guts have been upset ever since D-Day, but I doubt if there's any connection.

Some tried to cope by going absent without leave or deserting – even though there were few places to go and none of them safe. On any given day there were 60–70 deserters in 1st Division and nearly 100 for 5th Division. The Americans and Germans suffered similar sized losses. Others tried to manage by turning to drink. Paul Brown, an infantryman in 45th Division, confessed to his diary in March that he was often drunk – 'March 10: Drank vino again last night, sure got drunk . . .'; 'March 11: Was drunk again last night'. Over one five-day period in the front line he hardly ever seems to have been sober. Others became superstitious – 'I'd go nowhere without my lucky mug', said Jimmy Reed – and some turned to religion. Cor Longiotti of 45th Division wrote:

> The saying goes that there are no atheists in the foxholes, which is true, because I've seen soldiers who never prayed before make the sign of the cross, or pray the best they knew how, when it was a matter of life and death.

Norman Mohar had not paid much heed to religion until he fought at Anzio and recalls:

> I was suddenly in full realization that I was in the fray for real and that I must prepare my soul for whatever hereafter there was offered. Seeing a dead GI was the deciding factor. So at the first opportunity I visited our Chaplain Father Hanley. I asked him a lot of questions . . . I visited Father Hanley regularly after that . . . He sort of took me under his care.

To help deal with stress, the motivation and morale of the troops had to be attended to. Whilst patriotism, ideology, the Regiment and hatred of the enemy may have been motivational factors on the home front, they were not sustaining on the fighting front. 'I hated my sergeant far more than I hated the enemy,' says Peter Randall of the Special Service Force, 'but we had a job to do and that meant killing Germans – I wasn't allowed to kill my Sergeant.' Joachim Liebschner also felt little resentment towards those opposing him:

I cannot talk about hatred towards the enemy. We always thought that they were misguided people. We were quite convinced that we were fighting a just war. With regards to the British, they shouldn't be fighting against us anyway, because we were made more like the British than any other nation that we were fighting. The Americans were considered a little bit unintelligent and were doing the whole thing because they were paid and certainly didn't know what they were fighting for or why they were in Europe at all . . . When you went over the top and you didn't know what was going to be dished out at you, you fired in despair, anger . . . there was no choice. It was either them or you . . . you were firing at an unknown quantity . . . There was almost a camaraderie between the *Front Schwein* of your side, and the *Front Schwein* from the other side. They were people who were in the same kind of mess and one always had the feeling that one had much more in common with the Tommy or American lying opposite you than people sitting at the back of your lines dishing out the food, or distributing the mail or bringing forward ammunition . . . It was not a war we fought for Nazism, but a war that we fought for the Fatherland . . . we thought, 'Hitler knows what he is doing, better trust him and get on with the job.'

Most men did not fight for ethereal ideals; they may have fought because they believed that the war was just, but what sustained their motivation in the fighting was their comrades. Most soldiers wanted to do themselves justice and did not want to let their mates down. Corporal Lionel Waldergrave of 1st Armored Division says:

We went through a great deal in the beachhead. We just got on with it. I felt that I had a duty to do, not so much to my country, although that was important, but to myself and my comrades in arms. I didn't want to let myself or my friends down.

The Germans felt the same, with one officer writing in his diary: 'God help me to do my duty to the Fatherland, but above all give me the strength to be the leader that my men deserve.' The men that one fought with became a soldier's family, as British infantryman Ray Fort recalls:

> Our platoon was very close. We were all compact with each other. We all knew each other. What our failings were and our strengths, our likes and our dislikes. They were a good bunch and we looked after each other – that's what made it so terrible when someone was killed – it was like losing a very close brother. The Sergeant took me under his wing. He was a good man to me was Danny Deacon.

The American General Ernest Harmon later wrote that he felt a special and unique bond grew between the troops in the beachhead:

> It is true that all of us were in the same boat: we were there to stay or die. But it is not true that such a situation always creates brotherhood, I have never seen anything like it in the two World Wars of my experience. There was at Anzio a confidence in unity, an unselfish willingness among troops to help one another that I never saw again.

Whilst motivation requires a few key stimuli, sustaining morale is far more complex. In order for a soldier at Anzio to do his job under any circumstances and to the limit of his capacity, he needed a variety of mental and physical stimulants: food, shelter, camaraderie, medical support, good leadership and trust in weaponry included. The creation and maintenance of morale is an inexact science. A bottle of whisky could raise the morale of one man, but have no effect on another. However, letters from home were generally regarded to have an impact on everybody. A letter could boost a man's spirits ines-timably, but a 'Dear John' could send a man over the edge. Norman Mohar recalls:

> There was never any mail for me from home and I awaited the most important letter – from the girl I left behind. That day finally came. The orderly hollered MOHAR and I was stunned when he gave me a bag with the bottom part filled with letters! OH BOY! OH BOY! Now I can be replenished by reading some mushy stuff in a letter from 'you guess who'. I separated the letters according to postmarks and decided to read the last one first. Here it was, a 'Dear John'. I could have died on the spot. Such a feeling of hopelessness came over me . . . I decided to reconstruct the case as I read the oldest postmarked letter. It finally came out. The old 'lonesome bit' and it's been 'A long time' crap. Also, there was an Air Force guy with a cute cap that snowed her . . . I read the letters and tossed them into a little fire we had . . . . Later I wrote her a scathing letter, which she said 'made her cry'.

Officers received mail not only from family and friends, but also the family and friends of their men. Captain Felix Sparks was sent a letter from the mother of nineteen-year-old Corporal Robert L. Fremder pleading for information about her missing son:

> Oh My Dear Captain:
>
> Won't you please answer this letter and tell me something that isn't against the writing rules . . . Oh please do something or tell me something . . . Oh God, how I pray for this awful cruel war to end before it is too late. And oh please God bring my baby back home to me again some way or some how, please God . . . Oh Captain, I have dreamed of my baby son every night and sometimes where I work in a war plant . . . Why did this war have to be. He was only a

boy of 19 . . . . I will thank you so much. You will know how much
I will be grateful to you for being kind enough to answer this letter.
   Yours truly,
   Bob's Mother

Operation *Fischfang* had been a great demoraliser to the Germans.
Not only had they failed in their aims, but it became obvious that they
lacked resources whilst the Allies were strong, particularly in airpower. Anglo-American morale remained robust throughout, not
necessarily because their officers and NCOs were better, but because
they were stronger operationally and strategically. Thus whilst Hitler
blamed his commanders at the front, he was more to blame for their
failure than his commanders. In an attempt to undermine VI Corps's
morale, the Germans used air raids and shelling, but also psychological warfare. This took two main forms – the radio and leaflets. The
troops enjoyed listening to the sultry voiced 'Axis Sally' and her
companion, 'George' on 'Front Line Radio' broadcast from Berlin. It
was on the airwaves in the evenings when the forward troops could
receive it on wireless sets used to maintain communication with
forward units, and home made sets ingeniously constructed from
battlefield debris. The programme commenced with the signature
tune 'Between the Devil and the Deep Blue Sea', and was often
followed by Sally announcing tauntingly 'Hullo suckers'. The show
also played popular music, but was punctuated with propaganda. Sally
often declared that the beachhead was the 'largest self-supporting
prisoner-of-war camp in the world', and tried to raise doubts in the
minds of listeners about what their wives and girlfriends were up to
whilst they were away. George told horror stories of fighting at the
front: 'Have you heard about Private Fox', he said. 'He went out on a
patrol and stepped on a shoe-mine. Nasty things, shoe-mines. All his
guts were blown away. But he went on living another twelve hours.
You should have heard him yelling.' The programme ended with the

words, 'Think it over. Why should you be one of those rotting carcasses? Don't forget to listen in tomorrow. And a big kiss from Sall-y.' When Sally was eventually caught later in the war, the sultry voiced vixen was found to be both fat and ugly.

The radio failed to influence most Allied soldiers in the beachhead, and the leaflets dropped from aircraft were equally unsuccessful. The first were wordy and tried crudely to raise doubts in the minds of VI Corps about their abilities and the strength of the alliance between Britain and America. One dropped on 1st Division read:

> British soldiers, you are fighting against an opponent you know very well. You are not facing Italians but Germans. As gallant soldiers you have had the occasion to become acquainted with the courage and the grit of your German opponents . . . In the face of insurmountable odds a thousand men of crack British Guards surrendered. If they were forced to do so, then it is not dishonourable for you to lay down arms in case you are facing nothing but certain death. General Clark certainly played you a dirty Yankee trick! And who has got to bear the consequences?

But they became more subtle, playing on the similarities between Dunkirk and Anzio, and showing scantily clad women, representing sweethearts back at home, in compromising positions with shadowy figures. The most famous leaflet revealed a drawing of the Anzio beachhead in the shape of a skull, bearing the words: 'BEACH-HEAD – DEATH'S HEAD!' On the reverse it proclaimed:

> The Beach-Head has become a Death's Head! It is welcoming You with a grin and also those who are coming after you across the sea for an appointment with death. Do they know what they are in for? Yes, they feel that they are landing on a DEATH'S HEAD.

The troops used any piece of paper bearing the image of a pretty girl as pin-ups, and the others as toilet paper which was always in short supply.

Rest and relaxation away from the front line provided a welcome boost to the troops' ability to cope with the beachhead. As it was dependent on having sufficient resources to replace those recuperating, during the first weeks of the battle there was little prospect of this for either side. Nevertheless, as the weeks passed, Allied soldiers could expect to be in the line for between a week and ten days, in reserve for two days, followed by six days of complete rest. The Germans would spend three weeks in the line and then be withdrawn for ten days' construction work in the building of further defences before Rome – the Hitler Line between Cassino and Anzio. Joachim Liebschner had arrived in the beachhead on 22 January, but was not relieved for six weeks, by which time his company had lost 70 of its 120 men. Robert Dodge of 3rd Division had landed on 23 January and received a couple of days in the rear area after four weeks in the front line. Here he stayed for a couple of days enjoying a shower, some clean clothes, hot food, a motivational talk and a movie. 3rd Division was not pulled out of the line as a formation until 28 March after a full sixty-seven consecutive days there. Private George Avery wrote of the transformation that individuals underwent when relieved from the line:

> After not standing during the day, and always moving at a half crouch when you do move, as you work your way to the rear, you begin to feel more and more at ease so that when you reach the area where the tanks and artillery are stationed, you walk upright and unconcerned. By the time you reach the area where the cooks, medics, and ammunition handlers work, you walk upright, straight and tall, whistling that no one is trying to kill you.

The 3rd Division went into reserve for a few days, where they trained hard and learned some new skills, and were then given a rest. In the rear they caught up on some sleep and had a chance to read some of the many newspapers, such as *The Beachhead News,* and write letters. Letter writing was important, as Ernie Pyle recalls:

> I heard about one soldier who wrote to his girl that he had been wounded, and then wrote to his mother and tipped her off that he had just made it up. And another one who didn't fly at all wrote home that he had just shot down three Japanese Zeros. That was really good going, especially in Italy . . . .

One British officer wrote to *The Times* that he enjoyed playing cards in the beachhead. 'We have few distractions here and little enough time for relaxation, but we find bridge an excellent refreshment' and enclosed 'a deal which attracted some attention.' Many of the troops also liked to gamble, whether it was on cards or anything else. Beetle racing became very popular in April, as F.C.M. Reeves explains:

> Elaborate totes were constructed and really large money changed hands in bets. A champion beetle might fetch as much as three thousand lire or more . . . it was no mean price to pay for an insect. Runners were plentiful, for beetles seemed to be one of the chief products of the beachhead. Dig a slit trench, leave it for an hour, and the bottom would be black with beetles trying to get out. The system of racing was simple. Various colours were painted on the beetles' backs and the runners were paraded round the ring in jam jars. Just before the 'off', or I suppose one should say when they came under starter's orders, the beetles were placed under one glass jar in the centre of the 'course'. This was a circle about six feet in diameter. At the 'off' the jar was raised and the first beetle out of the circle was the winner. A difficulty arose when, for one reason or

another, it became necessary to change a beetle's colours in quick time; but one Gunner meeting the problem, solved it by attaching small flags to the beetles' backs with chewing gum.

One enterprising American corporal rounded up some mules, donkeys and horses and started the 'Anzio Beachhead Racing Association'. A number of races took place, including the 'Anzio Derby'. Fifth Army also arranged for singers and dancers to be shipped in to entertain the troops, but few went to the beachhead more than once, and a couple of performers left in mid-act when some shells landed a couple of miles away. Many different sports were played between units and divisions, including softball and football. The Royal Engineers once used their bulldozers to flatten the ground for a rugby match, but the rising dust attracted enemy artillery fire. The match was postponed due to 'Massive enemy bombardment'. An underground cinema was also constructed near Anzio and contained seating for up to thirty-five people. Occasionally a shell would explode within the rest area causing casualties, reminding everybody that they were still well within the range of the German heavy artillery. 'The only ways to get away from the guns', said Jimmy Reed, 'were death, a good wound or leave. Leave was far more difficult to get than the other two.' The Germans took their leave in Rome and could be there unwashed, unshaved and filthy within a few hours of patrolling at the front. Every four days a contingent of 750 Allied soldiers, the equivalent of a battalion of men, left by Landing Ship for rest camps near Naples. Naval vessels also took it in turns to have a break. Geoffrey Dormer wrote in his diary on 9 February: 'The lads can get ashore for the first time since January 12th. They'll all get pissed, and there will be the hell of a shindy . . .'. He was right, there was 'an almighty party', and he ended up putting his 'naked and vomiting' Commanding Officer to bed in the wee small hours. Once away from the beachhead some men ran wild, ending up in drunken brawls or losing all their money gambling, whilst others had a quiet drink and looked around for female companionship. Few of them, however, could abide the strict rules that applied to them in Naples. Many ended up in jail for visiting places that were off limits, or for being improperly dressed. Alan Whicker wrote about this: 'reality on the battlefield was living and dying. A few miles away, it was observing somebody's peacetime restrictions.' On 18 March, Vesuvius erupted for the first time in thirty-eight years and visitors to the city were treated to earth tremors as molten rock and ash were thrown thousands of feet into the air. 'It was like Armageddon had followed us', recalled one young British gunner, 'a volcano, the Germans still bombing us every night – we couldn't work out whether we were pleased to be there or wanted to get back to Anzio . . . I got extremely drunk one night and found the company of a young lady who took me to her room. We did the dirty deed, I fell asleep, she robbed me blind and gave me the clap.' Such was leave in Naples during the Battle of Anzio.

The Anzio beachhead had become a deadly place, sapping the strength of anybody and everybody that served there. The intensity of the experience – whether on land, sea or in the air – left men physically and mentally exhausted. The period of stalemate over the late winter and early spring had given both sides a chance to reassess their strategy and build some strength for the exertions to come. As the sleet and rain gave way to clearer skies and the warmer weather of May, the ground dried and VI Corps began to feel more confident in its capabilities, and more optimistic about the future. They knew as well as Adolf Hitler, still ensconced in his Berghof in the Bavarian Alps, that it was the eve of a new, and what could be decisive, campaigning season. The Germans looked not only at the prospect of another Fifteenth Army attempt to break the Gustav Line, and a breakout from the beachhead, but also at the probability of a cross-Channel invasion, and an assault against southern France. The outlook appeared bleak for Hitler, but

Albert Kesselring remained stoical. By early May his defences south of Rome had already achieved what they had been built to achieve, and he hoped that in his continued defiance to Alexander his forces could undermine Allied offensives in other areas. It was now up to the Fifteenth Army Group to move themselves into a position to destroy Tenth Army and then seize Rome.

They had the opportunity, but then opportunities had been wasted in Italy before.

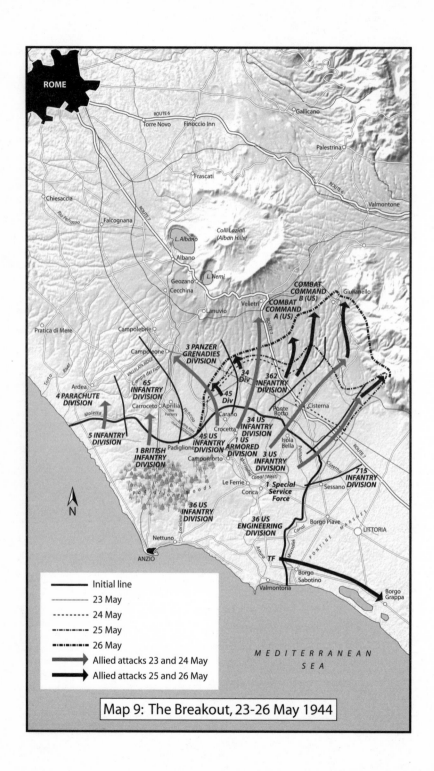

ROME

ROUTE 6
Torre Novo   Finoccio Inn

Gallicano

Palestrina

Frascati

Chiesaccia

Falcognana

ROUTE 7

Valmontone

ROUTE 6

Colli Laziali
(Alban Hills)

L. Albano

Albano

L. Nemi

Geozano
Cecchina

Lanuvio

Velletri

COMBAT
COMMAND
B (US)

COMBAT
COMMAND
A (US)

Giulianello

Pratica di Mere

Campolebrie

ROUTE 7

Rio Pefrosso

Campoleone

3 PANZER
GRENADIES
DIVISION

ROUTE 7

34
Div

362
INFANTRY
DIVISION

45
Div

Ardea

4 PARACHUTE
DIVISION

65
INFANTRY
DIVISION

Torto River

Carroceto Aprilia
          The
          Factory

Moletta

Crocetta

Carano

Cisterna

34 US
INFANTRY
DIVISION

5 INFANTRY
DIVISION

45 US
INFANTRY
DIVISION

Ponte
Rotto

1 US
ARMORED
DIVISION

Isola
Bella

ROUTE 7

1 BRITISH
INFANTRY
DIVISION

Padiglione

Campormorto

3 US
INFANTRY
DIVISION

Mussolini Canal (West)

715
INFANTRY
DIVISION

Cisterna

Le Ferrie

Conca

1 Special
Service
Force

Sessano

36 US
INFANTRY
DIVISION

P a d i g l i o n e   W o o d s

Torrina Canal

Nettuno

N

36 US
ENGINEERING
DIVISION

Mussolini Canal

Borgo Piave

Astura Canal

LITTORIA

P O N T I N E   M A R S H E S

ANZIO

TF

Borgo
Sabotino

Valmontoria

Borgo
Grappa

M E D I T E R R A N E A N
S E A

Map 9: The Breakout, 23-26 May 1944

CHAPTER 9

Diadem

(11–24 May)

Lieutenant Raleigh Trevelyan lay in 'wadi country', a claustrophobic and dangerous part of the beachhead. His position between the graves of its former occupants was in contaminated ground torn up by the German artillery. Here Trevelyan's craving to slay Germans reached its peak. He confessed in his diary on 11 May: 'Something has happened to me these last days; my mind has silted up. I kill with as much detachment as if I were a robot. Except that a robot wouldn't enjoy killing . . .'. The previous day whilst in an old trench, he had spied a German a couple of hundred yards away and immediately sought to kill him. But armed only with a grenade Trevelyan had to actively seek out a rifle before subsequently bagging his quarry. He watched as the man's head fell backwards, and was thrilled. Whilst searching for some binoculars that he had left in a shell hole he had stumbled across another target. This 'very blond Aryan' was combing his hair 30 yards away, presenting a prime target. Trevelyan dryly noted that, 'It was my duty to kill him, even in cold blood. Again I knew that the thought should revolt me, but again the hunter's urge was too powerful.' He took careful aim, squeezed the trigger, but his rifle jammed. Again, he went and sourced another weapon before satisfying his need. 'I fired at this wretched chap', Trevelyan explained. 'He threw up his hands with a gasp, which I clearly heard, and collapsed. Then the meaning of what I was doing hit me. Oh God, oh God, let me out of here before I do any more such things . . .'. The young officer had been polluted by the beachhead's merciless environment, ensnared until such time that he either became a casualty or was swept up in a breakout. Until then he struggled on, placated by the news that an attack had been launched against the Gustav Line and that plans were afoot for a massive VI Corps attack.

Allied deliberations about an offensive to break the deadlock on the Gustav Line and the Anzio beachhead began in February. They had led to Alexander's Chief of Staff, Lieutenant General Sir John Harding, producing an appreciation of the situation which was submitted to General Maitland Wilson at Allied Force Headquarters at the end of the month. Harding staunchly advocated a bold new offensive based around the concentration of Fifteenth Army Group's forces. Fifth and Eighth Armies would attack the Gustav Line followed by a breakout from the Anzio beachhead by VI Corps in an attempt to trap and destroy a large part of von Vietinghoff's Tenth Army. Once this had been achieved, Rome would be captured. It was a proposal which had potentially significant implications for Allied strategy as an Italian offensive would need to be heavily resourced. With the Americans adamant that the cross-Channel attack – Operation Overlord – was strictly off limits, the British set their sights on Operation Anvil. They argued that Italy offered a far better means of diverting the Germans from north-west Europe than the proposed invasion of the south of France and would wipe out far more of Hitler's formations. This proposition initiated a protracted period of debate and negotiation that would continue through to April. During this it gradually became clear that whilst London and Washington were in agreement that a spring offensive in Italy would be of some strategic benefit, they disagreed on the scope of the offensive. Angry that despite the deadlock, the British continued to want to feed their 'Italian beast', the Americans made their feelings clear. On 31 March Brooke entered in his diary:

> Telegram from American Chiefs of Staff came in, quite impossible to accept. Again arguing that after uniting Anzio bridgehead and main front we should go on the defensive in Italy, and start a new front in southern France. They fail to see that the forces available do not admit of two fronts in the Mediterranean.

Days later Brooke was again complaining: 'Difficulties again with our American friends who still persist in wanting to close down operations in Italy and open new ones in South of France, just at the most critical moment . . .' Time was passing and the British were unreceptive to American filibustering. The British pushed for a resolution by arguing that VI Corps had to be relieved, and that a new offensive would not only achieve this, but might also encourage further opportunities. The Prime Minister wrote to General George Marshall on 13 April:

> We should above all defeat the German army south of Rome and join our own armies. Nothing should be grudged for this. We cannot tell how either the allied or enemy armies will emerge from the battle until it has been fought. It may be that the enemy will be thrown into disorder and that great opportunities of exploitation may be open. Or we may be checked and the enemy may continue to hold his positions south of Rome with his existing forces.

A compromise was eventually reached. Operation Anvil was to take place sometime after 10 July which would give the proposed Italian offensive – code named Operation Diadem – ample time in which to mature. On 19 April the Combined Chiefs of Staff despatched a directive for the Italian offensive to General Maitland Wilson, the Supreme Allied Commander of the Mediterranean:

> OBJECT: to give the greatest possible assistance to Overlord by destroying or containing the maximum number of German formations in the Mediterranean.

The attack against the Gustav Line was to begin on 11 May – a mere three weeks before the cross-Channel invasion was due to be launched. This agreement was a major British coup, for the decision rendered Operation Anvil subservient to Diadem. The Americans recognised that the British had been given *carte blanche* in Italy, but Churchill was keen to impress on Franklin Roosevelt that his aims were honourable, directed solely towards the destruction of Germany. He never became tired of showing his support for Operation Overlord, but was always careful to add that the Germans must be sufficiently weakened in France if the Allies were not to find themselves in a position like that at Anzio – or worse. On 29 April in a note to FDR, Churchill wrote: 'I do not consider that the objective of the forthcoming battle in Italy called Diadem is the taking of Rome good though that would be or even the joining of the bridgehead which is indispensable. Its prime purpose is the destruction of the armed forces of the enemy . . . .' Having got what he wanted, the British Prime Minister did what he could to placate his ally and looked forward to success in Italy.

Operation Diadem required Fifteenth Army Group to concentrate its forces on two narrow fronts against the Gustav Line. Oliver Leese's Eighth Army – consisting of the XIII British Corps, I Canadian Corps and II Polish Corps – was to be centred on Cassino, whilst Mark Clark's Fifth Army – consisting of the French Expeditionary Corps and II US Corps – was to take up positions between the Liri Valley and the coast.

Alexander's aim was to stretch the Germans with a two Army attack, whilst retaining such concentration that a breakthrough was bound to occur. The first phase of Diadem was to be a four pronged assault: along the coast by II Corps; into the Aurunci mountains south of the Liri by the French Expeditionary Corps; across the Rapido by XIII Corps; and against the Monastery from the north by the Polish Corps. Alexander expected the first breach to be made at Cassino and it was here that he deployed his exploitation force, I Canadian Corps. A breakout from the Anzio beachhead was to take place once Kesselring had released his two reserve divisions, and was to strike out in a north-easterly direction to cut Route 6 and block Tenth Army's escape route. It was assumed by Alexander that once Tenth Army had withdrawn, it would do so only to other prepared defensive positions as the Germans had been busy constructing defences since the previous December. The Hitler Line, a belt of strong points protected by anti-tank ditches, mines and wire, stretched from five miles north west of Cassino down to the Gulf of Gaeta. Behind it lay the Caesar Line that started on the coast ten miles west of Aprilia and was strung through the Velletri Gap, across Route 6 and on for another forty miles. In its strongest sector (across the southern slopes of the Alban Hills) it comprised an almost unbroken barbed wire barrier (in some places ninety feet deep) with intricate trenches and gun pits. Von Mackensen did not believe that the Caesar Line was strong enough for anything other than a temporary stand, but Kesselring thought that it would provide the Fourteenth and Tenth Armies with the ability to fight south of Rome 'indefinitely'. The Field Marshal had begun to gain the reputation of a defensive genius; he had built his reputation – and two further defensive lines – on it. But Kesselring had become a victim of his own success, and by the spring of 1944 was expected to perform defensive miracles no matter what the circumstances. As such Cassino would remain a bulwark against Alexander, and Rome would not be gifted him without a fight.

The dislocation of the Germans had begun with Allied deception operations during the preparation for Operation Diadem. In order for the offensive to have the best possible chance of success, the reorganisation and movement of the attacking forces had to be carried out in great secrecy. This was achieved with such skill that the Germans had no idea what was being massed against them. Throughout the process Kesselring's eyes were drawn away from the Gustav Line to ports in North Africa, Sicily and Naples. Here he saw a build up of force that he was led to believe was for another amphibious attack against Italy, but in reality was for Operation Anvil. Thus, on the eve of the offensive, Tenth Army maintained just two mobile reserve divisions within striking distance of the Gustav Line with the Hermann Göring Panzer Division stationed at Leghorn to defend against the Allies' threat of an assault from the sea. The Field Marshal could not rely on any assistance of the once potent Luftwaffe in his quest to waylay the Allies for, by this time it had ceased to get involved in operations. However, the Allied air forces were extremely active. Operation Strangle was initiated by Wilson to 'deprive the enemy of the ability either to maintain his present positions or to withdraw his divisions out of Italy in time for Overlord' and targeted road, rail and sea communications. From mid-March to mid-May some 10,000 sorties delivered several thousand tons of bombs, leading Kesselring to report in early April that his two armies were receiving only 60 per cent of their minimum daily requirement of supplies. The damage that Strangle caused shifted valuable troops and resources into repair tasks, forcing the Germans to rely on less efficient road transportation. Its impact was impressive and helpful to the campaign, although not decisive.

Meanwhile, Lucian Truscott was making plans for a VI Corps breakout from the Anzio beachhead. Preparations for this included the arrival of more supplies, filling the dumps to capacity, and additional troops. 34th US Infantry Division had arrived in March,

Combat Command B of 1st Armored Division in late April and 36th US Infantry Division in early May. This brought the Corps up to a strength of five American and two British divisions plus the First Special Service Force. It was a considerable strike force, particularly as the five German divisions opposing them – 4th Parachute, 65th Infantry; 3rd Panzer Grenadier; 362nd Infantry and 715th Infantry Divisions – were weak in everything, including officers and NCOs. However, the Battle of Anzio had showed many times before that attacks against a well dug-in enemy struggled to gain momentum. Indeed, Mark Clark was so concerned that Truscott would not have the strength to break out and trap Tenth Army that he took his fears directly to Alexander. The Fifteenth Army commander reassured him that with the correct break out plan concentrating VI Corps's offensive power on the right to strike for the Velletri Gap and Valmontone, all would be well. Clark was unconvinced, and in any case, an attack to cut Route 6 would not fulfil his personal ambition to capture Rome before Operation Overlord pushed Italy off the front pages. Thus, in the 'interests of flexibility', Clark suggested that Truscott explore four different directions of attack when planning the breakout and told him to be ready on 48-hours' notice to take whichever became appropriate. Of the four only two were practicable, and Truscott drew up Operation Buffalo, an advance north eastwards through Cisterna to Valmontone, which would threaten the German Tenth Army withdrawal; and Operation Turtle, a northward attack through Campoleone and Albano, which would open Route 7 into Rome. When Alexander visited the beachhead and conferred with Truscott on 5 May, six days before the scheduled start date for Operation Diadem, he immediately selected Buffalo as the plan most likely to fulfil his aspirations. He informed the corps that it would be informed by Fifteenth Army Group headquarters when to launch its attack. That same day Clark received his orders from Alexander, and they were unambiguous:

To destroy the right wing of the German Tenth Army; to drive what remains of it and the German Fourteenth Army north of Rome; and pursue the enemy to the Rimini–Pisa line inflicting losses on him in the process.

This was an instruction which meant that Mark Clark would have to use all his cunning if VI Corps was to strike out for Rome. But he was resolute in his intention and later wrote:

We not only wanted the honour of capturing Rome, but felt that we deserved it . . . Not only did we intend to become the first army in fifteen centuries to seize Rome from the south, but we intended to see that the people at home knew that it was the Fifth Army that did the job, and knew the price that had been paid for it.

He wanted the Eternal City and the glory that went with it. What he did not want was for Alexander to manoeuvre Eighth Army into a position of taking Rome first. On 5 May a paranoid Clark confided to his diary:

I know factually that there are interests brewing for Eighth Army to take Rome, and I might as well let Alexander know now that if he attempts anything of that kind he will have another all-out battle on his hands; namely, with me.

In fact Harold Alexander had no intention of manipulating the battle in order to get the British into Rome first, and it also seems that he also had no intention of bringing Clark under control. He knew that Clark wanted to take the capital, and had heard his arguments about VI Corps being too weak to trap Tenth Army many times. But, when Clark called Alexander to complain about the Army Group commander directing a Fifth Army corps commander, he should have been 'gripped'. Clark recorded the conversation:

I told Alexander . . . that what I was guarding against was pre-conceived ideas as to what exactly was to be done and that I felt that he and Harding had such pre-conceived ideas. I told him that there was a chance for a great victory if we played our cards right . . . He kept pulling on me the idea that we were to annihilate the entire German Army and did it so many times that I told him that I did not believe that we had too many chances to do that; that the Boche were too smart . . . I am thoroughly disgusted with him and his attitude.

But instead of putting Clark firmly in his place as he should have done (and as Churchill would have wanted him to do) Alexander was typically conciliatory. Rather than making it clear he would not suffer any more mischief by the Fifth Army commander, he gave the impression that a push to Rome was still a possibility if Operation Buffalo ran into difficulties. This gave Clark the incentive that he needed to consent to Alexander's wishes, evade them and produce the aristocratic Anglo-Irish commander with a *fait accompli*. Indeed, on 6 May Clark told Truscott, 'the capture of Rome is the only important objective' and to be ready to execute 'Turtle' as well as 'Buffalo'.

Everything was set for a surprise attack. The deployments had gone well – there was a three to one superiority in the Cassino sector and two to one on the Garigliano. Fine weather had dried out the ground and German intelligence had not noticed anything out of the ordinary. Indeed, the day before Operation Diadem was launched, Kesselring was led to believe that an Allied strike was not possible before 24 May. In such circumstances the Field Marshal had no objections to von Vietinghoff flying back to Germany on the evening of 11 May to be personally decorated by Hitler. The XIV Panzer Corps's commander, Lieutenant General Fridolin von Senger und Etterlin, was already on leave as was his chief of staff and General Siegfried Westphal. The timing could hardly have been more fortuitous. On the morning of 11

May the Prime Minister cabled Alexander, 'All thoughts and hopes are with you in what I trust and believe will be a decisive battle, fought to the finish, and having as its object the destruction and ruin of the armed force of the enemy south of Rome.' To which Alexander replied:

All our plans and preparation are now complete and everything is ready. We have every hope and every intention of achieving our object, namely, the destruction of the enemy south of Rome. We expect heavy and bitter fighting, and we are ready for it.

That evening Alan Brooke wrote: 'Tonight at 11 pm the Italian attack starts. I pray to God that it may be successful. A great deal depends on it.' Both Churchill and Brooke were well aware that Diadem could very well prove to be their final Italian gambit.

The Cassino front exploded into action before midnight on 11 May when more than 1,500 guns fired the first of several million shells in support of Operation Diadem. The air rumbled, the ground tremored and out of the darkness the infantry rose up and struck. The Tenth Army beat away Alexander's renewed advances. In the Eighth Army the Polish Corps failed to take the monastery and XIII Corps struggled to obtain a foothold over the Rapido and Gari Rivers. In Fifth Army, the II Corps attack near the mouth of the Garigliano stalled, but the French Expeditionary Corps made significant progress south of the Liri and quickly drove behind enemy lines. General Alphonse Juin's specialist mountain troops had ripped a hole in the Gustav Line just where it was least expected and XIV Panzer Corps quickly began to lose its cohesion. As it did, II Corps began to make progress towards Formina again. Meanwhile, XIII Corps's tenacity was rewarded with a three-mile advance into the Liri Valley which unhinged LI Mountain Corps at its southernmost point. By 16 May, the Tenth Army was beginning to crumble and that evening Alexander signalled Brooke, 'we can now claim that we have definitely broken the Gustav Line.'

Kesselring acknowledged the fact too and telephoned von Vietinghoff advocating a withdrawal to the Hitler Line with the immortal words 'we shall have to give up Cassino'. Within an hour Tenth Army had issued directives for a general withdrawal and the bastion on Monte Cassino was prepared for evacuation – it fell on 18 May. Diadem had drawn first blood and the Germans if not reeling, were stunned. By this time the missing commanders had returned, but it was too late. Albert Kesselring was later to write, 'I look back on those days in horror.'

On 19 May, with II Corps just forty miles from the Anzio beachhead, Clark received an instruction from Alexander to attack 'from the Anzio bridgehead on Cori and Valmontone' no later than the morning of 22 May. This was eventually postponed by twenty-four hours, but its aim did not change. The crystal clear order was Alexander reminding his subordinate that he was unswerving in his ambition to trap and destroy Tenth Army. The news that VI Corps was soon to strike out of the beachhead for Valmontone was greeted with delight in London. The offensive was progressing well, and Alan Brooke allowed himself a rare moment of optimism when he wrote the following day:

Alexander's news of Italian fighting continues to be excellent. Thank heaven for it! I have staked a great deal on the Italian campaign in all our arguments with the Americans. I felt throughout that we had wonderful opportunities of inflicting a real telling defeat on the Germans which would be worth anything in connection with the cross Channel operations. The only danger was that the Americans should have their way and plan to withdraw forces from Italy at the critical moment. They nearly succeeded in ruining our strategy, and now I pray God we may be allowed to reap the full benefits of our strategy!

By this time the Germans were in retreat all along the Tenth Army front. They filled the Hitler Line opposite Eighth Army, but were too late to stop Fifth Army bursting through the position. Clark hoped that Leese would now make an assault before the Germans had a chance to establish themselves in their new defences, but he was to be disappointed. The Eighth Army was to take a couple of days to prepare for a set piece battle. Was this a British ploy to get the Americans to break Tenth Army prior to entering Rome themselves? Clark believed that it was and became more convinced than ever that he would have to be bold if his men were to enter the capital first. The momentum that Leese regained after eventually breaking through the German defences on 23 May was still not enough to convince Clark that the British were putting all that they could into the offensive. Despite the arrival of the two German reserve divisions, Fifth Army continued to make excellent progress, so why was Eighth Army so sluggish? Was Alexander allowing the French to clear the way for Leese prior to an Eighth Army dash for Rome? As Clark developed his conspiracy theories, Tenth Army seeped away towards the Caesar Line moving in a north-westerly direction to join Route 6 east of Valmontone.

At Anzio, there was an intensity to the atmosphere that had been missing for several weeks. The comings and goings at the various headquarters increased in frequency as the day of the VI Corps offensive drew nearer, and their staffs worked longer hours to ensure that the breakout was a success. Lucian Truscott had been driven round the beachhead in his jeep, right leg hooked laconically over the door. He was pleased with what he saw. On 22 May he arrived at 5th Division's headquarters – 'a shabby collection of tents full of sand near the beach' – to talk with Major General Gregson-Ellis. Major Kenneth Wright remembers the visit:

> The Corps commander turned up in a gleaming helmet and the most decrepit pair of boots I have ever set eyes on. He was all smiles and *bon ami*. We had been working incredibly hard putting together our attack and were tired. Truscott was like a breath of

fresh air – actually, more like a whirl wind – it was just what we needed . . . As he left he made a little speech. 'The Germans are gonna take one hell of a beatin'. It might take some little while to crack them, but then we'll be moving. Our boys are ready for this. They've waited a long time . . . I've no doubt that we'll stop the enemy in their withdrawal and crush them. No doubt at all.' With that he got back in his jeep and sped off. He was inspiring, and we all expected a great victory.

If great victories are based in meticulous planning and attention to detail then Truscott had developed sound foundations for success. The British were to attack along the coast using 5th Division and up the Via Anziate using 1st Division to pin 4th Parachute, 65th Infantry and 3rd Panzer Grenadier Divisions to the area. The Americans were to conduct the main attack on their right against the 362nd and 715th Infantry Divisions. 45th Division were to push to Campoleone, 1st Armored Division was to rupture the front and attack Velletri, and 3rd Division was to take Cisterna with 1st Special Service Force protecting its right flank. Cisterna was the first critical objective for VI Corps because with its capture Route 7 would be cut and a launch pad for further offensive action attained. Once Cisterna had fallen, 3rd Division was then to advance and take Cori, then turn north and complete the drive into the Valmontone Gap. Truscott did not under-estimate the difficulty of these tasks and ensured that the divisions had what they required. Miles of telephone line had been laid, huge stockpiles of ammunition waited in dumps, and there was plenty of fuel for the tanks and other vehicles. It was not easy in the confined space of the beachhead and with German observers watching from the Alban Hills to get ready for the battle, but by moving at night under the cover of artillery bombardments and with some clever camouflaging, the job had been done. George Avery, now promoted to the rank of corporal, wrote:

Every day was a busy day. Patrols every night, attempts to get behind enemy lines by both sides. The Germans working without let up to fortify their positions, we were sending out patrols to discover these strongpoints . . . Some of the nights were hauntingly beautiful: pitch darkness with flashes of light from the artillery pieces interrupting the darkness . . . .The time came when we were told to move the mortars to the railroad site and join the stockpile of shells waiting there. The following day our ditch was filled with first-aid men, litter bearers, combat engineers carrying mine sweepers, and riflemen from 3rd Division.

Truscott placed great emphasis on security. Orders were not given until the last moment, troops were not placed in positions where they were likely to be snatched by German raiding parties, and false radio transmissions were broadcast as a deception measure. Nevertheless, the Germans did expect an attack out of the beachhead at some point – particularly after Operation Diadem had begun – and were nervous. Corporal Ron Rhodes drove an ambulance to the front line one night full of ammunition, fuel and water and was to pick up the wounded. On his return journey he heard a shot and the engine raced:

I stopped and got out, lifted the bonnet and then felt something prodding my back. I looked round and saw a German officer with a Luger gun pointing at me. He said he had fired the shot and had got ten men in the ditch and wanted to inspect the ambulance. As we opened the doors the Anglo-Indian medic rolled his eyes and nearly crapped himself. The officer looked under the stretchers and at the top of his voice said in perfect English, 'We know that some of you are carrying ammo, petrol and other supplies in your ambulances and if we catch you, we will blast you off the face of the earth.' He then vanished into the night.

Truscott recognised that the 'break-in' battle would not be easy due to the strength of the German defences. During the stalemate period von Mackensen had overseen the development of sophisticated defence in depth across the beachhead. Near Cisterna, for example, the outpost zone line consisted of a series of platoon positions about 300 yards apart, each containing four to eight machine guns sited to fire a few inches above the ground and protected by dense wire and minefields. Several hundred yards behind this forward line lay the battle zone with reserve companies protected by dugouts along the ditches and supported by weapons pits and yet more machine gun nests. However, there was no counter-attacking reserve and so once the position was cracked, the Germans would have to either fight on unsupported or withdraw. To rock the very foundations of this defensive system Truscott had massed 1,500 guns, some a mere 500 yards from the front line. There was a huge emphasis on firepower, which impressed Robert Dodge waiting to attack with the 15th Regiment of 3rd Division:

> Everything was ready. We had got over huge numbers of artillery pieces in the beach-head, which was the greatest concentration ever assembled in so small an area. Just behind our position was a special unit of .50-calibre machine guns. They stretched as far as you could see, tripod to tripod, with ammo piled behind them. They were to give us overhead fire, and make the Jerries keep their heads down. In about every house, a tank had driven through the wall and was hidden.

Dodge and his comrades ate cold rations and remained motionless, some for several days, awaiting the start of the offensive. They had all been fully briefed, had scrutinised models and studied aerial reconnaissance photographs. Meanwhile, Raleigh Trevelyan, whose platoon of 1st Green Howards was to be in the vanguard of the 5th Division push, had to conduct a reconnaissance the night before the attack. It had been a bloody affair, as he wrote in a letter to his brother:

Suddenly there was an explosion, a hot flame seared my neck and I was dazzled by vivid streaks and sparks. The colonel, who was behind me on the same patrol, seemed to be lifted up and thrown into a bush. I was knocked over and lay stunned for a little. I must have stepped right over the mine. I got up and saw a figure behind me all quiet and dark, and another just behind groaning slightly. The first was a sapper officer, quite dead, with his face blown away. I lifted up the other who had stopped groaning. It was Lance-Corporal Atkinson with both his legs off. His breath came out with a great gurgling song and he died. Oh the smell of the hot thick blood on my hands and of the fumes of cordite. They haunt me still . . . I dread this attack . . . I am so afraid of disgracing myself.

Mark Clark arrived in the beachhead as the Green Howards were reorganising themselves the following day. At 2000 hours, less than 12 hours before VI Corps attacked, he held a press conference in which he declared that although the aim was 'to cut Highway 6 . . . with the ultimate objective of destroying as many Germans as possible' he had 'a flexible mind, and, depending upon what the Germans did, was prepared to meet several eventualities . . . one, a change in the direction of attack from due north to northwest.' The assembled correspondents were not surprised by what he said as this was the first time that they had heard any details about the operation, indeed they were distinctly impressed by Clark's confidence and the many possibilities open to the VI Corps. However, Major Mal Polton, one of Truscott's staff officers who had arrived in the beachhead only a week before, was intrigued by the Fifth Army commander's words. He recalls:

What struck me about what Clark said was not so much that there were other options to Operation 'Buffalo' – the attack to Valmontone – contingency plans were part and parcel of his job, but the stridency with which he articulated them. It seemed as though he were laying down a challenge, not only to the Germans, but to his superiors . . . He might as well have said, 'I don't think that we should be attacking north, we should be pushing north west to Rome'. I got the impression – and it may have been because I was so closely involved in certain aspects of the planning for the breakout and so was a little precious of 'Buffalo' – that Clark was using the press conference as another warning to VI Corps head-quarters that he was intent on Rome.

On the eve of battle, Clark was as fixated with the Italian capital as he had always been – possibly more so. Rome was now within his sights and as he said in answer to a question at the end of the press conference: 'I intend to take Rome, and to take it soon – nothing will stand in my way.'

At 0515 hours on 23 May, Mark Clark, Lucian Truscott and several members of the VI Corps staff were waiting in an artillery observation post just behind 1st Armored and 3rd Divisions. Truscott later wrote:

> Around us, we could see nothing. There was no sight or sound to indicate that more than 150,000 men were tensely alert and waiting. All was strangely quiet, and in the darkness that precedes dawn, the whole forward area seemed almost empty. There was tenseness in the air and little talk among us. For better or worse, the die was cast as the minute hands of watches moved slowly toward the zero hour.
>
> 0545! There was a crash of thunder and bright illuminating flashes against the sky behind us as more than one thousand guns, infantry cannon, mortars, tanks, and tank destroyers opened fire. That first crash settled into a continuous rumbling roar. Some distance ahead, a wall of fire appeared as our first salvos crashed into the enemy front lines, then the tracers move eerie patterns in streaks of light as hundreds of machine guns of every calibre poured a hail of steel into the enemy positions. Where we stood watching, the ground quivered and trembled.

Forty minutes later, as day broke, the guns ceased firing. Through the dust and smoke, fighter and light bombers attacked Cisterna. The town took a heavy pounding: buildings, roads and known defences were targeted in a ferocious five-minute raid. On its conclusion, there was a temporary silence, broken abruptly by an intense barrage in support of the attacking tanks and infantry. Robert Dodge wrote:

> Hell let loose its fury. Artillery, mortars, machine guns, and tanks. You never heard such noise. The battle of Armageddon had been joined . . . As the units in the initial assault moved out, it was awe-inspiring. Tanks emerged from everywhere: houses, straw piles, and ditches. The ground had dried out enough for them to maneuver. The force of the shelling really made it hard to breathe, and excitement mixed with fear made it hard to keep from trembling. The 50 calibre machine guns behind us all opened up, and the muzzle blast made your whole body vibrate.

With dry mouths, and lurching stomachs they stepped into No Man's Land. Spurred on by the sight of their comrades moving forward, they followed. Officers and NCOs shouted encouragement and the units managed to advance unmolested for 150 yards before the Germans, having risen from their shelters, began to cut them down. Norman Mohar says that the slaughter 'was as terrible as what was to happen on Omaha Beach in Normandy a couple of weeks later.' Firing from their trenches and pillboxes, the Germans had survived the attentions of bomb and shell and poured fire on the attacking infantry as they struggled through the wire. This barrier was largely unbroken and, in the teeth of the enemy's small arms, mortar and artillery fire, had to be broken with the wire-cutting 'Bangalore' torpedoes or hand-held cutters. In a few places, corpses were thrown on to the barbed wire to enable crossing points. As the Americans filtered through, the German machine guns trained their weapons on the gaps and more men fell. Norman Mohar was in one of the leading waves that morning:

> Vividly in my mind is the scene of the first wave strewn on the barbed wire. I recognized one of the GIs . . . I recognized his black curly hair. His helmet was blown off. All that remained was his upper torso, nude, lying across the concertina wire with his guts strewn over the wire. He must have gotten a direct hit. His squad was also killed by that blast or several blasts.

Those that managed to get through this first defensive obstacle, then had to run the gauntlet of an uncleared minefield covered by mortar, artillery and machine gun fire. Germans were occupying weapons pits and had to be removed in fierce hand to hand fighting. Above the soldiers 88-mm guns were firing air bursts. In such circumstances, the fire support of the Allied mortars was of great benefit. George Avery's mortars were following the infantry:

> The mortar can drop a shell from a few yards in front of us . . . to an extreme range of about two miles. So to be effective the mortars have to follow the infantry. From early sunrise to near noon, we had fired thousands of rounds at Germans who had been found by the infantry. But now the attacking forces were beyond us. The mortars were thrown into jeeps along with some shells and we rode cross-country. Destroyed tanks and dead littered the fields. The smell of the dead was in the air. But my sharpest memory was of being thirsty.

The division had pierced the German outpost zone and began attacking the main defences which would have to be ground down before Cisterna could be entered. Immediately the momentum of the attack began to falter. Private First Class John Dutko of 3rd Battalion of the 30th Regiment personally endeavoured to reinstall some impetus into the advance on his small sector of front when he attacked a troublesome 88-mm gun armed with his Browning Automatic Rifle. The 3rd Division historian describes what happened:

He ran 100 yards as machine gun bullets hit all around him and the 88 fired a couple of shells but he dived into a shell hole and the enemy machine guns converged their fire on it. Private Charles R. Kelley wrote: Dutko was a madman now. He jumped to his feet and walked toward the 88-mm firing his rifle from his hip. He had apparently forgotten the other two machine guns . . . When he had gone about halfway to the 88-mm he reached a point within ten yards of the weapon and wiped out the five man crew with a long burst of fire. Private First Class Dutko then wheeled on the second German machine gun and killed its two man crew with his BAR. The third machine gun opened fire . . . from twenty yards away and its first burst wounded him, making him stagger, but like a wounded lion he charged this gun in half run . . . killing the two man crew with a single burst.

It was his last act and he fell, mortally wounded. John Dutko was awarded a posthumous Medal of Honor. Having taken heavy casualties and tired after its lurch forward, John O'Daniel's men needed to be resupplied and reorganised before they could mount another attack on the town. Ensuring that the division got what it required to sustain itself in the offensive was a difficult job as the Germans cleverly laid a barrage behind the foremost American troops to stop movement. Private Daniel Goldstein of 15th Regiment dodged explosions all day in his role as a platoon ammunition man:

I had an awful job. I brought ammunition up, and took casualties back. By its very nature I was out in the open . . . It was often the case that the platoon would run out of ammunition when held up by an enemy strong point. Whilst they were all taking cover I would have to bob, duck and weave my way back to get whatever was needed . . . I'd then have to lug the ammo boxes, or sacks of grenades across the battlefield, often only to find that they had moved on leaving their casualties behind for me to recover . . . 23 May was a day that I'll never forget. Every time I moved there was a sniper, or a mortar barrage or an artillery bombardment . . . I could hardly do my job and there were many more like me, stuck in shell holes, wounded or dead.

Other American divisions had also found it difficult to impose themselves on the enemy during that first day. 1st Armored Division managed to advance two miles, but a thickly sown minefield initially slowed their advance and made them vulnerable to the German artillery. By noon Combat Command B had lost 23 tanks and seven tank destroyers. The armour managed to claw its way through to the Campoleone to Cisterna railway line, but here they ran into yet another minefield and carefully positioned anti-tank guns. Meanwhile, on their left flank, 45th Division took its limited objectives on the shoulder of the advance, but it too ran into a solid wall of German defenders. Lieutenant Gene Liggett, a Forward Observation Officer for the artillery, had a narrow escape that morning. Advancing with the infantry he had to lead two platoons through a minefield after their commanders had been killed, and then tried to reorganise the barrage to support them:

I was standing in a trench and looking around to see any activity that might take place ahead or to the sides of us. Obviously a German spotted me and fired a single round from an 88-mm gun that landed to the right side of me. A fragment from the exploding shell hit me on the right side of my head – coming through the steel helmet and plastic liner and hit the little metal clip holding the headband in. This little clip was bent almost double where the piece of steel had hit. It did fracture my skull as it hit just in front of and at about the top of my right ear. If I had had my head turned an eighth of an inch either way, it would have missed this little clip and killed me instantly.

As the Americans launched the main attack, the two British divisions began their feint. Trevelyan's platoon was nervous as it too had to negotiate a German minefield before it could get to grips with the enemy. On the way up to its jumping off point that morning, the radio operator shot himself. Reaching their designated position across the Moletta, Trevelyan gave the order: 'Fix bayonets. Cock your tommy-guns. Have your grenades ready.' When their barrage began, the platoon entered the minefield and the first casualties were taken. There was no time to stop for the wounded, the wall of shells was there for protection and could not be left to drift too far forward. A 'bloodcurdling yell – Charge!' was just what was needed to propel the men forward, but only eight were left standing having crossed No Man's Land. The platoon forged ahead regardless, and soon came across a German machine gun which opened fire at close range causing more casualties. Remarkably, Trevelyan was not amongst them in spite of leading the small group. His mind bent on revenge the Lieutenant and a few others tried to outflank the position. The barrage was 'falling with a retching crash in the trees and scrub . . . Clods of sand, scraps of branches, and white-hot shrapnel hurtled above us.' Before engaging the machine gun he was hit in the face, wrist, elbow and knee by fragments of hand grenades thrown by desperate Germans in the confusion. Nevertheless, as Trevelyan explained:

A furious, reckless excitement drove us on and at last Macdonnell and I reached the Jerry Spandaus. Macdonnell threw a grenade. After the explosion I ran to the edge of the dugout with my tommy-gun. There was still a German in it. I tried to use the tommy, but it was jammed. The German threw a grenade at my face, hitting me on the cheekbone. I was giddy, but could just see that the grenade had fallen back into the trench . . . A spout of earth and sand flew upwards. The German had gone.

This blockage removed, the platoon continued onwards as one of its number, Raymond Fort, describes:

We made our way forward mopping up the Germans, and when we got so far we had to stop because the casualties were so high and we were nearly out of ammunition . . . I finished up with a Bren gun because the Bren gunner was injured, and it didn't work . . . I had to literally get down and clean it and put it back together again before I could use it. It sounds crazy. I was laid on the floor with all this crap going on, but I had to do something with it . . . We couldn't see the lot in front of us. So it was a case of firing through the bushes at the attackers as they were attacking us.

The platoon took its objective, but as Trevelyan was at the Casualty Clearing Station having his wounds attended to, a German counter-attack pushed the Green Howards back across the Moletta.

By the end of 23 May, VI Corps had suffered some heavy losses. In the main attack, 3rd Division had lost 955 men (the largest number suffered by any one United States division in a single day during the war) and 1st Armored Division around 100 tanks and tank destroyers. However, in the Germans' stubborn defence, 362nd Division had lost half of its strength and two regiments of 715th Infantry Division were severely battered. Leutnant Gerhard Rahn, a platoon commander in 362nd Division who was to be awarded the German Cross in Gold for his performance at Anzio, recalls:

I experienced the Allied attack at Cisterna on 23 May 1944. Not counting the absolute hailstorm of bombs, the artillery preparatory fire – directed at the village and the surrounding buildings as well as the big road intersection and the supply roads – surpassed anything I had experienced up to that point, including the Russian theatre of war. Our grenadiers had set up packets of resistance in the ruins of the houses and farms. They fought bitterly . . . There was no shortage of courage on the part of our soldiers, not even the youngest ones. Even today, I am still convinced that it was a major accomplishment for our forces to have held up the enemy offensive for as long and as effectively as they did.

The Americans had not shattered the German defences, but they had put themselves in a position, as Truscott had hoped that they would, to take the attack further forward. The British diversionary attack had also fulfilled its objective and pinned 4th Parachute and 65th Divisions in the west. Von Mackensen was convinced that the main attack would be launched along the Via Anziate and the events of 23 May had not persuaded him otherwise. The second day of the offensive did not change his mind either, even though the British remained rooted to the Moletta, and VI Corps continued to take ground. By the end of 24 May, the Americans had rendered Cisterna highly vulnerable and eroded the German defences still further. Truscott was now on the verge of a breakthrough.

The fighting in the beachhead could be clearly heard in Rome. Having already received news that the Allies were approaching from the south, Romans allowed themselves to think about liberation for the first time since late January. With it came the fear that the city might become another Stalingrad as the Germans had not made it clear whether they intended to fight there or not. The final decision was Hitler's, although Kesselring had no desire to become embroiled in a prolonged and resource sapping urban battle. Nevertheless, it was rumoured that all the bridges and main public buildings had been mined and pillboxes had been built outside the walls. In these circumstances, the Italian Resistance prepared themselves for a new phase of their war, one that they hoped would lead to a popular uprising if it became necessary. However, whilst there was no doubt that the Romans were more fervently anti-fascist and anti-German than ever before, the population had become more submissive over the previous two months in the wake of the retribution meted out after the Via Rasella bomb. In this attack on 23 March orchestrated by Carla Capponi, a 40-pound bomb had been placed in a rubbish cart in the Via Rasella, and detonated when a company of German policemen marched past. Thirty-three had been killed and another seventy wounded. Hitler was livid and 335 Italians held in German prisons in Rome were shot two days later in the Ardeatine Caves just outside the city. A new wave of fear swept over the capital, the effects of which were still being felt at the end of May. There were more arrests, more sweeps of working class districts for forced labour, crippling price rises and a bread ration imposed that was the equivalent of two slices a day. The Resistance reacted with more bombings and shootings whilst Allied air raids continued to target barracks, marshalling yards and communication hubs. Fabia Sciarillo lived through this frightening time:

It was a dark period in Rome's history. We tried to get on with our lives, but it was impossible. I spent more and more time just trying to find food as all around the violence continued. I had one friend killed in March by a Gapist bomb, another in April in a shooting, and two killed in May during American air raids. The press talked about thousands perishing in these raids and I am sure that it was true. I saw the bodies lying on the pavement covered by blankets. Whole streets were demolished . . . Added to this were the German raids during spring which sought to uncover saboteurs and politicos.

We heard terrible stories about what happened to them . . . As the American and British troops got closer to Rome, there were more Germans on the street, and they became more brutal with the people. We hated them, but I suppose they were trying to frighten us into not rising up against them – it worked.

In mid-March the German dragnet searches dealt Peter Tompkins' OSS network a fatal blow when his radio operator Maurizio Giglio was arrested. The subsequent ending of transmissions to Fifth Army head-quarters was a blow to Mark Clark's intelligence, and even though Tompkins tried other methods of getting messages through, nothing now worked. Nevertheless, even as this particular method of assisting the Allies collapsed, another was developing with the organisation of partisan groups. The ambushes and demolitions conducted by the partisans had a demoralising effect on the Germans, and provided yet another challenge to their logisticians who were already at the end of their tether dealing with Operation Strangle. Private Pip Matthews had joined the partisans in November 1943. Matthews was taken prisoner in Sicily during July and subsequently sent to a prisoner of war camp near Parma. Released by the Italians on the announcement of the armistice, he then tried to make his way back to Allied lines. On one cold autumnal evening, he was sheltered by an Italian shepherd who, through contacts, introduced him to some members of the Resistance in Rome. With them, he established a partisan unit, armed with German weapons taken in ambushes conducted by other groups. The Cambridge-educated Matthews was a natural rebel who had turned down a Commission when he joined up in 1942, and had twice reached the rank of Sergeant only to lose it 'in a clash of personal-ities and of fists'. Pip Matthews recalls:

I was nominally the leader, but there wasn't much leading to do, we were all motivated and organised ourselves. I suppose I was the co-ordinator, making sure that we turned up at the right place, at the right time, with necessary kit to do the job . . . There were seven of us in total. Hairy beyond belief and scruffy looking just like partisans – or the hill farmers that we purported to be . . . There was me – an ex-prisoner of war, a Gapist chappie from Rome – very angry, a German deserter, a disillusioned lawyer, a laddie on the run for murdering a German soldier after some altercation or other, his brother and a fallen priest – he rather liked the ladies and his booze. Your average psychotic group of thugs and misfits . . . We were active in the Sabine Hills, not far from Kesselring's headquarters. We ambushed, raided, bombed, assassinated and demolished. We struck quickly, hard and legged it. None of us was ever caught. I doubt that any of us were ever seen. We had Jerry in all sorts of trouble – and there were many groups like ours doing similar things. Marvellous fun!

With partisan actions on the increase, Allied bombers enjoying the clear blue skies of an Italian spring and two Allied ground offensives developing south of Rome, Albert Kesselring was in an unenviable position during the last week of May. There was little that he could do about the partisans and the bombers, but his direction of Tenth and Fourteenth Armies would undoubtedly influence events. The Field Marshal had a clear idea of what Alexander was trying to do because – looking at the situation – it was exactly what he would have done: break out, block Route 7 and then strike into the Velletri Gap to cut Route 6. But how was he to counter this? The obdurate von Mackensen would not concede that the British push up the Via Anziate was a diversion. Kesselring later wrote that von Mackensen was 'unable to rid himself of a preconceived fixation as to the way the breakout from the beachhead would go.' Yet even if von Mackensen did shift his weight to a defence around Cisterna, Kesselring believed that it would be too late to stop an American breakthrough, and could lead to the collapse of the Fourteenth Army altogether. He therefore decided that von

Mackensen should defend for as long as possible against VI Corps to allow Tenth Army time to withdraw down Route 6 and take up defensive positions in the northern Caesar Line. General von Mackensen would, in the meantime, fight rearguard actions to allow him to conduct a staged withdrawal to the southern sector of the position. The greatest threat to this plan was if VI Corps broke through and blocked Route 6 at Valmontone before Tenth Army had withdrawn past it. Recognising this, Kesselring ordered the Hermann Göring Panzer Division to travel the 150 miles to Valmontone as soon as possible to hold the road open. It was going to be another race between VI Corps and the Germans. If Truscott won it, the Fifteenth Army Group would be in an excellent position to seek revenge on Tenth Army for all the difficulties that it had caused them since the previous autumn. But first Truscott had to break out. For every hour that he was not at Valmontone, more of von Vietinghoff's troops would escape.

By the evening of 24 May, Truscott was satisfied with his Corps's progress. The Germans had been stretched to breaking point and had not concentrated against the main attack. Most of the battle zone was in American hands and Cisterna was about to fall. With such solid progress, and the news that II Corps was at Terracina just thirty miles away, the prospects for VI Corps looked brighter than they had for months. Truscott was on the verge of cracking Fourteenth Army wide open, and Clark was on the cusp of a great victory. The destruction of a large part of Tenth Army looked achievable. But that night Clark was to directly ask Truscott, 'Have you considered changing the direction of your attack towards Rome?'

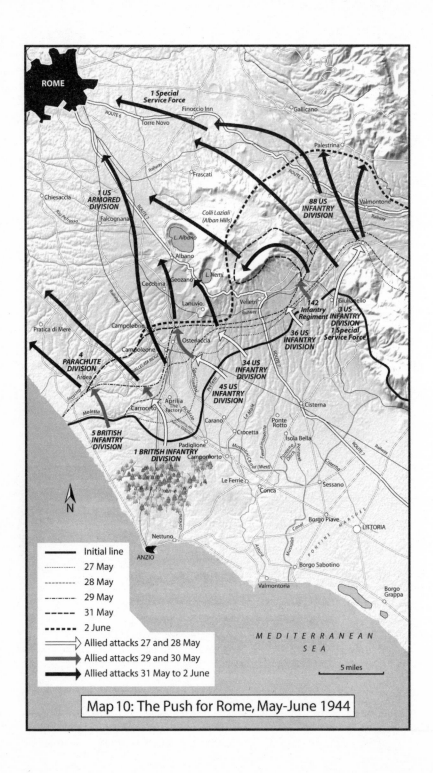

ROME

1 Special
Service Force

Finoccio Inn

Gallicano

ROUTE 6

Torre Novo

Palestrina

Chiesaccia

Rio Pel rosso

1 US
ARMORED
DIVISION

ROUTE 2

Falcognana

Frascati

Colli Laziali
(Alban Hills)

ROUTE 6

Valmontone

88 US
INFANTRY
DIVISION

Railway

L. Albano

Albano

Railway

Cecchina

Geozano

Lanuvio

L. Nemi

Campolebrie

Campoleone

Ostenaccia

Vallelata Ridge

4
PARACHUTE
DIVISION

Ardea

Spacciato

Fosso

34 US
INFANTRY
DIVISION

Velletri

Railway

36 US
INFANTRY
DIVISION

142
Infantry
Regiment

Giulianello

3 US
INFANTRY
DIVISION
1 Special
Service Force

ROUTE 7

Pratica di Mare

Incastro

Moletta

Carroceto

45 US
INFANTRY
DIVISION

Aprilia
The
Factory

Fosso

Carano

Crocetta

Lo Moletta

Ponte
Rotto

Isola Bella

Pontino

Cisterna

Railway

ROUTE 7

5 BRITISH
INFANTRY
DIVISION

1 BRITISH
INFANTRY
DIVISION

Padiglione

Camponforto

Mussolini Canal (West)

Le Ferrie

Conca

Fonte

Sessano

Borgo Piave

LITTORIA

N

Nettuno

ANZIO

Loricino

Wood

Astura

Canal

Mussolini

Fontine

Canal

Borgo Sabotino

Valmontoria

PONTINE MARSHES

Borgo
Grappa

	Initial line
	27 May
	28 May
	29 May
	31 May
	2 June
⇨	Allied attacks 27 and 28 May
➡	Allied attacks 29 and 30 May
➡	Allied attacks 31 May to 2 June

MEDITERRANEAN
SEA

5 miles

Map 10: The Push for Rome, May–June 1944

CHAPTER 10

The Eternal City

(25 May–5 June)

Captain Ben Souza's platoon of combat engineers were enjoying the first warming rays of the morning sun after a successful night's work. The previous evening Souza and his men had set out from the Anzio beach-head, and having crossed the Mussolini Canal, managed to push ten miles into the flooded Pontine Marshes. They had just passed through the village of Borgo Grappa south of Latina when a destroyed bridge over a narrow stream slowed their advance. Ben Souza had just picked his way across the debris to reach the opposite bank when a jeep roared up the road towards him. Its driver, Lieutenant Francis Buckley, offered a feeble salute. 'Where the hell do you think you're going?' inquired Souza. 'I'm trying to make contact with the Anzio forces,' replied Buckley. Souza grinned, 'Boy you've made it!' It was 0730 hours on 25 May. VI Corps had been reunited with Fifth Army, and the siege of the Anzio beachhead was over. It was a trivial event but of major importance, for within half an hour this inauspicious spot of coastal Italy was filling with reconnaissance troops from both VI and II Corps. At his Anzio command post Mark

Clark had been informed of the meeting of forces thirty minutes after the first hands had been shaken, and although delighted, continued with a scheduled conference with Lucian Truscott to talk about his plan to re-direct some of VI Corps formations towards Rome. However, Clark left for Borgo Grappa at the first opportunity and by 1030 hours was at the bridge mingling with the troops, insisting that the historic meeting be re-enacted for the twenty-five war correspondents and photographers he had in his entourage. In the subsequent photographs (that his public rela-tions staff ensured were immediately telegraphed around the world) Clark stands smiling, his back to the cheering troops behind him. As he posed the general kept repeating, 'It's a great day for the Fifth Army.' Alan Whicker looked on with amazement, later noting: 'For us, used to senior officers who were not expected to act, it was a new kind of actuality – as handled by Hollywood.'

It had been an important occasion for Fifth Army, and Mark Clark was determined to ensure that he was firmly associated with it. On his return to Anzio he issued instructions that he believed would guarantee his next major photo-call would be in the Eternal City. There was to be an attack by part of VI Corps to the north-west which would 'press vigorously towards Rome'. Clark sent a message to his Chief of Staff, Alfred Gruenther, back at his main headquarters which ended:

> I am launching this new attack with all possible speed in order to take advantage of impetus of our advance and in order to over-whelm the enemy in what may be a demoralized condition at the present time. You can assure General Alexander that this is an all-out attack. We are shooting the works.

Alexander certainly needed reassuring, for 25 May had been a successful day for Operation Buffalo. Even though the Fifteenth Army Group commander was concerned that Eighth Army was not putting General von Vietinghoff's men under the sort of pressure that would drive them remorselessly down Route 6 to their destruction, VI Corps was making progress. Under Truscott's pressure across the front the Fourteenth Army was disintegrating and Cisterna eventually fell. After three days of unwavering determination and 1,400 casualties, 3rd Division finally took the town that it had first hoped to capture at the end of January. At 1630 hours the Germans made their last radio transmission after an heroic stand. Rather than withdrawing, the brave men of General Greiner's 362nd Division had fought on without reinforcements and minimal resupply, forcing the Americans to winkle them out of the rubble-strewn streets building by building. In so doing the German formation had virtually ceased to exist, and John O'Daniel's men had attained a base from which to strike out into the Velletri Gap. The war correspondent Eric Sevareid entered the town soon after it had fallen and was shocked by the utter destruction that he found there. There was no longer any pattern to the streets, merely broken walls, brick dust and thousands of spent cartridge cases. In the wake of the tumult Cisterna had taken on an eerie stillness. Sevareid wrote:

> In the little park the palm trees lay blackened and uprooted. Over them a shining white victory statue stood erect on a pedestal. It was the figure of a woman holding aloft a torch in a gesture of triumph. Though her marble head and her torch were gone, in its present attitude of shocked surprise the statue seemed the only vital, living thing within the town.

But there was no time for the 3rd Division to relax thinking that its task was completed. This was only the beginning. No sooner had the last Germans been rounded up from their squalid cellars, than the bulldozers were clearing a path for tanks and tank destroyers to push forward. By the end of the day the formation had taken up a position between the Alban Hills and the Lepini Mountains near Cori. George Avery experienced the surge forward with the division's spearhead:

Cisterna was an utter ruin, not one building untouched. The rubble was so bad that the tanks had compacted a roadway above the original road when they passed through the city. Beyond the town in the open fields there were few Germans in sight. We were on the paved road to Cori . . . Here we dug in . . . We were within ten miles of Valmontone where the Germans had retreated and were preparing to make a stand.

On 3rd Division's left was Ernest Harmon's 1st Armored Division whose reserve, a task force commanded by the vigorous and colour-fully named Colonel Hamilton H. Howze, had struck out on the morning of 25 May to pierce the northern aspect of the Caesar Line and block Route 6. The only opposition that he found initially was a handful of German tanks falling back from the front into the Velletri Gap. Robert Dodge watching events unfold:

We got into some beautiful hills, where we could look across a broad valley. In the shelter of some rises, we had a mixture of everything. Cannon company light tanks with .75-mm howitzers were firing over the hill, medium tanks were regrouping, and infantry was lying waiting to move out. There was a tank battle taking place in a broad valley. I could see four Tiger tanks, sitting on knolls, firing at our Sherman tanks. Our tanks would sit behind knolls, revving their engines, dash to the top, fire, and be on their way down en masse at once. It was like a shooting gallery; the Jerries kept picking off our tanks. I watched the Shermans make hits in the Tigers, but the shells (tracers) just rico-cheted into the clouds. When one of our tanks was hit, it just sat there and burned. Sometimes survivors got out and made a run for cover, sometimes not. At one time four of our tanks were burning.

The Tigers were protecting the road running from Cori to Giulianello, then packed with over 600 Fourteenth Army vehicles in retreat. As the tank battle raged, Allied aircraft attacked the convoy. Howze later said he sent a battalion commanded by Lieutenant Colonel Bogardus S. Cairn to 'complete the job' of destruction and it revelled in 'chewing up' the Germans. Howze recalled:

> There were 15 Mark VI Tiger tanks on that road when I drove down a day or two later, as well as great quantities of guns and half tracks. At the head of our column, which was all mixed up with the destroyed German column . . . there was carnage indeed: bodies and pieces of bodies strewn about among the wrecked and burning vehicles. The air force added further excitement by strafing the entire area, without taint of discrimination, spraying German troops as well as American.

There were a number of 'friendly fire' incidents that afternoon and Dodge was wounded by a P-40 fighter bomber:

> When they started firing we dove from the truck. All the army trucks had yellow smoke grenades taped to the windshield to signal friendly forces. All you had to do was grab and throw. There was yellow smoke everywhere . . . Looking I saw four bombs leave the first plane as it roared down strafing. I dropped to the road beside the truck. One bomb landed on the other side of the road, right in the midst of my friends. I had a sapling beside me cut down by a bullet. I lay on my belly with my arms bent along my chest. My left arm was away from the blast. The blast must have picked me up, and the shrapnel went under me to hit my arm, I can't explain it. We had many casualties on the truck; five were killed.

That afternoon Howze's reconnaissance units pushed up to Artena, just three miles from Valmontone, encountering only the weak spearhead of the Hermann Göring Panzer Division arriving from Leghorn. The Colonel himself drove back to the division's headquarters that night to ask Harmon to throw 1st Armored forward to exploit the situation. In such circumstances Truscott became confident that by the 26th, Howze would be astride Route 6 leaving the road to Rome undefended.

On the evening of 25 May Operation Buffalo was proceeding to plan. The Americans were putting Fourteenth Army under extreme pressure across their front: 34th Division was striking towards Velletri at the foot of the Alban Hills, 45th Division was pushing at Campoleone whilst 3rd and 1st Armored Divisions were poised to strike towards Valmontone. There was a positive attitude abroad in Truscott's command, captured in a letter written by George Avery to his girlfriend that evening: 'I am writing this in the field my knee serving as a writing desk. I suppose it's old news to you but there is no longer an Anzio Beachhead . . . It's good to be moving. The fields are overrun with poppies.' Although VI Corps had suffered 3,357 casualties in less than three days' fighting, it was in an excellent position to penetrate to his objective and cut Route 6. It was, therefore, with some dismay that Truscott received notice from Clark that he was to move the focus of his attack to the south of the Alban Hills. This was the strongest part of the Caesar Line and was defended by three stalwart German formations: the 4th Parachute, the 65th, and the 3rd Panzer Grenadier Divisions. Clark had taken the decision to eviscerate Operation Buffalo, sacrificing it to satisfy his lust for Rome. He had convinced himself that he could obviate a number of difficulties by pushing a weakened force through to Valmontone whilst reassigning the power to Route 7: Alexander would be unable to complain that his order had not been carried out (for the remaining force would be strong enough to block Route 6) and would mean that Truscott need not undertake a tricky 90-degree turn for his forces to push down Route 6. Why court disaster when Route 7 offered a far more efficient and shorter route to Rome? Clark later rationalised his decision:

Alexander never gave me orders not to take Rome . . . I know he was concerned about my maintaining my thrust to Valmontone, but hell when we were knocking on its door we had already destroyed as much of the German Tenth Army as we could have ever expected . . . One thing I knew was that I had to take Rome and that my American army was going to do it. So in all the circumstances I had to go for it before the British loused it up . . . We had earned it you understand.

With no regard for the consequences, the Fifth Army Commander was willing to snatch what little glory the Italian front had to offer.

Truscott received his orders from Clark's Operations Officer, Brigadier General Don Brann: 'The Boss wants you to leave the 3rd Division and the Special Force to block Highway 6 and mount that assault you discussed with him to the north as soon as you can.' 3rd US Division, the Special Service Force and part of the 1st US Armored Division were to continue north eastwards to Valmontone while the 34th and 45th Divisions were to turn north towards Rome. The 36th Division was to strike between the diverging thrusts and would free the bulk of the 1st US Armored Division for an exploitation expected across the west side of the Alban Hills. Truscott had known that Clark was keeping his options open, indeed he had spoken to him that very morning about various scenarios, but was 'dumbfounded' at this development. A large part of VI Corps would not only have to turn on to a congested road system, which in itself would take days, but also realign its artillery, headquarters and artillery before endeavouring to break a heavily occupied sector of the Caesar Line. Truscott later lamented that:

I protested that the conditions were not right. There was no evidence of any withdrawal from the western part of the beachhead, nor was there evidence of any concentration in the

Valmontone area . . . This was no time to drive northwest where the enemy was still strong; we should pour our maximum power into the Valmontone Gap to insure the destruction of the retreating German army.

Clark knew that the order was difficult to justify and so had left Brann to notify Truscott and Gruenther to inform Alexander. Clark's Chief of Staff waited until the changes were a *fait accompli* before telegraphing Alexander late on the morning of 26 May:

The enemy forces opposing the beachhead in the Cisterna . . . area have been decisively defeated. The beachhead and main Fifth Army forces have joined. The overwhelming success of the current battle makes it possible to continue . . . towards Valmontone with powerful forces and to launch a new attack along the most direct route to Rome.

Harold Alexander was concerned at this news. He was rattled by Clark's impertinence and felt duped. Nevertheless, true to form, having digested the news and with stiff upper lip firmly in place, he replied to the Fifth Army headquarters: 'I am for any line which the army commander believes will offer a chance to continue his present success.' But he still couldn't help plaintively asking Gruenther, 'I am sure the army commander will continue to push towards Valmontone, won't he?' After the war Clark used the fact that, even at this late stage, Alexander did not overrule his decision as a way to justify it. In reality Alexander's muted response to his subordinate's decision was not tacit approval, it was impotence. It was too late to influence events. He had had his chance to reprimand Clark a few days earlier, and elected not to take it. Now he was paying the price. Truscott's divisional commanders were far less restrained in their reaction to the news of Clark's whim when the VI Corps commander presented the new plan to them. Harmon and O'Daniel in particular were furious. However, the assiduously loyal Truscott tried to justify a decision that he disagreed with by stating: 'The Boche is badly disorganized, has a hodgepodge of units and if we can drive as hard as we can tomorrow as we have done the last three days, a great victory is in our grasp.' The focus of the attack was now towards Velletri, Lanuvio and Campoleone and there was nothing that the VI Corps generals could about it for, as Brann had observed: 'There's no point in arguing. It's an order.' Howze was equally livid when he was awoken at 0200 hours on 26 May and told the news. He thought that Harmon was calling to authorise a thrust to Valmontone, but instead he was told that his force was to be cannibalised, with the larger part being assigned to the new push south of the Alban Hills. He later bemoaned the decision: 'I was sick about these orders, being very anxious to continue the deal of the day before.'

26 May became a day of reorganisation as Truscott rejigged his corps prior to carrying out orders. But whilst VI Corps was busy wasting its opportunity, the Germans true to form were calmly taking theirs. Kesselring threw elements of four divisions into the Velletri Gap in an attempt to stall the Allies. The Hermann Göring Panzer Division began its journey down to Valmontone from Leghorn on 23 May, but lost heavily en route at the hands of Allied aircraft. The division had been concerned that it was dangerous to move in daylight, and that they lacked fuel, but Kesselring was adamant that it had to take the losses and arrive before the Allies broke through. Peter Coup was a B-25 Mitchell bomber pilot flying out of Naples and recalls:

> The squadron was told that the Hermann Göring Division was on the move and we were sent to stop it. We attacked its convoys five times and did a great deal of damage . . . As we approached the Germans could hear us and would man their anti-aircraft guns, but rarely caused a problem . . . . Most ran for cover because bombs exploding in vehicles do terrible damage to bodies when the metal starts flying about . . . On one occasion a convoy was trapped at a

destroyed bridge and its tanks and lorries were pulverised. The next day we were sent again. The surviving vehicles, and perhaps some others, had managed to advance maybe ten miles. In the distance we could see the smoke from vehicles that we had hit the previous day.

General Wilhelm Schmalz's division lost 30 per cent of its fighting vehicles, 20 per cent of the heavy weapons, and 18 guns of the divisional artillery during its journey. It arrived over 26 to 29 May tired and shaken, but was thrown into battle piecemeal. Its first probe of the enemy took place during the night of 26 May and it was followed the next day by a determined attack to retake the weakly held Artena from 1st Armored Division. However, throughout the day 3rd Division and 1st Special Service Force were moving deeper into the Velletri Gap and by the evening, O'Daniel and Frederick were in firm control of the town, albeit under a storm of German steel from artillery, tanks and mortars around Valmontone. For four days the two sides slugged it out, neither giving ground, but on 30 May the Germans could not withstand the pressure and withdrew, although having achieved its aim of giving Tenth Army the space and time in which to withdraw. Seven of von Vietinghoff's divisions were pulled back east of Rome during the tête-à-tête between the two extemporised forces. The opportunity to destroy a significant number of Tenth Army divisions had been lost and Alexander was left to reflect sombrely on the signal that he had recently received from Churchill:

> I should feel myself wanting in comradeship if I did not let you know that the glory of this battle, already great, will be measured, not by the capture of Rome or the juncture with the bridgehead, but by the number of German divisions cut off.

Meanwhile, the attack south of the Alban Hills had begun against the Caesar Line outposts: 36th Division struck against Velletri, 34th Division towards Lanuvio, and 45th Division threatened Campoleone. 1st

Division, meanwhile, pushed up the Via Anziate whilst 5th Division held the Moletta. As Truscott expected, the resistance was fierce and Route 7 remained firmly closed. Ray McAllister of 45th Division regretted that the leadership of his unit was compromised by chronic casualties:

> We had lost our platoon Lieutenant and his replacement was a 90-day wonder. Without combat experience he was soon to destroy his whole platoon. We had taken over a German position abandoned as we pushed forward. I was in a covered foxhole with several wounded when he called the platoon into a football huddle to tell them what we would do next. The Germans had the place well zeroed in, something the old hands would have known, but by now most of the platoon was replacements. They dropped a couple of 90-mm mortar shells on the platoon . . . one mortar shell apparently hit the Lieutenant on the shoulder because his upper body was blown away. The whole platoon was hit and several killed. When I heard the shells and screams I raced out, too late for some but was able to get others into the covered bunker. By the grace of God I was in the bunker with the wounded or I'd have been blown away too.

The front line either stayed resolutely still, or just crept forward. The 'Factory' was taken on 28 May by 1st Division and, just like 3rd Division's capture of Cisterna, was a poignant moment, but it too found that there was barely the time to bury their dead from February than it was being used as a base from which to launch another attack. VI Corps made no significant impression on the Fourteenth Army defences until 1st Armored Division was finally in a position to attack on 29 May. Then Campoleone Station was taken followed by an advance into the main defences of the Caesar Line. However, even the armour ran into difficulties when it outran its support and was subsequently badly mauled by German anti-tank guns, losing 21 Shermans and 16 tank destroyers. Among those killed that day was General George Marshall's stepson, Lieutenant Allen T. Brown, with whom he was extremely close. The event did not improve his deeply held belief that Italy was a 'sideshow of a sideshow'. The carnage continued when Ernest Harmon's men threw themselves valiantly against the German 88-mm guns again the following day and another 23 tanks and tank destroyers were lost for no territorial gain. Sergeant Tony Glenister of Combat Command A recalls:

> An 88-mm round blew up the Sherman in front of us and we could hear the screaming inside. It was a tank man's worst nightmare, being burned alive . . . We saw one of our non-coms run up to the side of the tank and let loose with his machine gun at the side, between the treads until the screaming stopped. I doubt that his bullets penetrated the armor but it was terrible to listen to men being burned to death and not being able to help.

Burning tanks littered the battlefield, a poignant reminder of German resilience and Mark Clark's grandiosity and folly.

As May drew to a close Clark was facing the prospect of his front against the Caesar Line becoming stalemated. His change of direction had not led to a rapid breakthrough to Rome along Route 7, and was yet another wretched lesson in the need to concentrate forces. But just as the Fifth Army commander was beginning to think that his dream of seizing Rome before Operation Overlord was launched was fading fast, an unlikely saviour stepped forward. Major General Fred Walker's 36th Division was among the least respected formations under Clark's command and had been attacking Velletri for four days with little but heavy casualties to show for it. However, a reconnaissance force had managed to penetrate a gap in the Caesar Line and climb the steep slopes of Monte Artemisio behind the town to take up a strong position. Walker believed that if two regiments could be pushed up there, then Velletri would be rendered fatally vulnerable and fall. Neither Truscott nor Clark was convinced that this plan would work, but by 30 May they were willing to give it a try. Clark remarked to Walker, 'Fred, if you do it and succeed, we are on our way to Rome; but if you fail you will have to bear the brunt of what comes with the failure, and your action will be without my approval or the approval of Truscott.' But it did work, and by the time von Mackensen learned of the situation on 31 May, it was too late to do anything about it. Corporal David Stearns remembers:

> We climbed through the night, not knowing where the enemy were, up a steep slope. It was cold that night, and the rocks made us trip and stumble, but we just kept going . . . We climbed and climbed and by dawn we were standing on a long ridge overlooking Velletri. Boy what a view. We could see into the broad valley up to Artena and the Lepini Mountains, and down to the old beachhead . . . There were plumes of smoke rising all over, testament to the continued fighting for miles around.

Fred Walker had unlocked the front for, just as he predicted, the defending 362nd Division *Kampfgruppe* had been forced to withdraw.

This was a turning point. Truscott was delighted and Clark ecstatic. It also led to von Mackensen offering his resignation for the third time since his appointment to Fourteenth Army, and it being accepted just as Kesselring was about to sack him. Clark now sought an exploitation of the 36th Division penetration of the Caesar Line across the Alban Hills as the remainder of VI Corps continued to apply pressure to the south. He wished for an attack from the north-eastern side of the Alban Hills to be conducted under the auspices of II Corps which had arrived in the area having attacked along the coast and pushed north into the Velletri Gap. As 3rd Division advanced to Valmontone, First Special Service Force, spearheaded by Task Force Howze, was to turn onto Route 6 supported by 88th Division battalions, and with 85th Division advancing on its left across the northern slopes of the Alban Hills, push into eastern Rome. To facilitate this, the boundary with Eighth Army was moved to the north of Route 6 by Alexander as Leese was still twenty-five miles away at Frosinone. Clark felt that this was only fair after the sluggish British advance, caustically observing in his diary that: 'The Eighth Army has done little fighting. It has lacked aggressiveness and failed in its part in this combined Allied effort.' Rather than pushing into Rome on an open road, the Eighth Army was to push to the east of the city whilst II Corps took the lead. The French, meanwhile, several miles ahead of the British and coming through the Lepini Mountains, were to follow General Geoffrey Keyes's Corps and then swing to the north of Rome. With this decision Clark knew that Rome would be his.

The renewed offensive against the Caesar Line hit the Germans hard. In the north on 1 June, they were pushed out of the Velletri Gap, fighting furiously as they went, and that afternoon 3rd Division entered Valmontone. Private First Class Donny Wilson recalls:

At last we had taken the town that had caused us so many problems over the past days . . . We moved down a street, broken and pock marked buildings all around. There was a strange sort of silence, as though the town had died, it gave me the creeps. We could hear the sound of a Sherman tank coming up behind us, but nothing else moved. Then a single shot rang out and the head of the man in front of me exploded. The yell 'SNIPER!' went out. I ran for the cover of a doorway. There was a great deal of shouting. A medic ran over to the shot man, stayed a second, and joined me. 'Dead' he said . . . Then the tank that was behind us rolled past. The tank commander was very brave as he was taking instructions from our platoon leader with his hatch open. Then the tank's gun traversed left and 'BOOM!' – with one shot took down half a roof. There was no sniper after that.

As II Corps advanced on 2 June, the Caesar Line collapsed. As Howze and Frederick moved onto Route 6, Lanuvio fell on the southern slopes of the Alban Hills and 36th Division gave battle to the remnants of 362nd Division which had managed to withdraw from Velletri across the heights. But whilst there were no Germans to detain Keyes as Tenth Army receded into the distance, Fourteenth Army – which had lost three quarters of its strength since 23 May – was still withdrawing and required rearguard actions to protect them as they fled north. Joachim Liebschner of 4th Parachute Division was on a training course in the Alban Hills when he and his 120 colleagues were given charge of 350 new paratroopers and were formed into a *kampfgruppe* to slow the enemy. Liebschner recalls:

I was given 10 youngsters and one experienced man and two heavy machine guns and was ordered to defend, or stop the onslaught along the Via Appia – Route 7 . . . I took over very good fortified positions already dug. I put a machine gun nest either side of the road and stayed with one on the right hand side . . . At between 8 and 9 the following morning the whole field in front of us was filled with hundreds of Americans, their rifles slung across their shoulders or at their hip, walking towards us as though it were peacetime. We held our fire until they were 100 to 120 yards on top of us. Then we let go and caused an incredible amount of havoc. They were just falling like nine pins and the rest withdrew back into the woods. It took them about half an hour to sort out where we were and then they hammered us with their artillery and even heavy artillery, anything they had for half an hour or so and it was quite, quite devastating. I had never lived through anything like this as they had pin-pointed us quite exactly and now they were letting fly and the noise of it . . . We went down into the bunkers and we even then took the machine guns down as they would not have survived it.

The American infantry followed up the bombardment, but such was the devastation that they passed the bunkers:

We brought our machine gun into position again and started firing again and all we could see, the whole fore field was full of Americans and tanks and jeeps and lorries – above all tanks. We fired for another half a minute or a minute or two and the people who had already jumped over our trench came back. They opened fire, and three of us survived out of the 12 and surrendered. Of the other two one was badly wounded in his leg and the other was a tall uninjured youngster. We were chased through that field that we had been firing at by two Americans who were swearing at us. We were running along with our hands above our heads when they shot the tall fellow in front of me. He got a bullet right into his neck so that the main artery had been hit and the blood was spurting out and he ran another two or three steps and he turned around and then fell to the ground. I tried to kneel down in order to bandage him up, but I wasn't allowed to do that and was kicked away. He wouldn't have survived.

Liebschner and the other prisoner were ushered through the woods, then driven off to a prisoner of war compound in Anzio:

This was the first time that I thought that we could not win the war because all the war material I could see the Americans moving forward – the roads were simply full of tanks, lorries, jeeps – and moving during day time. We couldn't move a bicycle in the daytime without being shot at. The roads were jammed with traffic, they were moving this huge mass of war material, guns and tanks.

Back in London, Winston Churchill was spending an increasing amount of time in his Map Room, watching the course of the unfolding battle with varying degrees of exasperation. He had been outraged at Clark's diversion, saddened by Eighth Army's failure to chase the Tenth Army as hard as they might, and dispirited by the failure to destroy the Tenth Army divisions. Churchill was prone to tremendous highs and deep lows, but by 2 June he was in limbo. Although his head kept telling him that he should be concerning himself with the prospects for Operation Overlord, then just days away from being launched, his heart continually drew him towards the large map of Italy. The Mediterranean had been his love for so long, that he felt unfaithful whenever he spent time with the cross-Channel invasion. So restless had the Prime Minister become by the enormity of events, that on 3 June he took a train down to Southampton to watch troops embark for Normandy. There, noted Alan Brooke, he made 'a thorough pest of himself!' The same day Kesselring ordered that there would be no German defence of Rome. He had received direct instructions from Hitler: 'Führer decision. There must not be a battle for Rome. If necessary, the Army Group must swing back far enough to the north-west to ensure that the city in no circumstances becomes a battlefield.' This choice had been taken not so much out of regard for the Eternal City's cultural importance, but because the Führer feared another Stalingrad and did not want to give the Romans encouragement to initiate a popular uprising. The Allies did not want an insurrection either; they wished to march into a political vacuum which they could fill, rather than a bloody civil war between Rome's diverse political groups. Thus, on the morning of 3 June the Allies had dropped leaflets over the city from 'Headquarters of General Alexander'. In them Romans were asked 'to stand shoulder-to-shoulder to protect the city from destruction and to defeat our common enemies . . . this is not the time for demonstrations. Obey these directions and go on with your regular work. Rome is yours! Your job is to save the city, ours is to destroy the enemy.' As the Romans read, the Germans were fleeing the city. The hotel district became congested with staff cars, the pavements crammed with luggage. Trucks, troops and tanks were all on the move northwards and documents were being burned. The Italian Resistance were now ruthlessly hunting down known informants. There were to be some German rearguard actions in Rome to defend the bridges and protect the withdrawal of Fourteenth Army units, but that was all.

In the capital the Germans were withdrawing to the increasingly audible sound of battle. Throughout the day 34th and 45th Divisions traversed the southern slopes of the Alban Hills leading to the fall of Genzano, Albano and Castel Gandolfo as 1st Armored Division positioned itself on Route 7. Meanwhile, as 85th Division advanced over the northern slopes of the Alban Hills, Frederick and Howze forged fifteen miles down Route 6 to reach Finocchio a mere six kilometres north of Kesselring's former Frascati headquarters. 'Monty' Smith of the First Special Service Force recalls:

> I rode on a Sherman through the hilly countryside. It was a beautiful day, we were approaching Rome and I was feeling fine. After all that time in the beachhead, to be moving again was just fine. I felt that I was part of history, making a dramatic entrance on a tank. I thought that I'd be sipping espresso in a café by the following morning.

There was an early celebratory atmosphere developing which concerned Gruenther who informed Clark 'the Command Post has gone to hell. No one is doing any work here this afternoon. All semblance of discipline has broken down.' The Fifth Army commander sent messages to his subordinate commanders reminding them that the battle to break into Rome might well be a bloody one, and instructed both VI and II Corps to push mobile forces (comprising armour, engineers and infantry) into Rome the following morning to seize bridges which he feared were under threat of being destroyed by the Germans. The aptly named Charles Bridge, a newly arrived engineer First Lieutenant, wrote in his diary that night:

> We are to enter Rome tomorrow. My first action and it's breaking into the Italian capital. I don't know whether to feel privileged or cursed. We have been told to expect opposition. Some are talking about street fighting and the difficulty of moving tanks through narrow streets. I just want to get it over and finished with. Do or die.

The II Corps spearhead pressed forward again at dawn on 4 June, but soon became embroiled in a battle with a German unit defending the suburb of Centrocelle three miles from the centre of Rome. Anti-tank guns, riflemen and automatic weapons threw down a heavy curtain of fire which destroyed several tanks and wounded, among others, 'Monty' Smith who recalls nothing of the incident and woke up in a military hospital two days later having had an arm and a leg amputated. The battle raged for nine hours and necessitated an outflanking manoeuvre. That afternoon Mark Clark arrived on the scene with Geoffrey Keyes supposedly to find out why there was a hold up. But Clark's presence there bore all the hallmarks of another publicity stunt. Frederick briefed the men in the shelter of a ditch and then Keyes, led by Clark, sauntered over to a large 'Roma' city limits sign followed by photographers. His vanity nearly cost him his life, for as he posed, a single rifle round smacked against the sign and the party threw themselves to the ground. The photograph that was subsequently taken shows the sign with accompanying bullet hole and two sheepish looking generals beneath. Frederick was immediately instructed to take the sign down, as Clark wanted it as a souvenir.

The Fifth Army commander had hoped to burst through to central Rome that afternoon, but all attempts to infiltrate the German defences failed. Tanks, half-tracks, anti-tank guns and flak wagons barred roads and were often covered by infantry. These pockets of resistance would have to be eliminated or forced to withdraw before the city could be entered. Meanwhile, as 34th and 45th Divisions were still mopping up around the Alban Hills, 1st Armored Division advanced towards the southern suburbs on Route 7. But just as Truscott was beginning to think that his men would have the honour of entering the capital first, the tanks ran into Fred Walker's 36th Division. Having left the Alban Hills, the infantry were determined to use Route 7 to beat Harmon's troops to the capital. Walker dismissed the objections of the officer commanding the head of the armoured column, Lieutenant Colonel Louis V. Hightower, by pointing to the two stars on his helmet. It was a chaotic, unnecessary situation which further delayed the VI Corps advance. A furious Truscott was driven as fast as the traffic jam allowed to confront Walker and order him off the road. 1st Armored Division then continued its advance to the city boundary where it was stopped by similar positions to those frustrating Frederick. Harmon and Truscott were following the attack, and moved forward to explore the blockage and discuss a solution to the problem. As they talked over a map a German machine gun opened up on them from a nearby stone outhouse. Harmon recalls:

This, I thought, was the ultimate anticlimax. The two of us, who had gone through so much together, were to be killed by fire from an Italian privy. As we crouched there a Sherman tank came up the highway. I shouted and pointed. The Sherman tank didn't bother with its guns. It just turned at right angles and charged across the field and butted squarely into the building. When the tank had finished, there was neither machine gun, outhouse nor German. The tank commander saluted from his turret and rolled on. Truscott and I picked ourselves up, resumed the tattered vestments of our dignity and went back to being generals again.

There was to be no triumphal march into Rome on 4 June, but the German rearguards were gradually overwhelmed or thinned out and after dark, some infiltrations were made. It was an extremely confusing situation, with small groups from various units scampering through the dark, narrow streets, probing German pinch points and searching out routes for following troops. They were tentative at first, not knowing whether they were walking into a moonlit ambush or a street party. *Kampfgruppen* of the 362nd and 3rd Panzer Grenadier Divisions had to march quickly through the city to avoid being surrounded, and General Greiner only just avoided patrols of the 88th Division's Reconnaissance Troop as he drove through the centre. Homer Bigart wrote that evening:

> The entry of Allied troops into the heart of the Eternal City at dusk . . . was a moment of such wildly primitive emotion that . . . it is impossible to write soberly of the nightmarish scene along the Via Nazionale, where jubilation gave way to frozen panic and sudden death. The Nazis . . . sent a flak wagon charging into the lead column of American troops. We were passing the Bank of Italy when it happened. Just ahead, around the slope of Capitoline Hill, was the Palazzo Venezia and Mussolini's balcony. At the head of our column sprawled a Sherman tank, wearing a bonnet of hysterical Romans . . . As the hour of liberation approached, these flak wagons – heavy aircraft guns mounted on half-tracks – raced through the winding streets, shooting explosive bullets at intersections, attempting to cover the last-minute escape of Nazi snipers and demolition crews and to ambush the American vanguard . . . A flak wagon arrived, its guns streaming red tracers into the throng outside the Bank of Italy. I shall never forget that dreadful moment of panic . . . It was all over in a few minutes. The flak wagon, trying to dart past the tank and slaughter the infantrymen following it, was disabled by the second shell from the Sherman's 75. It lay like a

helpless black beetle while the Sherman crawled within a hundred feet and sent another shell crashing into its side. Two Nazis were killed outright and a third was dying. Three others were taken prisoner. The infantrymen had to fire their rifles into the air to save the captives from the infuriated throng.

On more than one occasion, American squads opened fire mistaking each other for the enemy. Indeed, in one such incident, Robert Frederick added to the wound that he had received earlier in the day to win his ninth Purple Heart of the Italian Campaign. He was, as one commentator has observed, 'the most shot-at-and-hit general in American military history.' Valhalla was not yet ready to receive Frederick, Clark, Keyes, Truscott and Harmon, for all could very easily have been killed on the outskirts of Rome that day.

In the early hours of 5 June Rome stirred and looked out on a dark scene devoid of Germans, but rapidly filling with Americans. Few Romans had dared to hope that Hitler would allow his troops to leave without fighting a pitched battle and that the Allies would have arrived so soon. Fabia Sciarillo recalls:

We were woken by trucks moving through the street. At first I thought that it was the Germans, but then I heard American accents. It was a wonderful feeling . . . After expecting General Clark to arrive days after Salerno and then hours after Anzio, we were apprehensive about becoming too hopeful for a swift liberation. But that is what we got. One day the Germans were here, the next they had been replaced by the Americans . . . By dawn people were lining the streets. I cried. I felt the tension leave me. There would be no more air raids, no more bombings or assassinations. We would be safe, and now that the Americans were here we expected food, electricity and everything else we had been lacking. It was a joyous occasion for Romans, but one tinged with sadness as the war continued.

It was very much an American party to which the British had not been invited. Harding later admitted that Clark had informed Alexander on 2 June that he would order 'his troops to fire on Eighth Army' if they approached Rome. Even so, Captain John MacAuslan from 5th Reconnaissance Regiment of 5th Division recalls driving into the city in a jeep:

> General Mark Clark had said no one was allowed into Rome except Americans – the British troops would be shot if they went near Rome. A patrol from my division of the Green Howards got in at half-past six – illegally – and I reckon I got in at half-past four. I wasn't quite in the centre, but we got quite a long way in. Then I turned round and came back again, because I had second thoughts. Common sense actually crept in, and I went back to Ostia. I found one of the troops putting up statues there and starting to shoot at them with machine guns, with a very agitated curator trying to stop them. They took no notice of him at all, so I stopped them doing that. I think that's quite the most useful thing I did during the whole war.

As dawn broke American Military Police were stationed at road junctions refusing British military personnel entry to the city. But, many American Fifth Army troops also missed the celebrations as they were either moved on to new objectives outside Rome before the festivities began, or by-passed the capital altogether. Robert Dodge, however, was lucky enough to be one of the feted, and recalls the heady atmosphere:

> My recollection of entering Rome was of crowds lining the streets, American flags being waved, cheering, flowers being tossed, and wine bottles being passed to us. We tossed candy to the children, and I believe the Italians felt a great relief.

Norman Mohar remembers a similarly joyous scene, but it very nearly ended in tragedy:

> We passed the Coliseum and entered the most beautiful sight of the war – it was like entering a big birthday cake! I remember the balconied apartments and high-rises with pastel colors and the cheering crowds waving and shouting . . . In the throng of people, with the shouting and cheering going on, the jeep driver had to make a quick turn to the right to avoid a collision with civilians. I was sitting on the right over the rear wheel. I lost my balance in the sudden swerve. I reached out to support myself and my hand found the pistol grip of a mounted 30-caliber machine gun! It was battle ready! I accidentally pulled the trigger! I fired a burst of about five rounds which struck a building about a foot apart beneath a window sill where about four persons were waving and cheering! They pulled back horrified! I saw the bullets hit and chew up the plaster. If they had hit only one foot higher I would have been some sort of killer.

The Times reported: 'Rome to-day is in a holiday mood. Shops are closed and the population is in the streets acclaiming the allied troops with almost embarrassing enthusiasm. Bunches of flowers are hurled into passing cars, and any allied soldier who stops for a moment immediately becomes the centre of an eagerly curious crowd.' But Mark Clark was unembarrassed. The Fifth Army commander had arrived in Rome at around 0800 hours having motored down Route 6 with his entourage including Gruenther and other staff officers. His stated intention was to find the Town Hall on Capitoline Hill and to hold a conference there with his four corps commanders. The truth was that he wished to be acclaimed the conqueror of Rome and have his picture taken by the waiting press. Clark's small convoy of jeeps got lost in the narrow streets packed with revellers, but his driver eventually found his way to St Peter's Square. Mark Clark later recalled:

As we stopped to look at the great dome of St Peter's a priest walking along the street paused by my jeep and said in English, 'Welcome to Rome. Is there any way I can help you?'

'Well,' I replied, 'we'd like to get to Capitoline Hill.'

He gave us directions, and added, 'We are certainly proud of the American 5th Army. May I introduce myself?' And he told me his name. He came from Detroit.

'My name's Clark,' I replied.

Led to the Town Hall by a youth on a bicycle, a serious-looking Clark then strode up its great staircase flanked by Keyes and Truscott. Alan Whicker photographed them and the iconic image was transmitted around the world. Clark later had a copy framed and hung in his home. He then proceeded to address the correspondents overlooking the Piazza del Campidoglio. Clark opened by declaring: 'Well, gentlemen, I didn't really expect to have a press conference here – I just called a little meeting with my corps commanders to discuss the situation. However, I'll be glad to answer your questions. This is a great day for Fifth Army and for the French, British, and American troops of the Fifth who have made this victory possible.' For the generals at his side, this was excruciating. Truscott later wrote: 'I was anxious to get out of this posturing and on with the business of war' – but they were required to stand next to their boss and nod and smile at what he said. Clark was grandstanding spectacularly, revelling in the attention. As far as the Fifth Army commander was concerned, he had achieved the aim. As he later wrote: 'We had won the race to Rome by only two days.' But whose aim had he achieved, and whose race had he just won?

In London and Washington there was considerable relief that the Italian capital had been captured, but with Overlord looming there was no time for self-congratulation. Indeed, on the morning of 5 June, Winston Churchill received a note from his wife, Clementine: 'I feel so much for you at this agonizing moment – so full of suspense, which prevents one from rejoicing over Rome!' On hearing the news Franklin Roosevelt broadcast to the nation exclaiming: 'One up and two to go', but sounded a note of warning by adding that Rome was not the end. 'Ultimate victory', he concluded, 'still lies some distance ahead.' But the circumstances in which Mark Clark achieved his conquest of Rome had removed its gloss. Operation Overlord was to be the beginning of the end of the war against Germany for the Western Allies, not Operation Diadem. The price of this pyrrhic Italian victory had been too high, with 44,000 Fifteenth Army Group casualties since 11 May, whilst a large proportion of Tenth Army had managed to escape to fight another day. Rome had always been of limited military value, and few people, apart from Mark Clark and the Italians, got overly excited about its capture. For most, Allies and German alike, the events of 5 June were to merely usher in a new phase of the war in Italy. In a remarkable case of strategic myopia, Clark had been blinded by the Eternal City.

Conclusion

The Battle of Anzio had been nightmarish. In its pure awfulness it stands comparison with any other battle of the Italian Campaign, or the Second World War for that matter. The stark casualty figures speak for themselves. Over four months the Allies lost 7,000 killed and 36,000 wounded or missing (totalling one third of the total VI Corps strength) and a further 44,000 non-battle casualties who were hospitalised due to injuries and sickness. German losses were at least as heavy. But whilst these statistics alone are suggestive of a ferocious battle, they fail to do justice to the intensity of the fighting. For a fuller picture one needs to consider that around 300,000 troops, together with their guns and fighting machines gave battle along a mere sixteen miles of front. The Germans enjoyed the advantage of observation over the beachhead from the Alban Hills, and used their artillery and bombers to pummel a VI Corps tightly packed into a vulnerable beachhead. The Allies, meanwhile, defended themselves with their own artillery – enhanced by the naval guns – and their deadly, demoralising air superiority. It was a battle fought with the ferocity of an encounter that neither side could afford to lose. For VI Corps the fear of being pushed into the sea was an obvious motivation, but for the Germans the impetus was the political importance that Hitler conferred on the fighting which far outstripped the need for Fourteenth Army to protect the rear of its Tenth Army comrades. The Battle of Anzio became a statement of intent for both sides at the beginning of a year pregnant with prospects for further Allied amphibious attacks and there was a consequential viciousness to the fighting in the beachhead which the combatants never forgot. Staff Sergeant Ross Carter wrote that any man that fought at Anzio 'got it seared in his brain like a burn with a blowtorch.'

Winston Churchill, Harold Alexander and the other supporters of Operation Shingle did not expect the intense, grinding encounter that eventually took place at Anzio. Far from being the dynamic operation to unlock the front that had been hoped for, the battle instead swiftly took up a special place in the pantheon of audacious military schemes that failed. Churchill admitted to Lord Moran in September 1944 that: 'Anzio was my worst moment in the war. I had most to do with it.' The operation remains as controversial now as it ever did and continues to provide both military historians and the armed forces with a relevant case study through which to explore the nature of alliances, general-ship, planning, risk assessment, logistics, motivation, morale, leader-ship, tactics and a plethora of other themes. The obvious question that most ask is: Why did it fail? It is tempting to look no further than the leaden footed John Lucas for the answer, but whilst his performance does demand scrutiny, for a balanced response one also has to examine the complex situation in which the VI Corps commander was working. The very concept of fighting in the Mediterranean was challenging to the Americans who initially only considered a brief foray into the region for the purposes of blooding its troops prior to the launch of the cross-Channel invasion. To the British, and to the British Prime

Minister in particular, the Mediterranean was always held in higher regard, offering exciting strategic opportunities. By the time that the Western Allies were fighting in Italy, Churchill not only sought to weaken the Germans prior to the launch of Operation Overlord, but also retained a hope of making the invasion of Normandy unnecessary with a drive up the Italian 'Boot' into the southern Reich. But the Americans never retained the same belief in the enterprise as the British. General George Marshall fought in Italy under sufferance, and was stretched to the limits when competition for precious strategic assets became intense, and with London continuing to demand a larger share for its faltering campaign. The fighting in Italy was not for the impatient or faint hearted.

In the end the Italian adventure was a disappointment, failing to deliver its more extravagant aims, and there is even some disagreement over whether it significantly diluted the German forces in north-west Europe. Although Alan Whicker correctly asserted that the campaign succeeded in 'tying down 25 German divisions in Italy for two years – and the fifty-five divisions deployed around the Mediterranean', one might still legitimately argue that Allied resources deployed to achieve this might have been more beneficially used elsewhere. Indeed, one is left wondering who was pinning whom in Italy for Kesselring's defensive brilliance demanded a far greater Allied investment there than had initially been anticipated. That investment included the launching of Operation Shingle which became the obvious means by which to try and break the Gustav Line induced deadlock that had beset the front by the end of 1943. The theory behind the assault had been sound, but only if requisite resources were made available. Neither Mark Clark nor John Lucas were ever convinced that they had the strength to attain Alexander's stated aims, but with Churchill's backing the operation seems to have obtained an unstoppable momentum. Indeed, the official British historian of the Mediterranean War has written that, 'the operation, largely owing to Mr Churchill's influence, was given quite an extraordinary degree of importance. It was fathered by wishful strategical thinking and was not made the subject of a searching tactical analysis.'

Fearing VI Corps's annihilation, the weaknesses that Clark perceived in Operation Shingle had drawn him to emphasise the need for caution after the landing. It was, however, Lucas's interpretation of that 'caution' which was to cause so many difficulties once battle was enjoined. Considering the paucity of German troops opposing the Allied force during the first couple of days of the attack, the VI Corps's commander's failure to push further and harder to obtain a substantial beachhead based on key towns from which he could attack or defend, was a grave mistake. Instead, Lucas carved out his vulnerable foothold at Anzio–Nettuno which lacked depth and any prospects for a rapid offensive realignment. Years after the battle Captain Felix Sparks of 45th Division wrote: 'Legend has it that Nero fiddled at Anzio while Rome burned. In 1944, it appears that General Lucas fiddled at Anzio while Winston Churchill and General Alexander burned.' Lucas did 'fiddle', but this was undoubtedly better than thrusting towards the Alban Hills prematurely and Lucas's commanders have subsequently partially vindicated his prudence. William Penney argued that an early breakout from the beachhead would have had disastrous consequences: 'We could have had one night in Rome and 18 months in P.W camps.' Gerald Templer later admitted that: 'I never understood how Anzio could possibly work. I am absolutely convinced that if Lucas had gone on (which he could have done) he could have got to Rome, but within a week or a fortnight there wouldn't have been a single British soldier left in the bridgehead. They would all have been killed or wounded or prisoners . . . we wouldn't have had a chance.' Lucian Truscott was of the same mind: 'any reckless advance to the Colli Laziali without first establishing a firm base to protect our beaches would have been sheer madness and would almost certainly have resulted in the eventual destruction of the landing forces.' Even as the battle was in progress the causes of the lack of movement were clear, with the astute war correspondent Homer Bigart reflecting on 26 March that:

> Again we were attempting too much with too little . . . To this observer it seems awfully late in the war to attempt so dangerous an operation without first securing such preponderance of strength that the outcome is never in doubt once the landings have been secured.

Albert Kesselring was to agree, opining after the war: 'it would have been the Anglo-American doom to over-extend themselves. The landing force was initially weak, only a division or so of infantry, and without armor. It was a half-way measure of an offensive that was your basic error.'

Yet despite the weight of support for Lucas's defensive mind-set, the theory that his 'unwarranted caution' was to blame for the failure of Operation Shingle still resonates. The idea that, in the words of SS Colonel Eugen Dollmann: 'The Americans put up their tents, said their prayers, had a good meal, and then lost a unique occasion for finishing the war within the year', is a difficult one to dispel largely because Lucas became the ideal scapegoat for a flawed plan. Crushed by his Anzio experience, Lucas was to die in 1949 before he could begin to set the record straight. Harold Alexander eventually confessed in his official despatch in 1950 that 'the actual course of events was probably the most advantageous in the end', but this was followed by Churchill's history of the war which was riddled with implied criticism of Lucas who 'confined himself to occupying his beach-head and having equipment and vehicles brought ashore.' It was a situation which led Lucas's brother to complain in a letter to Churchill that the late VI Corps commander was 'not the impotent, defense minded commander that your book portrays' and had 'obeyed his orders to the letter at Anzio.' This was indeed the case and was why when Clark could no longer withstand the pressure from Churchill and Alexander for Lucas's removal, he did so with considerable regret. Nevertheless, the advent of Truscott was useful for Clark who, by the end of February, had recognised that the sting had been taken out of the German threat and began to assess the offensive potential of VI Corps in the beachhead. During this time Mark Clark's thoughts ran contrary to those of Alexander for he believed that the plan to destroy Tenth Army was impractical, and had set his sights firmly on Rome. This would be achieved – once again – by the Fifth Army commander giving the impression that he was following his boss's wishes, but in reality conscientiously evading them.

It may well have been the case that Oliver Leese failed to push the German Tenth Army hard enough to crush it against the projected VI Corps push to Route 6, but Clark's decision to split the beachhead force ensured that von Vietinghoff's escape was complete. Indeed, Alexander later argued that had the thrust to Valmontone been maintained, 'the disaster to the enemy would have been much greater . . . I can only assume that the immediate lure of Rome for its publicity persuaded Clark to switch the direction of his advance.' Truscott concurred stating: 'There has never been any doubt in my mind that had General Clark held loyally to General Alexander's instructions, had he not changed the direction of my attack to the northwest on May 26th, the strategic objective of Anzio would have been accomplished in full. To be first in Rome was poor compensation for this lost opportunity.'

Alan Whicker, whose book about his wartime experiences in Italy is littered with gibes at Clark, declared: 'So Mark Clark, totally absorbed with self-publicity, remained the Germans' favourite enemy General: he always gave them an easier time than they expected – and with his strong personality, always got away with it.' For two days Clark did get away with it, basking in the glory of his capture of Rome being knocked off the front pages by the electrifying news of the invasion of

Normandy. Only then did he turn his attention back to the business of defeating Tenth Army. As Winston Churchill later ruminated: 'Such is the story of Anzio; a story of high opportunity and shattered hopes, of skilful inception on our part and swift recovery by the enemy, of valour shared by both.'

Epilogue

The old man smiles weakly. 'My name's Ted Jones', he says, 'I fought at Anzio with the Grenadier Guards.' He offers me a seat and lowers himself down onto a sofa with the aid of a walking stick. This is the first time that Ted has joined other veterans of the Italy Star Association on their annual weekend away. He was enjoying the bracing Sussex sea air, the entertainment and the opportunity to chat about the past. Maurice Cheadle, the Association's ebullient eighty-seven-year-old Founder tells me this will probably be the last time that members will hold such an occasion, but adds, 'we've been saying that for years. We may be fading', Maurice continues, 'but we're still fighting.' My instinctive reaction is to ask what they were still fighting, but I knew that the answer lay with men like Andrew Wilson, my veteran friend who had been a gunner at Anzio, a man who still limps from wounds he received in the beachhead and suffers recurring nightmares. Here was somebody not merely fighting his way through later life, but a veteran still fighting the battle's legacy. Through the Italy Star Association I had met many such men, and have always felt both privileged and humbled to be in their presence. Yet, with the becoming modesty of that generation, each seems astonished to find that someone half a century younger could be interested in their tales, let alone in them personally.

Ted Jones fought at the Factory, Carroceto, Buonriposo Ridge and in Anzio's 'wadi country'. I have read deeply into what happened at these places, and their very names fill me with curiosity. But for Ted they only provoke memories of sights, smells and sounds. Momentarily lost in the past, the distinguished-looking old man stares at the carpet. Then, with no prompting, he recalls the moment when a vicious German artillery bombardment shattered his company's position during an enemy counter-attack near the Via Anziate. From the perspective of his narrow slit trench he remembers the whine of approaching shells, the convulsive heave of explosions, the chest-pounding concussion. The smell of wet earth mixed with cordite. He remembers the buzz of a passing bullet and the staccato reply of the Bren guns. He remembers the screams of the wounded and the terrifying yells of the advancing German infantry. Ted Jones recalls his friend dying beside him with absolute clarity. 'He made a gurgling sound and was gone.'

As he relives the appalling ordeal he underwent as a twenty-year-old, I reflect that at twenty I was still a self-absorbed student, troubled by nothing more than playing rugby, or submitting my next essay on time, and feel moved to explain this to him. Ted looks at me with his pale blue eyes. 'But that's exactly what we fought for. For you to be able to get on with your life unburdened by such things.' He surreptitiously wipes a handkerchief across his face and changes the subject, asking if I am married. Yes, I tell him, with three young children. Freddie, my nine-year-old, enjoys reading books about the war and poring over documents with me. From his wallet Ted produces some photographs of his own. The dog-eared black and white pictures reveal him as a strapping soldier standing proudly next to a rather nervous looking, but pretty young woman with the trademark forties hairstyle – Ted's wife, Vera, whose name has been frequently dropped into our conversation. He runs his finger delicately over her image telling me that although the couple had been on holiday to Italy twice, he hadn't revisited Anzio. There was a short pause, then Ted continued, 'I'm ready to go now', he continues, 'to complete the circle, but . . .' His voice tails off and I offer to act as an escort for him, but he dismisses the suggestion, 'You don't want to act as nurse maid to me. No thanks.' But I can tell that he is interested and I scribbled my details on a piece of paper, asking him to call if he changed his mind. Ted shuffles off to play carpet bowls, but at the door he turns to me, raising the palm of his right hand, almost as if making an oath, and says 'I'll pray that your Freddie never has to fight in a war.'

Three days later a small package arrived at our house, with my name and address written in a shaky hand. Tearing open the wrapping, I pulled out the six pointed bronze medal hanging on its red, white and green ribbon. An Italy Star. There was a note from Ted Jones:

> Thank you for listening to my war stories and for being polite enough to sound interested in my ramblings. I enjoyed talking to you and I would like very much to go back to Anzio at your convenience. I have enclosed something for you. Please accept it. I have nobody to leave it to. Vera died 15 years ago and I am sure that you will look after it. You now know more about my wartime experience than anybody else ever has. I am grateful.

I picked up the telephone and dialled his number. Did he really want me to be the guardian of such a precious item, and when would he like to make the trip back to Anzio? My call was answered by a young receptionist at the retirement home, and I asked for Ted. 'I am sorry', she replied, clearly moved, 'he passed away last night.'

Notes

Introduction

p. xiii 'D-Day Dodgers' Daniel G. Dancocks *The D-Day Dodgers – The Canadians in Italy, 1943–45* McClelland and Stewart Inc. Toronto 1991, p. 382

p. xvi 'Everything is simple in war, but the simplest thing is difficult' Carl von Clausewitz, *On War* Wordsworth 1997, p. 66

Chapter 1: The Italian Job

p. 1 'Thirty seconds!' Richard Dawes interview, 16 January 2005

p. 2 'Rain, rain, rain . . .' quoted in Matthew Parker *Monte Cassino – The Story of the Hardest-Fought Battle of World War Two* Headline 2003, p. 35

p. 2 'This is just so awful . . .' Richard Dawes interview, 16 January 2005

p. 3 'they have been taught . . .' quoted in Matthew Jones *Britain, the United States and the Mediterranean War, 1942–44* Macmillan Press 1996, p. 12

p. 3 'Britain and America are partners . . .' quoted in Jones, *op. cit.*, p. 1

p. 4 'What I witnessed was the British power . . .' quoted in Michael Howard *The Mediterranean Strategy in the Second World War* Weidenfeld and Nicolson 1968, p. 25

p. 5   'Here is a true Second Front of 1942 . . .' quoted in Jones, *op. cit.*, p. 19

p. 5   'a momentous change of Grand Strategy' quoted in Howard, *op. cit.*, p. 32

p. 5   'hit and miss affair that would have spelled disaster . . .' quoted in Jones, *op. cit.*, p. 31

p. 6   'I am afraid that Eisenhower as a general is hopeless . . .' Alanbrooke diary, Liddell Hart Centre for Military Archives, King's College London

p. 6   'They simply do not know their job as soldiers . . .' quoted in David Fraser *Alanbrooke* William Collins 1982, p. 315

p. 6   'British commanders and staff officers impressed Americans . . .' Lt. Gen. L.K. Truscott Jnr *Command Missions – A Personal Story* Presido California 1990, p. 537

p. 7   'one of the constant sources of danger to us' quoted in Jones, *op. cit.*, p. 27

p. 7   'The Allies won a total victory . . .' Albert Kesselring *The Memoirs of Field-Marshal Kesselring* William Kimber 1953, p. 157

p. 7   'There were days when I sat in my tent alone . . .' Ernie Pyle *Here is Your War* Henry Holt New York 1944, p. 64

p. 8   'regarded the Mediterranean as a kind of dark hole . . .' quoted in Jones, *op. cit.*, p. 41

p. 8   'to establish a jumping-off base . . .' Kesselring, *op. cit.*, p. 157

p. 9   'We must tread very warily . . .' quoted in John Keegan ed. *Churchill's Generals* Warner Books 1991, p. 114

p. 9   'Americans instinctively liked him' quoted in Lloyd Clark *The Allies In Italy* in *History Makers* Journal of the North London History Association 1991, p. 3

p. 10   'haul Montgomery over the coals' quoted in Fraser, *op. cit.*, p. 348

p. 10   'So many brave young men going to their death tonight . . .' quoted in Martin Gilbert *Churchill – A Life* Heinemann 1991, p. 748

p. 11   'We get along very well as individuals . . .' John Steinbeck *Once There Was A War* Heinemann 1959, p. 84

p. 12   'This is a horse race in which the prestige . . .' quoted in WWII Campaign Brochures Sicily 1943 see www.army.mil/cmh-pg/Brochures/72-16/72-16.htm, p. 8

p. 12   'the Axis Command was mighty lucky . . .' Kesselring, *op. cit.*, p. 165

p. 12 'I think that everyone admitted . . .' Bernard Law Montgomery *The Memoirs of Field-Marshal The Viscount Montgomery of Alamein, K.G.* The Companion Book Club 1958, p. 173

p. 12 'perhaps the decisive one on the way to defeat . . .' Johannes Steinhoff *The Straits of Messina – Diary of a Fighter Commander* Andre Deutsch 1969, p. 255

p. 13 'an Allied physical victory' quoted in Carlo D'Este *Bitter Victory – The Battle for Sicily July–August 1943* Collins 1988, p. 551

p. 13 'Our last pictures of the Sicilian campaign . . .' Alan Whicker *Whicker's War* HarperCollins 2005, p. 67

p. 13 'only a few Italians still believed . . .' General Siegfried Westphal *The German Army in the West* Cassell 1951, p. 140

p. 14 'My dear Duce, it's no longer any good . . .' quoted in James Owen and Guy Walters *The Voice of War – The Second World War Told by Those Who Fought It* Viking 2004, pp. 337-8

p. 14 'The people in the street are going mad with joy . . .' quoted in Owen and Walters, *op. cit.*, p. 339

p. 14 'It was a wild time . . .' Alonzo Badotti interview, 5 March 2005

p. 15 'Over the course of the next few days . . .' Alonzo Badotti interview, 5 March 2005

p. 15 'would be intensified' Kesselring, *op. cit.*, p. 170

p. 16 'Marshall absolutely fails to realise . . .' Alanbrooke diary, Liddell Hart Centre for Military Archives, King's College London

p. 17 'quickly crushing Italy' Winston S. Churchill *The Second World War – Volume V – Closing the Ring* Cassell 1952, p. 36

p. 18 'Irresistibly the scene was like a regatta . . .' Alan Moorehead *Eclipse* Granta Books 2000, p. 20

p. 19 'peaceful . . . almost gentlemanly' Whicker, *op. cit.*, p. 81

p. 19 'I'm nearly dead. I have to talk to the P.M . . .' Jon Meacham *Franklin and Winston – A Portrait of a Friendship* Granta Books 2004, p. 237

p. 21 'The Italian Government having recognised the impossibility . . .' quoted in Owen and Walters, *op. cit.*, p. 353

p. 21 'It was clear that no one knew what awaited us . . .' Norman Lewis *Naples '44* Eland 1983, p. 11

p. 22 '. . . and so began a new chapter in our living nightmare' Fabia Sciarillo interview, 2 February 2005

p. 22   'poorly fitted to resist an attack from the sea' Westphal, *op. cit.*, p. 136

p. 23   'This was the third landing I had made . . .' quoted in Owen and Walters, *op. cit.*, pp. 354–5

p. 23   'The situation is extremely critical' Mark Clark diary, The Citadel Archives & Museum, Gen. Mark W. Clark

p. 23   'Nothing, I've no reserves. All I've got is a prayer' General Mark Clark *Calculated Risk – His Personal Story of the War in North Africa and Italy* George G. Harrap 1951, p. 194

p. 24   'I thought it over carefully as I walked along the beach . . .' Mark Clark, *op. cit.*, p. 193

p. 24   'If the Germans had pushed on to the sea . . .' Lloyd Clark *The Allies In Italy* in *History Makers* Journal of the North London History Association 1991, p. 3

p. 24   'assist in the defence of Army Headquarters . . .' Lewis, *op. cit.*, p. 17

p. 25   'Nearer and nearer the shells dropped . . .' quoted in Moorehead, *op. cit.*, p. 42

p. 25   'I hope that Eighth Army will attack . . .' Mark Clark diary, The Citadel Archives & Museum, Gen. Mark W. Clark

p. 25   'It looks as if you may be having not too good a time . . .' Mark Clark diary, The Citadel Archives & Museum, Gen. Mark W. Clark

p. 25   'Situation here well in hand' Mark Clark diary, The Citadel Archives & Museum, Gen. Mark W. Clark

p. 26   'We'd get reports from the BBC that . . .' quoted in Nigel Nicolson *Alex – The Life of Field Marshal Earl Alexander of Tunis* Weidenfeld and Nicolson 1973, p. 218

p. 26   'First, play up the Eighth Army progress henceforth . . .' quoted in Robert H. Adleman and Colonel George Walton *Rome Fell Today* Leslie Frewin 1969, p. 99

p. 27   'The Fifth Army is just a young Army . . .' Mark Clark diary, The Citadel Archives & Museum, Gen. Mark W. Clark

p. 27   'go to pieces in emergencies' Mark Clark diary, The Citadel Archives & Museum, Gen. Mark W. Clark

p. 27   'the finest division in this or any other theatre' Mark Clark diary, The Citadel Archives & Museum, Gen. Mark W. Clark

p. 27   'an outstanding battle leader' Mark Clark, *op. cit.*, p. 187

p. 28   'enormous ability, intelligence and drive' quoted in Lloyd Clark, *op. cit.*, p. 4

p. 28   'cold, distinguished, conceited, selfish, clever . . .' quoted in Lloyd Clark, *op. cit.*, p. 4

p. 28   'seemed false, somehow, too eager to impress . . .' quoted in Parker, *op. cit.*, p. 19

p. 28   'tall and dirty Western bandit on the prowl' Mark Clark, *op. cit.*, p. 192

Chapter 2: Viktor, Barbara, Bernhardt and Gustav

p. 32   'obnoxious, cackling ephemera' Letter from Gunther Maucke, 18 June 2005

p. 32   'The whole of Italy south of the Po is mountainous . . .' Westphal, *op. cit.*, p. 136

p. 33   'Our thirty-mile advance to Naples was anything but easy . . .' Mark Clark, *op. cit.*, p. 203

p. 33   'Ragged little boys from the slums finally rebelled . . .' quoted in Max Arthur *Forgotten Voices of the Second World War* Ebury Press 2004, pp. 360–2

p. 34   'anthill of humanity' Lewis, *op. cit.*, p. 27

p. 34   'We made slow progress . . .' *ibid.*, p. 23

p. 34   'I give you Naples for your birthday . . .' Mark Clark diary, The Citadel Archives & Museum, Gen. Mark W. Clark

p. 34   'He loved the attention . . .' Neil Tucker interview, 18 April 2005

p. 34   'If boiled long enough . . .' Lewis, *op. cit.*, p. 29

p. 35   'Allied crews were not geared up to deal with . . .' Whicker, *op. cit.*, p. 105

p. 35   'prostitution, black-marketing, racketeering . . .' Reynolds Packard *Rome Was My Beat* Lyle Stuart Inc New Jersey 1975, p. 110

p. 35   'I hope . . . by the end of the month or thereabouts . . .' quoted in Martin Gilbert *Road To Victory: Winston S. Churchill 1941–1945* Heinemann 1986, p. 520

p. 35   'All will be well . . .' Churchill, *op. cit.*, p. 135

p. 36   'He who holds Rome holds the title deeds of Italy' quoted in W.G.F. Jackson *The Battle for Italy* Batsford 1967, p. 162

p. 36   'Churchill is in a very dangerous condition, most unbalanced . . .' Alanbrooke diary, Liddell Hart Centre for Military Archives, King's College London

p. 36   'successive defensive positions . . .' Kesselring, *op. cit.*, p. 168

p. 37   'The pressure Kesselring now brought to bear . . .' Kenneth Macksey *Kesselring – German Master Strategist of the Second World War* Greenhill 1996, p. 184

p. 37   'narrow valleys were broken . . .' Lt. Gen. L.K. Truscott Jnr, *op. cit.*, p. 257

p. 38   'You must never fight the battle *his* way' quoted in Moorehead, *op. cit.*, p. 21

p. 38   'dread and foreboding as we sat . . .' Ross S. Carter *Those Devils In Baggy Pants* Signet New York 1951, p. 75

p. 38   'God must have made when He was mad . . .' Carter, *op. cit.*, p. 92

p. 39   'I threw dozens of hand grenades, and even rocks' quoted in Ernie Pyle *Brave Men* Henry Holt New York 1944, p. 102

p. 39   'Their life consisted wholly and solely of war . . .' Pyle, *op. cit.*, p.126

p. 40   'without parallel' Alexander in the Foreword to Anon. *Engineers in the Italian Campaign 1943–1945* No publisher 1946 (unpaginated)

p. 40   'On one mountain road where as usual . . .' Whicker, *op. cit.*, p. 109

p. 40   'we'd have to pull off the road . . .' Pyle, *op. cit.*, p. 91

p. 40   'the rain came down in torrents . . .' Mark Clark, *op. cit.*, p. 220

p. 41   'Cold and wet caused extreme discomfort . . .' Truscott, *op. cit.*, p. 276

p. 41   'comparatively few men *do* crack up . . .' Pyle, *op. cit.*, p. 106

p. 41   'give particularly careful attention . . .' Mark Clark diary, The Citadel Archives & Museum, Gen. Mark W. Clark

p. 41   'newly-made doughnuts . . .' Mark Clark diary, The Citadel Archives & Museum, Gen. Mark W. Clark

p. 42   'Haggard, dirty, bedraggled, long-haired, unshaven . . .' Truscott, *op. cit.*, p. 257

p. 42   'The strong glacial winds blowing off . . .' Carter, *op. cit.*, p. 66

p. 42   'They were terrifically big guns . . .' Pyle, *op. cit.*, p. 66

p. 43   'the destroying angel of . . .' Lewis, *op. cit.*, p. 23

p. 43   'Allied fighter-bombers were very effective . . .' quoted in Arthur, *op. cit.*, p. 270

p. 43   'I and my commanders were determined to have Rome . . .' John North ed. *The Alexander Memoirs 1940–1945* Cassell 1962, p. 117

p. 43 'of critical importance to make an amphibious . . .' Mark Clark diary, The Citadel Archives & Museum, Gen. Mark W. Clark

p. 44 'the letters "L.S.T." are burnt in upon the minds . . .' quoted in www.globalsecurity.org/military/systems/ship/amphib-ships.htm

p. 44 'restricted and distorted by the shortage . . .' Lloyd Clark, *op. cit.*, p. 7

p. 44 'It is becoming more evident that our operations in Italy . . .' Alanbrooke diary, Liddell Hart Centre for Military Archives, King's College London

p. 45 'I feel that Eisenhower and Alexander must have what they need . . .' Churchill, *op. cit.*, p. 221

p. 46 'vast and ugly' Moorehead, *op. cit.*, p. 72

p. 46 'found no suitable accommodation . . .' Whicker, *op. cit.*, p. 87

p. 46 'I sometimes felt that we . . .' Mark Clark, *op. cit.*, p. 222

p. 46 'an amphibious operation south of Rome . . .' Mark Clark diary, The Citadel Archives & Museum, Gen. Mark W. Clark

p. 47 'I was convinced that it would be unwise . . .' Mark Clark, *op. cit.*, p. 221

p. 48 'trained to do anything from making a ski assault . . .' *ibid.*, p. 227

p. 48 'Enemy has continued determined defense . . .' Mark Clark diary, The Citadel Archives & Museum, Gen. Mark W. Clark

p. 48 'It's by far the strongest area of defense . . .' quoted in Richard Tregaskis *Invasion Diary* University of Nebraska 2004, p. 195

p. 49 'it seemed to flood over me from above . . .' *ibid.*, pp. 208–9

p. 49 'Enemy gains contributed no great threat . . .' Parker, *op. cit.*, p. 59

p. 50 'It was the middle of November . . .' Letter from Edgar Weiss, 17 June 2005

p. 50 'military leadership without optimism is not possible' quoted in Kenneth Macksey, *op. cit.*, p. 186

p. 51 'I was not a superior officer . . .' quoted in Macksey, *ibid.*, p. 190

p. 51 'one slip and a strong defensive position . . .' *ibid.*, p. 192

p. 51 'would be able to do more . . .' Churchill, *op. cit.*, p. 167

p. 52 'We were flung out . . .' Antonio Zinzone interview, 3 February 2005

p. 52 'We were sometimes awoken by the sound . . .' Fabia Sciarillo interview, 2 February 2005

p. 54 'troops were struggling to overcome mines, wired booby-traps . . .' Mark Clark, *op. cit.*, p. 234

p. 54   'the ones that survived . . .' Moorehead, *op. cit.*, p. 65

p. 54   'always a little more needed, for a little longer . . .' Fraser, *op. cit.*, p. 394

p. 55   'I have been fighting with my hands tied behind my back' quoted in Gilbert *Churchill, op. cit.*, p. 759

p. 55   'Only a spark was needed to cause him to blow up' Lord Moran *Winston Churchill – The Struggle for Survival 1940–1965* Constable 1966, p. 132

p. 56   'Overlord remains top of the bill . . .' quoted in Jackson *The Battle for Italy, op. cit.*, p. 162

p. 56   'American drag on us has seriously affected our Mediterranean strategy . . .' Alanbrooke diary, Liddell Hart Centre for Military Archives, King's College London

p. 56   'Papa was really very tired and his voice almost completely gone' quoted in Gilbert *Road To Victory, op. cit.*, p. 569

p. 57   'Churchill's reputation as a statesman was founded . . .' Ted Morgan *FDR – A Biography* Grafton Books 1985, p. 704

p. 58   'He is a very, very, small man and cannot see big . . .' Alanbrooke diary, Liddell Hart Centre for Military Archives, King's College London

Chapter 3: The Anatomy of a Wild Cat

p. 62   'I shall have to stay with you longer than I have planned . . .' quoted in Gilbert *Road To Victory, op. cit.*, p. 603

p. 62   'My impression of the day is that we are stuck . . .' Alanbrooke diary, Liddell Hart Centre for Military Archives, King's College London

p. 62   'he seems to be planning nothing . . .' Alanbrooke diary, Liddell Hart Centre for Military Archives, King's College London

p. 62   'I was able to see quite clearly Mount Cassino . . .' Alanbrooke's 1950s note to his diary entry 17 December 1943, Liddell Hart Centre for Military Archives, King's College London

p. 63   'The total neglect to provide amphibious action . . .' quoted in Gilbert *Road To Victory, op. cit.*, p. 612

p. 63   'cannot be allowed to continue . . .' quoted in *ibid.*, pp. 618–19

p. 66   'The old boy presided . . .' Harold Macmillan *War Diaries – Politics and War in the Mediterranean January 1943–May 1945* Macmillan 1984, p. 338

p. 66 'we mourned with aching, hating hearts' Carter, *op. cit.*, p. 91

p. 66 'It was my first white Christmas . . .' Frank Kimble interview, 12 August 2005

p. 67 'Christmas day came . . .' John Swain *Destiny '39 – A Young Soldier's Experiences During World War II* Pen Press 2001, pp. 143–4

p. 67 'it should decide the battle of Rome . . .' quoted in Gilbert *Road To Victory*, *op. cit.*, p. 621

p. 67 'delay the departure of fifty-six LSTs . . .' quoted in Francis L. Loewenheim, Harold D. Langley and Manfred Jonas ed. *Roosevelt and Churchill – Their Secret Wartime Correspondence* Barry and Jenkins 1975, p. 399

p. 68 'so totally dislocated by the thrust . . .' quoted in Churchill, *op. cit.*, p. 391

p. 68 'It is easy to criticise, with justice, many of Churchill's . . .' Fraser, *op. cit.*, pp. 230–1

p. 69 'Fifth Army will prepare an amphibious operation . . .' The National Archives WO 204/6742 Operation Shingle: 5 US Army outline plan

p. 69 'Seize and secure a beachhead in the vicinity of Anzio . . .' WO 204/6742

p. 70 'Several higher ranking British officers . . .' Raleigh Trevelyan *Rome '44: The Battle For The Eternal City* Pimlico 2004, p. 42

p. 70 'I am far too tenderhearted ever to be a success . . .' John Lucas, U.S. Army Military History Institute, Carlisle Barracks, Pennsylvania

p. 70 'a peanut and a feather duster' Mark Clark, The Citadel Archives & Museum, Gen. Mark W. Clark

p. 71 'make a hearty and sustaining broth . . .' John Lucas, U.S. Army Military History Institute, Carlisle Barracks, Pennsylvania

p. 71 'surely the prize is worth it' quoted in Churchill, *op. cit.*, p. 395

p. 74 'Although the landing force . . .' quoted in Carlo D'Este *Fatal Decision – Anzio and the Battle for Rome* HarperCollins 1991, p. 98

p. 75 'without risk there is no honour . . .' quoted in *ibid.*, p. 99

p. 75 'A unanimous agreement for action . . .' Churchill, *op. cit.*, p. 396

p. 75 'the diminutive size of the proposed expedition . . .' John Lucas, U.S. Army Military History Institute, Carlisle Barracks, Pennsylvania

p. 76 'the whole affair has a strong odour . . .' John Lucas, U.S. Army Military History Institute, Carlisle Barracks, Pennsylvania

p. 76   'Apparently Shingle has become the most . . .' John Lucas, U.S. Army Military History Institute, Carlisle Barracks, Pennsylvania

p. 77   'Seize and secure a beachhead . . .' The National Archives WO204/10263 Operation Shingle Outline Plan

p. 77   'much thought had been put on the wording . . .' quoted in D'Este *Fatal Decision, op. cit.*, p. 113

p. 77   'I wish to hell he wouldn't' John Lucas, U.S. Army Military History Institute, Carlisle Barracks, Pennsylvania

p. 77   'They will end up by putting . . . .' John Lucas, U.S. Army Military History Institute, Carlisle Barracks, Pennsylvania

p. 78   'vital to the success of anything . . .' John Lucas, U.S. Army Military History Institute, Carlisle Barracks, Pennsylvania

p. 78   'Another week might save dozens of lives' John Lucas, U.S. Army Military History Institute, Carlisle Barracks, Pennsylvania

p. 79   'There was a great deal . . .' Bert Wickes interview, 8 March 2005

p. 79   'Boy we were nervous . . .' T.J. Anderson interview, 14 August 2005

p. 80   'I wrote three letters . . .' Clive Colley interview, 21 March 2005

p. 81   'At the present time there is not . . .' quoted in D'Este *Fatal Decision, op. cit.*, p. 126

p. 83   'We were biding our time . . .' Letter from Karsten Hoffmann, 2 April 2005

p. 84   'I have many misgivings, but am also optimistic . . .' John Lucas, U.S. Army Military History Institute, Carlisle Barracks, Pennsylvania

p. 85   'The army tried to coat . . .' Terry Reynolds interview, 22 March 2005

p. 86   'Aboard ship we were . . .' George Avery, Veterans History Project Collection, American Folklife Center, Library of Congress, Washington

p. 86   'It was only when we were at sea . . .' Letter from Leonard O. Peters, 18 August 2005

p. 87   'I walked through the decks . . .' Roger Hill papers, The Second World War Experience Centre, Leeds

p. 87   'We just wanted to get . . .' Terry Reynolds interview, 22 March 2005

p. 87   'Just back with Admiral . . .' quoted in Trevelyan *Rome '44, op. cit.*, p. 36

p. 87   'It was with tense . . .' Churchill, *op. cit.*, p. 425

p. 87   'The strain and fear which exist . . . .' Moorehead, *op. cit.*, p. 22

p. 88   'Nobody had a clear idea of what . . .' Major D.J.L. Fitzgerald *History of the Irish Guards in the Second World War* Gale and Polden 1949, p. 217

p. 88   'My only weapon of war . . .' Wynford Vaughan-Thomas *Anzio* Pan Books 1963, p. 14

Chapter 4: Style Over Substance

p. 91   'I am looking forward to some leave soon . . .' Letter in the possession of Berthold Richter's sister, Anna

p. 93   'I braced myself for the shock . . .' Vaughan-Thomas, *op. cit.*, p. 15

p. 93   'It was all very gentlemanly, calm and dignified' Fitzgerald, *op. cit.*, p. 217

p. 93   'We hit the beach and shook . . .' Email from Tom Joyce, 18 May 2005

p. 93   'We achieved what is certainly one . . .' John Lucas, U.S. Army Military History Institute, Carlisle Barracks, Pennsylvania

p. 93   'to make sure that the troops followed . . .' Denis Healey interview, 11 July 2005

p. 94   'The only Germans we saw . . .' Vaughan-Thomas, *op. cit.*, p. 16

p. 94   'a broad-shouldered, thick-chested man . . .' Tregaskis, *op. cit.*, p. 133

p. 94   'When I run out of the landing-craft . . .' quoted in Trevelyan *Rome '44*, *op. cit.*, p. 45

p. 95   'I was lucky not to be shot like him . . .' Ralph Leitner interview, 11 December 2004

p. 95   'he never heard a word of command' quoted in The National Archives WO 204/958

p. 95   'At a German command post . . .' *The Times* 25 January 1944

p. 95   'As our squad entered a gloomy narrow street . . .' Ran Williams interview, 20 April 2005

p. 96   'Once we knew that the division . . .' Oliver P. Roach interview, 16 August 2005

p. 97   'It was a little nervy being at the forefront . . .' Letter from B.A. Burke to Captain Archie Simmons dated 6 July 1945, Royal Military Academy Sandhurst archive

p. 97   'Personal and Most Secret for Prime Minister . . .' quoted in Lloyd Clark, *op. cit.*, p. 6

p. 98   'We have made a good start . . .' quoted in Gilbert *Road To Victory*, *op. cit.*, p. 661

p. 98 'Very good shoot, only 4 guns . . .' Alanbrooke diary, Liddell Hart Centre for Military Archives, King's College London

p. 99 'We have a problem . . .' Letter from Gunther Maucke, 18 June 2005

p. 102 'The deck of our LCI was crowded . . .' Carter, *op. cit.*, p. 95

p. 103 'The water was eight to ten feet deep . . .' *ibid.*, pp. 94–6

p. 103 'We doubled-time off the L.C.I . . . .' Robert E. Dodge *Memories of the Anzio Beachhead and the War in Europe* Vantage Press New York 2004, pp. 3–4

p. 104 'It gave me goose bumps . . .' 'Lofty' Lovett interview, 6 May 2005

p. 105 'Our farmhouse was sturdy . . .' Antonia Paolo interview, 5 February 2005

p. 105 'The battle was a mere few hundred . . .' Vaughan-Thomas, *op. cit.*, p. 153

p. 106 'The naval Lieutenant who commanded . . .' William Dugdale papers, The Second World War Experience Centre, Leeds

p. 107 'He brushed off the soil' Ted Jones interview, 8 May 2005

p. 107 'I don't feel safe except at sea . . .' quoted in Fitzgerald, *op. cit.*, pp. 218–19

p. 107 'General Alexander made a tour of the beach-head . . .' D. Erskine *History of the Scots Guards 1919–1955* 1956, p. 201

p. 108 'Goddam, General's fresh eggs all gone to hell . . .' quoted Truscott, *op. cit.*, p. 310

p. 108 'Don't stick your neck out, Johnny . . .' John Lucas, U.S. Army Military History Institute, Carlisle Barracks, Pennsylvania

p. 108 'We held the whole world in our hands . . .' Vaughan-Thomas, *op cit.*, p. 16

p. 109 'a withdrawal of Tenth Army . . .' Letter from Gunther Maucke, 18 June 2005

p. 109 'set up a temporary headquarters in Rome . . .' quoted in Lloyd Clark, *op. cit.*, p. 7

p. 110 'You must take your company and move them towards the Anzio beachhead . . .' Details taken from Edwin Wentz's diary and an interview conducted by an unknown person in 1962

p. 110 'The youngsters were like little children . . .' Edwin Wentz diary

p. 111 'The 1st Platoon opened fire . . .' Franz Kurowski *The History of the*

Fallschirm Panzerkorps Hermann Göring JJ Fedorowicz Publishing Inc Manitoba Canada 1995, p. 138

p. 112   'I was a runner which meant . . .' Joachim Liebschner interview, Sound Archive, Imperial War Museum, London

p. 112   'He lost his nerve altogether . . .' Joachim Liebschner interview, Sound Archive, Imperial War Museum, London

p. 113   'to push all units as they arrived . . .' Letter from Gunther Maucke, 18 June 2005

p. 114   'Every yard was important to me . . .' Kesselring, *op. cit.*, p. 194

p. 114   'the present line is shorter . . .' *ibid.* p. 194

p. 114   'Kesselring symbolised the German defense . . .' D'Este *Fatal Decision, op. cit.*, p. 132

p. 115   'D-Day Evening . . .' Geoffrey Dormer papers, The Second World War Experience Centre, Leeds

p. 115   'It has been a remarkable day . . .' Letter from Ivor Talbot, 13 March 2005

Chapter 5: The Nudge

p. 119   'poorly directed mob scenes in provincial operas . . .' Trevelyan *Rome '44, op. cit.*, p. 29

p. 119   'Your aunt is ill and about to die . . .' quoted in *ibid.*, p. 9

p. 120   'No . . . The Romans are not brave enough . . .' Letter from Gunther Maucke, 1 July 2005

p. 120   'an audacious and enterprising formation . . .' quoted in Martin Blumenson *Anzio – The Gamble That Failed* Weidenfeld and Nicolson 1963, p. 82

p. 121   'The first night I was sent out with booby-traps . . .' Norman Mohar, memoirs (unpublished)

p. 121   'an ominous harbinger of the trial . . .' Donald G. Taggart, ed. *History of The Third Infantry Division in World War II* The Battery Press Nashville 1987, p. 111

p. 122   'The thing that distinguished us . . .' Carter, *op. cit.*, unpaginated preface

p. 122   'The powerful *whoosh* of the projectile . . .' Carter, *op. cit.*, p. 100

p. 123   'higgledy-piggledy jumble . . .' Kesselring, *op. cit.*, p. 194

p. 123   'But when I got there . . .' Denis Healey interview, 11 July 2005

p. 123 'LANDING SOUTH OF ROME ESTABLISHED . . .' *The Times* 24 January 1944

p. 123 'being rapidly increased in depth' *The Times* 25 January 1944

p. 124 'As D-Day turned into D plus 1 . . .' Vaughan-Thomas, *op. cit.*, p. 73

p. 124 'The only excitement was . . .' William Dugdale papers, The Second World War Experience Centre, Leeds

p. 124 'I am doing my best, but it seems terribly slow . . .' John Lucas, U.S. Army Military History Institute, Carlisle Barracks, Pennsylvania

p. 125 'the first warning to the front line soldier . . .' Vaughan-Thomas, *op. cit.*, p. 81

p. 125 'Carroceto was in our hands . . .' Captain Nigel Nicolson and Patrick Forbes *The Grenadier Guards in the War of 1939–1945 Volume II The Mediterranean Campaigns* Gale and Polden 1949, p. 395

p. 126 'I cringed at the sight . . .' quoted in Arthur, *Forgotten Voices, op. cit.*, p. 267

p. 126 'a deadly game of hide-and-seek . . .' Vaughan-Thomas, *op. cit.*, p. 81

p. 126 'if I had that, I would be in Rome by now . . .' quoted in Peter Verney *Anzio 1944: An Unexpected Fury* Batsford 1978, p. 59

p. 126 'There was no choice but to attack again . . .' Nicolson and Forbes, *op. cit.*, p. 397

p. 127 'Captain Hohler rather carefully laid down . . .' *ibid.*, p. 397

p. 128 'I found Col. Gordon Lennox lying on a mattress . . .' William Dugdale papers, The Second World War Experience Centre, Leeds

p. 128 'The patience and gratitude shown by the wounded men . . .' Fitzgerald, *op. cit.*, p. 237

p. 129 'The squad had proceeded only a few steps . . .' Taggart, *op. cit.*, p.113

p. 130 'more power was needed' Truscott, *op. cit.*, p. 312

p. 131 'This is the most important thing I have ever tried to do . . .' John Lucas, U.S. Army Military History Institute, Carlisle Barracks, Pennsylvania

p. 131 'I am thinking of your great battle night and day' quoted in Trevelyan *Rome '44, op. cit.*, p. 69

p. 131 'not due to lack of urging from above' quoted in Lloyd Clark, *op. cit.*, p. 6

p. 131 'Churchill was full of doubts . . .' Alanbrooke diary, Liddell Hart Centre for Military Archives, King's College London

p. 131 'to urge General Lucas to initiate aggressive action at once' Mark Clark diary, The Citadel Archives & Museum, Gen. Mark W. Clark

p. 132 'Apparently some of the higher levels . . .' John Lucas, U.S. Army Military History Institute, Carlisle Barracks, Pennsylvania

p. 133 'Liberty ships lay tossing and the LCTs rolled . . .' John Herbert papers, The Second World War Experience Centre, Leeds

p. 133 '8.45 p.m. The biggest yet . . .' John Lucas, U.S. Army Military History Institute, Carlisle Barracks, Pennsylvania

p. 133 'All night the enemy dropped long-burning parachute flares . . .' Carter, *op. cit.*, pp. 110–11

p. 133 'With the glider bombs I found that if I started to turn . . .' Roger Hill papers, The Second World War Experience Centre, Leeds

p. 134 'Spartan lies on her side, the bilge just showing . . .' Geoffrey Dormer papers, The Second World War Experience Centre, Leeds

p. 134 'quiet, determined soldier, with broad experience' Blumenson *Anzio*, *op. cit.*, p. 139

p. 135 'Glad to see you. You're needed here' quoted in Major General E.N. Harmon *Combat Commander – Autobiography of a Soldier* Prentice-Hall New Jersey 1970, p. 161

p. 137 'He had already been through a great deal during the war . . .' Letter from 'An old soldier' 18 September 2005

p. 138 'Snoop and poop night work . . .' quoted James Altieri *The Spearheaders* Popular Library Toronto 1960, p. 168

p. 138 'My job was to summarise the intelligence . . .' David Williams interview, 12 May 2005

p. 140 'Such a lack of information, and no cover in those vines . . .' quoted in Trevelyan *Rome '44, op. cit.*, pp. 76–7

p. 140 'I'm going to send up our heavy friends . . .' William Breuer *Agony at Anzio – The Allies' Most Controversial Operation of World War II* Robert Hale 1985, p. 80

p. 140 'The most frightening moment . . .' Letter from Derek Williams, 6 June 2005

p. 141 'I had never been so frightened . . .' Ben Wallis interview, 2 May 2005

p. 142 'We were shelled and mortared throughout the hours of darkness . . .' David Harvey interview, 18 June 2005

p. 142   'We feel like the lead in the end of a blunt pencil . . . .' Clive Manley interview, 10 October 2005

p. 142   'I ordered an armored wrecker to pull them out . . .' Harmon, *op. cit.*, pp. 164–5

p. 143   'All we could see were the quick fountains . . .' Vaughan-Thomas, *op. cit.*, pp. 101–2

p. 144   'I was alone in my lonely world . . .' quoted in a letter by David Harvey, 26 June 2005

p. 145   'From that day on I vowed never to knock the Limeys again . . .' quoted in a letter by David Harvey, 26 June 2005

p. 145   'There were dead bodies everywhere . . .' Harmon, *op. cit.*, p. 165

p. 146   'We could have taken them . . .' interview in author's archive dated (illegible) 1944

p. 147   'I was told where I was to set . . .' Edwin Wentz's interview

p. 149   'Call received from 1st and 3rd Battalions . . .' Extract of *Rangers Battle Journal* 30 January 1944, author's archive

p. 149   'The Germans' first counterattack . . .' quoted in D'Este *Fatal Decision*, *op. cit.*, p. 165

p. 150   'It felt like I had been hit in the face . . .' interview in author's archive dated (illegible) 1944

p. 150   'I never thought that I'd survive . . .' Fred Davis interview, 30 August 2005

p. 150   'They were firing into us . . .' William O. Darby with William H. Baumer *Darby's Rangers – We Led the Way* Presidio 2003, p. 199

p. 151   'He sure had a lot of guts . . .' quoted in D'Este *Fatal Decision, op. cit.*, pp. 166–7

p. 151   'They're closing in on us, Colonel . . .' quoted in Taggart, *op. cit.*, p. 115

p. 152   'My men are helping to bury the dead . . .' quoted in D' Este *Fatal Decision, op. cit.*, p. 169

p. 152   'Clark is up here and I am afraid intends to stay . . .' John Lucas diary, U.S. Army Military History Institute, Carlisle Barracks, Pennsylvania

p. 153   'I don't blame him for being terribly . . .' John Lucas diary, U.S. Army Military History Institute, Carlisle Barracks, Pennsylvania

p. 153   'I have been disappointed for several days . . .' Mark Clark diary, The Citadel Archives & Museum, Gen. Mark W. Clark

p. 154 'News from Italy bad . . .' Alanbrooke diary, Liddell Hart Centre for Military Archives, King's College London

p. 154 'It seems to have been a bad show . . .' quoted in Lloyd Clark, *op. cit.*, p. 8

p. 154 'kind enough but I am afraid he is not pleased . . .' John Lucas, U.S. Army Military History Institute, Carlisle Barracks, Pennsylvania

p. 155 'He sat in his chair . . .' Vaughan-Thomas, *op. cit.*, p. 106

p. 155 'You push the accordion a certain distance . . .' Tregaskis, *op. cit.*, p. 167

p. 155 'I remember plainly a British officer screaming at us . . .' James Anderson unpublished and unpaginated memoir *World War Two Experiences*

Chapter 6: The Spring Released

p. 158 'The intensity of the fighting has been remarkable . . .' Felix Reimann diary and interview, 1 August 2005

p. 159 'It was good to feel that we would be striking back' Paul Franz interview, 8 October 2005

p. 159 'It was a struggle to keep anything dry . . .' Gerd Jebsen interview, 28 June 2005

p. 160 'Shells were falling all around with such frequency . . .' Lieutenant Edward Grace MC *Horror Farm*, an unpublished memoir

p. 161 'It had been raining that night and we were soaking wet . . .' Joachim Liebschner interview, Sound Archive, Imperial War Museum, London

p. 162 'The leading assault troop cleared out the first house . . .' *The Times* 7 March 1944

p. 162 'That salient – I'll tell you what it was like . . .' quoted in Vaughan-Thomas, *op. cit.*, p. 122

p. 164 'The P.M. is suffering from indigestion . . .' John Colville, *The Fringes of Power – Downing Street Diaries 1939–1955* Weidenfield and Nicolson 2004, p. 450

p. 164 'The operations in Italy are moving slowly . . .' *The Times* 4 February 1944

p. 165 'What we require is a thruster . . .' The National Archives, PREM 3, 248/4

p. 165 'had lacked some aggressiveness . . .' Clark diary, The Citadel Archives & Museum, Gen. Mark W. Clark

p. 165 'Penned in as they were on the low-lying . . .' Kesselring, *op. cit.*, p. 195

p. 166 'The frost and the wet meant that wherever the enemy went . . .' William Dugdale papers, The Second World War Experience Centre, Leeds

p. 167 'Well, if he was as tough on the Germans . . .' Vaughan-Thomas, *op. cit.*, p. 136

p. 167 'We all knew our end was nigh . . .' James Reeder papers, The Second World War Experience Centre, Leeds

p. 168 'Before you are taken prisoner . . .' Joachim Liebschner interview, Sound Archive, Imperial War Museum, London

p. 168 'Every time our gun fired . . .' Felix Reimann interview, 1 August 2005

p. 168 'The steady, deliberate, thump-thump-thump of Bren-guns . . .' The National Archives WO169/ 16271

p. 169 'three and a half hours of sheer hell . . .' Felix Reimann interview, 1 August 2005

p. 169 'I wish I had an American Division in there . . .' John Lucas, U.S. Army Military History Institute, Carlisle Barracks, Pennsylvania

p. 170 'Any movement provoked a tornado of German spandaus . . .' William Dugdale papers, The Second World War Experience Centre, Leeds

p. 170 'We pulled out of our cover to support . . .' Felix Reimann, 1 August 2005

p. 171 'The British are badly disorganized . . .' John Lucas, U.S. Army Military History Institute, Carlisle Barracks, Pennsylvania

p. 171 'There is a fucking great German tank . . .' quoted in D'Este *Fatal Decision, op. cit.*, p. 216

p. 172 'I asked to see him and a sister . . .' William Dugdale papers, The Second World War Experience Centre, Leeds

p. 172 'A real flurry. Would you believe it? . . .' quoted Trevelyan *Rome '44, op. cit.*, p. 153

p. 173 'a travesty, pathetic and tragic' Papers of Major General Sir William Ronald Campbell Penney, Liddell Hart Centre for Military Archives, King's College London

p. 173 'I have a feeling that you may have hesitated . . .' quoted Trevelyan *Rome '44, op. cit.*, p. 145

p. 174 'Alexander never sees the logistics of a problem . . .' John Lucas, U.S. Army Military History Institute, Carlisle Barracks, Pennsylvania

p. 174 'I am disappointed with VI Corps Headquarters . . .' quoted in Trevelyan *Rome '44, op. cit.*, p. 156

p. 174 'I am afraid the top side . . .' John Lucas, U.S. Army Military History Institute, Carlisle Barracks, Pennsylvania

p. 174 'Even . . . without putting in a full counter-offensive . . .' *The Times* 8 February 1944

p. 175 'FIERCE EFFORTS AGAINST BEACH-HEAD . . .' *The Times* 11 February 1944

p. 175 'The situation in the bridgehead is grim . . .' quoted in D'Este *Fatal Decision, op. cit.*, p. 252

p. 175 'For once he was not his urbane self . . .' Vaughan-Thomas, *op. cit.*, p. 161

p. 176 'The enemy landings at Nettuno are the start . . .' quoted in Kurowski, *op. cit.*, p. 143

p. 177 'I think this means my relief . . .' John Lucas, U.S. Army Military History Institute, Carlisle Barracks, Pennsylvania

p. 178 'Every artillery piece on the beachhead . . .' Peter Graffagnino, memoirs (unpublished)

p. 178 'As the barrage lifted, I peered out of my foxhole . . .' quoted in Emajean Buechner, *Sparks – The Combat Diary of a Battalion Commander (Rifle), WWII, 157th Infantry Regiment, 45th Division, 1941–1945* Thunderbird Press Metairie, Louisiana 1991, pp. 84–85

p. 179 'By nightfall, we still held our position' quoted in *ibid.*, p. 85

p. 180 'We fired all day, from dawn until dusk, without a break . . .' Letter from Charlie Franklin, 16 July 2005

p. 180 'It was a massive morale boost to see a huge formation . . .' Letter from T.D. Morgan, 18 July 2005

p. 181 'The shelling was awful . . .' Gerd Jebsen interview, 28 June 2005

p. 181 'a special, intricate kind of obstacle, hell to attack, hell to defend' quoted in Trevelyan *Rome '44, op. cit.*, p. 144

p. 182 'many events occurred which will never be part of recorded history' John Lucas, U.S. Army Military History Institute, Carlisle Barracks, Pennsylvania

p. 182 'It was a turkey shoot . . .' Rick O'Toole interview, 18 June 2005

p. 182 'The full power of the allied air forces . . .' *The Times* 18 February 1944

p. 184 'There we were only two squads . . .' Cor Longiotti, memoirs (unpublished)

p. 185 'There we stayed for the next several days . . .' quoted in Buechner, *op. cit.*, p. 86

p. 185 'Emerging out of the morning mist . . .' Norman Clarimont interview, 12 May 2005

p. 185 'Waves of German infantry poured across . . .' *History of the First Division Anzio Campaign January–June 1944* Jerusalem 1946, p. 82 (author unknown)

p. 186 'Shortly after daybreak . . .' Cor Longiotti, memoirs (unpublished)

p. 187 'Sir, I guess you will relieve . . .' quoted in D'Este *Fatal Decision, op. cit.*, p. 244

p. 188 'calculate and direct artillery fire . . .' Francis Eugene Liggett, Veterans History Project Collection, American Folklife Center, Library of Congress, Washington

p. 189 'My only recourse was to attack . . .' quoted in Trevelyan *Rome '44, op. cit.*, p. 166

p. 189 'Our eyes stung with tiredness . . .' Letter from Gunter Pollmann, 15 May 2005

p. 190 'We were out of plasma, morphine and bandages . . .' Peter Graffagnino, memoirs (unpublished)

p. 190 'There was a loud cheer as the Shermans . . .' Nathaniel Duncan, memoir (unpublished)

p. 191 'By the afternoon of 19 February we had had enough . . .' Letter from Gunter Pollmann, 15 May 2005

p. 191 'German dead were piled in heaps . . .' John Lucas, U.S. Army Military History Institute, Carlisle Barracks, Pennsylvania

Chapter 7: Changes

p. 195 'conspiring to undermine the effectiveness of his brave troops' Letter from Gunther Maucke, 28 July 2005

p. 196 'ebullient and full of praise for what the troops had achieved' Letter from Klaus Hide, 2 June 2005

p. 197 'Message from Clark. He arrives with eight generals . . .' John Lucas, U.S. Army Military History Institute, Carlisle Barracks, Pennsylvania

p. 198 'It is difficult to escape the feeling . . .' Jackson, *The Battle for Italy, op. cit.*, p. 201

p. 198 'I had for some time been considering a change . . .' Mark Clark, *op. cit.*, p. 291

p. 198 'I thought I was winning something of a victory' John Lucas, U.S. Army Military History Institute, Carlisle Barracks, Pennsylvania

p. 198 'My orders were, to me, very clear . . .' John Lucas, U.S. Army Military History Institute, Carlisle Barracks, Pennsylvania

p. 199 'I was not blind to the fact . . .' Truscott, *op. cit.*, p. 320

p. 199 'Lucas was absolutely full of inertia . . .' quoted in Trevelyan *Rome '44*, *op. cit.*, p. 154

p. 199 'I left the finest soldiers in the world when I lost the VI Corps . . .' John Lucas, U.S. Army Military History Institute, Carlisle Barracks, Pennsylvania

p. 200 'We've got a new head at Anzio . . .' Vaughan-Thomas, *op. cit.*, p. 200

p. 202 'Our predicament . . . .was still critical . . .' Peter Graffagnino, memoirs (unpublished)

p. 202 'It was a curious experience . . .' Letter from Paul van der Linden, 1 July 2005

p. 204 'All hell broke loose . . . suddenly there were Germans everywhere . . .' R.E. Bullen, *History of the 2/7th Battalion The Queen's Royal Regiment* Exeter 1958, pp. 100–1

p. 204 'stumbled flushed and wild-eyed into the caves . . .' Peter Graffagnino, memoirs (unpublished)

p. 204 'After ten days of underground darkness . . .' Peter Graffagnino, memoirs (unpublished)

p. 205 'I only lasted two or three days . . .' Murray Levine, memoirs (unpublished)

p. 207 'That proved Allied superiority . . .' Joachim Liebschner interview, Sound Archive, Imperial War Museum, London

p. 207 'People lived like savages, faces smeared with mud . . .' quoted in Trevelyan *Rome '44*, *op. cit.*, p. 189

p. 207 'It was a savage, brutish troglodyte existence . . .' Fitzgerald, *op. cit.*, p. 335

p. 210 'Traffic through Rome going south on 15th . . .' quoted in Trevelyan *Rome '44*, *op. cit.*, p. 107

p. 210 'a major psychological mistake . . .' *ibid.*, p. 96

p. 211 'Sabotage goes steadily forward' quoted in *ibid.*, p. 56

p. 211 'I heard some shots' quoted in *ibid.*, p. 56

p. 211 'The Allies' bombers were hated . . .' Fabia Sciarillo interview, 2 February 2005

p. 212 'Everyone knows the Nazi record on religion . . .' quoted in *ibid*, p.179

p. 213 'The Hermann Göring are reporting . . .' Letter from Gunther Maucke, 28 July 2005

p. 213 'a mysterious and unsettling experience . . .' Letter from Eric Montrose, 13 August 2005

p. 214 'I suppose that we had been given a fairly easy ride . . .' Edwin Wentz interview 1962

p. 215 'Four or five hundred yards away . . .' Carter, *op. cit.*, pp. 112–13

p. 215 'He grabbed the telephone . . .' Carter, *op. cit.*, p. 106

p. 216 'Dawn was breaking and we could see the shapes of tanks . . .' Letter from Eric Montrose, 13 August 2005

p. 216 'By the second day of the attack . . .' Edwin Wentz interview 1962

p. 217 'There was flight after flight of four-engined Liberators . . .' John Herbert papers, The Second World War Experience Centre, Leeds

p. 219 'At the end the Führer said . . .' Westphal, *op. cit.*, p. 160

p. 219 'remorseless pressure must be put on the enemy . . .' quoted in David Irving *Hitler's War* Hodder and Stoughton 1977, pp. 609–10

p. 221 'a large second front in Italy . . .' quoted in Blumenson *Anzio, op. cit.*, p. 150

p. 221 'Naturally I am very disappointed . . .' Churchill, *op. cit.*, p. 436

p. 222 'I thought we should fling . . .' Colville, *op. cit.*, p. 456

Chapter 8: Entrenchment

p. 225 'squatted down and just cowered . . .' Pyle *Brave Men, op. cit.*, pp. 169–71

p. 226 'The buildings near the harbour resemble . . .' John Herbert papers, The Second World War Experience Centre, Leeds

p. 227 'On our infrequent trips to the rear . . .' Carter, *op. cit.*, pp. 107–8

p. 227 'the guy in the Red Hat' quoted in Whicker, *op. cit.*, p. 147

p. 227 'in a most suspicious manner . . .' John Herbert papers, The Second World War Experience Centre, Leeds

p. 228 'First you heard a distant, almost discreet cough . . .' Vaughan-Thomas, *op. cit.*, p. 149

p. 228 'He gave me an injection and started to drill . . .' Ron Rhodes papers, The Second World War Experience Centre, Leeds

p. 228 'We went down six feet . . .' Swain, *op. cit.*, p. 153

p. 229 'The bottom was squashy . . .' quoted in John Ellis *The Sharp End of the War – The Fighting Man in World War II* David and Charles London 1980, p. 43

p. 229 'Major Young's "brolly" . . .' Fitzgerald, *op. cit.*, p. 326

p. 229 'Subconsciously I started to count . . .' Ron Rhodes papers, The Second World War Experience Centre, Leeds

p. 230 'We have just sunk a mine . . .' Geoffrey Dormer papers, The Second World War Experience Centre, Leeds

p. 230 'on the look out for any E-boats . . .' John Herbert papers, The Second World War Experience Centre, Leeds

p. 231 'Much advance publicity of the horrors of Anzio . . .' M.W.L. Wood papers, The Second World War Experience Centre, Leeds

p. 232 'our first problem is the literal rebirth . . .' quoted in D'Este *Fatal Decision, op. cit.*, p. 311

p. 232 'Son, you ain't flyin' nowhere, you ain't jumpin' . . .' Letter from David Cohen, 28 May 2005

p. 232 'The truckload of replacements turned off . . .' Homer Bigart *Forward Positions – The War Correspondence of Homer Bigart* Compiled and edited by Betsy Wade The University of Arkansas Press Fayetteville 1992, p. 39

p. 233 'They were afraid of the unknown . . .' Moorehead, *op. cit.*, p. 64

p. 233 'I know it ain't my fault that they get killed . . .' quoted in Pyle *Brave Men, op. cit.*, p. 135

p. 234 'We pitied the scared, bewildered, shy, eager youngsters . . .' Carter, *op. cit.*, p. 123

p. 234 'The Anzio Experience has remained with me . . .' Whicker, *op. cit.*, p. 115

p. 234 'Just returned from Anzio . . .' David Harris diary

p. 235 'We got to change our underwear very rarely . . .' Raymond Fort papers, The Second World War Experience Centre, Leeds

p. 236 'We used our helmets for everything . . .' Ray McAllister, memoirs (unpublished)

p. 237 'It was remarkable . . .' Jimmy Reed telephone interview, 6 March 2005

p. 237 'We stayed away from the Americans . . .' Douglas Vickers interview, 14 April 2005

p. 237 'We had nothing to do with the British . . .' Letter from T.D. Morgan, 18 July 2005

p. 237 'They were a good bunch . . .' Jimmy Reed telephone interview, 6 March 2005

p. 238 'The Americans were brash, but jovial . . .' William H. Lewis interview, 5 April 2005

p. 238 'The Yank came in one day . . .' Ron Rhodes papers, The Second World War Experience Centre, Leeds

p. 238 'In the evenings we could hear Tommy . . .' Joachim Liebschner interview, Sound Archive, Imperial War Museum, London

p. 239 'On Easter Sunday I was up with the infantry . . .' Francis Eugene Liggett, Veterans History Project Collection, American Folklife Center, Library of Congress, Washington

p. 239 'I remember a BAR . . .' Dodge, *op. cit.*, p. 17

p. 240 'The German was most indignant . . .' Fitzgerald, *op. cit.*, p. 339

p. 240 'When we were sent to the stores for something . . .' Letter from Bernie Kirchoff, 1 May 2005

p. 240 'Life was tense as it always is . . .' quoted in Trevelyan *Rome '44, op. cit.*, p. 236

p. 241 'My first shock was the sight . . .' quoted in *ibid.*, p. 196

p. 241 'I looked in their pockets . . .' Norman Mohar, memoirs (unpublished)

p. 241 'Dog tired and overworked . . .' Ray McAllister, memoirs (unpublished)

p. 242 'Looking back to Anzio, I can hardly believe that it was me . . .' Letter signed 'JPL, a 3rd Division Sergeant at Anzio' 12 July 2005

p. 242 'nothing very spectacular . . .' John Herbert papers, The Second World War Experience Centre, Leeds

p. 242 'American parachutists – devils in baggy pants – are less than 100 meters . . .' *Combat Record of the 504th Parachute Infantry Regiment April 1943–July 1945* The Battery Press Nashville 2004, unpaginated

p. 243 'unemotional cutthroats' Robert H. Adleman, and Colonel George Walton, *The Devil's Brigade* Corgi 1968, p. 3

p. 243 'They are all around us every time we come into the line . . .' Adleman and Walton, *ibid.*, p. 116

p. 243 'At the beginning . . .' Joachim Liebschner interview, Sound Archive, Imperial War Museum, London

p. 243 'Dusk, and these awful nights . . .' quoted in Trevelyan *Rome '44, op. cit.,* p. 236

p. 244 'It was a carefully planned fighting patrol . . .' Letter from Fred Mason, 26 January 2005

p. 246 'We'd wait until midnight . . .' Joachim Liebschner interview, Sound Archive, Imperial War Museum, London

p. 246 'Ten yards away from me there was a distinct movement . . .' quoted in Trevelyan, *Rome '44, op. cit.,* p. 196

p. 246 'I had to pick up these dead bodies . . .' Norman Mohar, memoirs (unpublished)

p. 247 'Jerry hit an ammunition dump . . .' Ron Rhodes papers, The Second World War Experience Centre, Leeds

p. 247 'It was sometimes necessary to leave the wounded . . .' Joachim Liebschner interview, Sound Archive, Imperial War Museum, London

p. 248 'The wounded lay in two rows . . .' J.A. Ross *Memoirs of an Army Surgeon* William Blackwood & Sons Ltd. 1948, p. 209

p. 249 'We passed an excellent evening . . .' Whicker, *op. cit.,* p. 132

p. 249 'The worst task we had to do . . .' H. Bretherick papers, The Second World War Experience Centre, Leeds

p. 250 'foresaw his own death in an attack . . .' Carter, *op. cit.,* p. 106

p. 250 'We lost 8 dead and 11 wounded . . .' Norman Mohar, memoirs (unpublished)

p. 250 'I got up at first light as usual . . .' Swain, *op. cit.,* p. 157

p. 251 'I saw a number of those cases . . .' Arthur Malinson interview, 12 May 2005

p. 251 'Tonight I feel the strain of this existence . . .' Geoffrey Dormer papers, The Second World War Experience Centre, Leeds

p. 252 'March 10: Drank vino again last night, sure got drunk . . .' Sergeant Paul Granville Brown journal, 45th Infantry Division Museum, Oklahoma

p. 252 'The saying goes that there are no atheists in the foxholes . . .' Cor Longiotti, memoirs (unpublished)

p. 252 'I was suddenly in full realization . . .' Norman Mohar, memoirs (unpublished)

p. 252 'I hated my Sergeant far more than I hated the enemy . . .' Letter from Peter Randall, 12 June 2005

p. 253 'I cannot talk about hatred towards the enemy . . .' Joachim Liebschner interview, Sound Archive, Imperial War Museum, London

p. 253 'We went through a great deal . . .' Lionel Waldergrave interview, 22 June 2005

p. 254 'God help me to do my duty to the Fatherland . . .' Frederick Lammers diary and letter, 22 August 2005

p. 254 'Our platoon was very close . . .' Raymond Fort, The Second World War Experience Centre, Leeds

p. 254 'It is true that all of us were in the same boat . . .' quoted in D'Este *Fatal Decision, op. cit.*, p. 299

p. 255 'There was never any mail for me from home . . .' Norman Mohar, memoirs (unpublished)

p. 255 'Oh My Dear Captain . . .' quoted in Beuchner, *op. cit.*, p. 99

p. 256 'Have you heard about Private Fox . . .' quoted in Trevelyan *Rome '44, op. cit.*, p. 158

p. 257 'British soldiers, you are fighting against an opponent . . .' leaflet given to the author by David Hardy

p. 257 'The Beach-Head has become a Death's Head! . . .' leaflet in author's archive

p. 258 'After not standing during the day . . .' George Avery, Veterans History Project Collection, American Folklife Center, Library of Congress, Washington

p. 259 'I heard about one soldier who wrote . . .' Pyle *Brave Men, op. cit.*, p. 94

p. 259 'We have few distractions here . . .' *The Times* 29 March 1944

p. 259 'Elaborate totes were constructed and really large money . . .' quoted in Owen and Walters, *op. cit.*, pp. 393–4

p. 260 'The only ways to get away from the guns . . .' Jimmy Reed telephone interview, 6 March 2005

p. 260 'The lads can get ashore for the first time . . .' Geoffrey Dormer papers, The Second World War Experience Centre, Leeds

p. 261 'reality on the battlefield was living and dying . . .' Whicker, *op. cit.*, p. 170

p. 261 'It was like Armageddon had followed us . . .' Jonathan Forbes interview, 3 September 2005

Chapter 9: Diadem

p. 265 'Something has happened to me these last days . . .' Raleigh Trevelyan *The Fortress* Collins 1956, p. 91

p. 265 'It was my duty to kill him . . .' Trevelyan *The Fortress*, *op. cit.*, p. 92

p. 266 'I fired at this wretched chap . . .' Trevelyan *Rome '44*, *op. cit.*, p. 243

p. 267 'Telegram from American Chiefs of Staff . . .' Alanbrooke diary, Liddell Hart Centre for Military Archives, King's College London

p. 267 'Difficulties again with our American friends . . .' Alanbrooke diary, Liddell Hart Centre for Military Archives, King's College London

p. 267 'We should above all defeat the German . . .' quoted in Blumenson *Anzio*, *op. cit.*, p. 166

p. 268 'OBJECT: to give the greatest possible assistance . . .' quoted in Arthur Bryant *Triumph In The West 1943–1946* Collins 1959, p. 183

p. 268 'I do not consider that the objective . . .' The National Archives, PREM 3/472

p. 270 'deprive the enemy of the ability . . .' quoted in Jackson *The Battle for Italy*, *op. cit.*, p. 206

p. 272 'To destroy the right wing of the German Tenth Army . . .' quoted in *ibid.*, p. 223

p. 272 'We not only wanted the honour . . .' Mark Clark, *op. cit.*, p. 332

p. 272 'I know factually that there are interests brewing for Eighth Army . . .' Mark Clark diary, The Citadel Archives & Museum, Gen. Mark W. Clark

p. 273 'I told Alexander . . . that what I was guarding . . .' Mark Clark diary, The Citadel Archives & Museum, Gen. Mark W. Clark

p. 273 'the capture of Rome is the only important objective' Mark Clark diary, The Citadel Archives & Museum, Gen. Mark W. Clark

p. 274 'All thoughts and hopes are with you . . .' quoted in Churchill, *op. cit.*, p. 529

p. 274 'All our plans and preparation are now complete . . .' Churchill, *op. cit.*, p. 529

p. 274 'Tonight at 11 pm the Italian attack starts . . .' Alanbrooke diary, Liddell Hart Centre for Military Archives, King's College London

p. 274 'we can now claim that we have definitely broken the Gustav Line . . .' quoted in Molony, *op. cit.*, p. 126

p. 275 'we shall have to give up Cassino' quoted in Dominick Graham and

Graham Bidwell *Tug of War – The Battle For Italy: 1943–45* Hodder and Stoughton 1986, p. 282

p. 275   'I look back on those days in horror' quoted in Trevelyan *Rome '44*, *op. cit.*, p. 267

p. 275   'Alexander's news of Italian fighting continues to be excellent . . .' Alanbrooke diary, Liddell Hart Centre for Military Archives, King's College London

p. 276   'a shabby collection of tents full of sand near the beach' Letter from David Munford, 12 June 2005

p. 276   'The Corps commander turned up in a gleaming helmet . . .' Major Kenneth Wright diary

p. 278   'Every day was a busy day . . .' George Avery, Veterans History Project Collection, American Folklife Center, Library of Congress, Washington

p. 278   'I stopped and got out, lifted the bonnet . . .' Ron Rhodes papers, The Second World War Experience Centre, Leeds

p. 279   'Everything was ready . . .' Dodge, *op. cit.*, p. 21

p. 280   'Suddenly there was an explosion . . .' quoted in Trevelyan *Rome '44*, *op. cit.*, p. 279

p. 280   'to cut Highway 6 . . . with the ultimate objective . . .' Mark Clark diary, The Citadel Archives & Museum, Gen. Mark W. Clark

p. 280   'What struck me about what Clark . . .' Notes made by Mal Polton in 1953 supplied by his wife

p. 281   'I intend to take Rome . . .' Mark Clark diary, The Citadel Archives & Museum, Gen. Mark W. Clark

p. 281   'Around us, we could see nothing . . .' Truscott, *op. cit.*, p. 371

p. 282   'Hell let loose its fury . . .' Dodge, *op. cit.*, pp. 22–3

p. 282   'was as terrible as what was to happen on Omaha Beach . . .' Email from Norman Mohar, 19 February 2005

p. 283   'Vividly in my mind is the scene of the first wave strewn . . .' Norman Mohar, memoirs (unpublished)

p. 283   'The mortar can drop a shell from a few yards . . .' George Avery, Veterans History Project Collection, American Folklife Center, Library of Congress, Washington

p. 284   'He ran 100 yards as machine gun bullets . . .' Taggart, *op. cit.*, p. 157

p. 284   'I had an awful job . . .' Daniel Goldstein interview, 28 August 2005

p. 285 'I was standing in a trench and looking around . . .' Francis Eugene Liggett, Veterans History Project Collection, American Folklife Center, Library of Congress, Washington

p. 286 'Fix bayonets. Cock your tommy-guns . . .' Trevelyan *The Fortress*, *op. cit.*, p. 109

p. 286 'falling with a retching crash . . .' *ibid.*, p. 110

p. 286 'A furious, reckless excitement drove us on . . .' *ibid.*, p. 111

p. 287 'We made our way forward mopping up the Germans . . .' Raymond Fort papers, The Second World War Experience Centre, Leeds

p. 288 'I experienced the Allied attack at Cisterna on 23 May 1944 . . .' quoted in Kurowski, *op. cit.*, p. 223

p. 289 'It was a dark period in Rome's history . . .' Fabia Sciarillo interview, 2 February 2005

p. 290 'I was nominally the leader . . .' Pip Matthews interview, 12 May 2005

p. 291 'unable to rid himself of a preconceived fixation . . .' Kesselring, *op. cit.*, p. 203

p. 292 'Have you considered changing the direction of your attack towards Rome?' quoted in D'Este *Fatal Decision*, *op. cit.*, p. 366

Chapter 10: The Eternal City

p. 295 'Where the hell do you think you're going? . . .' Adleman and Walton *Rome Fell Today*, *op. cit.*, pp. 218–19

p. 296 'It's a great day for the Fifth Army' *ibid.*, p. 219

p. 296 'For us, used to senior officers . . .' Whicker, *op. cit.*, p. 169

p. 296 'press vigorously towards Rome' Mark Clark diary, The Citadel Archives & Museum, Gen. Mark W. Clark

p. 296 'I am launching this new attack with all possible speed . . .' Mark Clark diary, The Citadel Archives & Museum, Gen. Mark W. Clark

p. 297 'In the little park the palm trees lay blackened and uprooted . . .' Eric Sevareid *Not So Wild a Dream* Alfred A. Knopf New York 1946, p. 401

p. 298 'Cisterna was an utter ruin, not one building untouched . . .' George Avery, Veterans History Project Collection, American Folklife Center, Library of Congress, Washington

p. 298 'We got into some beautiful hills . . .' Dodge, *op. cit.*, p. 26

p. 299 'There were 15 Mark VI Tiger tanks on that road . . .' quoted in D'Este *Fatal Decision*, *op. cit.*, p. 362

p. 299 'When they started firing we dove from the truck . . .' Dodge, *op. cit.*, p. 26

p. 300 'I am writing this in the field . . .' George Avery, Veterans History Project Collection, American Folklife Center, Library of Congress, Washington

p. 301 'Alexander never gave me orders not to take Rome . . .' quoted in D'Este *Fatal Decision*, *op. cit.*, p. 371

p. 301 'The Boss wants you to leave the 3rd Division . . .' quoted in Blumenson, *Anzio*, *op. cit.*, p. 183

p. 301 'I protested that the conditions were not right . . .' Truscott, *op. cit.*, p. 375

p. 302 'The enemy forces opposing the beachhead in the Cisterna . . .' quoted in Blumenson *Anzio*, *op. cit.*, p. 185

p. 302 'I am sure the army commander will continue . . .' quoted in *ibid.*, p. 185

p. 303 'The Boche is badly disorganized . . .' quoted in *ibid*, p.184

p. 303 'There's no point in arguing . . .' quoted in Truscott, *op. cit.*, p. 375

p. 303 'The squadron was told that the Hermann Göring Division . . .' Peter Coup interview, 25 May 2005

p. 304 'I should feel myself wanting in comradeship . . .' Churchill, *op. cit.*, p. 536

p. 305 'We had lost our platoon Lieutenant and his replacement . . .' Ray McAllister, memoirs (unpublished)

p. 306 'An 88-mm round blew up the Sherman . . .' Tony Glenister interview, 29 May 2005

p. 307 'Fred, if you do it and succeed . . .' quoted in Trevelyan *Rome '44*, *op. cit.*, p. 301

p. 307 'We climbed through the night . . .' Letter from David Stearns, 12 June 2005

p. 308 'The Eighth Army has done little fighting . . .' Mark Clark diary, The Citadel Archives & Museum, Gen. Mark W. Clark

p. 308 'At last we had taken the town that had caused us so many problems . . .' Donny Wilson telephone interview, 18 March 2005

p. 309 'I was given 10 youngsters and one experienced man . . .' Joachim Liebschner interview, Sound Archive, Imperial War Museum, London

p. 311 'a thorough pest of himself!' Alanbrooke diary, Liddell Hart Centre for Military Archives, King's College London

p. 311 'Headquarters of General Alexander . . .' Leaflet in author's archive

p. 312 'I rode on a Sherman . . .' Monty Smith interview, 18 August 2005

p. 312 'the Command Post has gone to hell . . .' Mark Clark diary, The Citadel Archives & Museum, Gen. Mark W. Clark

p. 313 'We are to enter Rome tomorrow . . .' Charles Bridge diary

p. 314 'This, I thought, was the ultimate anticlimax . . .' quoted in D'Este *Fatal Decision*, *op. cit.*, p. 395

p. 315 'The entry of Allied troops into the heart of the Eternal City at dusk . . .' Bigart, *op. cit.*, pp. 47–9

p. 316 'the most shot-at-and-hit general in American military history' Adelman and Walton *Rome Fell Today*, *op. cit.*, p. 253

p. 316 'We were woken by trucks moving through the street . . .' Fabia Sciarillo interview, 2 February 2005

p. 317 'his troops to fire on Eighth Army . . .' quoted in Trevelyan, *Rome '44*, *op. cit.*, p. 303

p. 317 'General Mark Clark had said no one was allowed into Rome . . .' quoted in Arthur, *op. cit.*, p. 275

p. 317 'My recollection of entering Rome was of crowds . . .' Dodge, *op. cit.*, p. 31

p. 318 'We passed the Coliseum and entered the most beautiful sight of the war . . .' Norman Mohar, memoirs (unpublished)

p. 318 'Rome to-day is in a holiday mood . . .' *The Times* 6 June 1944

p. 319 'As we stopped to look at the great dome of St Peter's . . .' Clark, *op. cit.*, p. 345

p. 319 'Well, gentlemen, I didn't really expect to have a press conference here . . .' quoted in D'Este *Fatal Decision*, *op. cit.*, p. 398

p. 319 'I was anxious to get out of this posturing . . .' Truscott, *op. cit.*, p. 380

p. 319 'We had won the race to Rome by only two days' Mark Clark, *op. cit.*, p. 346

p. 319 'I feel so much for you at this agonizing moment . . .' quoted in Gilbert *Road To Victory*, *op. cit.*, p. 791

p. 320 'One up and two to go . . .' *The Times* 6 June 1944

Conclusion

p. 322 'got it seared in his brain like a burn with a blowtorch' Carter, *op. cit.*, p. 95

p. 322 'Anzio was my worst moment in the war . . .' Moran, *op. cit.*, p. 210

p. 323 'tying down 25 German divisions in Italy for two years . . .' Whicker, *op. cit.*, p. 5

p. 323 'the operation, largely owing to Mr Churchill's influence . . .' Molony *op. cit.*, p. 772

p. 324 'Legend has it that Nero fiddled at Anzio while Rome burned . . .' quoted in D'Este *Fatal Decision, op. cit.*, pp. 278–9

p. 324 'We could have had one night in Rome . . .' quoted in D'Este *Fatal Decision, op. cit.*, p. 405

p. 324 'I never understood how Anzio could possibly work . . .' John Cloake *Templer – Tiger of Malaya* Harrap 1985, p. 130

p. 324 'any reckless advance to the Colli Laziali . . .' Truscott, *op. cit.*, p. 311

p. 325 'Again we were attempting too much with too little . . .' Bigart, *op. cit.*, p. 41

p. 325 'it would have been the Anglo-American doom to over-extend themselves . . .' quoted in Fred Majdalany *The Battle of Cassino* Longmans 1957, p. 86

p. 325 'The Americans put up their tents . . .' quoted in Trevelyan *Rome '44, op. cit.*, p. 49

p. 325 'the actual course of events was probably the most advantageous . . .' quoted in David Reynolds *In Command of History – Churchill Fighting and Writing the Second World War* Penguin 2005, p. 191

p. 325 'confined himself to occupying his beach-head . . .' Churchill, *op. cit.*, p. 426

p. 325 'not the impotent, defense minded commander . . .' quoted in Reynolds *In Command of History, op. cit.*, p. 390

p. 326 'the disaster to the enemy would have been much greater . . .' quoted in Trevelyan *Rome '44, op. cit.*, p. 292

p. 326 'There has never been any doubt in my mind that had General Clark . . .' Truscott, *op. cit.*, p. 550

p. 326 'So Mark Clark, totally absorbed with self-publicity . . .' Whicker, *op. cit.*, p. 182

p. 327 'Such is the story of Anzio . . .' Churchill, *op. cit.*, p. 437

Select Bibliography of Published Sources

NB Place of publication London unless stated.

Adleman, Robert H. and Walton, Colonel George *The Devil's Brigade* Corgi 1968

Adleman, Robert H. and Walton, Colonel George *Rome Fell Today* Leslie Frewin 1969

The Alexander Memoirs 1940–1945 Edited by John North Cassell 1962

Allen, William L. *Anzio: Edge of Disaster* E.P. Dutton 1978

Altieri, James *The Spearheaders* Popular Library Toronto 1960

Anzio Beachhead 22 January–25 May 1944 Center of Military History Washington 1990

Aris, George *The British Fifth Division 1939 to 1945* The Fifth Division Benevolent Fund 1959

Arthur, Max *Forgotten Voices of the Second World War* Ebury Press 2004

Avery, George *I Remember Anzio* (unpublished)

Barzini, Luigi *The Italians* Penguin 1968

Bennett, Ralph *Ultra and Mediterranean Strategy 1941–1945* Hamish Hamilton 1989

Bigart, Homer *Forward Positions – The War Correspondence of Homer Bigart* Compiled and edited by Betsy Wade The University of Arkansas Press Fayetteville 1992

Black, Robert W. *Rangers in World War II* Presidio Books New York 1992

Blaxland, Gregory *Alexander's Generals – The Italian Campaign, 1944–45* William Kimber 1979

Blumenson, Martin *Anzio – The Gamble That Failed* Weidenfeld and Nicolson 1963

Blumenson, Martin *Mark Clark* Jonathan Cape 1985

Breuer, William *Agony at Anzio – The Allies' Most Controversial Operation of World War II* Robert Hale 1985

Bryant, Arthur *Triumph In The West 1943–1946* Collins 1959

Buechner, Emajean Jordan *Sparks – The Combat Diary of a Battalion Commander (Rifle), WWII, 157th Infantry Regiment, 45th Division, 1941–1945* Thunderbird Press Metairie Louisiana 1991

Bullen R.E., *History of the 2/7th Battalion The Queen's Royal Regiment* Exeter 1958

Burhans, Lieutenant Colonel Robert D. *The First Special Service Force – A War History of the North Americans 1942–1944* The Battery Press Nashville 1996

Cancelli, Diego *Aprilia 1944* privately published 1994

Carter, Ross S. *Those Devils In Baggy Pants* Signet New York 1951

Carver, Michael *Harding of Petherton* Weidenfeld and Nicolson 1978

Carver, Field Marshal Lord *War In Italy 1943–45* Pan Books 2001

Center of Military History United States Army *Anzio Beachhead 22 January–25 May 1944* Washington D.C. 1990

Cheetham, A.M. *Ubique* Freshfield Books Formby 1987

Churchill, Winston S. *The Second World War – Volume V – Closing the Ring* Cassell 1952

Clark, General Mark *Calculated Risk – His Personal Story of the War in North Africa and Italy* George G. Harrap 1951

Clark, Lloyd *The Allies In Italy* in *History Makers* Journal of the North London History Association 1991

Clarke, Rupert *With Alex at War – From the Irrawaddy to the Po 1941–1945* Leo Cooper 2000

Cloake, John *Templer – Tiger of Malaya* Harrap 1985

Colville, John *The Fringes of Power – Downing Street Diaries 1939–1955* Weidenfield and Nicolson 2004

Combat Record of the 504th Parachute Infantry Regiment April 1943–July 1945 The Battery Press Nashville 2004

Cottingham, Peter Layton *Once Upon a Wartime* Manitoba 1996

Cowdrey, Albert E. *Fighting for Life – American Military Medicine in World War II* The Free Press New York 1994

Crosby, Donald F. *Battlefield Chaplains – Catholic Priests in World War II* University Press of Kansas 1994

Curtis, Geoffrey *Salerno Remembered* The Queen's Royal Surrey Regimental Association 1988

Dancocks, Daniel G. *The D-Day Dodgers – The Canadians in Italy, 1943–45* McClelland and Stewart Inc. Toronto 1991

Darby, William O. with Baumer, William H. *Darby's Rangers – We Led the Way* Presidio California 2003

D'Este, Carlo *Bitter Victory – The Battle for Sicily July–August 1943* Collins 1988

D'Este, Carlo *Fatal Decision – Anzio and the Battle for Rome* HarperCollins 1991

De Belot, Raymond *The Struggle for the Mediterranean 1939–1945* Princeton University Press New Jersey 1951

Danchev, Alex and Todman, Daniel *War Diaries 1939–1945 Field Marshal Lord Alanbrooke* Weidenfeld and Nicolson 2001

Dodge, Robert E. *Memories of the Anzio Beachhead and the War in Europe* Vantage Press New York 2004

Doherty, Richard *Ireland's Generals in the Second World War* Four Courts Press Dublin 2004

Dorling, Taprell *Western Mediterranean 1942–1945* Hodder and Stoughton 1947

Ellis, John *The Sharp End of the War – The Fighting Man in World War II* David and Charles 1980

Engineers in the Italian Campaign 1943–1945 Anon. 1946

Erskine, David *History of the Scots Guards 1919–1955* The Naval and Military Press 1956

Fehrenbach, T.R. *The Battle of Anzio* Monarch Books Connecticut 1962

The First Divisional Artillery at Anzio October 1944

Fisher, Ernest F. Jnr *United States Army in World War II – The Mediterranean*

Theater of Operations – Cassino to the Alps Center of Military History, United States Army, Washington D.C. 1977

Fitzgerald, Major D.J.L. *History of the Irish Guards in the Second World War* Gale and Polden 1949

Foot, M.R.D. *Resistance – European Resistance to Nazism 1940–45* Eyre Methuen 1976

Fraser, David *Alanbrooke* William Collins London 1982

Gilbert, Martin *Churchill – A Life* Heinemann 1991

Gilbert, Martin *Road To Victory: Winston S. Churchill 1941–1945* Heinemann 1986

Gooderson, Ian *Air Power at the Battlefront – Allied Close Air Support in Europe 1943–45* Frank Cass 1998

Graham, Dominick and Bidwell, Graham *Tug of War – The Battle For Italy: 1943–45* Hodder and Stoughton 1986

Harmon, Major General E.N. *Combat Commander – Autobiography of a Soldier* Prentice-Hall New Jersey 1970

Healey, Denis *Time of My Life* Michael Joseph 1989

Hibbert, Christopher *Anzio – The Bid For Rome* Macdonald and Co 1970

Hinsley, F.H. et al *British Intelligence in the Second World War – Its Influence on Strategy and Operations Volume Three Part 1* HMSO 1984

Historical Division, War Department *Fifth Army at the Winter Line* Washington 1945

History of the First Battalion The King's Shropshire Light Infantry February 1943–May 1945 (No details)

History of the First Division Anzio Campaign January–June 1944 Jerusalem 1946

History of the 157th Infantry Regiment (Rifle) 4 June '43–8 May '45 Baton Rouge Louisiana 1946

A History of 2/6th Bn. Queen's Royal Regiment in the Italian Campaign The Dog Press (No date)

Holden Reid, Brian *The Italian Campaign, 1943–45: A Reappraisal of Allied Generalship* in Gooch, J. (ed.) *Decisive Campaigns of the Second World War* Frank Cass 1990

Howard, Michael *The Mediterranean Strategy in the Second World War* Weidenfeld and Nicolson 1968

Irving, David *Hitler's War* Hodder and Stoughton 1977

Jackson, W.G.F. *The Battle for Italy* Batsford 1967

Jackson, W.G.F. *Alexander of Tunis As Military Commander* Batsford 1971

Jones, Matthew *Britain, the United States and the Mediterranean War, 1942–44* Macmillan Press 1996

Katz, Robert *Fatal Silence – The Pope, the Resistance and the German Occupation of Rome* Cassell 2003

Keegan, John ed. *Churchill's Generals* Warner Books 1991

Kesselring, F.M. Albert *The Memoirs of Field-Marshal Kesselring* William Kimber 1953

Kurowski, Franz *Battleground Italy 1943–1945: The German Armed Forces in the Battle for the 'Boot'* JJ Fedorowicz Publishing Inc Manitoba Canada 2003

Kurowski, Franz *The History of the Fallschirm Panzerkorps Hermann Göring* JJ Fedorowicz Publishing Inc Manitoba Canada 1995

Lamb, Richard *War In Italy 1943–1945 – A Brutal Story* John Murray 1993

Lewis, Norman *Naples '44* Eland 1983

Loewenheim, Francis L., Langley, Harold D. and Jonas, Manfred ed. *Roosevelt and Churchill – Their Secret Wartime Correspondence* Barrie and Jenkins 1975

Lutz, Gunther *Panzer Platoon: Attack Anzio!* Sphere Books 1980

Macksey, Kenneth *Kesselring – German Master Strategist of the Second World War* Greenhill 1996

Macmillan, Harold *The Blast of War 1939–1945* Macmillan 1967

Macmillan, Harold *War Diaries – Politics and War in the Mediterranean January 1943–May 1945* Macmillan 1984

Majdalany, Fred *The Battle of Cassino* Longmans 1957

Marshall, Charles F. *A Ramble Through My War – Anzio and Other Joys* Louisiana State University Press Baton Rouge 1998

Mauritz, Michael *The Secret of Anzio Bay – A True Story of an American Fighter Pilot in World War II in Italy* Word Association Publishers Pennsylvania 2002

Meacham, Jon *Franklin and Winston – A Portrait of a Friendship* Granta Books 2004

Mitcham Jnr, Samuel W. *Hitler's Legions – The German Army Order of Battle, World War II* Dorset Press New York 1985

Molony, Brig C.J.C. et al *The Mediterranean and the Middle East Volume V The Campaign in Sicily 1943 and the Campaign in Italy 3rd September 1943 to 31st March 1944: History of the Second World War United Kingdom Military Series* HMSO 1973

Molony, Brig C.J.C. et al *The Mediterranean and the Middle East Volume VI Victory in the Mediterranean Part I 1st April to 4th June 1944 History of the Second World War United Kingdom Military Series* The Naval and Military Press 2004

Montgomery, Bernard Law *The Memoirs of Field-Marshal The Viscount Montgomery of Alamein, K.G.* The Companion Book Club 1958

Montgomery, Field Marshal The Viscount Montgomery of Alamein *El Alamein to the River Sangro* Hutchinson (no year of publication given)

Moorehead, Alan *Eclipse* Granta Books 2000

Moran, Lord *Winston Churchill – The Struggle for Survival, 1940–1965* Constable 1966

More, Jasper *The Land of Italy* Batsford 1953

Morgan, Ted *FDR – A Biography* Grafton Books 1985

Morison, Samuel Eliot *History of United States Naval Operations in World War II Volume Nine: Sicily–Salerno–Anzio: January 1943–June 1944* University of Illinois Press 2002

Morris, Eric *Circles of Hell – The War in Italy 1943–1945* Hutchinson 1993

Morton, H.V. *Southern Italy* Methuen 2002

Nicolson, Nigel *Alex – The Life of Field Marshal Earl Alexander of Tunis* Weidenfeld and Nicolson 1973

Nicolson, Captain Nigel and Forbes, Patrick *The Grenadier Guards in the War of 1939–1945 Volume II The Mediterranean Campaigns* Gale and Polden 1949

Norfolk, Reginald N. *Operation Corkscrew – Operation Shingle – An Account of Two Combined Operations* privately published 2002

Owen, James and Walters, Guy *The Voice of War – The Second World War Told by Those Who Fought It* Viking 2004

Packard, Reynolds *Rome Was My Beat* Lyle Stuart Inc New Jersey 1975

Parker, Matthew *Monte Cassino – The Story of the Hardest-Fought Battle of World War Two* Headline 2003

Picknett, Lynn, Prince, Clive and Prior, Stephen *Friendly Fire: The Secret War Between the Allies* Mainstream Publishing Edinburgh 2005

Pyle, Ernie *Brave Men* Henry Holt New York 1944

Pyle, Ernie *Here is Your War* Henry Holt New York 1944

Reynolds, David *In Command of History – Churchill Fighting and Writing the Second World War* Penguin 2005

Richards, Denis and Saunders, Hilary St George *Royal Air Force 1939–1945* HMSO 1954

Rings, Werner *Life With the Enemy – Collaboration and Resistance in Hitler's Europe 1939–1945* Weidenfeld and Nicolson 1982

The Rise and Fall of the German Air Force 1933–1945 – Issued by the Air Ministry 1948 PRO 2001

Roe, Tom *Anzio Beachhead – Diary of a Signaller* privately published 1988

Rosignoli, Guido *The Allied Forces In Italy 1943–45* David and Charles 1989

Roskill, Captain S.W. *The War At Sea 1939–1945 Volume III The Offensive Part I 1st June 1943–31st May 1944* HMSO 1960

Ross, J.A. (JAR) *Memoirs of an Army Surgeon* William Blackwood & Sons Ltd. 1948

Schorer, Alvis D. *A Half Acre of Hell – A Combat Nurse in WWII* Galde Press Minnesota 2002

Schwentker, Otto *Fallschirm-Pioneer-Bataillon 4* privately published Hameln 1982

Senise, Paolo *Lo sbarco ad Anzio e Nettuno 22 gennaio 1944* Mursia Milan 1994

Sevareid, Eric *Not So Wild a Dream* Alfred A. Knopf New York 1946

Sheehan, Fred *Anzio Epic of Bravery* University of Oklahoma Press Oklahoma 1964

Staiger, Jörg *Anzio–Nettuno: Eine Schlacht der Führungsfehler* Neckargemünd 1962

Steinbeck, John *Once There Was A War* Heinemann 1959

Steinhoff, Johannes *The Straits of Messina – Diary of a Fighter Commander* Andre Deutsch 1969

Stoler, Mark A. *Allies and Adversaries – The Joint Chiefs of Staff, The Grand Alliance and US Strategy in World War II* The University of North Carolina Press 2000

Stoler, Mark A. *Why George Marshall? A Biographical Assessment.* An essay on the George C. Marshall Foundation website www.marshallfoundation.org/pdf/-01Stoler--Marshall.pdf

Strabolgi, Lord *The Conquest of Italy* Hutchinson 1944

Swain, John *Destiny '39 – A Young Soldier's Experiences During World War II* Pen Press 2001

Taggart, Donald G. ed. *History of The Third Infantry Division in World War II* The Battery Press Nashville 1987

Tidyman, Ernest *The Anzio Death Trap* Belmont Books New York 1968

Tobin, James *Ernie Pyle's War* University Press of Kansas Lawrence 1997

Tregaskis, Richard *Invasion Diary* University of Nebraska 2004

Trevelyan, Raleigh *The Fortress* Collins 1956

Trevelyan, Raleigh *Rome '44: The Battle For The Eternal City* Pimlico 2004

Truscott Jnr, Lt. Gen. L.K. *Command Missions – A Personal Story* Presidio California 1990

Vaughan-Thomas, Wynford *Anzio* Pan Books 1963

Verney, Peter *Anzio 1944: An Unexpected Fury* Batsford 1978

von Clausewitz, Carl *On War* Wordsworth 1997

von Senger und Etterlin, General Frido *Neither Fear Nor Hope – The Wartime Career of General Frido Von Senger und Etterlin Defender of Cassino* Macdonald 1963

Warlimont, Walter *Inside Hitler's Headquarters 1939–45* Weidenfeld and Nicolson 1964

Wells, Lloyd M. *From Anzio to the Alps – An American Soldier's Story* University of Missouri 2004

Westphal, General Siegfried *The German Army in the West* Cassell 1951

Whicker, Alan *Whicker's War* HarperCollins 2005

Whitlock, Flint *The Rock of Anzio From Sicily to Dachau: A History of the U.S. 45th Infantry Division* Westview Press Colorado 1998

Woodruff, William *Vessel of Sadness* Abacus 2004

Ziegler, Philip *Soldiers – Fighting Men's Lives 1901–2001* Chatto and Windus 2001

Order of Battle

ALLIED FORCES IN ITALY

Allied 15th Army Group
General Sir Harold Alexander

British Eighth Army
General Sir Bernard Montgomery
Lieutenant General Sir Oliver Leese (from 31 December 1943)

British V Corps
British XIII Corps
Canadian I Corps
New Zealand Corps
Polish II Corps
French Expeditionary Corps

United States Fifth Army
Lieutenant General Mark Clark

US II Corps
US VI Corps
British X Corps

VI Corps at Anzio
Major General John P. Lucas
Major General Lucian K. Truscott (from 23 February 1944)

BRITISH FORCES

1st British Infantry Division
Major General W.R.C. Penney

24th Guards Brigade	1/Irish Guards
	1/Scots Guards
	5/Grenadier Guards
2nd Infantry Brigade	1/Loyal Regiment
	2/North Staffordshire Regiment
	6/Gordon Highlanders
3rd Infantry Brigade	2/Sherwood Foresters
	1/Duke of Wellington's Regiment
	1/King's Shropshire Light Infantry

56th British Infantry Division
Major General G.W.R. Templer

167th Infantry Brigade   8/Royal Fusiliers
9/Royal Fusiliers
7/Oxfordshire and Buckinghamshire Light
     Infantry

169th Infantry Brigade   2/5 Queen's Royal Regiment (West Surrey)
2/6 Queen's Royal Regiment (West Surrey)
2/7 Queen's Royal Regiment (West Surrey)

168th Infantry Brigade   10/Royal Berkshire
1/London Scottish
1/London Irish Rifles

18th Brigade   1/Buffs (West Kent)
14/Sherwood Foresters
9/King's Own Yorkshire Light Infantry

5th British Infantry Division
Major General P.G.S. Gregson-Ellis

13th Infantry Brigade   2/Cameronians (Scottish Rifles)
2/Royal Inniskilling Fusiliers
2/Wiltshire Regiment

15th Infantry Brigade   1/Green Howards
1/York and Lancaster Regiment
1/King's Own Yorkshire Light Infantry

17th Infantry Brigade   2/Royal Scots Fusiliers
2/Northamptonshire Regiment
6/Seaforth Highlanders

2nd Special Service Brigade

Brigadier R.F.J. Tod

9 Commando

43 Royal Marine Commando

UNITED STATES FORCES

3rd US Infantry Division

Major General Lucian K. Truscott

Brigadier General John W. O'Daniel (23 February 1944)

7th Infantry Regiment

15th Infantry Regiment

30th Infantry Regiment

45th US Infantry Division

Major General William W. Eagles

157th Infantry Regiment

179th Infantry Regiment

180th Infantry Regiment

1st US Armored Division

Major General Ernest N. Harmon

Combat Command A

Combat Command B

Combat Command C

First Special Service Force
Brigadier General Robert T. Frederick

First Regiment
Second Regiment
Third Regiment

Ranger Force
Colonel William O. Darby

1st, 3rd and 4th Ranger Battalions

504th Parachute Infantry Regiment
Colonel Reuben H. Tucker

Three Parachute Infantry Battalions

509th Parachute Infantry Battalion
Lieutenant Colonel William P. Yarborough

GERMAN FORCES IN ITALY

German Army Group C
Field Marshal Albert Kesselring

Tenth Army
General Heinrich von Vietinghoff

XIV Panzer Corps
LI Mountain Corps

Fourteenth Army at Anzio
General Eberhard von Mackensen

I Parachute Corps
General Alfred Schlemm

4th Parachute Division – Major General Heinz Trettner

29th Panzer Grenadier Division – Lieutenant General Walther Fries

65th Infantry Division – Major General Helmuth Pfeifer

715th Infantry Division – Major General Hans-Georg Hildebrandt

114th Jäger Division – Lieutenant General Karl Eglseer

LXXVI Panzer Corps
General Traugott Herr

3rd Panzer Grenadier Division – Lieutenant General Fritz-Hubert Gräser

26th Panzer Division – Lieutenant General Smilo von Luettwitz

Hermann Göring Panzer Division – Major General Paul Conrath

362nd Infantry Division – Lieutenant General Heinz Greiner

71st Infantry Division – Major General Wilhelm Raapke

Glossary

Avalanche – Code name for the landing at Salerno

Baytown – Code name for the landing at Reggio di Calabria

CCS – Casualty Clearing Station

COS – Chiefs of Staff

Husky – Code name for the invasion of Sicily

LCI – Landing Craft Infantry

LCT – Landing Craft Tank

LST – Landing Ship Tank

OKW – Oberkommando der Wehrmacht – High Command of the German Armed Forces

Overlord – Code name for the invasion of North West Europe (previously called Roundup)

Roundup – Code name for the invasion of North West Europe (later called Overlord)

Shingle – Code name of the landings Anzio–Nettuno

Slapstick – Code name for the landing at Taranto

Torch – Code name for the landings in North Africa

Index